Psychical Realism
The Work of Victor Burgin

The Lieven Gevaert Series is a major series of substantial and innovative books on photography. Launched in 2004, the Series takes into account the ubiquitous presence of photography within modern culture and, in particular, the visual arts. At the forefront of contemporary thinking on photography, the books offer new insights on the position of the photographic medium within art historical, theoretical, social and institutional contexts. The Series is produced by the Lieven Gevaert Research Centre for Photography, Art and Visual Culture (www.lievengevaertcentre.be) and covers four types of approaches: publication of outstanding monographic studies, proceedings of international conferences, book length projects with artists, translations and republications of classic material. The Lieven Gevaert Series is published by Leuven University Press, and distributed in North America by Cornell University Press.

Psychical Realism
The Work of Victor Burgin

Alexander Streitberger

Leuven University Press

Table of Contents

Acknowledgments

I am most grateful to all my colleagues, students, and friends, whose encouragements and helpful critiques were vital to the completion of this book. First, I would like to thank Nathalie Boulouch and Valérie Mavridorakis for inviting me to a conference related to the exhibition on work by Victor Burgin at the Galerie Art & Essai, University of Rennes 2, in 2007. Even though the art and views of Victor Burgin already played a role within my former research on language theory and Conceptual art, my participation in the conference at Rennes provided the basis for my book project's explicit focus on psychical reality.

For suggestions, fruitful exchanges and shared experiences—be it in personal conversations or in the professional context of conferences, workshops and seminars—I warmly thank Stefanie Diekmann, Danièle Méaux, Katharina Sykora and the members of the research project "Das fotografische Dispositiv", Leszek Brogowski, Kaja Silverman, Raphaël Pirenne, Brianne Cohen, Sébastien Fevry, Marcel Marburger, Pamela Scorzin, Dieter Massa, as well as the members of the Lieven Gevaert Research Centre for Photography, Art and Visual Culture, and all the others who contributed more or less directly to the project and who hopefully will forgive me for not having mentioned them by name. Many thanks also to Ton Brouwers for his careful language editing and his encouraging feedback. A special thanks goes to Guillaume Le Gall, Stéphane Symons and Erik Verhagen for their attentive reading of the manuscript and for their inspiring suggestions and comments. For her invaluable advice, her constant and continuous academic and human support, and her sometimes critical but always positive and constructive attitude towards my project, I owe a great debt of gratitude to Hilde Van Gelder.

I am further grateful to Eva Schmidt and the Museum of Contemporary Art in Siegen for having given me the opportunity to contribute, as author, a monograph on Burgin's series *Gradiva* to the museum's prestigious publication series. I want to thank Galerie Zander, Cologne, for their support and, in particular, for giving me the opportunity to make the opening speeches for two exhibitions about the work of Victor Burgin, *Dovedale* in 2010 and *Some Cities* in 2017. This was tremendously helpful to gain a deeper understanding of Burgin's projection works. I further wish to thank Galleria Lia Rumma, Naples, for kindly receiving me at the exhibition *Dear Urania* (2016-2017), which became a crucial work for my argument in this book. I also want to thank the various other institutions, archives and foundations that facilitated the research for this project.

I am immensely grateful and indebted to my family, in particular to my daughters Laura and Irene, for their understanding and patience, as well as my wife, Chiara Nannicini, who always sustained me both emotionally and intellectually throughout all the years I was struggling to develop my ideas into a coherent and readable format. She was also the one who introduced me to the literary universe of Italo Calvino, whose poetic image of the city as a dream rebus, concealing desires and fears, wonderfully connects with the idea of a psychical realism.

Finally, I am particularly grateful to Victor Burgin for his availability and the many fruitful exchanges we had at every stage of the project.

The publication of this book was made possible through financial support from the Fonds de la Recherche Scientifique-FNRS, the Institut des civilisations, arts et lettres (INCAL/UCLouvain), and the Centre de recherche en théorie des arts (CERTA/UCLouvain).

… the logical small change is in the interstices. (Barthes, 1975: 9)

With cities, it is as with dreams: everything imaginable can be dreamed, but even the most unexpected dream is a rebus that conceals a desire or, its reverse, a fear. (Calvino, 1974: 44)

Introduction

"psychical reality" […] is the ground of my actions. (EAT: 198)

Within the category of the "other" on the horizon of responsibilities specific to the artist I would include not only other individuals, and other groups of individuals, but also the "other" that is the unconscious, and the "other" that is the "real"—not the preformatted "reality" of documentary "realism," but that which is uncanny in experience, that which resists signification. (PT: 149)

To write a book about Victor Burgin's artistic practice entails covering a period that spans some fifty years and a wide variety of tendencies (conceptualism, postmodernism, feminism, …) and media (text, photography, projection, computer modelling, …). It further requires taking into account his prolific and influential writings on photography, art, and visual culture, writings that constitute a kind of "parallel text"—to invoke the title of Burgin's book of "interviews and interventions about art"—a text that, albeit rarely dealing explicitly with his artistic work, is always involved in a fruitful dialogue with it, thus contributing to what Burgin himself called the "uncertain" location of his art, "'between:' between gallery and book; between 'visual art' and 'theory'; between 'image' and 'narrative'—'work' providing *work* between reader and text." (BN: 6)

In this study I want to take up the challenge of tracing back the parallel unfolding of artistic practice and theory in Burgin's work since the late 1960s. To avoid the pitfalls of using the visual work as a simple illustration of the theory, or, alternatively, of misunderstanding the theory as an explanation of the visual work, I will emphasize the "between-theory-and-art" as a productive space. As a consequence, my approach entails a constant shifting between close observation, description, and analysis of the artistic work and recourse to concepts and ideas as they occur in the theoretical writings within the broader discursive field of visual culture. Furthermore, my ambition in this book is to consider the various historical contexts of artistic practices and critical debates against the backdrop of which Burgin's work and thinking has evolved over the past five decades. From the early conceptual text works to recent digital projection works, from documentary-based photography to the virtual space of computer imaging, I examine the ways in which Burgin has reacted, and still reacts, in and through his work, to the artistic, intellectual, social, economic, and political conditions of his time. Over the course of five chapters, I trace the distinct and consecutive, but often also complementary and interwoven, trajectories that together constitute a whole despite their multiple and fragmentary character, much like—to borrow an image from Walter Benjamin— the pieces of a mosaic. In terms of art history and practice, this journey takes me from Modernism, Minimalism, Conceptual art, and appropriation art to video art and, more recently, computer-based imaging. Concerning visual culture in general, I situate Burgin's work within the broader fields of media and techniques such as painting, photography, cinema, the Internet, computer games, and virtual reality. From a theoretical-philosophical perspective, logical positivism, phenomenology, semiotics, poststructuralism, critical theory, and, of course, psychoanalysis have to be considered, for these approaches not only serve as the bedrock of Burgin's theoretical writing but also inform his artistic practice, albeit in much more associative and suggestive ways.

A decade ago, I began my introduction to *Situational Aesthetics. Selected Writings by Victor Burgin*, with an observation by Walter Benjamin about the treatise:

> Tirelessly the process of thinking makes new beginnings, returning in a roundabout way to its original object. The continuous pausing for breath is the mode most proper to the process of contemplation. For by pursuing different levels of meaning in its examination of one single object it receives both the incentive to begin again and the justification for its irregular rhythm. Just as mosaics preserve their majesty despite their fragmentation into capricious particles, so philosophical contemplation is not lacking in momentum. (Benjamin, 1992: 28-29)

I accorded such a prominent place to these words because, I argued, they are apposite to Burgin's writing as an intellectual process that does neither coalesce into a closed homogeneous body of theory nor provide a teleological model for the understanding of images: "Although there is an overarching and consistent theme present throughout his writings— that of the *space of visual representations*—Burgin always orbits around it towards something new, interrupting a thought in order to take it up again elsewhere and place it within a different context." (Streitberger, 2009: xi) The same may be said of Burgin's artistic work. Instead of evolving in one direction in terms of a continuous progression, it circles around a common origin, theme, or focus from which it departs and to which it returns in a constant process of layering and varying perspectives according to the shifting cultural, technological, and socio-political situation. In his 1984 essay "Diderot, Barthes, *Vertigo*," Burgin observes that the *mise-en-scène* of desire and fantasy "circles back" on itself in "a *spiral*, perpetually renewing itself by conquering new territory while nevertheless tracing the same *figure*." (EAT: 128) This also applies to his art. Moreover, the *mise-en-scène* of desire and fantasy—of psychical reality—is at the very heart of his artistic practice. As he claimed in an interview with John Roberts, "it's all about psychical space. That's all my work was ever about." (Roberts, 1997: 102-103) More recently, Burgin has compared the spiraling process of his projection pieces with practices of psychoanalysis (as described in Freud's essay "Remembering, Repeating and Working Through"), as well as with the way fantasies and daydreams manifest themselves in the form of "short sequences, most often fragmentary, circular and repetitive." (VBP: 78; Laplanche and Leclaire, 1972: 162-163) If the space of visual representations provides the general context of Burgin's work, the main focus of his work is psychical reality, which he defines with reference to Freud as the unconscious processes at work in the construction of the social *and* political subject. Burgin's interest in interior processes and their consequences for the way we see the world and act within it does not appear only in the early 1980s, when he turned to psychoanalysis in order to address "questions of gender and sexuality in relation to images." (PT: 166) A main aim of this book is to demonstrate that psychical space has always been a major concern in Burgin's work. As I argue in Chapter 1, by the end of the 1960s the psychical conditions of the work's perception are crucial to his conception of art already. For example, works such as *VI* (1973) and *Lei Feng* (1974), which are based on the rhetorical figure of antanaclasis, in which "the same word is repeated with a different signification" (TP: 49), anticipate the idea of the spiral as an endless psycho-semiotic displacement of meanings and identities. I therefore suggest that the term "psychical realism," coined by Burgin in 1987 as "the code name of a project" to describe the environment of mass media (Lewis, 1987/88: 63), may well be understood as a kind of umbrella term for his artistic work as well.

Before developing this point in more detail, I would like to come back to Benjamin's discussion of the treatise in order to stress another aspect that seems crucial to me for Burgin's artistic practice: the question of the viewer and her or his relation to the work. For Benjamin, contemplation, rather than being a passive devotional state, is a restless process of thinking that endlessly repeats, taking its momentum from the recurring reorganization of its fragments. This not only reflects how Burgin organizes his own work; it also corresponds to the way he conceives of its viewing in terms of a mode of contemplation that requires active interpretation—"'work' providing *work* between reader and text." (BN: 6) This position anchors Burgin's conception of the work of art in the tradition of Marcel Duchamp's famous statement about the spectator's contribution to the creative act, as well as in poststructuralist ideas drawing on Umberto Eco's concept of the open work and Roland Barthes' advent of the reader at the cost of the death of the author (even though the latter's death never seemed to be of particular interest to Burgin). The work as a text—or intertext—weaving together different existing narratives, stories, and discourses is not only a product of the artist's imagination; it also potentially includes the memories, fantasies, and reflections of the spectator as a "contemplator." It would be wrong, however, to understand Burgin's works as texts, even though he himself draws this analogy in his writings of the 1970s and 1980s. They are as much texts as they are images. As Valérie Mavridorakis puts it, Burgin "has never dissociated the textual and the visual." (SCR: 13) Burgin himself confirms this when writing: "From its beginnings my work has been most fundamentally concerned with relations between words and images, with hybrid 'scripto-visual' forms in which neither picture nor text predominates, in which the text itself is the vehicle for an image." (CP: 11) Just as the text works of the early 1970s are not mere intellectual exercises that deny visuality (in reality the words perform visual perception), so the photographs and projected images of the later works do not rely strictly on visual perception. In neither case do they simply depict the real world but rather show how the world is *mise-en-scène* through verbal *and* pictorial representations. As such, they may contribute to what W.J.T. Mitchell has called the "redemption of imagination":

> Perhaps the redemption of the imagination lies in accepting the fact that we create much of our world out of the dialogue between verbal and pictorial representations, and that our task is not to renounce this dialogue in favor of a direct assault on nature but to see that nature already informs both sides of the conversation. (Mitchell, 1986: 46)

More specifically, Burgin emphasizes the empty space between words and images, the space that is included "in anticipation of the work of the viewer-reader in the same space." (Bishop and Cubitt 2013: 215) This in-between space or interstice may take the form of semantic gaps, spatial distances, or—in the recent projection works—sequences during which no image is seen, no sound is heard. Such interstitial zones function similarly to Roman Ingarden's spots of indeterminacy (*Unbestimmtheitsstellen*) or Wolfgang Iser's blank spaces (*Leerstellen*) as virtual voids or ambiguities that transform the text into "a puzzle which we have to solve ourselves." (Iser, 1978: 129; Ingarden, 1973)

The complexity of the image-text relations in Burgin's work is perhaps best illustrated by a personal anecdote about a misreading.

Browsing the English translation of Jacques Rancière's 2003 book *Le destin des images* (*The Future of the Image*), I stumbled over the term "sequence-image," as a concept of the intertwined yet conflictual relationship of image and text—a "coupling power of the uncoupled." (Rancière, 2007: 59) I was surprised to find in Rancière's text the identical term that Burgin coined in 2004 for something else: a fleeting mental image that is indeterminately (n)either still (n)or moving, acting in a space *between* memory and perception, past and present, stillness and movement (see Chapter 5). Only then I realized my linguistic error that the English translation of Rancière's "phrase-image" was of course not "sequence-image" but "sentence-image." Yet the way Rancière defined the sentence-image comes very close to Burgin's "scripto-visual" works: they are paratactical, in that they juxtapose disparate elements of which the relations are not given but have to be actively inferred. To put it in Rancière's terms, they develop an "active, disruptive power" because of their combinatory capacity and their openness "to being combined with any element from a different sequence to compose new sentence-images *ad infinitum*." (Rancière, 2007: 46 and 31) In Burgin's psychical realism, however, the undoing of "the representative relationship between text and image" (46), is not only an aesthetic function, as it is for Rancière, but additionally reflects the way memories, fantasies, and desires mingle and interact with perceptions of the material world.

Realism has been a major preoccupation in Burgin's thinking from the outset. In his writings of the 1970s, he identified realism as one of the two main forces of modern art and historiography. For its exclusive emphasis on content and subject matter, he argued, realism has generally been defined in radical opposition to formalism's unique concern with style and form, thus forcing a radical disjunction of signifier (form) and signified (content). (EAT: 11) When he began to teach photography at the Polytechnic of Central London in 1973, he observed this gulf between pure visual form and transparency of the sign also in the domain of photography in the guise of the two prevailing attitudes of aestheticism and sociologism, the latter perceiving the photograph as a document, "a window on the world." (TC: 9-10) In contrast to such a "naïve" understanding, Burgin's search for a different realist project responded to a debate on aesthetic realism in the Winter 1971 issue of *Screen* magazine, in which the editors argued against the uncritical use of the term "realism" in traditional film theory. Drawing on this debate, Burgin employed the concept of realism against the tradition of Modernism in the field of art. By exposing the deficiencies of the prevalent, purely formalistic interpretation of the Russian avant-garde, and pointing toward a functionalist tradition of thought, he arrived at a concept of realism that made it possible for him to construct a counter-model in response to formalist Modernism.

Understanding realism as being part of a larger Marxist socialist project, Burgin, in a 1975 paper, quoted from Bertolt Brecht's essay "The Popular and the Realistic": "Realism is [...] a major political, philosophical and practical issue and must be handled and explained as such— as a matter of general human interest. [...] Realism means: revealing the mesh of causes in society. Unmasking the dominant viewpoints as viewpoints of those who dominate." (Burgin, 1976a: 363) In this light, realism does not refer to photography's putative ability to produce a copy of some aspect of the external objective reality. A realist use of photography would rather mean to reveal how the medium takes part in the construction of reality in the service of the dominating ideology. As I argue in Chapter 2, this is exactly what Burgin tried to do in his works of the 1970s. His photo-texts of this period pursue a "critical realism" in the sense of Hilde Van Gelder and Jan Baetens' definition of the term as "a practice, [...] as a way of seeking to understand the social reality by critically 'making notes' of it." (Baetens and Van Gelder, 2006: 9)

While questions of perception and memory have always been an issue in Burgin's early works (his critical realism might also be described as a "latent" psychical realism), by the end of the 1970s, in the wake of feminism, he adopted an explicitly psychoanalytical stance linked to his increasing interest in questions of sexual difference and power relations within representation. As of the early 1980s, Burgin embraced Freud's idea of another locality ("die Idee einer anderer Lokalität"), this other space that Lacan described as the *between perception and consciousness.*" (BN: 6) The concept of a "psychical realism" responds to this new orientation in Burgin's work:

> My use of the expression "psychical realism" however most particularly invokes the work of Freud, who began by trying—in the manner of a detective—to determine the actual historical truth of what his patients told him, but who subsequently came to realize that the historically real event is not all that is real for us, and that what he called 'psychical reality' plays as great a part in our perception of the world, and the formation of symptoms, as does physical reality. (SA: 110)

This emphasis on psychical reality is not least the result of a feeling that in a postmodern and postindustrial capitalist society, characterized by the ever-changing laws of the market and the scattered and fragmented space of representation induced by the mass media, the Marx-inspired project of aesthetic realism fails. (Lewis, 1987/88: 63) As I argue in Chapters 3 and 4, the works of the 1980s and 1990s are reflecting Burgin's insight that the complex imbrication of constantly overlapping heterogeneous temporal and spatial realities within the Western media society of the spectacle find their analogue in the functioning of unconscious fantasies and dreams. Psychical realism is then the answer to "a feeling of being inside a new space today—socially, politically, technologically, psychically." (63)

If Burgin described his work *Office at Night* (1985-86) as a "*re*-viewing of art through a prism of contemporary concerns" (BN: 182), the same can be said to apply to his entire work. These contemporary concerns are threefold: investigating the male gaze and pleasure within feminist debates, posing the question of the place of art and painting within a late capitalist society, and exploring the complex interrelationship of physical experience and imaginary associations within the heterogeneous environment of the mass media. Burgin's most recent works can be understood in terms of an expanded psychical realism in which the latest technological developments and techniques, in particular the Internet and virtual reality, are taken into account. Opening up an imaginary, psychical space where heterogeneous temporal and spatial layers are condensed and scattered across the virtual space of computer-generated images and the real space of the gallery, the projection works, which are analyzed in Chapter 5, investigate our experience of the world today, constantly oscillating between fiction and fact, fantasy and the real. In the age of the globalized space of television broadcasts and the Internet, Burgin argues that, "our everyday encounter with the environment of the media is the formal analogue of […] 'interior' processes as inner speech and involuntary association." (RF: 14) Reacting to current trends, phenomena, and discussions in the fields of digital technologies and social media, Burgin's use of 3-D computer modeling software and his thematization of virtual worlds such as Second Life suggest that in the twenty-first century a psychical realism has to come to terms with the fact of being a kind of second order realism, intercalating the algorithm "between the calculating subject and the object calculating." (Uricchio, 2011: 31) Echoing Lev Manovich's famous dictum of 1997 that "what computer graphics has (almost) achieved is not realism, but only *photorealism*," Burgin corroborates that today the "prevailing standard of realism in computer modelling is not the world as such, it is rather the world as it appears to the camera." (Manovich, 1997: 63; SDZ: 266) Consequently, *Afterlife* (2018) imagines a multiverse of alternative realities in which the thin line between the real, the virtual, and the psychic seems to be definitely erased, establishing the digital object as a pure psychical object. Yet this fantasy of an afterlife in the virtual metaverse is countered by the reintroduction of materiality and physical experience. Conceived as a classic book, *Afterlife* is a haptic object meant to be manipulated by the viewer-reader. This resistance to the purely virtual can also be observed in *Dear Urania* (2016), in which the computer-generated projection loops are integrated into the spatial display of the gallery through which the "peripatetic viewer" has to navigate her or his real body in order to gather the different elements of the work and organize them into a whole within her or his imagination (see Chapter 5, The Peripatetic Mode of Spectatorship). By addressing a physically *and* psychically active spectator and by leaving it up to her or him to reassemble the disparate fragments and narratives of the work, Burgin may be seen as taking a political stance against the highly capitalized productions of the film and videogame industries, in which the creation of computer-generated virtual spaces offers the spectator or the user total immersion into a perfectly simulated world. Operating at the threshold between the physical and the virtual, Burgin understands his psychical realism as a form of resistance: "Resistance to the assimilation of critical language to the neo-liberal cultural doxa is intrinsic to the various work of interstice creation." (SDZ: 33 and 39)

The particular focus of this book and the limits set by its length make it impossible to provide an exhaustive overview of Burgin's artistic work or to address all the issues at stake in it. I could not include a discussion of several works for lack of space, and I also had to put aside a variety of aspects worthy of consideration. For example, although the significance of the role of cinema, literature, music, and painting in Burgin's work recurs repeatedly, my argument in this book does not offer a systematic analysis of such influences.[1] Also, some readers may object that voices critical of Burgin's work are insufficiently addressed. Burgin's sometimes trenchant critique of certain artistic practices (for example, documentary political art and postmodernist painting) and his feminist and psychoanalytically informed approach has provoked some strong reactions indeed. In my view, however, these tend to be unbalanced and fail to do justice to the complexity of Burgin's work. When Jessica Evans, for example, objected that Burgin "prioritizes the intellectual labour of thinking over the pleasure of the text," (Evans, 1994: 216) she omitted the fact that it is precisely the reintroduction of visual pleasure that preoccupied Burgin in the early 1980s and that this led him to produce works which operate on an aesthetic level as much as on an intellectual one. Régis Durand, when asking himself whether knowledge of theory is a prerequisite for understanding Burgin's work, commented as follows: "*No*, for these works of art do not have a true meaning, which needs to be discovered by means of vast knowledge and expertise […]. *Yes*, in that the lack of such knowledge may cause great frustration in some spectators, as if they lacked the keys to the work." (Durand, 1991: 71) Burgin himself replied to the critiques of his psycho-realistic works of the 1980s: "You *don't* need a knowledge of psychoanalytical theory to deal with work like this—you simply need to know how to dream." (BN: 109) This is not to deny the fact, of course, that Burgin's works demand a considerable intellectual effort if one is to grasp the multiple layers of meaning contained in them. But it would certainly be wrong to disregard the associative and intuitive structure underlying his artistic work, causing it to be much closer to poetry than to intellectual demonstration.

Evans further argued that the rejection of a representation of politics in favor of a politics of representation would lead to a kind of universalist formalism that neglects content for the sake of the reflection of (formal) representational modes. (Evans, 1994: 206) Yet rather than being merely a formal exercise, a politics of representation will always interrogate the *meanings* of representations as well. If Burgin refutes the efficacy of art as a form of political activism, this does not mean that his work is not socially committed or without political content.[2] In this respect, Burgin rather endorses Jacques Rancière's dialectical concept of political art: "Suitable political art would ensure, at one and the same time, the production of a double effect: the readability of a political signification and a sensible or perceptual shock caused, conversely, by the uncanny, by that which resists signification." (Rancière, 2011: 63) Another critique that has been leveled at Burgin's artistic and theoretical work concerns his engagement with feminism. As also argued by Evans: "How can a male theorist use feminist theory without being part of the problem?" (Evans, 1994: 207) This is a thorny question indeed, one that probably does not allow a definite answer. The issue can even be taken one step further by asking: "how can a male art historian write on a male artist using feminist theory without being part of the problem?" But would the only way out of this conundrum be neither to use feminist theory nor—as an artist—to represent the female body? As discussed in Chapter 3, Burgin is perfectly aware of this problem and, rather than eluding it, he attempts to address and problematize it from his (heterosexual male) position, as one of a dialect of respect and desire for the woman. To borrow Burgin's own words about the project of a psychical realism: "impossible, but nevertheless…" (IDS: 56)

This brings me back to the book's primary concern, which is to suggest that Burgin's work contains the *possibility* of a psychical realism as an artistic project that rejects a clear distinction between the exterior physical reality and the interior psychical imagination; as a project that operates *between* memory and perception, fantasy and fact; as a project, finally, that adopts mechanisms of psychical processes and psychoanalytical theory in order to show how representations in our digital media society work—by analogy with unconscious discourses—while at the same time offering an alternative form of dreaming: an "interstice creation" (SDZ: 33) that resists easy assimilation to the flow of mass-media images within a neo-liberal consumer culture.

Chapter 1
Situational Aesthetics

1.1. Beyond Minimalism: From Object to Perception

Growing up in the industrial working-class town of Sheffield, Victor Burgin began his artistic training in London at the Royal College of Art (RCA), where Iris Murdoch was his tutor in philosophy. As once declared by Burgin, it was Murdoch who "introduced me to an intellectual rigour that was anathema to the entire institution of art as I had experienced it to that time." (Godfrey, 1982: 3) The philosopher's classes on British Empiricism and the reading of her book on Jean-Paul Sartre had a significant influence on Burgin's interest in theories of sensory perception and phenomenological ideas about experience of real-life situations. (CP: 15) Yet, it was from 1965 to 1967, during his studies at the Yale School of Art and Architecture, that Burgin found fertile ground for his artistic and intellectual growth, when he took classes in phenomenology and studied with artists such as Donald Judd, Robert Morris, Ad Reinhardt, and Frank Stella.

In the beginning of his years at Yale, the more expressive approach of his earlier paintings made way for a reduction of painterly means to simple geometrical all-over patterns and variations of flat grey paintings. (Godfrey, 1982: 3) (Fig. 1.1. and Fig. 1.2.) In 1965, Burgin describes his painting from his time at the RCA, before he went to Yale, as follows:

> I paint in series, each series representing an addition to my vocabulary. Generally, this present series investigates the way in which anonymous forms free colour: to what extent the function of the painted areas may be taken over by the areas which are bare, and in what sequences space may be made to shift by means of built-in alternative readings. Particularly, I hope by limiting my technical and formal means to achieve a purer presentation of the "things" about which I am unable to verbalise. (*Four Young Artists*, 1965: n.p.) (See Plate 1)

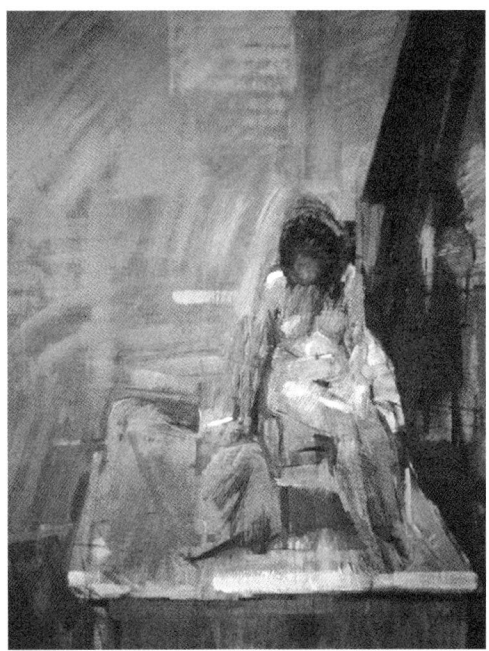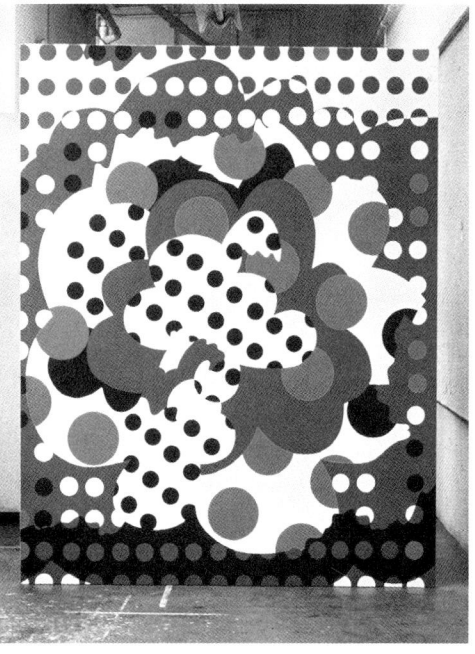

On the one hand, this comment situates Burgin's work within modernist painting concerned with the expression of the specific qualities of an artistic medium, in this case liberated color and figure-ground problems. On the other hand, the serial approach and the reasoning about his painting in terms of "thingness" indicate a new orientation toward Minimalism. The "Minimal sculpture programme" (Seymour, 1972: 74) and its phenomenologically informed theoretical framework, as developed in the writings by Robert Morris and Annette Michelson, had a decisive influence on Burgin's thinking in his Yale years, resulting in a shift in his artistic conception from the production of material objects to the mental organization of perceptions. This Minimalist approach culminated in several sculptures Burgin produced in his New Haven studio. Set against the wall or laid on the floor, these "paintings reduced to frames" consisted of wooden bars arranged to create angles. (CP: 16) Despite their material character, these works are neither sculptural objects nor pictorial frames. Being rather fragments of frames than closed rectangles, they open up to the environment and the situation in which they are placed and in which they may be interpreted either as a pictorial framing device or a window (if mounted to the wall) or an architectural ground plan (if put on the floor). In other words, they are contextual markers, which deflect the spectator's attention from the materiality of the art object to its function within a particular setting. (Fig. 1.3.)

Figure 1.1. (Left)
Life Study, 1958.

Figure 1.2. (Right)
Untitled, 1962

To use a central term of Burgin's seminal 1969 essay "Situational Aesthetics," these sculptural frames are actually "situational cues," that is, "substantial materials located in exterior space-time" which "subvert their objectness" by highlighting their function within a particular spatio-temporal situation. (SA: 10) I will come back to this crucial concept later on, but for now it suffices to say that Burgin's disapproval of the art object in favor of an emphasis on the problem of the frame's function as structuring device situates him within discussions taking place in the American art scene of the 1960s. In particular the dominance of Abstract Expressionism in the 1950s, including the accompanying modernist discourse, triggered a highly polarizing debate within the art world. This prompted artists who today we associate with Minimal art to oppose modernist ideas of autonomy, medium specificity, and formal composition, as well as to redefine sculpture as "real space" unity (Donald Judd), as "place" (Carl Andre), as a "function" of its environment (Robert Morris), or as "serial process." (Sol LeWitt)[3]

Although they seemed to reject the object as a unique, autonomous formal entity, it would still linger in exhibition spaces, often as massive, opaque matter demonstrating its material physical properties. Just think of Richard Serra's heavy steel plates or Donald Judd's huge indoor and outdoor pieces. Drawing on Judd's comment on geometrical forms and Morris's interrogation of the artwork's contextual framework, Burgin paved his way out of the Minimalist paradox of defining the work as a contextual function, while at the same time insisting on its material appearance. Referring to Judd's pondering "the discovery of a form which was neither geometric nor organic" (Seymour, 1972: 76), Burgin reasoned that such a form could only be a mental or

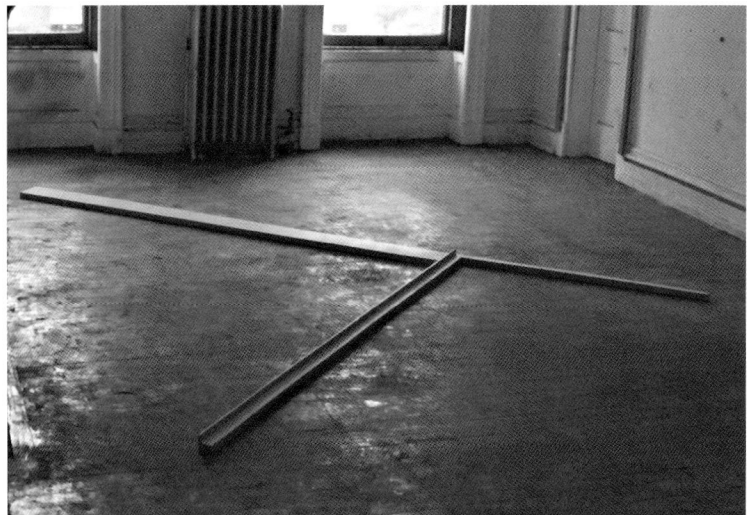

Figure 1.3.
Floor Piece, c. 1965.

psychological one. (Seymour, 1972: 76; Roberts, 1997: 80) And in re-sponse to Morris' definition of the work as merely one of the "terms" in the room, he asked: "If the work is a term no more important than any other term, why bother making it?" (Godfrey, 1982: 4)

This view fits in quite perfectly, of course, with the position of many of his artistic peers later associated with Conceptual art. As claimed by Soll LeWitt in his famous "Paragraphs on Conceptual Art" from 1967: "The idea itself, even if not made visual, is as much a work of art as any finished product." (LeWitt, 1999: 14) Lucy Lippard and John Chandler have described this highlighting of the immaterial idea at the expense of the physical object as a process of dematerialization, observable since the 1960s with the emergence of Minimal art and Conceptual art. In their influential essay, "The Dematerialization of Art," published in *Art International* in 1968, they wrote: "The studio is again becoming a study. Such a trend appears to be provoking a profound dematerialization of art, especially of art as object, and if it continues to prevail, it may result in the object's becoming wholly obsolete." (Lippard and Chandler, 1968: 31)

Burgin was unequivocal about his intention "to go beyond Minimal-ism and do away with the physical object entirely." (CP: 16) In 1967, he begun to write instructions on file cards, but two years later, after he realized that these pieces still contained an unresolved tension between their mental, linguistic character and the material objects that may re-sult from the instructions' execution, he introduced his pure text-works, which did not require any physical act to be performed at all. However, Burgin was never really interested in the dematerialization of the object by merely replacing it by the idea. In line with the sharp critique leveled by some conceptual artists at Lippard's position (Atkinson, 1999, 52-58), his main focus was rather on questions of perception and memory than on linguistic instructions or propositions concerning the act of making art. This can be illustrated by comparing the instructions that Burgin wrote on file-cards in 1967 with Lawrence Weiner's 1968 pub-lished small book *Statements* which contains twenty-four typewritten descriptions of works. Peter Osborne has related the work of both artists to the "performative character of the earliest (proto-fluxus) works of Conceptual art from 1961-62." (Osborne 2002a: 67-68) Osborne is right to observe that both Burgin and Weiner avoid the commanding imper-ative of many Fluxus scores and instructions, such as Georges Brecht's *Word Events* from 1961, in favor of a more neutral, indirect tone, often in the past tense. (68) However, the similarities end there, as can be shown by juxtaposing two seemingly similar statements on a room's al-teration by adding a material surface or skin to it. Where Weiner makes a reference to a "sheet of plywood secured to the floor or wall," Burgin talks about an "interior wall of a room to be concealed by a skin," say-ing that the "skin is parallel with and an eight-inch above the surface it conceals" and that the skin's color "simulates that of the concealed surface." Evidently, the two artists aim at completely different aesthetic purposes and effects. Weiner refers to the act of making a work, to the transformation of material matter to art by putting it on the wall (like a painting) or on the floor (like a sculpture). For him, making a work of art is a question of "expending a certain amount of material and a certain amount of energy."(Junker, 1968: 44; Alberro and Zimmerman, 1998: 46) Burgin, in contrast, avoids this figure-ground problem by concealing the real wall by a kind of mimicry skin. What is at stake here is not the production of an aesthetic object; instead, this is about the very conditions under which the act of perception takes place.

This shift from object to perception, from work to context, is clearly formulated in "Situational Aesthetics," published in 1969 in the October issue of *Studio International*. The essay begins with some observations on recent art's attention to "the conditions under which objects are perceived and to the process by which aesthetic status is attributed," emphasizing thus the linguistic character of "art as message, as software" and insisting on its systemic rather than objective nature. (SA: 7) While the problems of perception and the work's conditions relate to Minimalism, the definition of art in terms of language, information, and system clearly hints at the preoccupations of a new generation of conceptual artists, including Mel Bochner, Lawrence Weiner, Joseph Kosuth, Art and Language, and others. At this point, it is worth noticing that Joseph Kosuth's influential essay "Art after Philosophy," a kind of manifesto of linguistic Conceptualism, was published in the same *Studio International* issue as "Situational Aesthetics." But whereas Kosuth, drawing on analytical linguistic philosophy, declares art to operate on analytic propositions which tautologically "express definitions of art," denying the relevance of everything outside the art system (Kosuth, 1991: 21), Burgin, in contrast, insists on the relational character of art, including the spatiotemporal, perceptual, and psychical conditions as pivotal components of the work:

> [T]he specific nature of any object formed is largely contingent upon the details of the situation for which it is designed; through attention to time, objects formed are intentionally located partly in real, exterior space and partly in psychological, interior space. (SA: 7)

As the essay's title suggests, the concept of "situation" is crucial for both Burgin's theoretical thinking and his artistic practice. Robert Morris' abovementioned "Notes on Sculpture" certainly had a decisive influence on Burgin's concept of situational aesthetics. In this essay, in fact, Morris describes the work of art as an interaction of the object, its spatial context, and the beholder's subjective perception: "The better new work takes relationships out of the work and makes them a function of space, light, and the viewer's field of vision." (Morris, 1995: 232) Elsewhere, in the same text, Morris qualifies the work as "a term in the expanded situation" that has to be subjected to control in order to coordinate the variables of object, light, space, and body. (234) The theoretical notion on which Morris builds his relational concept of art is that of "gestalt." He argues that the simpler a geometric form is, the better it can be visualized and experienced as a unified whole, a gestalt. Only when the gestalt is established as a constant mental form can one be "both free of the shape and bound to it." (228) This means that the gestalt of a simple (regular or irregular) form makes one aware of the way one perceives the object within a given situation.

1.2. Role-playing: Behavior and Memory

This shift from object to perception was certainly of importance for Burgin's conception of situational aesthetics. However, he is less interested in the mental reconstruction of a physical object encountered in the present space-time than in the way this encounter acts on the spectator in terms of behavior and memory. The perception of the work, then, concerns not only the experience of the work in the present time, but it also relates to the psychological time of memories and recollections from the past. Consisting of two rope triangles displayed in Greenwich Park, London, *Memory Piece* from 1969 perfectly illustrates this "recognition of a multiplicity of times, the concentration on process and behavior." (SA: 13) (Fig. 1.4. and Fig 1.5.) As the general instructions read:

Figure 1.4.

Memory Piece,
Two similar units
36×36×36 ft, 1967.

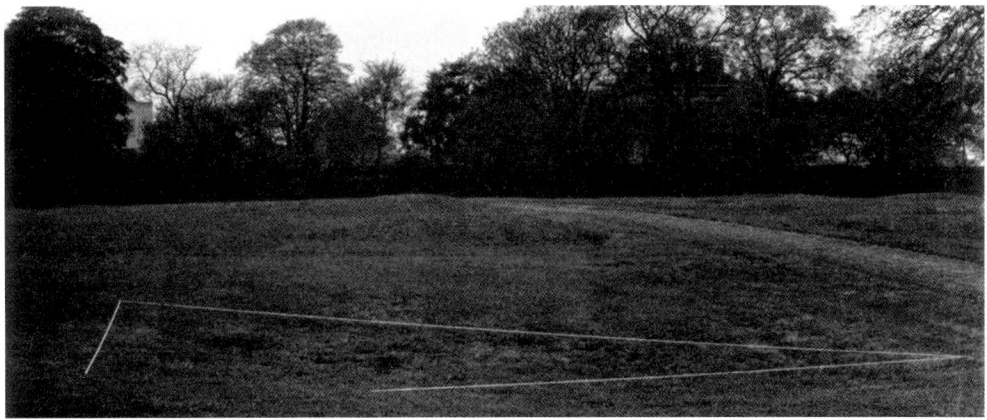

1. Two units co-exist in time
2. Spatial separation is such that units may not simultaneously be directly perceived.
3. Units isomorphic to degree that encounter with second is likely to evoke recollection of first.

The fact that the work consists of two temporally and spatially separated fragments situates it in both the exterior physical space and the subjective interior space of personal associations and memories. It is thus not surprising that Burgin's principal argument against Michael Fried's modernist agenda of medium specificity pertains primarily to the time aspect. If the perception of all works of art—be it music, theatre, painting, or sculpture—is based on a temporal process of confronting actual present experiences with recalled images and memory data, it follows that the distinction between "arts of space" and "arts of time" is misleading.

In Burgin's *Memory piece*, the spectator discovers the work successively while crossing the park. But what exactly is discovered depends largely on his behavior, which is determined by his momentary mood, attitude, and attention, as well as on his general knowledge and sensibility. Due to the Minimalist form of the work, a distracted or preoccupied person may see nothing at all, or he may pass the first triangle more or less unconsciously, only to remember its existence when encountering the second isomorphic structure. In contrast, an attentive observer, familiar with contemporary art, may recognize the triangles

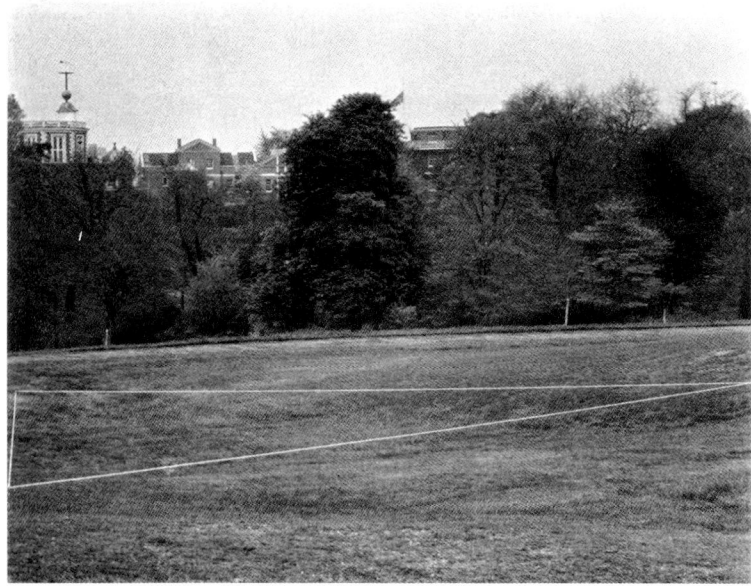

Figure 1.5.

Memory Piece, Two similar units 36×36×36 ft, 1967.

as part of a work of art. In all cases, however, it is impossible to have a unique, immediate experience of the work as advocated by modernist critics Clement Greenberg and Michael Fried. In terms of the issue of behavior within situational aesthetics, it is nevertheless instructive to have a closer look at Fried's polemical critique of Minimalism. In his much-discussed essay "Art and Objecthood" (1967), Fried rejects minimal or "literalist" art as non-art, as a kind of theater that involves real space and includes the experience of the spectator. His conception of Minimalism as a theatrical event "capable of achieving remarkable effects of 'presence' […by] deploy[ing] and isolat[ing] objects and persons in 'situations,'" brings in the notions of behavior and role-playing. (Fried, 1998: 171)

Even though the conclusions drawn by Fried from his observations concerning the definition of art are highly problematic, it is remarkable that his association of "situational" art and theater seems to make a significant point. In this respect, it is worth mentioning that in the very same year of the publication of Burgin's "Situational Aesthetics" the American writer and artist Michael Kirby independently used exactly the same expression in his book *The Art of Time: Essays on the Avant-Garde*.[4] As he writes:

> [A]n object seen as a work of art is psychologically placed in a cultural-historical context that determines the characteristics of the experience. Traditional aesthetics asks that the perception of a work of art exist "out of time," as it were. Situational or historical aesthetics sees the work in the context of time where the trans-sensory elements are of fundamental importance. (Kirby, 1969: 45–46)

In opposition to Greenberg's modernist formalism, Kirby insists on the artwork's "significance as a *quality of perception*" (26), emphasizing "the subjective aspects of experience rather than […] the thing experienced. (23) Kirby develops his anti-essentialist considerations on aesthetic experience in terms of relation, interaction, and situation on the basis of his theoretical and practical involvement with performance art and theater. Yet, aside from common interests in phenomenology and perception theory, Burgin seems more concerned with questions of memory and behavior.

As the first scientific reference in "Situational Aesthetics," Burgin quotes the cognitive psychologist Karl H. Pribram: "Somewhere between the retina and the visual cortex the inflowing signals are modified to provide information that is already linked to a learned response." (SA: 9; Pribram, 1969a: 76) In other words, perception is never only a matter of reproduction (of the external world), but depends, to a large extent, on patterns pre-structured by past experiences and memories. Accordingly, Burgin posits, aesthetic objects "are located partly in real space and partly in psychological space." (SA: 9) Memory, therefore, is a fundamental aspect of the constitution of an aesthetic object. In another paper, "The Physiology of Remembering," Pribram further suggests that "changes in patterns of organization—coding—are as important to the process of effective remembering as is storage *per se*." (Pribram, 1969b: 80) *Memory piece* functions as a demonstration of this, as the spectator automatically superposes on the second triangle, present to the retina, the "memorized configuration" of the first triangle that he encountered shortly before. (SA: 12) The process of recollection alters the perception of both the first triangle and the second one:

> Consciousness would be sent back through its memory data assembling *en route* an object analogue composed of recalled images, the relationships between these fragments to be governed by personal associative propensities. The life of this conceptual element might be brief though repeated path-tracing between the two cues would probably favour a particular sequence of forms and impress them on the memory. (SA: 11)

Shifting appearances, then, interact with shifting memories. From this follows that Burgin's interest in perception and memory, rather than being reduced to the cognitive process, implies the behavior of the perceiver. This leads him to Morse Peckham's widely discussed book *Man's Rage for Chaos. Biology, Behaviour, and the Arts*. In a footnote, Burgin quotes Peckham as writing that "art is not a category of perceptual fields but of role-playing." (SA: 14) In fact, Burgin's essay appears to owe a lot to Peckham's book regarding terminology and aesthetic concepts, specifically with respect to the definition of art as a form of behavior and the recommendation to use substantial materials as "situational cues" rather than for their objective qualities.

Peckham defines works of art as consequences or deposits of cultural patterns of behavior. (Peckham, 1965: 11) According to him, the work of art and its specific context give the perceiver "an orientation involving socially standardized behavior." Within this situation, the perceiver is playing a "particular social role, a culturally transmitted combination of patterns of behavior." (40) Peckham understands this idea of role-playing in terms of stage-acting. (52) While the actor plays his role on-stage, the audience re-acts to the particular situation in which he finds himself and plays his own role as audience. The term Peckham uses to establish the connection between situation and role involves a theatrical metaphor as well. In order to know what kind of social role we have to play in a given situation, we pick up "cues" implicit in that situation: "In all human behavior we take our cues not only from other performers but also from the situation. It is the situation that tells us how we are supposed to behave." (64) This shift in the definition of art from object to cue, entailing an emphasis on the perceiver's space, is crucial for Burgin's concept of situational aesthetics. A work of art, then, is *an occasion for a human being to perform the art-perceiving role in the artistic situation, that is, on the artistic stage.*" (66)

Burgin's borrowing of theatrical terms from Peckham—such as "situation," "cue," and "role-playing"—might prompt the conclusion that his works of this period have in common with Minimalism what Michael Fried called "stage presence." (Fried, 1998: 155) But while Fried refers to the anthropomorphic character of Minimalist works and their quality as objects experienced in time, Burgin goes one step further by reducing the work to a set of cues within a situation.

1.3. Photography between Reflection and Recollection

Burgin's use of photography in this period is particularly revealing in this respect. Displayed for the first time at the London edition of Harald Szeemann's landmark show *When Attitudes Become Form*, *Photopath* consists of twenty-one photographs constituting a path along the floor. (Fig. 1.6. and Fig. 1.7.) Printed to actual size, the images represent exactly what they hide: the floor on which they are placed. Tony Godfrey described this piece as "a dematerialized version of Carl Andre's Lever." (Godfrey, 1998: 205) Actually, Andre wrote about his work: "My idea of a piece of sculpture is a road. That is, a road doesn't reveal itself at any particular point or from any particular point." (Tuchman, 1970: 57) But unlike Andre's physical objects, Burgin's path is a virtual one. The fragile character of the photographic print implies that it is not to be walked on, but to be looked at. The work cannot be removed without being destroyed.

In "Situational Aesthetics," Burgin describes this kind of work as "an immaterial object […] which is solely a function of perceptual behavior, but which yet inducts attributes of physicality from its material setting." (SA: 8) In this respect, Peter Osborne has observed that photography "functions

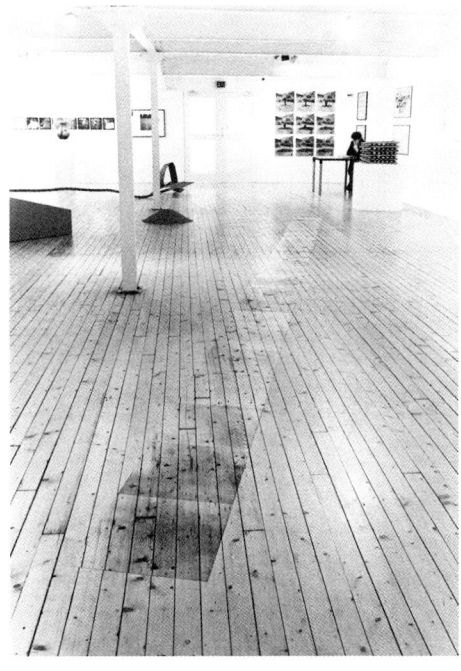

Figure 1.6.

Photopath, 1967–1969.

Installation view, Fruitmarket Gallery, Edinburgh, 1985.

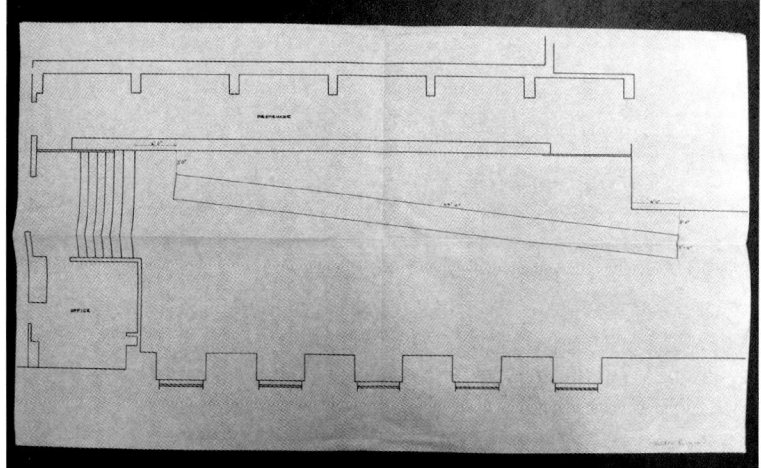

Figure 1.7.

Photopath, Sketch for ICA
exhibition, London, 1969.

here as a new kind of blank form." (Osborne, 2002a: 67) His conclusion, however, that the photograph, rather than pointing to its own qualities, functions as a means to "'select' a portion of the environment" seems to be too reductive. Insofar as the floor's concealment beneath the photographs questions the myth of photography's transparency, while the setting further reveals the medium's dependency of its spatial and institutional context, *Photopath* can also be interpreted as a work *about* photography. Different from other conceptual artists using photography, Burgin understands the medium neither as "technical data like industrial photography" (Ed Ruscha, quoted in Lippard, 2001: xiv), nor as a "deadpan version of the photographic document" (Batchen, 2003: 177) or merely a "tool with which to initiate ideas." (Alloway 1970: 3-4)[5] The photographs of *Photopath* are both reflexive of their own function and exploratory of the spatio-temporal conditions in which they occur and to which they refer as "situational cues." In this particular work, as pointed out by Burgin in an interview, he was "using photography to signify recollection." (Seymour, 1972: 74) Photography, in other words, is not reduced to its documentary function to store past events; it draws the viewer's attention to the very act of recollection in showing something that is there and not there at the same time.

An unpublished proposal for the ICA exhibition reveals clearly the tension between the psychological space-time of recollection and the material experience of real space-time. In a letter to Charles Harrison, the organizer of the London show, Burgin writes: "Proposal for ICA—A conceptual object concerned with a space/time path having its terminal points in Nash House and a private house in Nottingham." After listing the already well-known steps that have to be followed to create the ICA terminal's segment, he adds: "The Nottingham terminal is constructed and situated in a similar manner and is one third the size of the ICA terminal."[6]

This means that, originally, Burgin intended to connect the ICA photopath over a distance of around 130 miles with a smaller version of it, adapted to the conditions of a private house at Nottingham where from 1967 to 1973 he taught as a lecturer at the Trent Polytechnic. As in *Memory piece*, it is impossible for the spectator to experience both parts at the same time. But unlike the former work, the ICA proposal introduces a social dimension in the form of the institutional and private aspects of scale, while it also questions the role of photography, as a means of representation, in terms of the relationship between perception and recollection.

As Burgin states in an interview with John Roberts, *Photopath* is "a gesture to draw attention to the conditions of perception without actually altering the environment too much." (Roberts, 1997: 82) The work, then, is neither a transparent document nor a material object, but rather a gesture, or a situational cue, which is meant to invite the viewer's critical reflection on modes of perception. This use of photography is, of course, completely different from the way most other conceptual artists employ the medium. Lawrence Weiner's proposal for the ICA show, for instance, was also based on an instruction, reading: "A RIVER SPANNED." After indicating that, in the exhibition, only a small card with those written words was to be displayed, the realization of the work being without importance, Weiner goes on as follows:

> If you decide to build the piece the choice of spanning used again rests with you. Please—Under no circumstances are there to be photographs of the piece shown in the exhibition area. If the piece is constructed I do not mind photographs in any media. My only concern is that photographs are not exhibited as Art. (Letter to Charles Harrison, Tate Archive, London)

Documentation is undoubtedly an issue in Burgin's early photographic work. *25ft two hours* (1969) consists of twenty-five photographs registering a file-card container being moved in a straight line and by one foot stages, through twenty-five feet. (Fig. 1.8.) Further, the apparently identical photographs were identified with the index cards from the box and filed in the box under the respective letter of the alphabet. Aside from the unresolved question of whether the instruction has to be executed or not, the status of the photographs is ambiguous. They are documents, insofar as they represent a segment of reality in a neutral, unexpressive way. They may further be related to serial photography in the tradition of Eadweard Muybridge's chronophotography, highly recommended by conceptual artists Sol LeWitt and Dan Graham for its capacity "to fixate the *real* mobile to be reproduced as an illusion by means of the immobile." (Graham 2001: 104) Unlike Renaissance perspective, Graham observes, "[t]here is no single, fixed point of view. The changes are positional and only involve the motion of the *reader's* eye." (106) This shift from the single photograph as a fixation of objects in space toward an understanding of the medium as temporal process involving the viewer's perception is a crucial point in Burgin's photographic work. In the case of *25ft two hours*, another aspect is of major interest: the systematic submission of the making of the work, including the photographs, to the alphabetic writing system. Similar to Robert Morris' *Card-file* from 1962, in which the artist categorizes the material and conceptual conditions of the work's production according to the alphabetic index cards of the file, Burgin's piece records the steps of its own making. Still, it would be wrong merely to describe *25ft two hours* as a piece about artistic production and behavior. It is more about language and the process of perception. In "Situational Aesthetics," in which the work is printed in order to illustrate the text (Seymour, 1972: 74), Burgin describes perception as "a continuum, a precipitation of event fragments decaying in time." (SA: 10) The photographs in *25ft two hours* are succeeding fragments of an event, and as such they are also cues or metaphors for the continuous flux of perception.

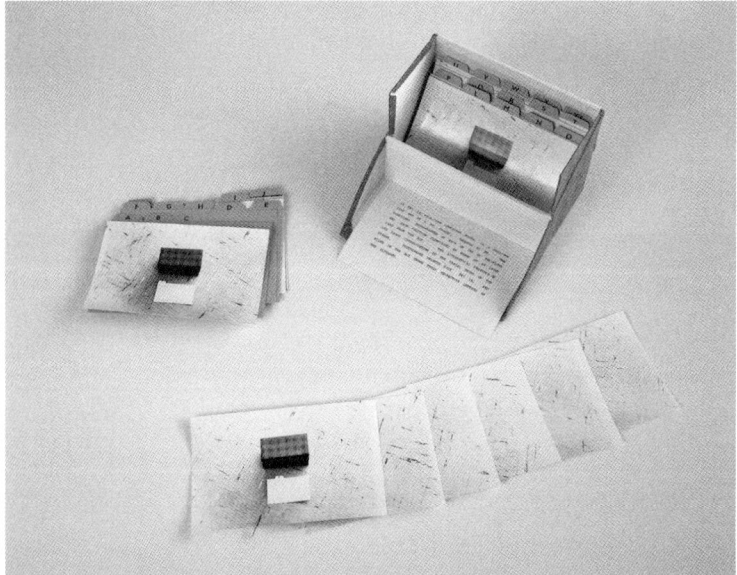

Figure 1.8.

25ft Two Hours, 1967.

1.4. Serial Art and Systems

As demonstrated by *25ft two hours*, perception is not a single thing, but organized serially. In his essay "Constancy and Invariance in Perception," James Gibson argues that "visual perception is unbounded. We are aware of a world that surrounds us like a panorama, not a cone of rays." (Gibson, 1965: 63) The panoramic character of *Photopath* and many other early pieces may be related to this idea of the 360-degree mode of perception as suggested by Gibson, an author to whom Burgin refers repeatedly in his earlier writings.[7] The first file-card work printed in the catalogue of the ICA show provides the following instruction: "Back to the wall, take a polaroid photograph of the door. Pin the print to the wall immediately behind your head. Move along the wall repeating the procedure five times."

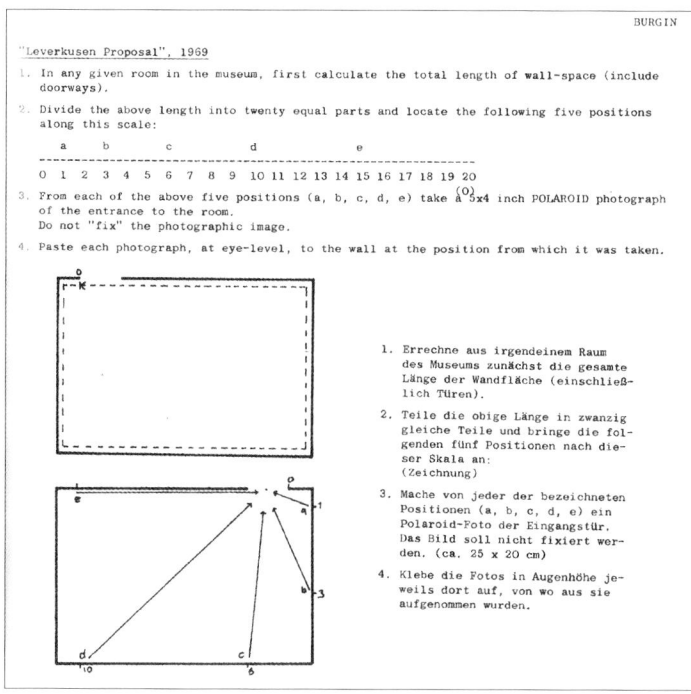

Figure 1.9.

Leverkusen Proposal, 1969.

In: Rolf Wedewer (ed.), *Konzeption—Conception*, cat. Städtisches Museum Leverkusen, Schloß Morsbroich, 1969.

A similar piece, *Leverkusen Proposal*, printed in the catalogue of the exhibition *Konzeption-Conception*, held in 1969 at Museum Morsbroich in Leverkusen, specifies that the five positions from which the photographs are to be taken must be defined according to a division of the total length of the wall-space into twenty equal parts. (Fig. 1.9.) The polaroids, pasted on the wall, at eye-level, according to the position

from which they were taken, thus demonstrate the panoramically organized vision
of the room by a spectator entering the
room. I will come back to the panorama
as a means to organize vision and perception in Chapter 5. Another important
aspect of the work is its serial, systematic,
and informational character. Reproduced
on the two pages immediately preceding
the *Leverkusen Proposal*, the work *Carton
Programme, March 1968* is based on a set
of numeric and graphical configurations.
(Wedewer 1969: n.p.)

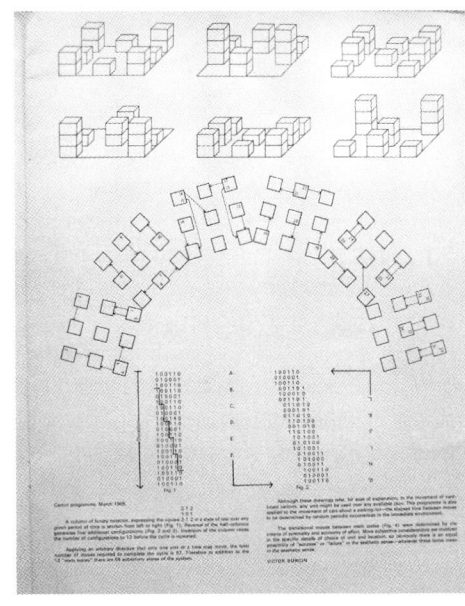

First published in 1968, in the fourth issue of *Control Magazine, Carton Progamme*
is Burgin's first work conceived for and
printed in a magazine. (Fig. 1.10.) In consists of a column of binary notations which
express a configuration of cubes plus ad-
ditional configurations generated by a procedure of reversal of the
half-column. As a permutational system determined by a set of pre-
defined data rules, *Carton Progamme* may be compared to conceptual work that emerged out of Minimalism dealing "with idea systems
of logical, mathematical and spatio-temporal relations." (Osborne,
2002b: 23) Sol LeWitt's description of his *Serial Project No. 1 (ABCD)*
(1966) is also valid for Burgin's piece:

Figure 1.10.

Carton programme,
March 1968. In: *Control
Magazine*, 4, 1968.

> It would be a finite series using the square and cube as its syntax.
> […] The evidence given him or her [the spectator] by the other
> pieces in the set, and by reference to the other sets will inform
> the viewer as to what should be there. (LeWitt, 1978: 170)

In the second half of the 1960s, artists and critics interrogated the
notion of "serial art," including its relation to systems. In 1967, Mel
Bochner published his article "Serial Art, Systems, Solipsism," in
which he claimed the abstract, self-contained, and non-referential character of serial art. Referring to works by LeWitt, Don Judd, Hanne
Darboven, Dan Graham, and himself, Bochner emphasizes the pre-
determined, systematic logic of serial art, "without adjustments based
on taste or chance," in order to avoid subjective personal decision
making. (Bochner 1968: 100) In the following year, Jack Burnham introduced the expression "Systems Aesthetics," claiming that "we are
now in transition from an object-oriented to a system-oriented culture."
(Burnham, 1968: 31) Referring, like Burgin, to Peckham's *Man's Rage*

for Chaos, Burnham notices a shift from art as material entity to art as a function of the relation between people and their environment. (31) This position is much closer to Burgin's than LeWitt's or Bochner's. Bochner may have tried to overcome such traditional artistic values as subjective expression, hierarchical composition, and the autonomy of the material object, but eventually he got stuck in modernist assumptions of self-reflexivity. Burnham, in contrast, would stress the situational, interactive component of art and its embeddedness in a broader cultural and social context.

At first glance, *Carton Programme* and LeWitt's *Serial Project* seem to be inspired by control systems, as they are described in terms of cybernetics and communication theory. Norbert Weiner's definition of the ideal computing machine reads like an instruction for such works:

> The ideal computing machine must then have all its data inserted at the beginning, and must be as free as possible from human interference to the very end. This means that not only must the numerical data be inserted at the beginning, but also all the rules for combining them, in the form of instructions covering every situation which may arise in the course of the computation. Thus the computing machine must be a logical machine as well as an arithmetic machine and must combine contingencies in accordance with a systematic algorithm. (Weiner 1961: 118)

Since the mid-1960, cybernetics and theories of communication, information, media, and system became increasingly popular in art and aesthetic theory. Two exhibitions from 1970, *Software, Information Technology: Its New Meaning of Art* curated by Jack Burnham and *Information* curated by Kynaston McShine, emphasized the new "sense of communication" in recent art at the time. (McShine, 1970: 141) With its focus on the relationship between art and technology, Burnham's show drew on the notion of "software" as a metaphor for the way artists deal with "information systems and their devices." (Shaken, 2002: 434) In Les Levine's *Contact: A Cybernetic Sculpture* (1969) or Hans Haacke's *Photo-Electric Viewer-Programmed Coordinate System* (1966-68), the strong affinity with new technologies and communication theories is suggested already in the title. In the short statement that accompanies *Carton Programme* in *Control Magazine*, Burgin evokes explicitly cybernetics and media theory as relevant points of reference. However, he resolutely rejects the categorical analogy often drawn between science and art in general, and cybernetics and the artwork's function in particular. "Art, unlike science," he writes, "does not investigate—it produces." And some lines further on, Burgin states:

[I]t would be wrong to say that art itself is a "control" in the cybernetic sense as it disrupts, rather than encourages, stability. Art is neither a control in the cybernetic sense nor in the strongest literal sense as "the power of command." Art may be honestly said to exert social control only within the limitations of its being a structuring factor in the perceived environment, responsible for modifications in our perceptual role-playing, and a general influence as an activity amongst the community of activities which constitute society. (Burgin, 1968: n.p.)

This is, of course, Morse Peckham's aesthetics of discontinuity, according to which the artist's role is to create disorder and unexpected situations in order to make the perceiver aware of the disparity between his conventional experiences and orientations and "the data his interaction with the environment actually produces." (Peckham, 1965: 313)

Carton Programme reflects both aspects: the technological, scientific and the social, behavioral. In creating an apparently logical system mimicking procedures of scientific technological programs (binary notation, pre-determination, numerical combination), Burgin, like other conceptual artists, dashes the expectations of traditional aesthetic values such as uniqueness, subjectivity, and expression. But he also questions the then pervasive identification of art with science or of artworks with pre-defined, operational technological communication systems that operate independently of external influences. The arbitrary directives to generate new constellations (reversal of the half-columns or the directive that only one unit at a time may move) do not have any function or purpose other than making the spectator aware of his own role-playing when re-constructing in his mind the various sets which occur from this process. The system is neither self-fulfilling, like LeWitt's *Serial Project*, nor self-contained and non-referential, as Bochner would like to have serial art. Burgin includes the possibility to apply his program to social contexts ("the movement of cars about a parking-lot") or to involve subjective considerations, as in game-playing with unpredictable results.

1.5. The Text Works and the Perceptual Field

At the end of 1969, Burgin showed his "first self-sufficient written work, in a small show in Nottingham." (Seymour, 1972: 74) *This Position* was the response to the problem of how to deal with the tension between (linguistic) instruction and (material) execution, still unresolved in the file-card works. (Fig. 1.11.) The work comprises a sequence of eleven sentences, glued on the walls of the room in a way that the gallery visitor has to move along the walls in order to read them. The 1974 catalogue of the Art Council's new acquisitions contains the following concise description of the piece:

> The viewer stands at each place to read a sentence beginning "This position…" which directs his attention to a specific aspect of himself in relation to a time interval and, or to other people or things. The sequence is introduced by means of a hypothetical point in time, x and terminates at another, later point, x'. All the other refer to the interval between these two, an analogy of the fact that they are read in the time which elapses between reading the first and last sentences themselves. (*Art as a Thought Process*, 1974: 24)

The bodily experience of the environment is thus connected with the mental act of reading. Exterior space and interior space coalesce in the mind of the spectator who is invited to relate the position of his body with all kinds of physical and psychological actions and projections experienced within a given duration. The complete elimination of material components is also crucial for the question of the relation between interior and exterior time, which becomes increasingly important in the text works. As Burgin states in a short text published in the journal *Architectural Design*: "In the absence of objects we become more aware of duration, revealed through changes in our perceptual field." (Burgin, 1970a: 388) Sentences six to eight propose to the reader a reflection on the complex layers of time involved in our experience of duration, passing from exterior time ("all time external to self") to interior time of the self ("all integration of interior time of self with exterior time") and concluding with the comparison of one's own temporal experience with that of the other ("similarly integrated with interior time of another"). This shift from real (exterior) time-space to psychological (interior) time-space is also a crucial issue in *Room*, made for the exhibition *Idea Structures*, held in 1970 at Camden Arts Centre, London. Similar to *This Position*, the work was pasted at equal intervals on the walls of an empty room.

As observed, this kind of panoramic arrangement is reflective of Gibson's reasoning on "unbounded perception." A continuous, horizontal structure without closure, the panorama expresses further Burgin's preoccupation to avoid composition and "the unique art work status." (Burgin, *The Tate Gallery Report*, 1975: 95) This is perfectly in line with other conceptual artists' concern to reject traditional values of form and substance in favor of content and abstract ideas. In the very same year as *Room*'s presentation at the *Idea Structures* show, Joseph Kosuth installed his *Information Room* as "Special Investigation" in Donald Karshan's exhibition *Conceptual Art and Conceptual Aspects* at

THIS POSITION SIGNIFIES ANY MOMENT IN DURATION OF SELF (X)

THIS POSITION SIGNIFIES ALL INTERIOR TIME OF SELF SUBSEQUENT TO X AND PREVIOUS TO X'

THIS POSITION SIGNIFIES ALL INTERIOR MODIFICATIONS PERFORMED BY SELF UPON EXTERIOR PHENOMENA SUBSEQUENT TO X AND PREVIOUS TO X'

THIS POSITION SIGNIFIES ALL PROJECTIONS OF CONCEPTS AND GOALS OF SELF ONTO ANOTHER SUBSEQUENT TO X AND PREVIOUS TO X'

THIS POSITION SIGNIFIES ALL PROJECTIONS OF FANTASY PROTOTYPES CONCEIVED BY SELF ONTO ANOTHER SUBSEQUENT TO X AND PREVIOUS TO X'

THIS POSITION SIGNIFIES ALL TIME EXTERNAL TO SELF SUBSEQUENT TO X AND PREVIOUS TO X'

Figure 1.11.

This Position, 1969.

In: Victor Burgin, *Work and Commentary*, London, Latimer, 1973.

THIS POSITION SIGNIFIES ALL INTEGRATION OF INTERIOR TIME OF SELF WITH EXTERIOR TIME SUBSEQUENT TO X AND PREVIOUS TO X'

THIS POSITION SIGNIFIES ALL INTEGRATION OF INTERIOR TIME OF SELF WITH EXTERIOR TIME SIMILARLY INTEGRATED WITH INTERIOR TIME OF ANOTHER SUBSEQUENT TO X AND PREVIOUS TO X'

THIS POSITION SIGNIFIES ALL SENSORIMOTOR REFLEXES OF SELF SUBSEQUENT TO X AND PREVIOUS TO X'

THIS POSITION SIGNIFIES ALL EXCHANGES OF CODED MOTOR ACTION BETWEEN SELF AND ANOTHER SUBSEQUENT TO X AND PREVIOUS TO X'

THIS POSITION SIGNIFIES ANY MOMENT IN DURATION OF SELF WHICH IS LATER THAN X, (X') the New York Cultural Center. Containing all kinds of books, art magazines, and newspapers, Kosuth's personal library transformed the exhibition space into "a venue for knowledge rather than a container for objects." (Rorimer, 2004: 100) In contrast with Burgin's work, the experience and perception of the situation in which art takes place, the exhibition room, is completely disregarded in Kosuth's room piece. Reduced to an "environment for intellectual consumption" (100), *Information Room* finally brackets the spatial and perceptual conditions of the encounter with the work for the sake of mere (and unilateral) transmission of information.

While still concerned with questions of perception within a given situation, the eighteen parts of *Room* put increasing emphasis on inner processes. From "substantial things" (1), the text passes to "duration" (2), from "appearances" (4) to "recollections" (5), from "bodily acts" (8) and "bodily sensations" (12) to "emotions" (13) and "inner experiences" (16). The general, objective diction of the sentences, deliberately used in allusion to "British Empiricist philosophy" (*The Tate Gallery Report*, 1975: 95), as well as the rising complexity, caused by the more extensive logical deductions made each time from the previous propositions, contribute to the displacement of the spectator's attention from body to mind. Rather than relating to a specific spatio-temporal experience, the work is conceived as a "mental set" (96) that provides general "cues" for both perception and how we (re)construct perception through language.

The shift in focus from present, exterior actions to interior and recollected perceptions culminates in the following two text-works, *All Criteria* and *Any Moment*, both published in 1970 in contexts of printed matter. (Fig. 1.12.) *All Criteria* was "an answer to the problem of placing a piece like that [*Room*] in a catalogue." (Seymour, 1972: 74) Burgin was aware that *Room*, if printed in the catalogue, could be encountered in whatever space the reader would be located at the moment of his reading. As the page may potentially be read in any situation, a new piece, specifically created for the catalogue, should avoid any reference to anything that might not be present to the reader. Consequently, he conceived for the catalogue a completely new work, *All Criteria*, in which he invites the reader to compare and define acts and events happening in time rather than in space. This step from the exhibition room to the page has far-reaching consequences for the work's conception. While Burgin insists on the "second-order" character of his file-card instructions (Seymour, 1972: 74), these catalogue and magazine text-works suspend the hierarchical distinction between word (instruction or description) and object (final work).

The problem of the proportionate inclusion of primary and secondary information in relation to the use of the printed page as artistic format was very popular in this period. From the mid-1960s, numerous conceptual artists produced work for magazines in order to move away from traditional exhibition spaces, such as galleries and museums, and to replace the material art object by a text- and information-based concept of art. Dan Graham's *Poem Schema* (March 1966), printed in May 1969 in the first issue of *Art-Language*, is representative of this tendency. Listing a series of component variants to which the actual data are to be added according to each published appearance, *Poem Schema* defines itself as information about its own conditions and context. (Graham, 2001: 95) It was Seth Siegelaub who drew the consequences from this in replacing the exhibition space by the catalogue. In the introduction to the catalogue of the group exhibition *January 5-31, 1969 (Barry, Huebler, Kosuth, Weiner)*, he suggests: "The exhibition consists of (the ideas communicated in) the catalogue; the physical presence (of the work) is supplementary to the catalogue." (Siegelaub, 1969: n.p.) In a conversation with Charles Harrison, published in December 1969 in Studio International, Siegelaub added:

> The use of catalogues and books to communicate (and disseminate) art is the most neutral means to present the new art. The catalogue can now act as primary information for the exhibition, as opposed to secondary information about art in magazines, catalogues, etc., and in some cases the "exhibition" can be the "catalogue." (Harrison, 1969: 202)

When Burgin evokes the "second-order" character of his instruction cards, this has to be considered against the backdrop of the outlined context. With *All Criteria*, he uses for the first time the printed page as a work in its own right, as "first-order" information. It is thus not surprising that Charles Harrison selected *Any Moment* for his 8-page section of Seth Siegelaub's "48-page exhibition" included in the *Studio International* edition of July-August 1970. Like Graham's *Poem Schema*, *Any Moment* reflects the conditions under which the work is encountered. But while Graham refers to the piece's own properties and to the media context in which it appears, Burgin draws the attention away from the text as fact toward the reader's immediate perceptual experience of objects, bodily acts and sensations, as well as emotions and memories.

In the catalogue of Kynaston McShine's exhibition *Information*, the same piece, printed on the left-hand side, is juxtaposed, on the right-hand page, to a list of the locations situated on the 51.28 degrees North latitude, which the artist extracted from *The Times Atlas of the World*. (CP: 44) (Fig. 1.13.) The subjective, local experience of the reader is thus contrasted with the global horizon of scientifically collected, objective data.

1
ALL CRITERIA BY WHICH YOU MIGHT DECIDE THAT ANY SERIES OF BODILY ACTS, DIRECTLY KNOWN TO YOU AT ANY MOMENT PREVIOUS TO THE PRESENT MOMENT, CONSTITUTES A DISCRETE EVENT

2
ALL CRITERIA BY WHICH YOU MIGHT ASSESS THE SIMILARITY OF ANY ONE EVENT TO ANY OTHER EVENT

3
ANY SERIES OF SIMILAR EVENTS DIRECTLY KNOWN TO YOU PREVIOUSLY TO THE PRESENT MOMENT

4
ANY OBJECT WITHIN 3 WHICH YOU KNOW TO BE THE SAME INDIVIDUAL THROUGHOUT 3 AND TOWARDS WHICH ANY BODILY ACTS WERE DIRECTED

5
ALL CRITERIA BY WHICH YOU MIGHT ASCRIBE INDIVIDUALITY TO THINGS OTHER THAN OBJECTS

6
ALL INDIVIDUALS WITHIN 3 OTHER THAN OBJECTS

7
A HYPOTHETICAL EVENT IN SERIES WITH 3 OCCURRING LATER THAN THE PRESENT MOMENT

8
AN OBJECT WITHIN 7 WHICH IS THE SAME INDIVIDUAL AS 4

Figure 1.12.

All Criteria, 1970.

In: Victor Burgin, *Work and Commentary*, London, Latimer, 1973.

9
ALL HYPOTHETICAL INDIVIDUALS WITHIN 7 OTHER THAN OBJECTS

10
ALL INDIVIDUALS WHICH ARE BOTH MEMBERS OF 9 AND OF 6

11
ANY OBJECT DIRECTLY KNOWN TO YOU AT THE PRESENT MOMENT TOWARDS WHICH ANY BODILY ACT IS DIRECTED

12
ALL INDIVIDUALS DIRECTLY KNOWN TO YOU AT THE PRESENT MOMENT OTHER THAN OBJECTS

13
THE SUBSTITUTION OF 11 FOR 8 AND FOR 4

14
THE SUBSTITUTION OF 12 FOR 9 AND FOR 6

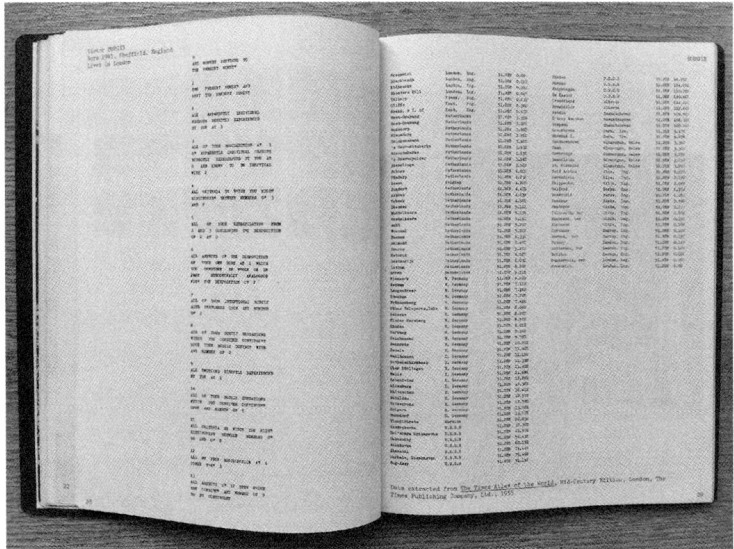

Figure 1.13.

Any Moment (1970) and data extracted from *The Times Atlas of the World*. In: Kynaston McShine (ed.), *Information*, cat., Museum of Modern Art, New York, 1970.

1.6. Linguistic Art and Ideology

The linguistic character of the text-works and their use of language in the style of logical empiricism situate them clearly in the context of analytic conceptualism. In "Language and Art," published in 1970 in David Lamelas' conceptual book *Publication*, Burgin insists on the "*informational* nature of art." (Burgin, 1970b: 11) He argues moreover that a linguistic work, according to Wittgenstein's remark on the structural correspondence between sentence and fact, "must be to some extent homologous in structure with that of the type of experience to which it refers." (10) But while analytic conceptualists such as Joseph Kosuth and Art & Language were using language either as a self-referential artistic form or as a general model for the definition of art, Burgin was more interested, as Peter Osborne put it, in "using language as an artistic means for investigating conceptual structures of perception." (Osborne, 2002a: 69)

Like Kosuth and other conceptual artists, Burgin refers to language theory and, in particular, to Wittgenstein, A. J. Ayer, Rudolf Carnap, and other exponents of logical positivism. Claiming a *linguistic turn* for the arts, many conceptualists borrowed from these philosophers the idea of replacing metaphysical statements about matters of facts by the logical analysis of the linguistic frameworks that structure the experience and perception of the world, in order to counter Modernism's essentialist myth of the artwork considered as a material substance. Drawing on Ayer's *Language, Truth and Logic* (1936), Kosuth, in "Art after Philosophy," defines works of art as analytic propositions, which are tautological in the sense that they wouldn't "describe the behavior of physical, or even mental objects; they express definitions of art, or the formal consequences of definitions of art." (Kosuth, 1991: 21) Burgin agrees with this kind of linguistic conceptualism on two points: first, that art is not a question of material substances but of information, and, second, that a work's meaning does not reside in its status as an autonomous object but in the relations of its appearances which constitute the work as an aesthetic object. In this respect, Ayer, in *Language, Truth and Logic*, has argued: "Logical analysis shows that what makes these 'appearances' the 'appearances of' the same thing is not their relationship to an entity other than themselves, but their relationship to one another." (Ayer, 1952: 42) Kosuth's works from the end of the 1960s function in this sense as propositions which are not meaningful in themselves, but "operational units […] designed to function (operate 'meaningfully') in unison with other units." (Kosuth, 1999: 341) In analogy to Carnap's *The Logical Structure of the Word* (1928), Kosuth's objective is no less than revealing "the logical structure of art" as a logical—and tautological—system of interrelated propositions. Actually, in his highly influential book, Carnap's aim was "to establish a 'constructional system,' that is, an epistemic-logical system of objects or concepts" according to which the application of logical methods allows for translation of each concept from natural language or science to formally purified concepts. (Carnap, 2003: 5)

Although Burgin also quotes Ayer and Carnap in his essays from around 1970, he does so in a manner quite differently from Kosuth. Rather than defining art as the logical construct of an artificial meta-language, he is more interested in the way that both philosophers describe words as part of a symbolic system with "fluent transitions between physical and psychological orientation." (Burgin, 1970b: 11) Carnap's concept of "psychological objects," in particular, plays a crucial role in Burgin's thinking at that time. In "Rules of Thumb," he rejects the idea that the aim of art can be concerned with "the construction of formal systems *independently* of empirical references." (Burgin, 1971: 238) Although claiming that the instrumental rather than expressive use of language in Conceptual art is closer to science than to literature, Burgin contests the equation of artistic practice and scientific method. As a cultural object, art cannot be understood separately from other social practices and contexts, as Kosuth would like to have it; instead, art manifests itself within the global structure of "culture-as-a-whole." (238) Hence Burgin's rejection of Kosuth's analogy between art and analytical philosophy, describing art in terms of an artificial language as a purely logical, self-contained meta-system. Rather than Carnap's search for a method to explain the mathematical, logical structure of the world,

Burgin zooms in on what this philosopher has to say about the relation between cultural objects and psychological objects. Carnap's psychological objects are "acts of consciousness: perceptions, representations, feelings, thoughts, acts of will, and so on." (Carnap, 2003: 32) As such, they are not entities of the real world (physical objects), but interior processes within some individual subject. Carnap distinguishes physical and psychological objects from cultural objects, which are historically and sociologically determined: "groups, institutions, movements in all areas of culture, and also properties and relations of such processes and entities." (39) As a cultural object comes alive through psychological occurrences which are its manifestations, it follows that "*every cultural object is reducible [...] to psychological objects.*" (90) In "Rules of Thumb," Burgin refers to this inference and quotes Carnap's example of religion:

> We ascertain the religion of a given society through representations, emotions, thoughts, volitions of a religious sort which occur with the members of this society; also, documents in the form of writings, pictures, and buildings are considered. Thus, the recognition depends upon the manifestation and the documentation of the object in question. (Burgin, 1971: 238; Carnap, 2003: 89)

Instead of being an analytic proposition, then, an artwork is a cultural object that manifests itself in the form of psychological processes and interrelated documents.

The implications for Burgin's text-works in this period are two-fold. On the one hand, it is possible to observe a shift from perception to emotions and fantasy, from "appearance" to "feeling." While *Any Instantaneous Appearance* (1970) is still concerned with questions of gestalt and appearance in relation to mental images and external objects, *From Feel* (1971) proceeds from the encounter with physical objects toward the interrelatedness of bodily sensations and psychological states of emotion and mood. This position corresponds to Carnap's "analogism," according to which autopsychological objects (in regard to oneself) determine our knowledge of physical objects, while heteropsychological objects (in regard to the other) must always be referred back to the perception of the physical world. (Carnap, 2003: 94) In *Bracketed Performative* (1971), Burgin actually gives his work a psychological bias, based on Carnap's philosophical distinction, when requiring, respectively, "A description of an autopsychological object" (V 1.1.) and "A description of a heteropsychological object." (V 3.1.) Even though the psychological dimension is approached in analytical rather than in psychoanalytical terms, it appears that these references to Carnap's concepts already announce Burgin's orientation toward a psychical realism in the early 1980s.

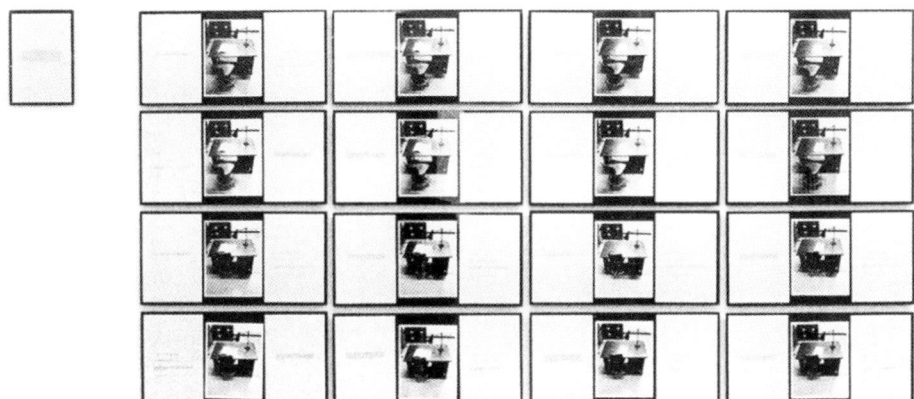

On the other hand, the acknowledgment that art cannot be approached independently of a broader social context leads to a new interest in human relations and the ways these relations are performed, narrated, and documented. *Performative/Narrative* (1971) is the first work that represents this shift from a conceptual approach based on general statements about perception toward an orientation interested in interactions in the social world. (Fig. 1.14.) The work comprises a series of sixteen photographs accompanied by verbal text. An introductory note, written in the manner of game instructions, fixes the general rules according to which events, material things, and participants may be related to each other—or not—within a spatio-temporal framework. Each of the panels consists of three parts: a narrative text, relating some events and actions performed by a boss, his son, and their secretary; a black and white photograph of a typical office setting in which these events might have occurred; and four sentences which invite the reader to think about his knowledge of the preceding narrative and the preceding photograph, and how they might be interrelated. For each of the four sentences, a positive or a negative option exists ("YOUR KNOWLEDGE" or "NOT YOUR KNOWLEDGE OF"), so that all combinations determine the number of the panels of the work. The resulting variations are indicated above the narrative text by means of binary digits from 1111 to 0000. (Fig. 1.15.) The work relies on a matrix of permutations of these digits, which also determines the way the objects in the photographs are displayed: the chair pushed away from the desk or pushed under it; the lamp switched on or off; the desk drawer pulled out or not; the file on the desk open or closed. As Burgin puts it: "What went on inside and outside the photograph was structured according to the same rules; in the process 'narrative' was generated." (Godfrey, 1982: 5)

Figure 1.14.

Performative/Narrative, 1971. 16 parts, each 34×67 cm. Installation view. Paul Maenz Gallery, Cologne, 1971.

In a neutral, descriptive tone, the text relates a set of events occurring in the office. Not unlike the preceding text-works, the story of *Performative/Narrative* evolves around objects, bodily actions, temporal and spatial experiences, sensations, emotions, and recollections—the difference being that the former pieces consist of general terms and sentences which address the reader's proper experiences. Relating to John Austin's speech act theory, Burgin describes these instructional pieces in terms of "performative utterances," because "it requires you to do something." (Godfrey, 1982: 5) However, *Performative/Narrative* adds the performance of the narrative's protagonists to this performative form of reader address. While the text of the first two panels describes objects and actions of the secretary (1111) and her boss (0111), some of the following panels address mental states (the boss thinking of her: 1011), memories ("a sunset that reminded him of a postcard": 0011), and emotions ("then, recalling a certain remark, she laughed": 1110). Yet, these events are not woven into a continuous storyline. Appearing throughout the work in changing combinations and contexts, they form a fragmentary narrative in which alternative interpretations of a situation are suggested and contradictions not excluded. Panel 14 (0100), for example, relates the following actions of the three protagonists:

> Before reaching the door he had stopped his hitherto rapid progress down the darkened room and was now examining a folder by the light of a solitary lamp. A year later his son was to stride by that same desk, gaze fixed on the connecting door behind which, had he only been there that morning, he might have heard the laughter of their secretary as she recollected a certain remark.

The motive of the laughing secretary was already introduced in panel 9 (1110), which informed the reader about what she did shortly before the act of recollection. Next, in panel 13 (1100) the actions performed by the boss and his son in the adjacent room are added, but, contrary to the following set of descriptions, son and father are in the same room at the same time. While from panel 9 to panel 13 a shift in perspective takes place from the viewpoint of the secretary to that of her employers, the text of panel 14 leaves the reader puzzled about the contradictory assertions about the moment of the son's presence in the room.

The piece is not about the reader's experience of his own actions, feelings, or recollections. It is more concerned with the reader's knowledge about representational systems (photography and text) and the way he interprets a fictitious, fragmentary narrative about actions, feelings, and recollections that occur in a typical social constellation (office, employer, secretary). It is with this shift from perception to representation, from general terms to social relations, that photography reappears in Burgin's work.

In *IV 2* (1972), displayed at Documenta 5 Kassel in 1972, Burgin's interest in the "*social* world" (Godfrey, 1982: 6) becomes even more explicit. The first of twenty parts leaves no doubt that the piece deals with social behavior rather than perceptual behavior: "Norms of behaviour supported by informal, unorganised, yet more or less uniform social pressures; *mores*; and not norms of behaviour supported by formal, organized, and uniformed social sanctions, systems of penalties; laws." Mental states, emotions, actions, and perceptions are now considered against the backdrop of institutional norms, moral judgments, and ethical considerations. In an interview with Anne Seymour, Burgin pointed out that the term "Situational Aesthetics" originates from a pun on "Situational Ethics." (Seymour, 1972: 74) If this allusion to John Fletcher's moral theory about the law of love—published in 1966 under the title *Situation Ethics: The New Morality*—should not be overestimated, his idea to ground his ethical model not in fixed law or moral absolutes, but on the basis of a "method of 'situational' or 'contextual' decision-making," may also be relevant for *IV 2*, in which the particular situation and experience of the reader are bracketed within social norms and ethical questions. (Fletcher, 1966: 11)

This interest in social reality went completely against the grain of the "analytic" position defended by Kosuth and the British Art & Language group. In an issue of their journal *Art-Language*, they attacked Burgin for failing to distinguish between "the extensional 'object' and certain aspects of the referential apparatus."[8] In his response, entitled "In reply," published in the following issue of the same journal, Burgin countered by criticizing "analytic art" for its "*l'art pour l'art* position" and insisting on a pragmatic approach that characterizes art not in terms of philosophical definitions but in terms of its use:

> What counts as art varies through history and between societies, as does art's function. A de-reified notion of art places it [...] as socio-culturally contingent, implying we should seek formation rules for art within the complex of synchronous social practices contemporary with the given work. (Burgin, 1972a: 33)

Burgin now rejects resolutely any comparison between art and "artificial languages evolved within science." And when he claims that art would be concerned with "the social mediation of the physical world through the agency of signs" rather than with the physical world as such (33), it is obvious on what methodological ground he from then on will search for formation rules in art and other kinds of representation: semiotics.

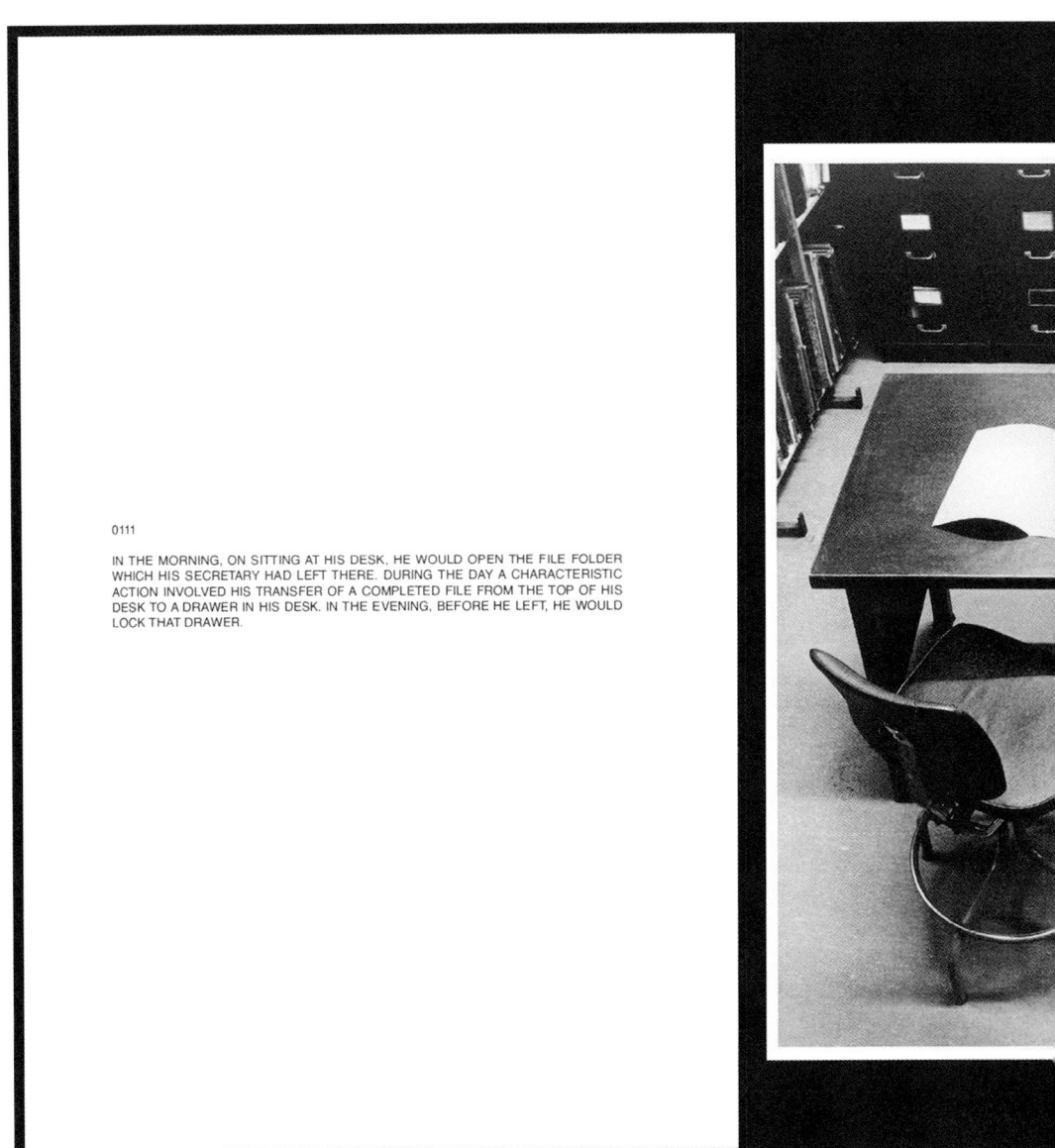

0111

IN THE MORNING, ON SITTING AT HIS DESK, HE WOULD OPEN THE FILE FOLDER
WHICH HIS SECRETARY HAD LEFT THERE. DURING THE DAY A CHARACTERISTIC
ACTION INVOLVED HIS TRANSFER OF A COMPLETED FILE FROM THE TOP OF HIS
DESK TO A DRAWER IN HIS DESK. IN THE EVENING, BEFORE HE LEFT, HE WOULD
LOCK THAT DRAWER.

Figure 1.15. *Performative/Narrative*, 1971. Part 2.

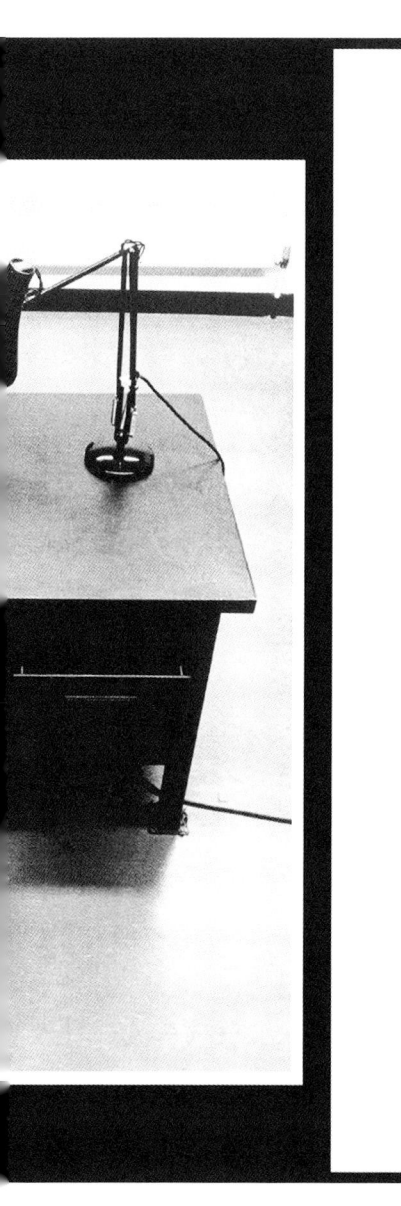

1

NOT YOUR KNOWLEDGE OF THE PRECEDING NARRATIVE

2

YOUR KNOWLEDGE OF THE PRECEDING PHOTOGRAPH

3

THE CRITERIA BY WHICH YOU MIGHT DECIDE THAT ASPECTS OF 1 ARE ANALOGOUS
TO, CORRELATE WITH, OR MAY BE PLACED IN SOME COMMON CONTEXT WITH,
ASPECTS OF 2

4

YOUR INFERENCES FROM 1 AND 2 ON THE BASIS OF 3

Ferdinand de Saussure, whose distinction of langue and parole Burgin evokes in his essay "In Reply," declared in the first edition of his *Course in General Linguistics* that semiology (*sémiologie*) has to be conceived as "a science which studies the role of signs as part of social life. It would form part of social psychology, and hence of general psychology." (Saussure, 1983: 15) As such, it provides Burgin precisely with what he is looking for in this period: a theoretical framework that permits him to apprehend art as part of social and psychological life in general. Quoting Saussure's definition of langue as a system of rules and conventions in which the individual signs only make sense through their relationships with other signs, Burgin emphasizes a structural and relational conception of meaning that he found already in Carnap's scientific categories of relational descriptions and structural descriptions. (Burgin, 1972b: 17) For this reason, Carnap's analytic approach aiming at a general model of the logical construction of the world now makes room for a structuralist view in which structural descriptions are not provided directly from our knowledge, but are made, as claimed by Claude Lévi-Strauss, quoted in Burgin's "Margin Note," in respect to "culture as 'an assembly of symbolic systems.'" (Margin Note, 17) In *Work and Commentary* (1973), however, Burgin cautions against the danger of a structuralism for its own sake, that is, as a methodology that transcends particular contents by integrating them in a self-defining and self-regulating system. (SA: 38) Structuralist-inspired semiotics serves him above all as a tool to understand the place of art and other symbolic systems within culture as a whole. The reading of Barthes' *Elements of Semiology*, after his return from Yale to Britain in 1967, had a decisive influence on Burgin's increasing interest in art as part of a signifying system of representations constitutive of society: "What was crucial about it for me was that here was a theory which was able to turn its attention, almost indiscriminately, to advertising, to cinema, to literature." (Roberts, 1997: 97)

This exposure to French structuralist thinking caused him to move away from analytical Conceptualism's art-as-definition-of-art position and toward a definition of art as a social practice reflecting ideological convictions and preferences: "As the domain of art therefore is the domain of those very sign systems by whose means social reality, that is to say ideology, is constituted and disseminated then it cannot be 'value-free.'" (Burgin, 1972b: 18) The task of art, then, is neither to produce aesthetic objects merely concerned with problems of art—this would be the modernist *l'art-pour-l'art*-position—nor to succumb to an anything-goes relativism or "*laissez-faire* subjectivism." The artist's task is instead to "dismantle existing communication codes and to recombine some of their elements into structures which can be used to generate new pictures of the world." This means an interdisciplinary approach that crosses "traditional lines of demarcation in the arts," and, as a consequence, a critical examination of "today's technological pluralism and its manifestation as 'mass media.'" (SA: 18-19; 40)

As mentioned, *Performative/Narrative* is a first step toward an artistic practice in which questions of social relations (text) and modern technologies of documentation (photography) are addressed and correlated. Yet, the narrative and the photographs are still subjected to a logical system based on the combination of binary digits. The photographs are made in a strictly documentary mode without explicit reference to the external world of mass media. However, in the panel texts 0011 and 0010, the man is reminded of a postcard depicting, respectively, a sunset and a city scene. The particular relevance of this becomes clearer by drawing a link with another, unpublished, narrative text-work from this period, *A Period of Interruption*.[9] As in *Performative/Narrative*, the juxtaposition of a landscape with an image seen before appears twice within a slightly different context. But here the object of comparison is not a postcard but a painting: "By evening, the landscape reminded him of a painting he had once seen of Christ in the desert, the sun had been low." This almost inconspicuous switch from art (painting) to popular culture (postcard) announces Burgin's new orientation toward the realm of the social and the mass media. In his artistic practice, commercial photography has replaced painting as medium of reference.

Chapter 2
Toward a Politics of Representation

As indicated above, Burgin's work in the period between 1973 and 1977 is defined by two fundamental issues: semiotics as theoretical tool for analyzing all sorts of representation as part of a social and ideological formation, and photography as both the object of such analysis and artistic means appropriate to challenge the myths of romantic aestheticism and the rhetoric of advertising encountered through the mass media. Burgin's response to the question he raised in a lecture from 1975, "Why Photography?," is twofold. The first reason pertains to the fact that photography, as language, can be understood by everyone in the sense that we learn it "in the normal course of acculturalisation—no special training needed." (Burgin, 1976a: 361) The second reason has a decidedly political and ideological dimension, involving critique of capitalism as a competitive, profit-oriented ideology. Such critique is only possible through the ways it "presents itself continually, in every moment of our waking lives, in the form of advertising billboards, T.V. commercials, in newspapers and magazines… it's framed using, characteristically, the photograph and the text." (364) As a consequence, two crucial shifts characterize this period in Burgin's work. In terms of theoretical aspects, the focus is less on analytical philosophy and theories of perception than on semiotics and Marxist-inspired cultural critique. Simultaneously, aesthetic and perceptual considerations on the work's dependency on a specific situation give way to more general reflections on the relationship between representation and ideology within Western capitalism's media society. In short, context is still a major concern, but whereas around 1970 the underlying key concept of Burgin's artistic practice was that of "situational aesthetics," a shift can be observed in the following years toward the idea of the "environment of the media," which became an umbrella term to reintegrate art "into the broader field of cultural criticism." (BN: 12; Roberts, 1997: 97)[10]

Another important preliminary remark has to be made at this point. The photographic works of Burgin from the early 1970s are exclusively concerned with advertising, the imagery and rhetorical codes of which he appropriates and recycles. By reintegrating advertising photographs within critical text-image collages, he re-actualizes the socio-political project of Dadaism and the Russian avant-garde.[11] At the same time, however, he shares the view of many conceptualist artists at the time that it is more urgent in a media-saturated world to provide critical reflection on the already existing images than to add new images to the world. (Durand, 1988: 21)[12] The year 1976 marks a turning point insofar as the series *UK 76* reintroduces self-made photographs that refer to photographic traditions other than advertising, such as social documentation and street photography. In his writings from this period, two essays, both published in 1976, illustrate this shift from advertising to photography in general in a subtle, but nonetheless striking way. Drawing on a materialist-oriented semiotic approach, "Socialist Formalism" first appeared in *Studio International* in March/April 1976 as a plea against modernist formalism. In opposition to Modernism's history of pure form, Burgin highlights the political and cultural commitment of Russian Formalism engaging in the public domain by means of text-image works designed for placards, journals, and advertising. Wondering why British intellectuals, at that time, tended to put a lot of emphasis on cinema while having disproportionally little interest in advertising—despite the latter's massive ideological interventions in contemporary culture—Burgin posits: "whereas the cinema readily constitutes itself as an object, advertising is received as an environment and as such tends to pass unremarked." (Burgin, 1976b: 151) Published later that same year, in the December issue of *20th Century Studies*, "Modernism in the *Work* of Art" further develops the issues raised in the earlier essay, even though advertising seems to have lost its central position, clearing the way for a more general approach to photography as medium. Now we read:

> While films and paintings readily constitute themselves as *objects*, thus facilitating critical attention, photography, as constituted in the mass media, is received as an *environment* and passes relatively unremarked. Photography is encountered, in most aspects of daily life, as a fragmented or partial object: photojournalism, amateur, advertising, documentary …, etc. Semiotically, these cannot be said to be the manifestations of a single fact. There is no single *signifying system* (as opposed to technical apparatus) upon which all photographs depend, in the sense in which all texts in English ultimately depend upon the English language; there is no "language of photography" in the sense of *langue*. There is rather a heterogeneous complex of codes upon which photography may draw. (EAT: 20)

It is precisely the heterogeneity and the broad contextual character of photography in which Burgin grew interested. This aspect will be developed toward the end of this chapter, but first I will take a closer look at the way in which Burgin addresses the relationship between photography, rhetoric, and ideological formations in society. It is not a coincidence that he produced his first work that included appropriated advertising photographs in 1973, the year that he started to teach in the Department of Film and Photography at the Polytechnic of Central London. The antagonistic positions he found there between the formalist belief in the "purely visual" of fine art photography and the documentary approach, conceiving the photographic image as a transparent "window on the world," triggered critical discussion of photography's place within the inherited ideologies of Western society, encompassing his teaching and writing as much as his artistic practice. (PT: 208)

2.1. The Politicization of Art in Britain

The relationship between politics and art was a crucial issue in the leftist art scene of Britain in the 1970s. As John A. Walker puts it: "During the early and mid-1970s, in New York, a politicization of art and theory took place comparable to that which occurred in London at the same time." (Walker, 2002: 139) The conference *Art:Politics | Theory:Practice*, held in May 1974 at the Royal College of Art London, brought together artists, activists, and intellectuals, discussing the artist's position vis-à-vis the problem of class struggle as well as possibilities of social or political change through art. (Wilson, 2016: 87) Institutions like the ICA and magazines such as *Control* and *Studio International* increasingly included work and essays with a social and political agenda.

Stephen Willats' *Control* Magazine, for instance, launched in 1965 as a platform for artists "which make up the new attitude in visual communication," shifted its focus, in the course of the 1970s, from a main interest in conceptual models, behavioral situations, and learning systems toward the search for solutions to new social functions of art.[13] As mentioned above, Burgin contributed a text and a work to issue 4 of 1968, which was dedicated to "the artists relation to society, and the controls that are available to them." (*Control*, editorial, issue 4, 1968: n. p.) Subscribing to the theoretical framework of the magazine at this time, Burgin relates the question of social control to aspects of communication, the object-audience relationship, and situational behavior. Drawing on Morse Peckham's concept of art as role-playing, Burgin defines the artist's role as "that of the designer of 'activity clusters' formed for specific social and environmental situations." The essay ends with a strong political claim: "In a materially satiated and goal-less society the role-creating capacity of art might lead it into government!" (Burgin, 1968: n. p.) This merely implicit political stance—changing social conditions by changing the mode of perceptual behavior—becomes explicit as early as 1973, when Burgin begins his critical investigation of advertising as a powerful carrier of ideology in works such as *VI* (1973) and *Lei Feng* (1974).

It was also Willats who pioneered projects exploring the relationships between social structures and behavior, such as *The West London Social Resource Project* and the *Cognition and Control Project*, set up in 1972 at Gallery House. (Wilson, 2016: 89; Willats, 1976a: 100-107; Willats, 1976b) Yet, Burgin kept a critical distance from these kinds of activist neighborhood projects with their "task-oriented methods" in which the participant should be involved in a process of learning by being confronted with gradually "more difficult and less familiar conceptual territory." (Willats, 1976b: 9) His attitude was not that of an activist setting out to change the world by organizing activities with the aim "to stimulate a reordering of social structures and behaviour." (Wilson, 2016: 89) As an artist, he preferred to intervene from within the art institution as part of what Althusser named the Ideological State Apparatuses (Godfrey, 1982: 7), i.e., a set of distinct institutions that subject the individual to socially constructed rituals and beliefs taken to be natural. (Althusser, 1971: 127-186) In a *Studio International* issue dedicated to the relation of art spaces and alternative spaces, Burgin writes:

> The gallery then is to be seen as one amongst a number of institutional spaces of the broader ideological institution "art." It is within, as much as beyond, such spaces that the politically aware art-worker—whatever his or her specific practice—may work for cultural change, albeit in the knowledge that the ideological inertia of the institution is massive and that "in all good faith" it will seek to repress all forms of practice which threaten the hegemony of its present vested interests. (Burgin, 1980: 26)[14]

Burgin's socialist political views as well as his emphasis on the relationship between representation and ideology were shared by other artists in Britain. As explained by John A. Walker, the St. Martin's Group (SMG), a federation of artists and writers which among others included John Stezaker, Rosetta Brooks, John Tagg, and Walker himself, aimed to analyze "the relation between ideology and systems of visual representation such as perspective (vantage and vanishing points), the common mechanisms of pictorial rhetoric (visual metaphors, similes, hyperbole, personification, etc.) and the vexed relation of the avant-garde to official and mass culture." (Walker, 2002: 163) This thematic and theoretic orientation, as well as the resulting decision to explore news photographs and advertising images as privileged means of dominant ideology, agreed quite well with Burgin's preoccupations at the time.

2.2. Guerrilla Rhetoric: The Antanaclastic Works[15]

> Paradox and ambiguity are interesting figures as they present a
> contamination of content relation by form relation: the content
> relation is at fist seen as homologous with the form relation, then
> on closer inspection this reading is inverted. (TP: 74)

2.2.1. The *Discordance* of Ideologies

The final work reproduced in *Work and Commentary* is the first in which
Burgin appropriates an advertising photograph. *VI* (1973) consists of
ten parts, each comprising three distinct elements: the photograph of
a nuclear family taken from a British mail order catalogue, a caption
to that photograph, and a text similar to those of the preceding text-
works. (Fig. 2.1.) Whereas the photograph remains the same throughout the whole series, the two verbal parts change, thus offering alternative possibilities to interpret the image. The advertising photograph
represents the typical cliché of a Western family: The woman in the
foreground, flanked by a boy and a girl, cares for the children while the
husband is standing behind his family members in order to protect and
sustain them. His gaze is directed to his wife, who looks down to the
boy as their legitimate son and heir. At first glance, the large type captions, dealing with questions of value in respect to objects, actions, and
goals, are completely disconnected from what is happening in the image
they are expected to explain. But that is precisely what Burgin intends.
The difficulty of bringing together image and caption destabilizes the
taken-for-grantedness of the family cliché; it de-naturalizes it. In reality,
the words of the caption do not aim at the visible content of the image.
They rather redirect the reader's attention toward the underlying ideological structure of the family as a social convention while at the same
time denouncing advertising as a tool to legitimate and spread such
shared beliefs in the name of the dominant social order. (SA: 36) The
first caption, "Any physical object is to be positively valued only if it may
be instrumental in the achievement of a goal," refers, then, to the advertising photograph as ideological object. What is important is not what it
depicts, but the purposes for which it is used: to sell a particular product,
and, on a more general level, to consolidate the social role of the family
as one of the main pillars of Western capitalist consumer society.
   As Burgin writes in 1975:

> The desirability, the "closeness," and the joy of family life are
> centrally important concepts in legitimating and supporting this
> unit. In an environment of billboards, popular press, television,

and commercial cinema it is difficult to pass a single day without encountering some visual representation of the family.
(TP: 65-66)

The dichotomic divisions into personal and collective, perpetuation
and perpetual revision, objective deliberation and subjective intuition,
and circumspection and precipitance, invite the reader to think about
how the roles of the family members are distributed in society and confirmed through images in the media. In this case, the words "objective,"
"circumspection," and "goal" may be ascribed to the man, while "intuition," "precipitance," and "subjective" are qualities associated with the
woman and children blithely rushing forward.

The text juxtaposed with the photograph, in contrast, begins with
a statement on the perception of a gestalt, similar to those of earlier
text-works such as *Any Instantaneous Appearance* (1970). But already
in the second panel, the parallel text introduces basic concepts of semiotics such as "signifier," "unmotivated" and "motivated" signs, "code,"
and "message," which can be used as tools of interpretation. Panel six
is of particular interest, because here Burgin describes the two possible functions of an image's caption: anchorage and relay. Introduced
by Roland Barthes in his classical essay "The Rhetoric of the Image"
(1964) in order to analyze advertising images, "anchorage" occurs
when the linguistic message directs the reader towards a preferred
meaning, whereas "relay" signifies a complementary relationship between text and image, in which "the unity of the message is realized
at a higher level." (Barthes, 1977: 41)[16] Apparently, Burgin suggests the
application of Barthes' terminology to the image-text combination on
the left-hand side. (Fig. 2.2.) As the caption provides no cues for a specific meaning of the image, the reader tends to understand the caption
as a relay function. Yet the overt contradiction between the image's
emphasis on the family as a stable unit and the caption's suggestion
to value positively the perpetual revision of all extant goals and their
means makes it nearly impossible to find a "higher level" of meaning,
other than in fact to revise values commonly associated with the family.
Consequently, the texts of panels seven to nine are concerned with the
way individual actions are pre-determined by the ideological framework of values commonly accepted by a given society. The final panel
exposes the three possibilities of congruence between the sub-codes of
sender and receiver: complete congruence signifies "full *concordance*
of ideologies"; in the case of partial congruence, the interpretation of a
message would only be successful to some extent; and, finally, complete
incongruence leads to "*discordance* of ideologies."

In the end, it becomes clear that Burgin is not concerned with describing or explaining the image by means of verbal language. The work

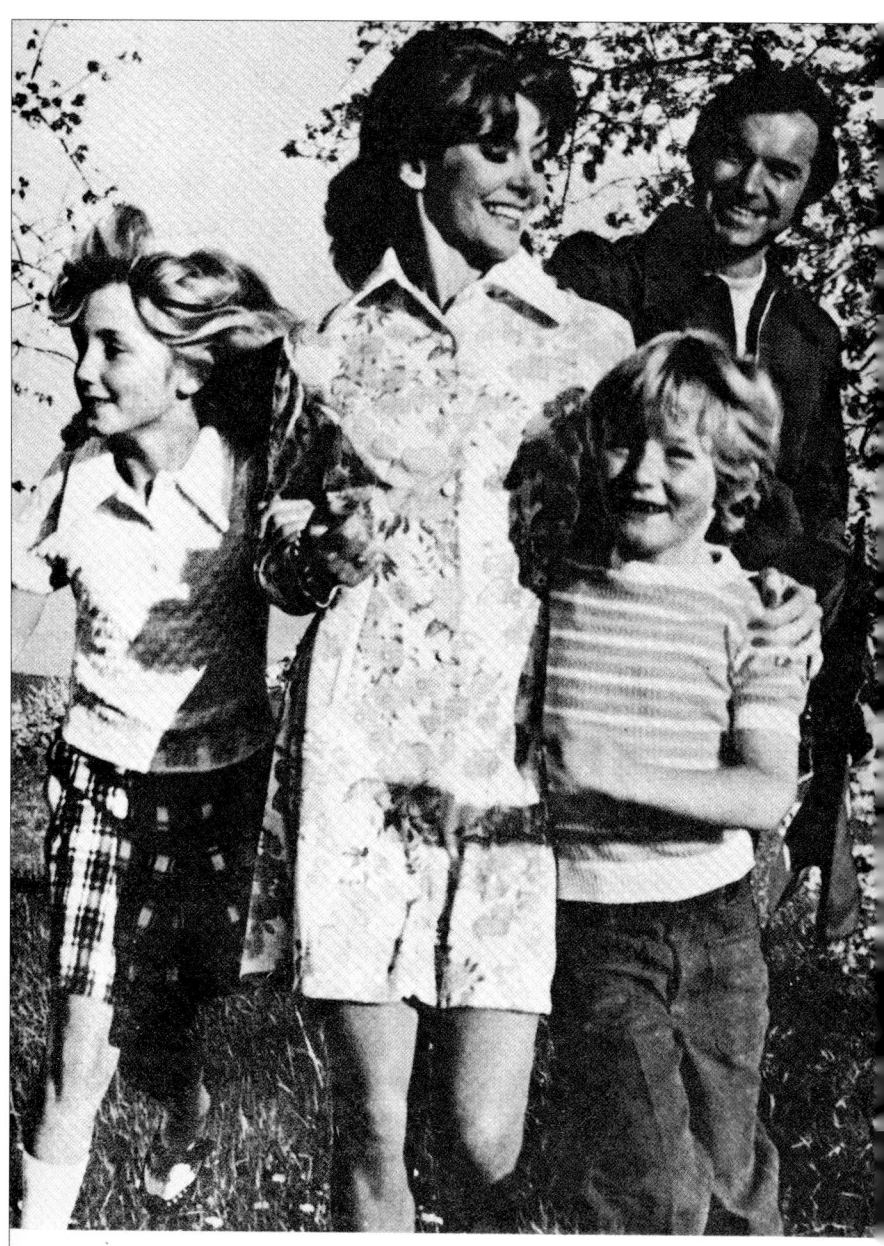

Any physical object is to be positively valued only if it may be instrumental in the achievement of a goal.

I

A complex of phenomena so integrated as to be seen as a unit with properties not derivable from the parts of that unit in summation; a sector of a given perceptual field identified, at a given moment, as a whole and as having attributes more extensive than the sum of the attributes of its constituent elements; a *gestalt*

Figure 2.1.

VI, 1973 (Panel I), *Work and Commentary*, London, Latimer, 1973.

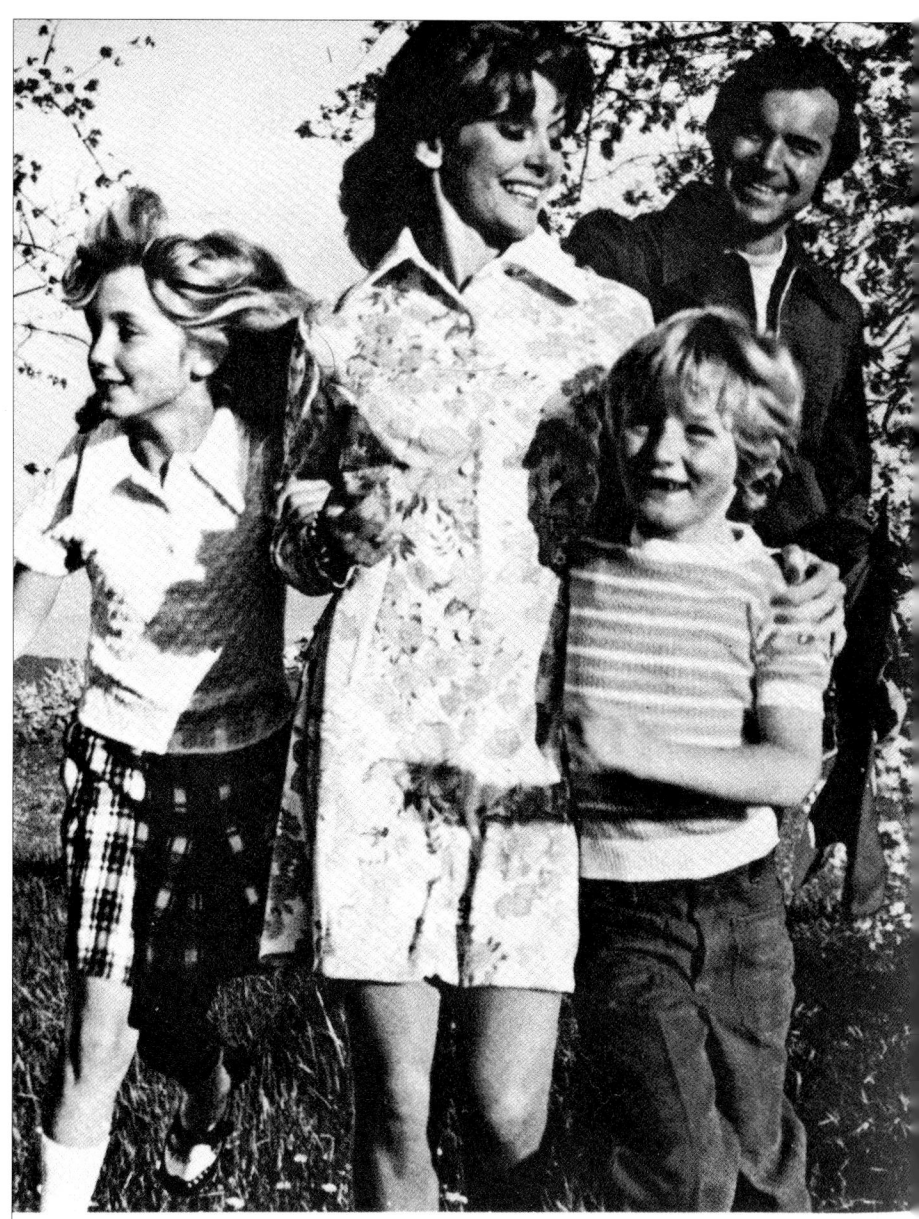

The perpetual revision of all extant goals and their means of achievement is to be positively valued.

VI

1
The juxtaposition of a visual image and a supplementary linguistic message, this latter indicating prefered meanings from amongst the connoted meanings of the former; *anchorage*

2
The juxtaposition of a visual image and a complementary linguistic message indicating a meaning not signified by either of the component messages; *relay*

Figure 2.2.

VI, 1973 (Panel VI), *Work and Commentary*, London, Latimer, 1973.

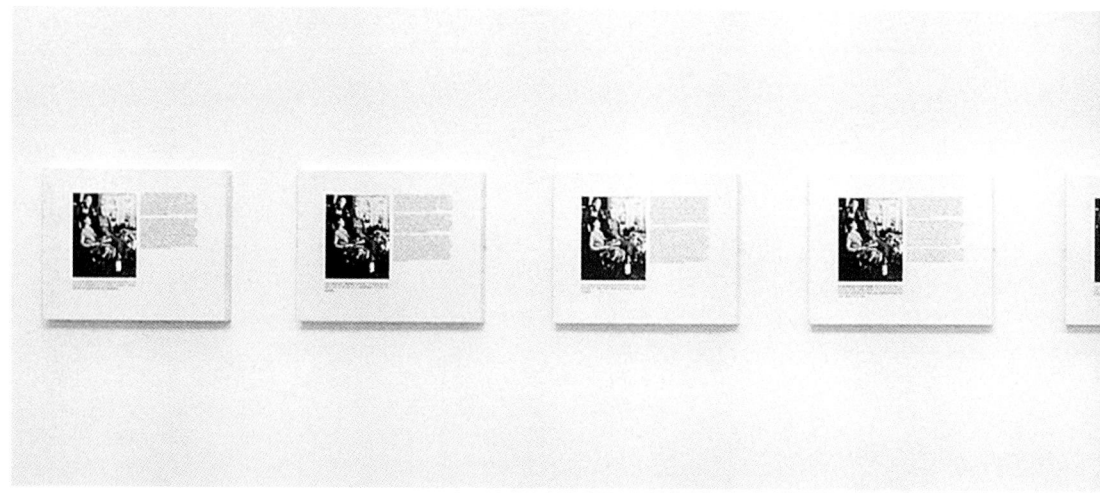

is rather a critical comment on the complex ways in which ideologies are established through visual and verbal forms of representation. The repetition of one and the same photograph through all ten panels reveals the standardized character of advertising, while the unrelated, changing and sometimes contradictory value statements of the captions destabilize the reader's expectations and prevent easy interpretation. The text on the right-hand side provides a theoretical meta-text that "anchors" the family-photograph within the general context of ideology. The final aim of the work is perhaps to encourage the reader to reflect upon the question to what point she or he is in concordance or discordance *with* the dominating ideology and the values it carries.

2.2.2. Semiotic Theory and Artistic Practice

The decontexualization and recontextualization of appropriated advertising images as well as the confrontation of images with different kinds of verbal texts are also strategies employed in the photo-text series, entitled *Lei Feng*.[17] (Fig. 2.3.) Similar to *VI*, this series consists of nine panels that are each composed of an advertising photograph for sherry accompanied by a caption and excerpts of a theoretical text. Again, the photograph remains the same, while the texts change from one panel to the next. Differently from the previous work, the captions of *Lei Feng* add up to a coherent narrative of a didactic-moral character. The inclusion of two great figureheads of Maoist propaganda, Lei Feng and Zhang Side, exemplifies the Maoist myth of altruistic selflessness in the name of the people. The photograph is another idealized

The Work of Victor Burgin

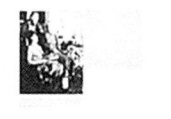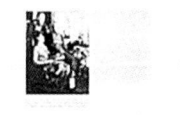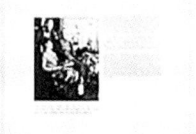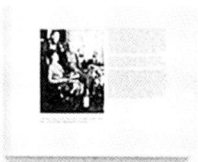

representation of modern family life, showing proud parents toasting with sherry to the success of their daughter who has made it onto the cover of *Vogue* magazine. The ideological contradiction could not be more explicit: the socialist myth of unconditional selflessness in the service of a transcendent idea versus the celebration of another myth, that of the capitalist American dream, according to which prosperity and recognition are the results of individual effort.

Figure 2.3.

Lei Feng, 1974.

9 parts, each 50×75 cm. Installation view, Lisson Gallery, London 1974.

The text blocks to the right of each of the photographs again provide a semiotic meta-text to the work. But differently from VI, the text now deals with the problem of photographic representation. When the text in the first panel explains that "a photograph of three people grouped together may, in reality, have comprised a live model, a two-dimensional "cut-out" figure, and a wax dummy," one unavoidably asks oneself the question regarding the "real" referent of the advertising photograph. (Fig. 2.4.) As the reproduction of a reproduction, the *Vogue* cover obviously confronts us at a second-level reality. In view of the stylized poses of the depicted family members, one might certainly ask the question of whether these might not, in fact, be wax figures. And who can truly say that the *Vogue* portrait is actually a picture of the young woman portrayed in the advertising photo and not a different woman or even a cutout or a wax dummy? Over the course of the other panels, the text addresses the possible applications of semiological theory in order to reveal the ideological implications entailed in the construction of meaning through photographic images.

This is also the aim of "Photographic Practice and Art Theory," an essay published in 1975 in *Studio International*, in which Burgin offers a detailed semiotic analysis of photography. The theoretical fragments

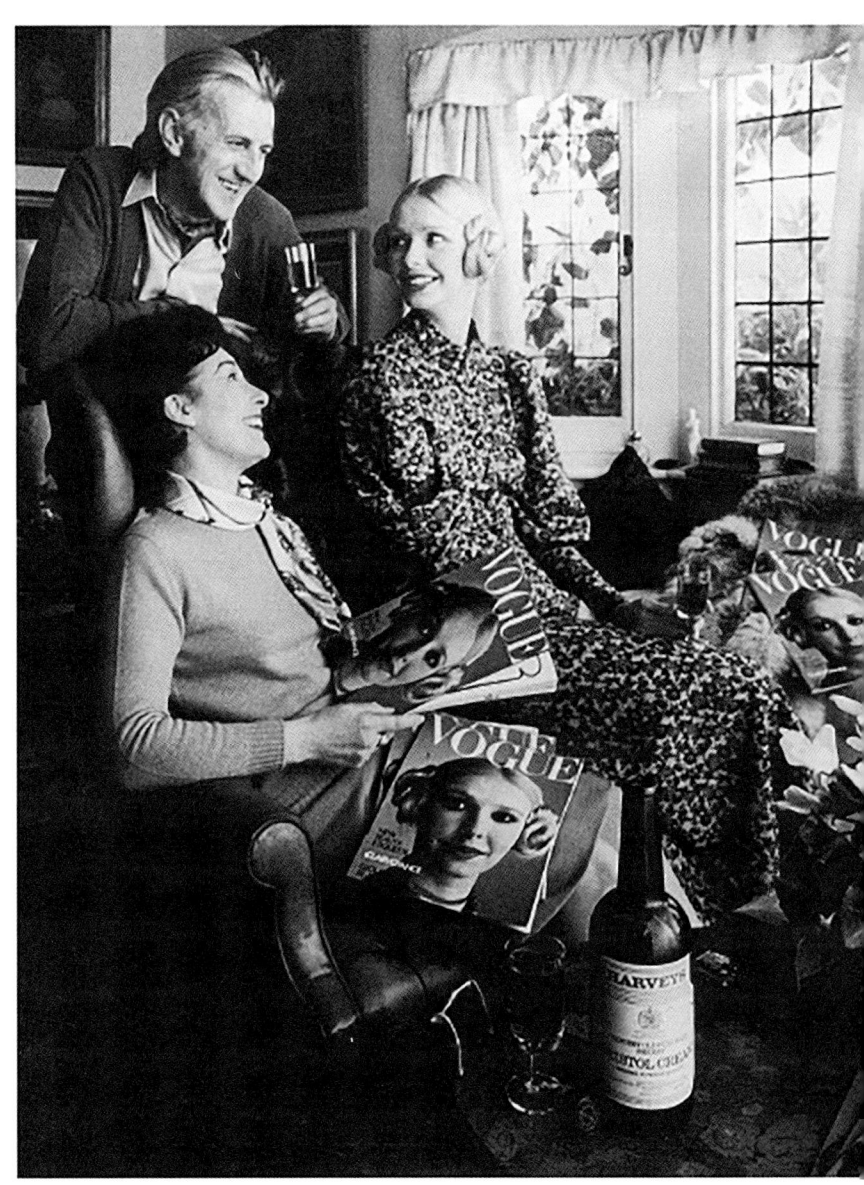

The young soldier Lei-Feng asks his instructor if he may be assigned to a combat mission. When refused he cannot hide his impatience.

e difference between language and iconic imagery is most marked
the case of the photograph. The linguistic sign bears an arbitrary
ationship to its referent, the photographic image does not. There is
 law in nature which dictates that the linguistic sign 'tree' (or 'arbre'
'baum') should be associated with the thing with which it is in fact
ociated, this is a matter of cultural convention. In the case of the
otograph on the other hand the image is in a sense caused by its
erent. Just as there is a causal relation between the presence of an
-current and the direction in which a weathervane points, so a
oto-sensitive emulsion *necessarily* registers the distribution of light
 which it is exposed, leading Pierce to describe the photograph as a
asi-predicate' of the light which stands to it as 'quasi-subject'.

e *chiaroscuro* of the photographic image replicates, *mutatis*
tandis, that present to the exposed film. What lines and volumes
en emerge to our eye are related to their referents, as Volli has
phasised, strictly according to geometrical principles of projective
nsformation. In an ingenuous assumption the photograph is held to
produce its object. However, the relationship between a
otographic image and its referent is one of reproduction only to the
ent that Christopher Wren's death-mask reproduces Christopher
en. The photograph abstracts from, and mediates, the actual. For
imple, a photograph of three people grouped together may, in
lity, have comprised a live model, a two-dimensional 'cut-out'
ure, and a wax dummy. In the actual presence of such an
embly I would quickly know them for what they were. No such
tainty accompanies my cognition of the photographic group.
thes found in photography ' . . . a precious miracle, a reality from
ich we are sheltered,' but if photographs shelter us from reality it
y nothing more ineffable than a shortage of information.

Figure 2.4.
Lei Feng, 1974 (Panel I).

from *Lei Feng* are here woven into a linear, academic paper, which investigates the rhetorical nature of advertising photographs. Right at the beginning of the essay, the very same Sherry advertising is reproduced to illustrate the family as "perhaps the most important basic structural unit in society." (TP: 41) Some pages later, Burgin discusses repetition as a fundamental rhetorical operation in advertising and gives the example of antanaclasis as a special variant of repetition in which "the same word is repeated with a different signification." (78) Referring to a car advertisement, in which each of four identical images is differently captioned, Burgin shows that antanaclasis is also a frequently used rhetorical figure in advertising in order to highlight the multiple functions and qualities of a single product: the Citroën as a "family shopping car," a "practical state car," a "luxury saloon," and an "overnight sleeper."

In *VI* and *Lei Feng*, Burgin employs this "figure of ambiguity," but in opposition to the Citroën advertising, the changing captions and text fragments do not indicate properties or qualities of the represented object (the family). What they do offer are alternative narratives and general theoretical reflections on society and representation. Unlike advertising photography, Burgin's pieces do not conceal the rhetorical structure of the image. The (stereo)typical presentation of the family resulting from social and ideological values is rather revealed through the confrontation of heterogeneous visual and verbal components within a fragmentary, critical text. In this respect, both pieces lay the foundation for the socio-political, semiotically inspired approach of the photographic works of the following years. In a public discussion held in 1977, Burgin actually outlined an aesthetic program that aims to raise the contradictions in social life by fragmenting the wholeness of the texts of which a given society is composed:

> And one way of doing that is to make texts out of components which won't marry happily together, so that there are cracks in the structure, and this text then becomes a sort of critique of the other texts; So I think it is possible to avoid the trap of straightforward realism, straightforward representationalism, which is already ideologically loaded. (Burgin, 1978: 137)

This is exactly how *VI* and *Lei Feng* proceed, announcing a new critical aesthetics, an aesthetics of cracks and fragments.

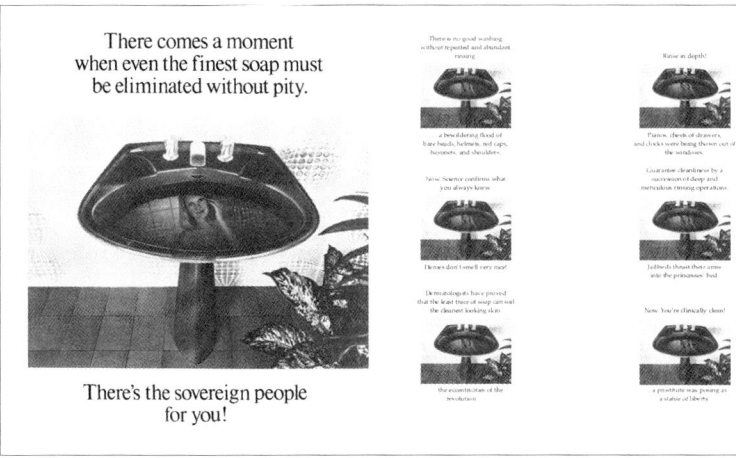

Figure 2.5.

Hussonet, 1974.

7 parts, each 119×85 cm.

2.2.3. Heroes Don't Smell Very Nice!

The last work in which Burgin uses antanaclasis in order to create an ambiguous message based on contradicting narratives is *Hussonet* from 1974. (Fig. 2.5.) The piece is composed of seven parts. In the center of each panel the same photograph represents a sink situated in a bathroom and reflecting the face of an attractive woman. The image thus conflates the flawlessness of the woman's skin with the cleanness of the sanitary area as if real beauty could only become visible through washing operations. It goes without saying that in the imagery of Western societies both the beautiful body and the activity of cleaning are inextricably associated with women. In their laconic style, the texts that accompany the image, at first glance, mimic conventional advertising. And indeed, the changing headings placed above the image all refer to a typical vocabulary of detergent advertisement: "finest soap," "good washing," "science confirms," "dermatologists have proved," "guarantee cleanliness," etc. But the authoritarian, relentless, occasionally even paradoxical tone makes the reader become suspicious. "There comes a moment when even the finest soap must be eliminated without pity" does not only contradict the image's rhetoric of cleanness; it also has an aggressive connotation that fits much better with the revolutionary discourse actually evoked in the subtitles: "There's the sovereign people for you!" pulls the reader out of the tidy world of advertising and bourgeois stereotypes of cleanness and confronts her or him with the ironic, distanced point of view that Gustave Flaubert takes vis-à-vis the French Revolution of 1848 through the bohemian theater critic Hussonet, a fictional character in his novel *Sentimental Education*.

While the main character of the novel, Frédéric Moreau, is impressed by the heroics of the uprising of the people, Hussonet reacts with sarcasm when commenting on the grotesque situation of a number of proletarians handing on the throne to each other in order to take a seat on the place of power, as articulated in the first sentence quoted in Burgin's work: "There's the sovereign people for you!" (Flaubert, 2004: 313) All following subtitles are also quotations from Hussonet as, for example, his remark in view of the crowd taking the Tuileries: "The heroes don't smell good!" (313) In Burgin's piece, this disdaining comment on the people is used as the quite astonishing reply to the heading "Now. Science confirms what you always knew." Whereas the image and the advertising context would suggest a logic such as "beauty depends on cleanness and cleanness can only be achieved by using a particular detergent," the actual words stand in ironic contradiction with both the seriousness of scientific assertions and the image's rhetoric of cleanness. The heading of the last panel concludes with the redundant observation "Now. You're clinically clean!," while the subtitle describes another grotesque passage from Flaubert's novel in which "a prostitute was posing as a statue of liberty." (314) Contrasting the housewife and the whore as two female stereotypes, Burgin deconstructs the representational system of patriarchy as it operates in the Western world. This feminist concern will become more explicit in his work of the late 1970s, starting in 1977 with the photo-text-series US 77.

In *Hussonet*, Burgin certainly does not share the elitist attitude of Flaubert who disparaged "the people" as a credible political ideal, and who wrote to his friend George Sand: "I believe that the crowd, the mass, the herd, will always be detestable." (Jonsson, 2008: 54) But Flaubert's warning about the prejudices and stereotypes—the "idées reçues"—which find all too often fertile ground in collective movements is also a concern of Burgin's critique of ideology and advertising as one of its most powerful tools in Western media society. Burgin in fact turned the sarcasm with which Flaubert's Hussonet comments on the people's uprising in the 1848 revolution against the stereotypes conveyed in advertising. It is not "the people" or "the group" that is the seedbed for "idées reçues," but the representations with which these collectives are fed.

The task of semiotic analysis, then, is to isolate the rhetorical structures of advertising in order to understand the ways in which ideological purposes are transmitted through representation. This is the agenda of Burgin's theoretical writing of the 1970s. The works discussed above, built upon this critical analysis of the rhetoric of advertising in the service of the dominating ideology. Quoted by Burgin in his essay "Socialist Formalism," Anthony Wilden claims that the first line of defense against the violence of the rhetoric of the establishment is to learn something about rhetoric. […] But a line of defense is not enough; […] What is required […] is a guerrilla rhetoric. And for a guerrilla rhetoric, you must know what your enemy knows, why and how he knows it, and how to contest him on the ground." (Burgin, 1976b: 151)

And elsewhere Burgin adds retrospectively that his strategy in this period would have been "a kind of *guerrilla semiotics*: capturing images and turning them against themselves." (PS: 24) That is exactly what Burgin does in his three advertising-text-works of 1973-1974. While in his theoretical writing, rhetorical devices are isolated and analyzed for their contribution in the construction of ideology, these three works mimic antanaclasis, as a typical rhetoric figure in advertising, and deconstruct its ideological structure by contrasting the image with heterogeneous verbal texts which insist ironically on the paradoxical ambiguity of the message. When Burgin writes in "Art, Common Sense and Photography" that "there is no reason why, once the devices of advertising have been isolated by semiotic analysis, they may not be 're-cycled' in counter-ideological message-making," he points precisely to this function of the artwork as a form of guerrilla rhetoric. (Burgin, 1976c: 2)

The claim that concludes the theoretical text portion of *Lei Feng* in panel nine actually confirms the position that Burgin takes in both his theoretical writings and his artistic practice: "In this recognition we may therefore opt for a theoretically self-conscious intervention in the production of photographic rhetoric, for a 'critical practice' where semiotics, ideology and aesthetics meet." Behind this claim one can readily recognize Benjamin's dictum, according to which social transformation is only possible if the traditional (bourgeois) division between theory and practice is suspended. This will be one of the bedrocks of Burgin's Marx-inspired photo-pieces of the following years.

2.3. The Author as Producer

2.3.1. Work Outside and Inside the Gallery

The works Burgin produced in the mid-1970s are all based on recycled advertising imagery combined with short texts imitating the rhetoric of advertising copy. In this period, the space outside the gallery or the museum became once again a site of artistic presentation—the difference being that now the magazine or public space no longer appeared as alternative spaces to the gallery (as in *All Criteria*, *Carton Programme*, or *Memory Piece*), but as their logical counterpart in the production of ideology through representation. In *Between*, Burgin writes:

> Part of the intention was to deconstruct the ideological division between the inside and the outside of the gallery. On the one hand, the work on the gallery walls looked like the sort of image-text constructions you encounter in the street, and in magazines. On the other hand, I did do work which was placed actually in the street, and in magazines. (BN: 12)

Reflect, Contradiction (1976) was first published in the January 1976 issue of *Artforum* as Burgin's first solo show in New York. (BN: 12) It is also the announcement of his show at the ICA in London that took place from January 14 to February 8, 1976. The piece consists of two photographs accompanied by text. The left image shows a pensive woman sitting at a desk overstuffed with paperwork, while the right image depicts an elegant woman apparently on a shopping tour. The combination of image, caption, and short text overtly mimics advertising in magazines. But rather than explaining or connecting the two images, the words printed above them leave the reader in doubt because of their ambiguity. Whereas "Reflect" may refer to the activity of the woman at the office desk, the link between the word "Contradiction" and the second image remains ambiguous. It is uncertain whether the contradiction lies in the discordance between word and image, refers to the relationship between the two images, or simply alludes to "contradiction" as a rhetorical device of direct opposition between things compared. In the light of Burgin's interest in Barthes' essay "The Rhetoric of the Image," it may also be understood as a somewhat didactical demonstration of the above-discussed two fundamental functions in the text-image relationship according to the French semiotician: while in the first case the caption orients the reader to one in the maze of possible meanings of the image (anchorage), in the second case the word adds meaning to the image (relay).

In "Art, Common Sense and Photography," Burgin actually describes the rhetorical structure of an advertisement in the journal *Psychology Today* as one of relay, because the photograph, depicting a courtyard scene with an impoverished family, is in no way anchored by the caption which reads "It's all in your mind." And he concludes: "The rhetorical structure of the text/image relation in this case is that of *paradox*." (Burgin, 1976c: 2) Contradiction, ambiguity, and paradox are also the rhetorical devices Burgin uses in his magazine work. As in *Hussonet*, he re-cycles the rhetorical structure of advertising in order to create a counter-ideological message. According to the semiotician Jacques Durand, "rhetoric is in sum a repertory of the various ways in which we can be 'original.' It is probable then that the creative process could be enriched and made easier if the creators would take account consciously of a system which they use intuitively." (Burgin, 1976c: 2) Burgin does not only deliberately use the rhetorical devices of advertising; he also names them ("contradiction") and subverts their original function—i.e. persuading and seducing the consumer—by confronting the unresolved image-caption-relation with a laconic text contrasting the problem of class consciousness ironically with concerns about radical change as they might occur in both advertising and revolutionary discourse.

In a similar way, other works such as *Sensation* (1975), *Going Somewhere?* (1976), and *Think about it* (1976) confront appropriated advertising imagery with verbal elements raising questions of property, capitalism, and class consciousness. *Think about it*, for instance, appeared in the March/April 1976 issue of *Studio International* on the spread preceding Burgin's essay "Social Formalism," in which parts of "Art, Common Sense and Photography" are included and further developed. (Fig. 2.6.) Once again, the work features the photograph of the thinking woman, this time isolated from her office surrounding and juxtaposed with a text deconstructing the idea of middle-class people as classless and independent of capitalist exploitation. On the left side, the oversized head of Rodin's *Thinker* is monumentally staged as a symbol of the free-thinking heroic artist.[18] Burgin uses here the figure of hyperbole (overstatement) in order to create an ironic contrast between bourgeois values of autonomy epitomized by Rodin's modern male sculpture and a critical reflectiveness about existing social differences represented by the photographic portrait of the woman. The construction of gender through representation, albeit implicitly, already lurks beneath the surface of Burgin's socialist project. Drawing on Georg Lukács' definition of "false consciousness" as a problem of perception and knowledge that could be countered by new theoretical orientation, (Eyerman, 1981: 49) Burgin aims to dismantle photography and advertising as a manipulative instrument of the dominant ideology, and from there to establish a counter-rhetoric which invites the viewer/reader to skepticism and to a questioning of the existing social order.

As a consequence of this socialist agenda, Burgin leaves the institutional context of art (gallery, magazine) in favor of the street. In 1977, Paul Maenz asked seven politically oriented artists, including Burgin,[19] the following question: "What do you expect—ideologically, commercially, technically—from an art gallery functioning within the current cultural/economic structure?" As Burgin responded:

> The gallery then is to be seen as one amongst a number of institutional spaces of the broader ideological institution 'art.' It is

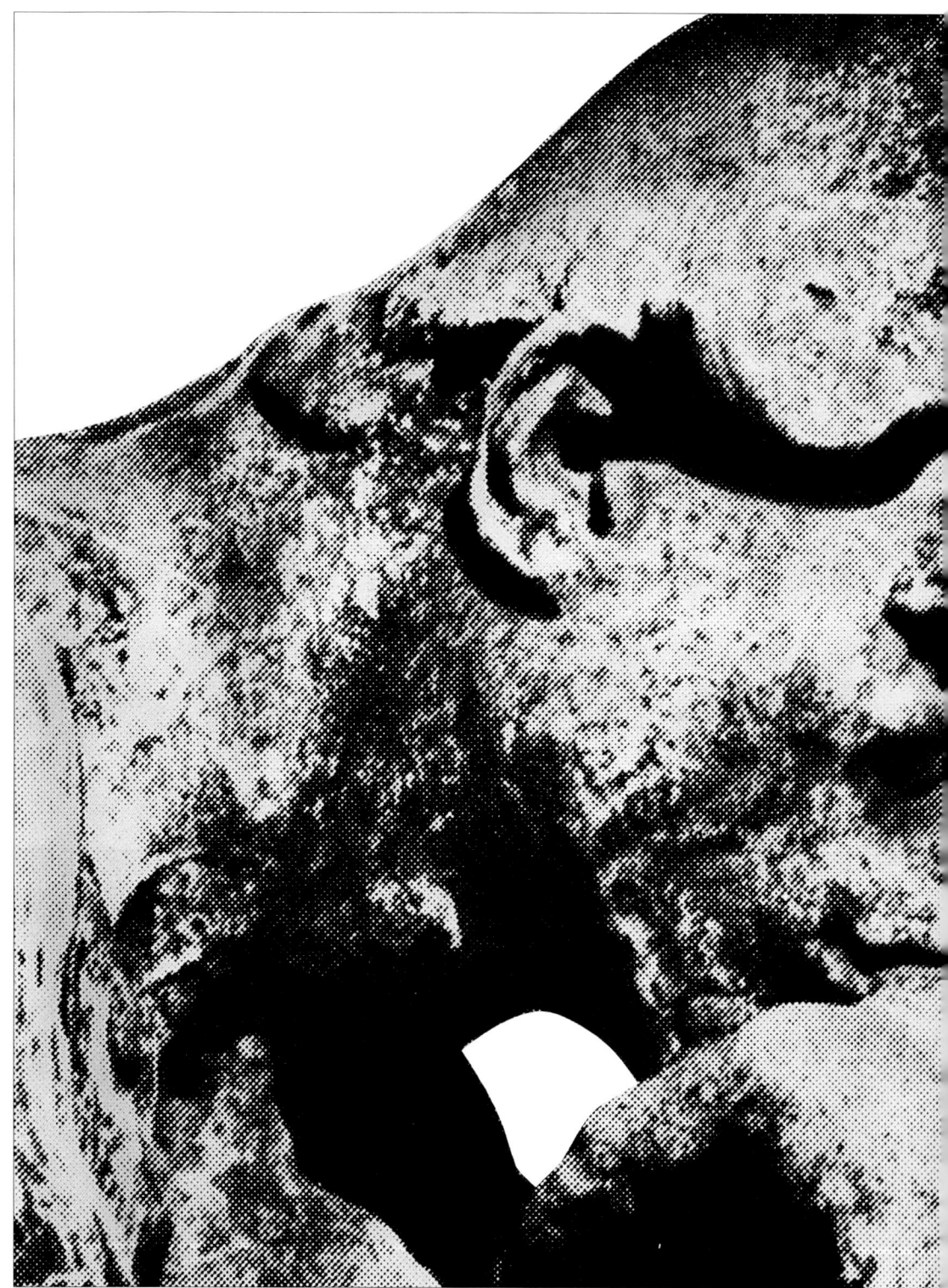

Figure 2.6. *Think About It*, 1976. 121,9×167,6 cm.

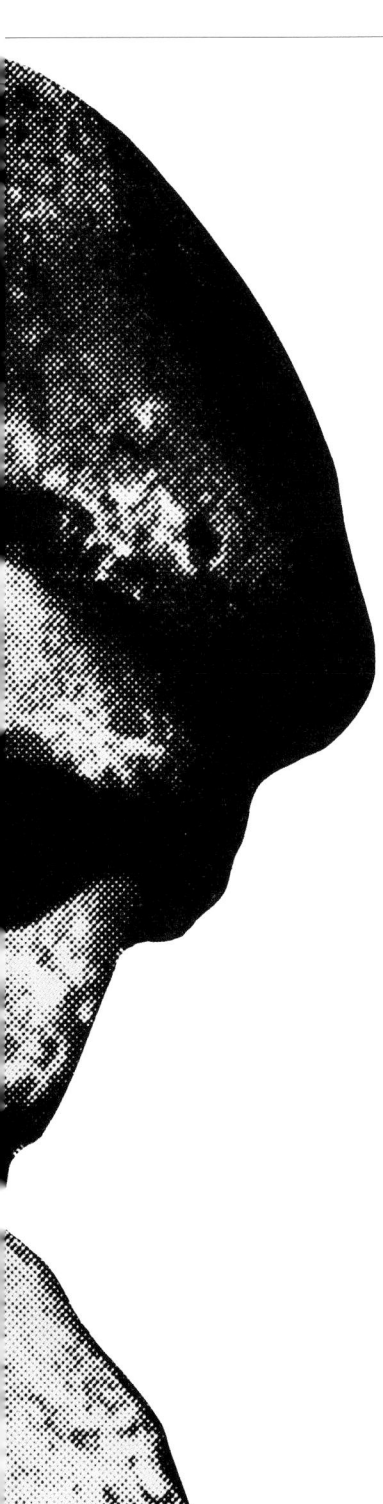

It's worth
thinking about . . .

To finance the system of conspicuous expenditure,
an extraordinary credit network has been set up,
which, when considered, reveals much of our real
class situation. The earners of wages and salaries are
alike in this, that most of them become quickly
involved in a system of usury which spreads until it is
virtually inescapable.

How many supposedly middle-class people really own
their houses, or their furniture, or their cars? Most of
them are as radically unpropertied as the traditional
working class, who are now increasingly involved in
the same process of usury.

In part it is the old exaction, by the
propertied, from the needs of the
unpropertied, and the ordinary
middle-class talk of the property
and independence which make
them substantial citizens is an
increasingly pathetic illusion.

One factor in maintaining the
illusion is that much of the capital
needed to finance the ordinary
buyer comes from his own
pocket, through insurance and
the like, and this can be
made to look like the
sensible process of
accumulating social
capital.

What is not usually
noticed is that established
along the line of this
process are a group of
people using its
complications to make
substantial profit out of
their neighbours' social
needs.

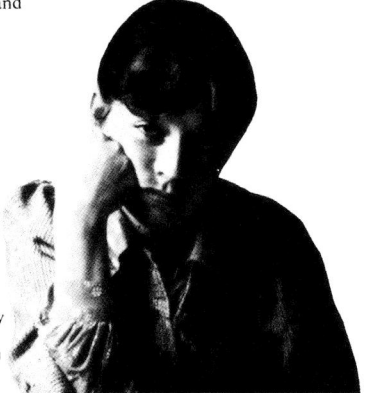

As we move into this
characteristic contemporary
world, we can see the
supposed new phenomenon
of classlessness as simply
a failure of consciousness.

Class consciousness
think about it

within, as much as beyond, such spaces that the politically awake art-worker—whatever his or her specific practice—may work for cultural change. (Maenz, 1977: n. p.)

The poster *Possession* was originally designed for a group exhibition at the Fruitmarket Gallery in Edinburgh in 1976. (Fig. 2.7. and Plate 2) In the summer of the same year, 500 copies were posted in the streets of the center of Newcastle upon Tyne. (BN: 20; Wilson, 2016: 101) Reproducing the conventions of advertising, Burgin wanted to produce a message that "anybody could understand." (Lewis, 1987/88: 59) For that reason Burgin opted for a very economical and effective solution with a stock photograph of a young couple embracing in the center, to which he added two short and straightforward sentences that were easily readable and understandable for anyone passing by in a hurry: a question, "What does possession mean to you?," and a reply in the form of a quotation from *The Economist*: "7% of our population own 84% of our wealth."

On a basic level, the hurried reader would grasp the central message of social and economic inequality, after which she or he, when pondering the relationships of the three elements, would consider the more complex connotative meanings, including "all sorts of questions about property relationships, sexual relationships that become property relationships, and so on." (BN: 21) As later on a survey revealed, however, the reactions of the people did not quite match with Burgin's ideal "reflexive" reader. They were rather diverging and rarely subtle or nuanced, ranging from some confusion about the words "possession" and "passion," and formal considerations about the quality of the picture and the question of whether the image would fit with the text or not, to general claims about the injustice in the world. (BN: 16) Consequently, Burgin decided to go back to the gallery as the institutional domain in which he, as an artist, recognized his original roots. Because the determinant framing context of the meaning of an artwork—whether shown in a gallery, on the street, or wherever—would always continue to be the art system, it was futile to try to escape the institution. (Lewis, 1987/88: 59)

Burgin's approach of the mid-1970s has often been compared with that of other British artists using images appropriated from the media, such as Susan Hiller, Margaret Harrison, and John Stezaker. In particular the latter's text-image-collages, confronting photographs of newspapers and cinema with ironic captions and texts, are often cited in this context. (Wilson, 2016: 91-93; Roberts, 1997: 32-34; Cork, 1976: 326-327) For some of Stezaker's works, such comparison seems justified. *Liberty Misleading the People* (1975), for example, juxtaposes car advertising with a woman, a text on a man's erotic experience with love dolls, and a quotation by Marx saying "Value…is a relation between

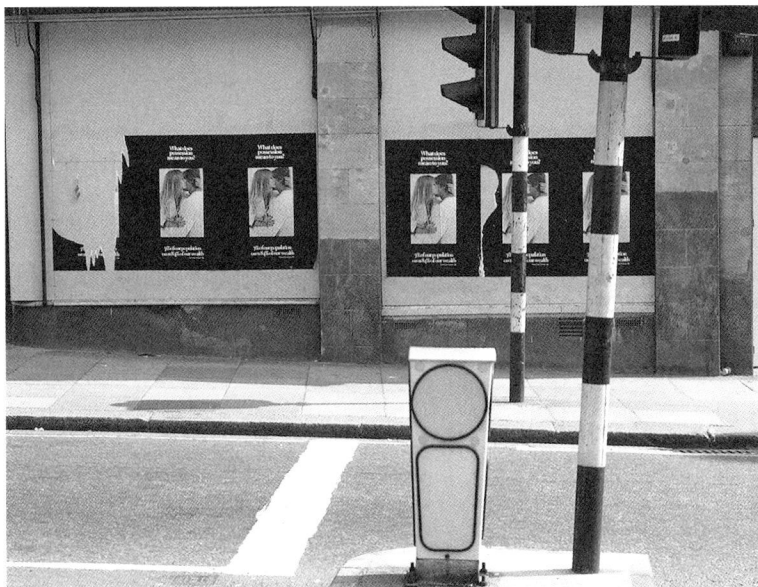

Figure 2.7.

Possession, Newcastle, 1976.

109×84 cm.

persons expressed as a relation between things." In this context, Marx's aphoristic formula becomes an ironic comment on the transformation of the woman's body in a commodity object of desire. This way of exposing "social values inherent in modes of communication" (Stezaker in: *Arte Inglese Oggi*, 1976: 399) is at the heart of one of Burgin's works from the mid-1970s. *Going Somewhere?* shows an attractive, confident young lady beside a Jaguar. (Fig. 2.8.) The text identifies her as Jane, 23, "a fast mover […] heading in the right direction." Next to this incarnation of speedy successfulness, a photograph of a female factory employee, Jean, also 23, is described as "a fast worker […] the faster she works the more she earns." Along the metonymic chain of Jane—Jaguar—Jean—Job, the contradictions of capitalist society embodied by class differences and female stereotypes are unmasked and critically questioned altogether. These kinds of works are part of a socialist art project, whose task, according to Burgin,

> is to unmask the mystifications of bourgeois culture by laying bare its codes, by exposing the devices through which it constructs its self-image. Another job for socialist art is to expose the contradictions in our class society, to show up what double-think there is in our second-nature. Qualifications for the first job include a knowledge of semiotics; qualifications for the second job include a knowledge of politics and economics. (Burgin, 1976b: 154)

Going somewhere ?

Jane, 23, 0-60 in 6.8, is a fast mover.
Fast round the curves, turning heads, and heading
in the right direction . . . nice work.

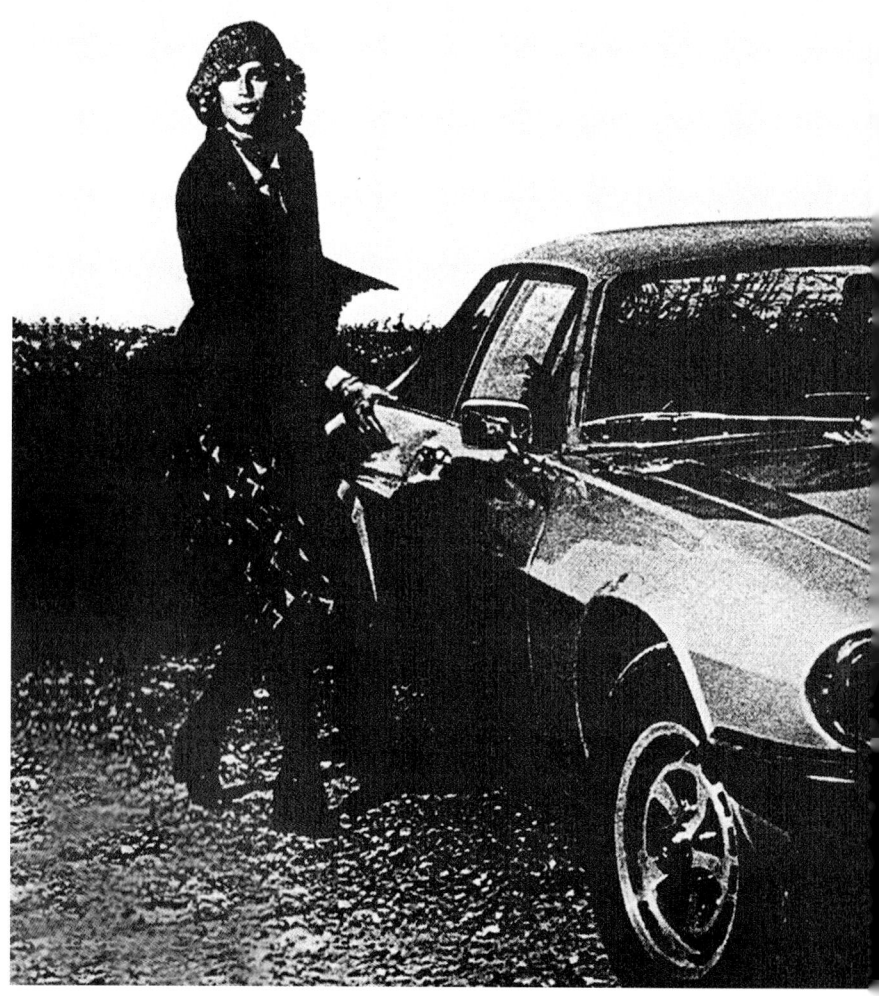

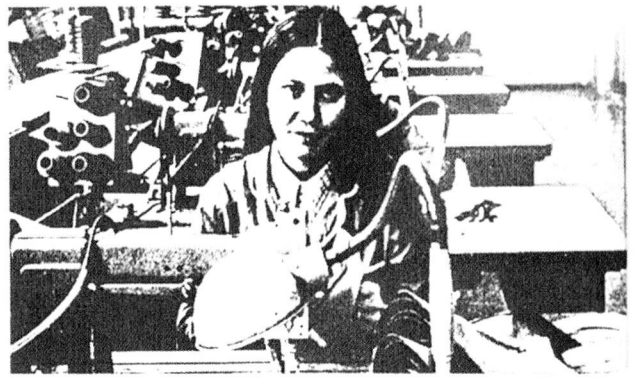

Jean, 23, 07.00-17.30, is a fast worker.
Fast on the job she has to be, the faster she works
the more she earns . . . piece work.

Class consciousness
you're nowhere without it!

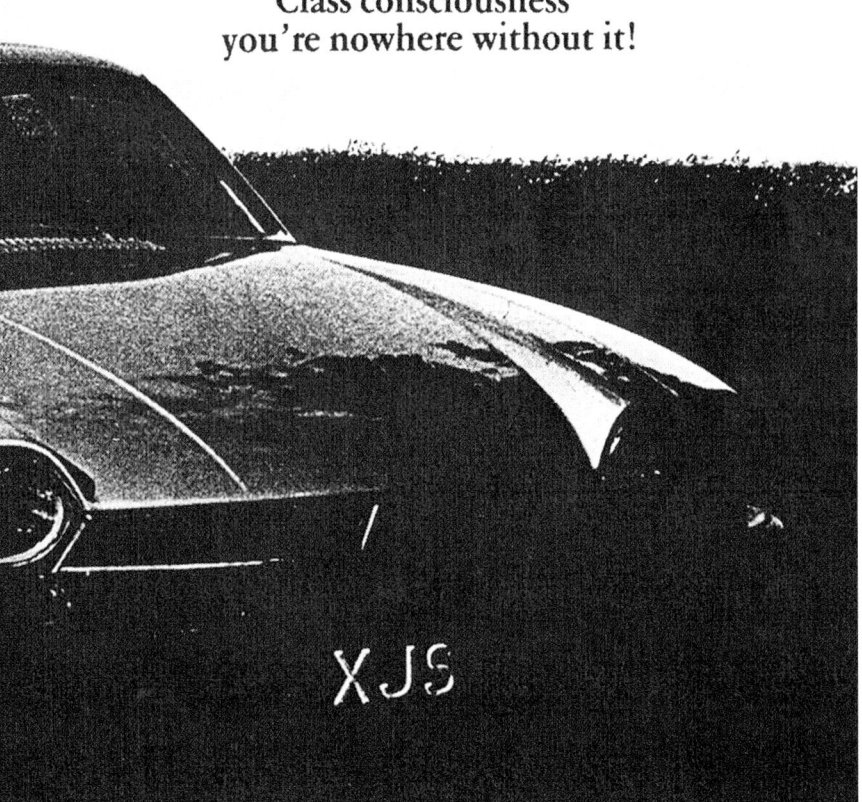

XJS

Figure 2.8.

Going Somewhere?
122×168 cm. 1976.

Burgin himself has indicated, however, that his exchanges with other British artists were all but intense at the time. (Roberts, 1997: 95) His interest in the political use of photomontage by the Russian avant-garde and Dadaism, as well as his reference to Brechtian and Benjaminian ideas about authorship, creation, and the role of the artist in society situates him closer to some critical positions as developed in the United States by artist-writers such as Martha Rosler and Allan Sekula.

2.3.2. The Tradition of Political Photocollage

Burgin discovered John Heartfield and the Russian formalists when he began to teach photography in the Department of Film and Photography at the Polytechnic of Central London in 1973. (Roberts, 1997: 94) In this period, he realized that in the practice and teaching of photography two antagonistic factions were pitted against each other, one defending a documentary approach based on the belief in the medium's transparency for the sake of objective content and the other insisting on a modernist approach based on the idea of photography as an autonomous form of art with its proper stylistic specificities. "Socialist Formalism" and "Modernism in the *Work* of Art," both published in 1976, address the problem of the historic legitimation of photographic discourse. Both essays begin with the observation that Modernism's successful dissemination of its version of art history as an evolution from realist, content-based work to abstract, autonomous art for its own sake has only been possible by means of the obliteration or assimilation of artistic tendencies with different, if not antagonistic, artistic programs—i.e., Russian Formalism and Dadaism.

> The consolidation of conceptualist practices along the socialist lines which have been implicit from their inception demands a reading of formalist aesthetics, of history, and of current priorities, different from that now predominating in the Western art community. (Burgin, 1976b: 148)

For a critical re-positioning of Russian Formalism in art history, Burgin's recent discovery of the film journal *Screen* has been of major importance. (Streitberger, 2009: xvii) The winter 1971 issue of *Screen* was dedicated to the Russian avant-garde journal *Novy Lef* of which documents about Russian film were published triggering a debate around realism in terms of a theoretical interrogation of the application(s) of the concept. ("Realism is used in many ways," Editorial, vol. 13, 1) Even though Burgin's interest in the Russian avant-garde, and his own use of the concept of realism, must be seen against the backdrop of this debate, it should be noted that his frame of reference was very different from that of the *Screen* authors. Rather than turning against a congealed mono-dimensional use of the concept of realism within film studies, he was seeking to employ a different idea of realism against the tradition of Modernism in the field of art. By exposing the deficiencies of the prevalent purely formalistic interpretation of the Russian avant-garde, and pointing to the latter's functionalistic and political orientation, Burgin could now suggest to integrate Russian Formalism within a modern Western art practice engaged with "those codes and contents which are *in the public domain.*" (Burgin, 1976b: 151)

In "Modernism in the *Work* of Art," Burgin focuses on the use of photography within Russian Formalism and other European avant-garde movements of the 1920s and 1930s, such as Dadaism and German Constructivism, in order to show to what extent specific bourgeois ideas of art history based on the distinction between 'high' and 'low' culture were, at this particular historical conjuncture, irrelevant to an international artistic project that, situated between aestheticism and utilitarianism, as well as form and fact (content), insisted on its active participation in political and social life by means of a close relationship between art and the mass media. As Burgin emphasizes, photocollage, as used by Rodchenko, Heartfield, Moholy-Nagy, and many others, not only was a major visual instrument in the formation of mass culture, but also marked a critical moment in the history of representation:

> The use of photocollage in the deconstruction of monocular perspective thus appears as historically "over-determined," doubly concerned with that which was *critical* in visual art at that particular historical conjuncture: that it should resist the return of imaginary for which idealist abstraction and photographic "realism" alike were preparing it. (EAT: 19)

The use of techniques of collage and montage as means to reject romantic and modernist concepts of photography alike, was also a concern in the work and writing of American artists Allan Sekula and Martha Rosler. Like Burgin, both artists saw a real danger in recent tendencies of a fetishistic notion of photography within the art institutions. In an essay from 1975, republished in Burgin's edited volume *Thinking Photography*, Sekula delivers a sharp critique of the romantic notion of the photographer as genius who expresses unique essences. He warns for the "symbolist folk-myth" of the photographer as "seer," as "expressive genius" who produces "spiritual significance" as opposed to another popular myth, the "photographer as witness" who represents "empirical truth." (Sekula 1982: 108) Notably in the United States, a formalist approach to photography became increasingly dominant in the institutional discourse since the 1950s. Beaumont Newhall's highly influential *History of Photography*, in which the founder of the Museum of Modern Art's photography department aimed to retrace the evolution of the medium from craft to independent art, culminated in the 1960s in Szarkowski's claim to concentrate on the characteristics and problems intrinsic in the medium. (Newhall, 1978; Szarkowski, 1997: 7) As Sekula put it: "The invention of the photograph as high art was only possible through its transformation into an abstract fetish, into 'significant form.'" (Sekula, 1982: 103)[20] And in her article "Lookers, Buyers, Dealers and Makers," Martha Rosler observes this shift from documentary value to expressive value, taking as an example Dorothea Lange's photographic work for the FSA, which, appropriated by the art institutions, left social documentation behind to become the creation of an expressive, solitary genius. (Rosler, 2004: 36-37) Burgin, too, cautions against the formalism of Szarkowski, who, ignoring the context of production and presentation, reduces the photographic image to a formal composition that is dependent on cardinal rules such as detail, framing, and perspective. (Szarkowski, 1997; Burgin, 1980: 73-75) In their theory and practice, these artists therefore set about deconstructing the shift from documentary photography to aesthetic expression, from reporter to genius, a shift that—they believed—serves the liberal politics of capitalism in which the image, removed from its political context, becomes a product that is appreciated for its inherent formal and material qualities. This is why Burgin, Sekula, and Rosler dismiss intuitive and expressive creation in favor of an artistic practice that is contextual and socially-engaged and takes account of the ideological forms operating in a society at the aesthetic, social, and political level.

2.3.3. The Author as Producer

The model for this practice is clearly inspired by the model of author as producer conceived by Walter Benjamin in the wake of Bertolt Brecht's reflections on his concept of epic theater. Indeed, to define artistic practice and the artist's role in society, all three authors refer explicitly to Benjamin's essay "The Author as Producer," based on a 1934 lecture given at the Institute for the Study of Fascism in Paris. From the passages in which Burgin, Rosler, and Sekula overtly quote Benjamin, three aspects form the basis of a theoretical-practical artistic practice. When Rosler, quoting Benjamin, writes that "to supply a productive apparatus without trying […] to change it is a highly disputable activity," she is highlighting the artist's responsibility towards society. (Benjamin, 1998: 93-94; Rosler, 1984: 335) And Sekula, quoting Brecht, emphasizes the necessity to maintain a critical distance from the production apparatus, and adopt a meta-reflexive attitude:

> The muddled thinking which overtakes musicians, writers and critics as soon as they consider their own situation has tremendous consequences to which too little attention is paid. For by imagining that they have got hold of an apparatus which in fact has got hold of them they are supporting an apparatus which is out of their control. (Sekula, 1978: 869)[21]

So, the artist is expected to develop a body of work that implies its own critical reflection within the context of its aesthetic and social discourse. In accordance with this position, Burgin, drawing on Benjamin, suggests a "pan-discursive" attitude whereby photography and writing, artistic and political tendencies, intertwine to embrace technical progress:

> And we shall lend greater emphasis to this demand if we, as writers, start taking photographs ourselves. Here again, therefore, technical progress is, for the author as producer, the basis of his political progress. (Benjamin, 1998: 95; TP: 216)

Social transformation, meta-reflection, and interdisciplinarity are all vital components of a creation that is radically opposed to the romantic orientation of Modernism based on concepts of intuition, autonomy, and purity. Basing his theory of the artist as producer on Brecht's principles of epic theater, Benjamin suggests that the quality of the work does not lie in formal, symbolic values but in a dialectic link between literary trends and socio-political reality: "the rigid, isolated object (work, novel, book) is of no use whatsoever. It must be inserted into the context of living social relations." And he continues: "Before I ask: what is a work's position *vis-à-vis* the production relations of its time, I should like to ask: what is its position *within* them?" (Benjamin, 1998: 87) If the artist wishes to exert influence on his era, aspiring to change the society in which he lives, he must apply and enter into a dialogue with the very means of production and technologies of this society: photography, film, and radio.

The principles underpinning a critical exploration of society are interruption and alienation (*Verfremdung*), as introduced by Brecht in his epic theater and, later on, claimed by Benjamin for montage as the basic process in film, radio, the press, and photography. Drawing on John Heartfield's use of the book jacket as "a political instrument," Benjamin highlights, in fact, "the technique of montage, for montage interrupts the context into which it is inserted." (99) By interrupting the action,

Brecht aims to surprise the audience. Due to the fact that "the interruption of the action [...] always works against creating an illusion among the audience," the audience is distanced from "the conditions of our life." The spectators are therefore invited to take a step back from the play and are compelled to "take up a position towards the action," referring to the position of the actors as well as to the spectators' own situation. (99-100) The creative process thus requires the artist to adopt the processes of the dominant production apparatus and, in transforming them, encourage the attitude of maintaining critical distance toward the production conditions in art and society.

Martha Rosler's definition of art as a "practice of critical photography and text" as well as her "quotational ('appropriational') and ironic" approach, in works such as *Bringing the War Home* (1967-1972) and *The Bowery in two inadequate descriptive systems* (1974/75), aiming at a "critical engagement with the images of mass culture, visual and verbal, and with those of photography (and art) as a practice," are perfectly in line with Benjamin's position. (Rosler, 2004: 139) So are Sekula's works of the 1970s, most notably *Aerospace Folktales* (1973), conceived as a "disassembled movie" built up from heterogeneous visual, verbal, and auditory components in order to provide a critical meta-commentary of the myths of photographic realism and capitalist liberalism alike. (Sekula, 2003: 92)

Burgin's works of this period, as Rosler's and Sekula's, concur with all the decisive points of the model of the author as producer. First, their hybrid character, oscillating between text and image, photo and film, contrasts with the formalist tendency in photography already criticized by Benjamin, such as New Objectivity, which he believes, "has turned the struggle against misery into an object of consumption." (Benjamin, 1998: 96) Instead of expressing essential values, the photographer should frame the images with language to anchor, contradict, reinforce, subvert, supplement, specify, or extend the meanings depicted by the images themselves. (Sekula, 1978: 866) From this perspective, Burgin's "aesthetics of fragments and cracks," constitute an analytical device in which the creative process contains its own process of reflection. (Burgin, 1978: 137) Montage and interruption are the key components of this approach, which is diametrically opposed to the modernist aesthetic model. While Modernism champions the autonomy and self-reflexivity of the artistic medium, which, removed from the social context, references only its own formal qualities, Burgin's critical montages, often juxtaposing the advertising image with a theoretical metatext, suggest that a medium is defined, on the one hand, according to the social and economic context in which it is used and, on the other, by the interactions, rivalries, and reciprocal influences between it and another medium.

Finally, this contextual approach must include the spectator. As in Brecht's epic theater, interruption (medium, genre, style) invites the spectator, who is constantly pulled out of the narrative, to distance himself from what he sees. The impact created by the brusque juxtaposition of photography and film, family photographs and bureaucratic documents, advertising copy and laconic commentary, encourages the spectator to become a politically-aware "pensive spectator." (Bellour, 2007) If the question of creation is essentially the place for art to reflect on itself, its own operations and practices, the works discussed here are that very place, not in the sense of the closed aesthetic place of modernist self-referentiality, but as a place of social and aesthetic struggle in which reflection on art is inextricably linked to reflection on society because aesthetic, social, and political discourses are bound by the same ideological conditions.

2.4. Toward a Rhetoric of the Unconscious

Between 1976 and 1978, Burgin realized three photo-text-series, *UK 76*, *US 77*, and *Zoo 78*, which mark an important turning point in his work. A crucial difference with the former appropriation works concerns the nature and the presentation of the photo-texts. Burgin abandons the recycling of existing advertising images in favor of photographs he took himself at the places where he worked or traveled. He then printed the images with a superimposed text on large panels (40×60 inches for *UK 76* and *US 77*), which were arranged along the walls of the gallery. This way of adapting the format and the display of the panels to the conditions of the gallery space is to be understood as a response to his above-mentioned incursion in the street with the poster *Possession*. As a result of his "wish to address […] those expectations which have accumulated in the form of the art institution," Burgin begins to concentrate on the gallery space as the legitimate institutional domain of the artist. (Lewis, 1987/88: 59)[22]

2.4.1. The Rhetoric of Art Photography and Advertising

UK 76 is based on photographs Burgin took on the occasion of a commission he received by the Coventry Workshop to take pictures in factories around Coventry. (Godfrey, 1982: 19) (Fig. 2.9.) In adding short texts to these strictly documentary images, Burgin combines ironically two systems of representation, "the thematic and pictorial conventions of socially 'concerned' documentary photography" and "graphic and rhetorical conventions derived from glossy magazines." (CP: 48)

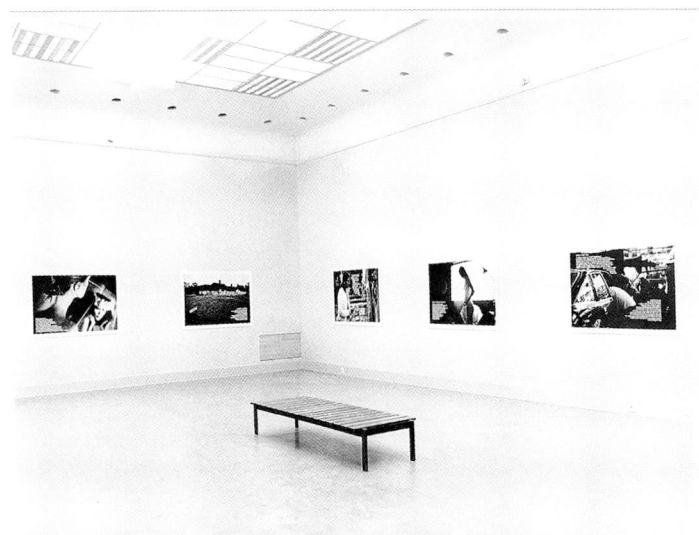

Figure 2.9.

UK 76, 1976.

11 parts, each 100×150 cm.
Installation view, John
Weber Gallery, New York,
1977.

The purpose of this confrontation of contradicting social formations—capital versus labor—with their respective styles—fashion journalism versus social documentary photography—was to demystify the different codes of representation (advertising and social documentary) by "constructing a rhetorical antithesis to map a social antithesis." (Lewis, 1987/88: 56) The St. Laurent-panel, for instance, juxtaposes the picture of a female immigrant worker with a text derived from the fashion page of a newspaper. (Fig. 2.10.) St. Laurent's "whole new lifestyle" is here confronted with the working conditions of the Pakistani factory worker. Retrospectively, Burgin took his distance from this kind of political work, which, according to him, does not provide any additional value to the source material apart from ironic antagonism. (PT: 214) However, there are other examples in the series, which address in a more subtle and complex way the construction of ideology through the dominant social discourse and its representations. "It's only natural," reads the heading of a commentary about the proletariat's dependency of actual and historical context, printed on the photograph of a picturesque British landscape shrouded in a misty atmosphere. The contradiction nature/ideology relates to both the proletarian who thinks to be a sovereign master of his own destiny while being completely dependent of the social conditions in which he lives, and the belief in an either expressive, spontaneous, or objective, neutral value of the representation of nature as propagated by, respectively, romanticism and realism. In a certain sense, this idea of landscape as formed by and in representation follows in the tradition of the picturesque. As early as in 1768, William Gilpin defined *picturesque* as "a term expressive of that peculiar kind of beauty, which is agreeable in a picture." (Gilpin, 1802: xii) A landscape, rather than being a naturally given segment of topography, is a function of the viewer's perception in which it pre-exists as a specific type of painting. (Krauss, 1985: 163-164) But whereas in British romanticism the representational character of landscape relies on aesthetic categories such as the beautiful and the sublime, Burgin situates the problem of representation in ideology and plays the "romantic" myth of aesthetic autonomy against the proletarian myth of self-determination. As many earlier works, *UK 76* is still "based on certain assumptions about the nature of ideology as 'false consciousness,'" in this case the assumption that one is free to decide his or her own destiny while the latter is merely a function of the dominant ideological system. (Godfrey, 1982: 22)

2.4.2. Framing Sexual Difference

In *US 77* the previously prevailing ironic antithetic rhetoric, generating a moral message from the collision of contradictory visual and verbal elements, is superseded by a more equivocal approach based on the "'interpenetration' of word and image" to avoid an all too clear meaning, leaving thus much more to the viewer's imagination and interpretation. (Lewis, 1987/88: 56) (Fig. 2.11.) Burgin now rejects the idea of "false consciousness," arguing that there is no "true consciousness" that could exist outside of ideology. From this, he draws the conclusion, that if "ideology isn't a matter of 'false consciousness,' but is a matter of representations—then the forms of representations—visual, verbal, kinesic, or whatever—become something to examine for their ideological implications." (Godfrey, 1982: 16) Consequently, his focus shifts from the representation of politics to a politics of representation. As Burgin suggests, the difference between the representation of politics and a politics of representation is that while the former is concerned with the critical depiction of "the political issues of the day" and may thus be compared with propaganda and agitation, the latter asks about the unconscious structures which inform the re-presentations of the empirical realm.

> We don't simply *inhabit* a material reality, we simultaneously inhabit a psychic reality—the former, in fact, being "known" only *via* the latter. Psychic reality, the register of the subjective, of emotion (including, of course, pleasure), is organised according to the articulation of sexual difference. (Godfrey, 1982: 26)

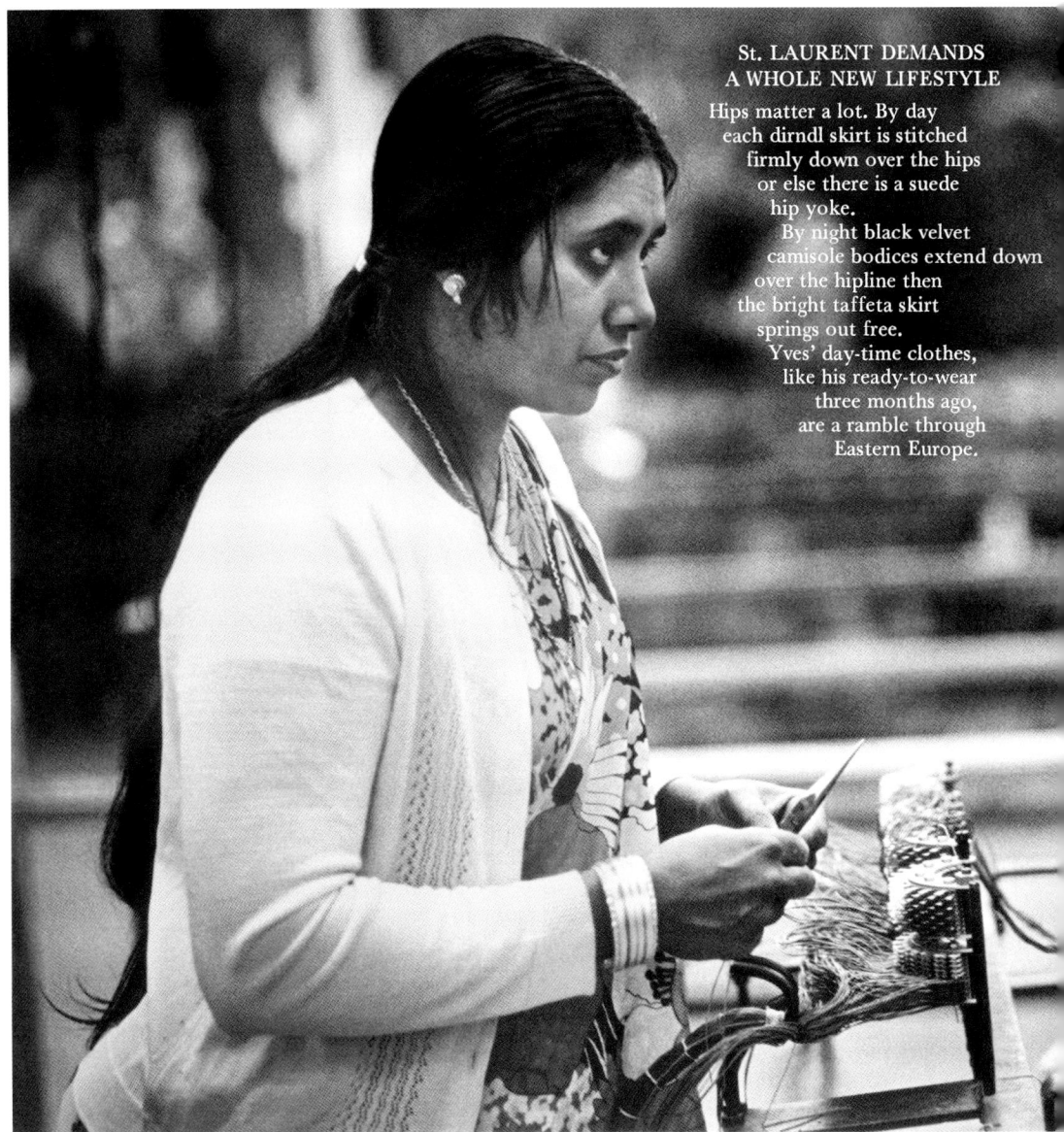

St. LAURENT DEMANDS
A WHOLE NEW LIFESTYLE

Hips matter a lot. By day
each dirndl skirt is stitched
firmly down over the hips
or else there is a suede
hip yoke.
By night black velvet
camisole bodices extend down
over the hipline then
the bright taffeta skirt
springs out free.
Yves' day-time clothes,
like his ready-to-wear
three months ago,
are a ramble through
Eastern Europe.

Figure 2.10.
UK 76, 1976 (ST LAURENT DEMANDS A WHOLE NEW LIFE STYLE).

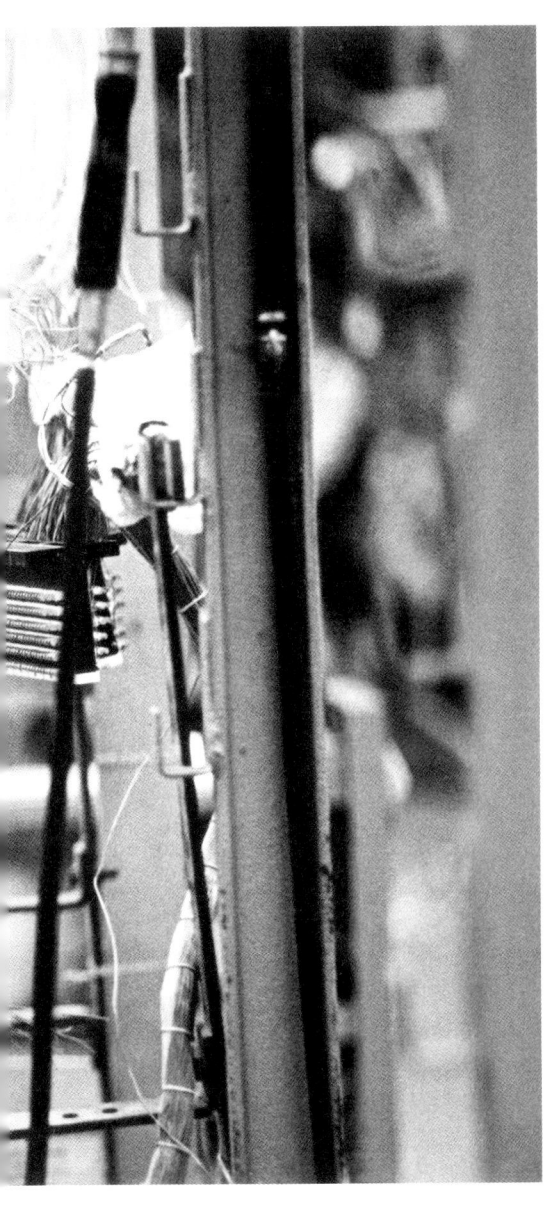

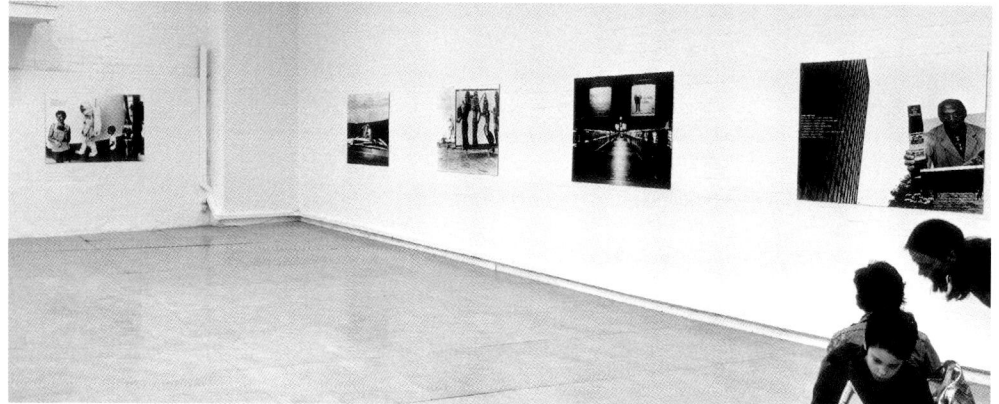

While earlier works such as *Lei-Feng*, *Hussonet*, and *Going Somewhere* touch on questions of gender clichés in a more implicit way, *US 77* raises sexual difference in representation as a crucial issue. (Between: 40) This entails also a move toward Freudian and Lacanian psychoanalytic theory as an instrument to analyze "the rhetoric of the unconscious." (Lewis, 1987/88: 56) The shift from "image of sexual difference" to "sexual-difference-as-image" manifests itself in how advertising is shown in the photographs. In six out of the twelve panels, billboards with advertising are represented within their urban setting. While in former works the advertising imagery was isolated from its original context and integrated in a new image-text configuration, it is now shown *as* image deployed within a particular socio-cultural context.

Most of the panels are overtly addressing questions of gender and sexuality. In "Patriarchitecture," for instance, the text is a direct quotation from Freud's essay "On the Universal Tendency to Debasement in the Sphere of Love," in which the psychoanalyst comments on man's unresolved problem of distinguishing women in categories of sexual object and respected, and therefore undesirable, subject, caused by the supposedly unacknowledged idea of incest with mother or sister. (Freud, 1912/1957: 185) (Fig. 2.12.) The image shows the desert of the periphery of Las Vegas with desolate trees and industrial structure in the background. The foreground is dominated by a billboard advertising of a strip club, which is deliberately cropped on the right by the photograph's edge. The placard represents one and the same pin-up model in four different seductive poses while performing a strip-tease that ends with the woman in lingerie. If we read the term "Patriarchitecture" as a name for structures built by men for men, then we might be inclined, on a first level, to establish an analogy between the architecture of patriarchy and the female body as a representational construction created by man to

Figure 2.11.
US 77, 1977.
12 parts, each 100×150 cm. Installation view, Museum of Modern Art, Oxford, 1978.

satisfy his sexual desires. But the image contains an uncanny moment that is hard to grasp. The image is decentered; it slips away revealing a deserted, hostile environment in which nothing thrives and prospers. Is this the gloomy nightmare of patriarchal ideas of sexuality that lurks behind the façade of an imaginary fantasy of the perfect female body? Repeated four times, this body is not real. It appears like a clone or like Freud's uncanny *doppelgänger* that haunts our dreams "and forces upon us the idea of something fateful and inescapable where otherwise we should have spoken of 'chance' only." (Freud, 1919/1955: 237)

In "Patriarchitecture," the billboard functions as a projection screen for man's sexual desire and potency; but its dark border provides also a frame of behavior for woman, transforming her into a fetishized object. Drawing upon Laura Mulvey's seminal essay "Visual Pleasure and Narrative Cinema," published in 1975 in *Screen*, Burgin writes in 1976: "The photograph stands to the subject-viewer as does the fetishised object: it is to be looked at; the look gives pleasure; it affirms an existence beyond itself; it simultaneously denies the presence of that existence." (EAT: 19) Burgin takes up Mulvey's argument, formulated for Hollywood cinema, that "fetishistic scopophilia builds up the beauty of the object transforming it into something satisfying in itself," and applies it to glossy advertising and fine print art photography. (Mulvey, 1975: 14) In *US 77*, Burgin quotes and undercuts both tendencies. While the motives and the black-and-white aesthetic of the photographs follow in the tradition of street photography, the grainy, harsh quality of the images, due to a complex production process based on various prints in different sizes, runs counter to fine art photography's preference for detail and fine grain. (Godfrey, 1982: 9) If the superposition of short texts on the images contributes to refusing the pleasure of looking at a fine art print, it first and foremost imitates another photographic genre: advertising as encountered in magazines. But once again, the fetishizing effect of the image is subverted on various levels. In "Patriarchitecture" this happens through the verbal message, the decentering of the billboard, which is contrasted with a desolate landscape, and the literal doubling of the frame of reference (placard within magazine advertising).

The panel "Framed" addresses the question of the relationship between ideological and representational framing in a much more explicit and complex way. (Fig. 2.13.) Burgin retrospectively described this panel as "the end of the beginning" of his practice, bringing together most elements of his subsequent work: "relation of image to text; the interpenetration of real and imaginary space; the intersections of sexuality and politics." (CP: 38) In his 1979 interview with Tony Godfrey, he offers the following commentary on it:

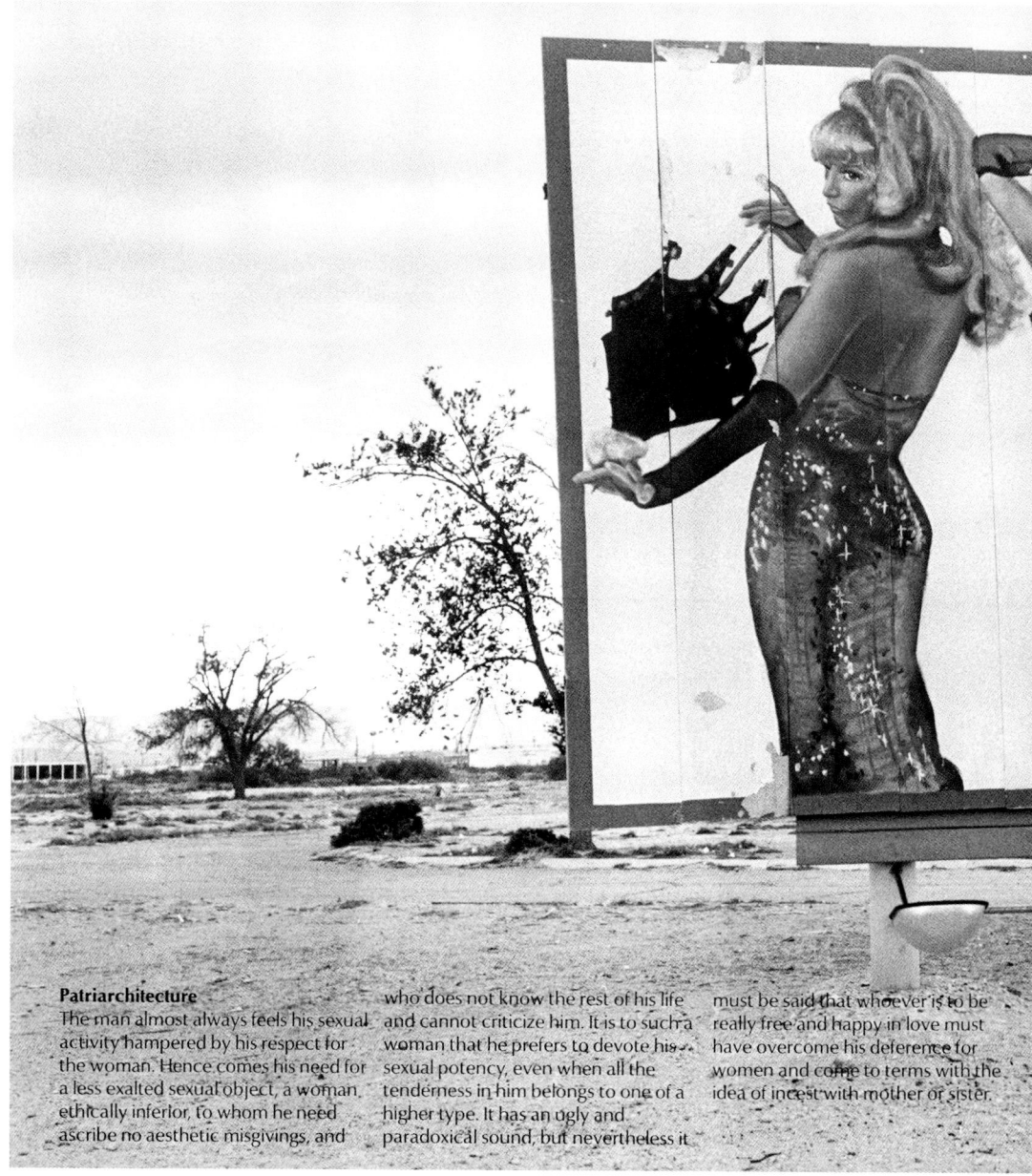

Patriarchitecture
The man almost always feels his sexual activity hampered by his respect for the woman. Hence comes his need for a less exalted sexual object, a woman, ethically inferior, to whom he need ascribe no aesthetic misgivings, and who does not know the rest of his life and cannot criticize him. It is to such a woman that he prefers to devote his sexual potency, even when all the tenderness in him belongs to one of a higher type. It has an ugly and paradoxical sound, but nevertheless it must be said that whoever is to be really free and happy in love must have overcome his deference for women and come to terms with the idea of incest with mother or sister.

Figure 2.12.
US 77, 1977 (PATRIARCHITECTURE).

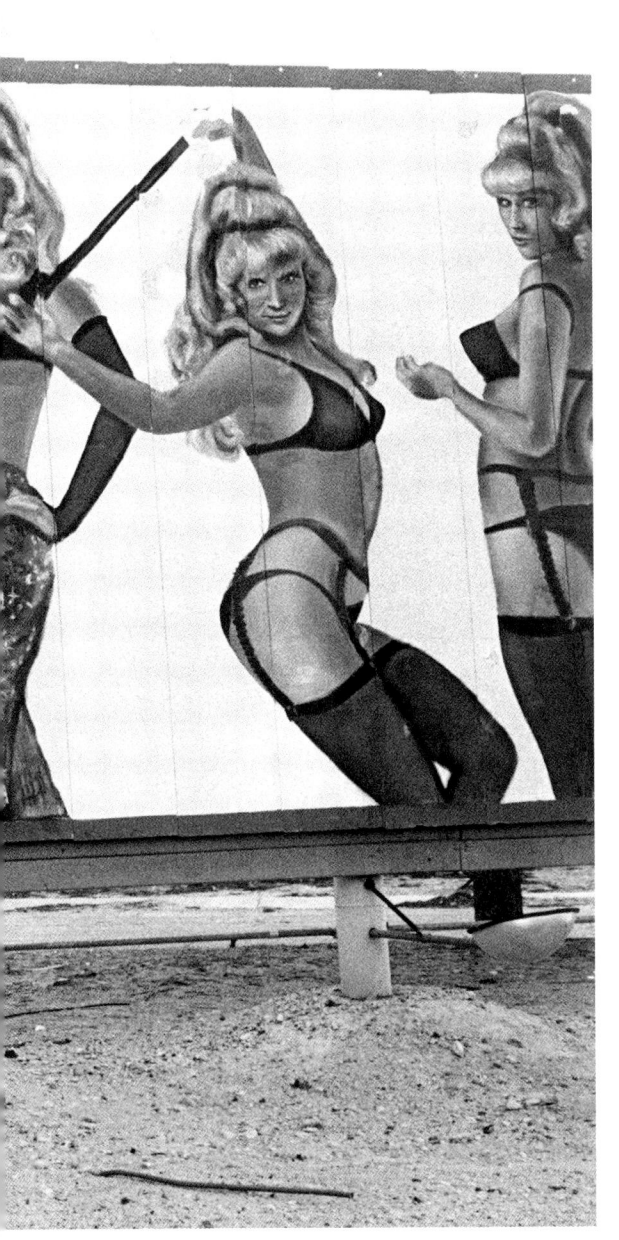

the "keyword" Framed is used to relate together a number of pictured and "written" frames: the frame of the panel itself; the frame of the Marlboro poster, the frame of the photograph described in the text; and the frame of the mirror in which the woman watches herself. Secondly the word "framed"—in the language of gangster and cowboy films—has the meaning of the misrepresentation of an individual: the good guy is "framed" by the bad guys. The cowboy in the poster helps this reading. Now this idea of being framed, of having a certain "picture" of yourself imposed on you by others against your will, can then be attached to the stereotypes which are arranged as oppositions: young girl/middle-aged woman; male hairdresser/cowboy—these are clearly distinguished cliché representations of people used in the media, and in culture in general. (Godfrey, 1982: 18)

The text-image combination, Burgin continues, could encourage one to pursue further associations, such as "cigarette—fag—homosexuality" or "bag (depicted in the photo)—elderly woman," and he concludes: "These sorts of 'literalisations' of elements in an image aren't often picked up consciously, but I think that they contribute to what we might call the 'unconscious' of an image." (Godfrey, 1982: 18)

The photographic frame Burgin alludes to is certainly not the one identified by John Szarkowski, drawing on Greenberg's definition of specificity, as a characteristic feature of the medium. In *The Photographer's Eye*, Szarkowski writes:

While the draughtsman starts with the middle of the sheet, the photographer starts with the frame. The photograph's edge defines content. It isolates unexpected juxtapositions. By surrounding two facts, it creates a relationship. The edge of the photograph dissects familiar forms, and shows their unfamiliar fragment. It creates the shapes that surround objects. The photographer edits the meanings and patterns of the world through an imaginary frame. (Szarkowski, 1997, n. p.)

Considering Burgin's critical discussion of modernist ideas about photography in his theoretical work, "Framed" can certainly be understood as a response to Szarkowski's interpretation of the frame as a formal device that transforms the world into an image. Rather than operating on a "depictive level," (Shore, 2007: 37) Burgin's frame is an ideological device that structures the perception and the representations of the world. As Victor Burgin points out in "Looking at Photographs," (1977) every representational framing of the world is subjected to ideological assumptions: "The structure of representation—point-of-view and frame—is intimately implicated in the reproduction of ideology (the 'frame of mind' of our 'point-of-view'). More than any other textual system, the photograph presents itself as 'an offer you can't refuse.'" (TF: 146) In another essay he adds:

> To speak of the "sense" and "story" of a photograph is to acknowledge that the reality-effect of a photograph is such that it inescapably implicates a world of activity responsible for, and to, the fragments circumscribed by the frame: a world of causes, of "before and after", of "if, then…", a narrated world. (EAT: 69)

This position may be related to Jean-Louis Baudry's apparatus theory as applied to cinema. In modern media society, Baudry holds, the frame is a decisive device of the dominant ideological apparatus established to manipulate the perception and the self-conception of the subject: "The world is no longer only an 'open and indeterminate horizon.' Limited by the framing, lined up, put at the proper distance, the world offers up an object endowed with meaning, an intentional object, implied by and implying the action of the 'subject' which sights it." (Baudry, 1974-75: 43) As a proper means to resist this "offer you can't refuse" (Burgin), Baudry suggests that it is necessary to reveal the mechanisms of image-making and framing in the work itself (as an example he cites Vertov's *Man with a Movie Camera*). This is precisely what Burgin does in *US 77*. He shows how the framing of the world takes place by imbricating various verbal and visual frames, including the photographic panel itself, the poster of the Marlboro man, the picture of the beautiful young woman, and the mirror in the hair salon. Together they represent diverse sites of the production of ideology: art and documentary photography, magazine and street advertising, portraiture and beauty salons. The text of "Framed" ends by revealing the unsettling effect of the mirror as a surface where ideology becomes visible: "But the woman continues sitting, continues staring at her reflection in the mirror." And with Baudry we may add: "And the mirror, as a reflecting surface, is framed, limited, circumscribed. *An infinite mirror would no longer be a mirror.*" (Baudry, 1974-75: 45)

Yet, Burgin's mirror is not merely a limit imposed by aesthetic or social conventions; it is rather a framing device delineating the unconscious as the virtual playground of ideology. The woman remains petrified in front of her mirror reflection, turning into an object, being aware that her attempt to look like the beautiful young woman cannot keep up with her expectations; on the contrary, her identity dissolves in the image of the mirror. In Jacques Lacan's reinterpretation of Freud, the mirror is the very locus for the constitution of a self in the human infant. According to the French psychoanalyst, the mirror stage is

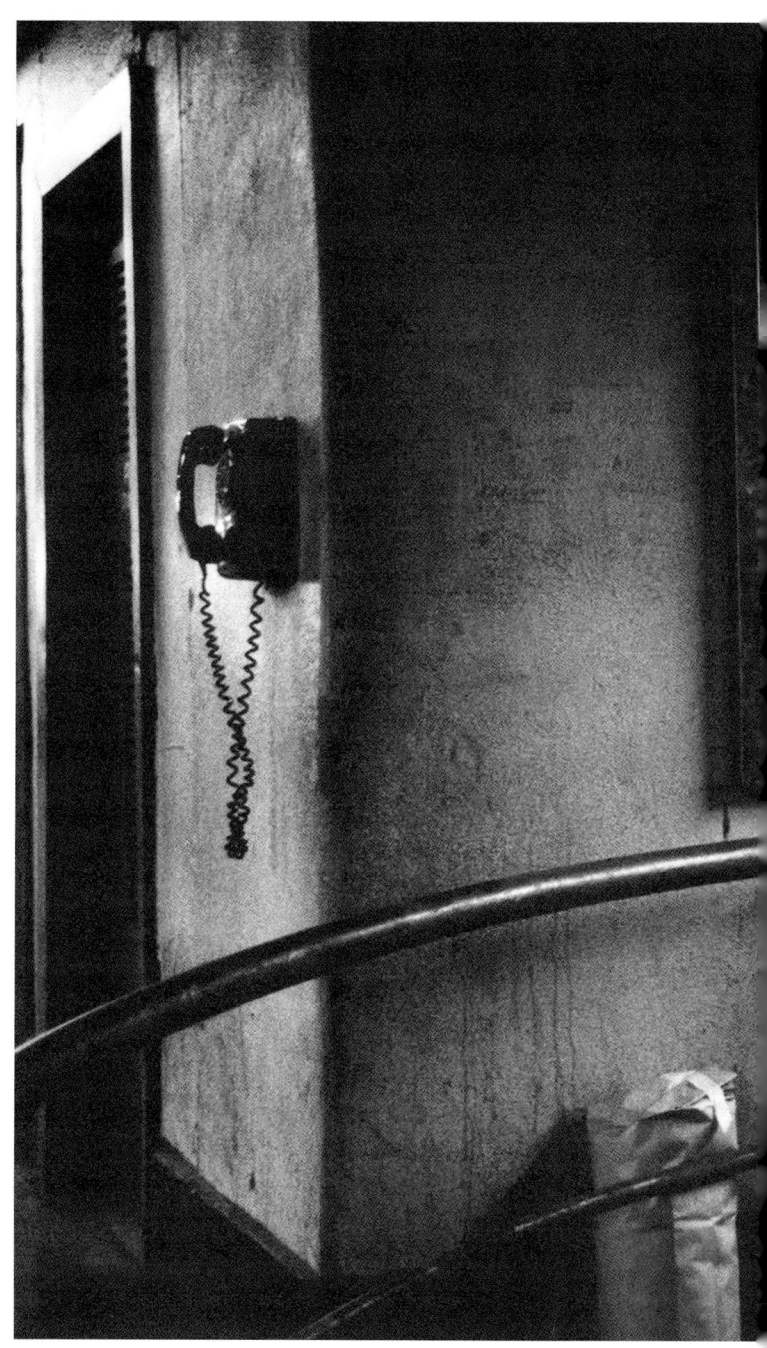

Figure 2.13.
US 77, 1977 (FRAMED).

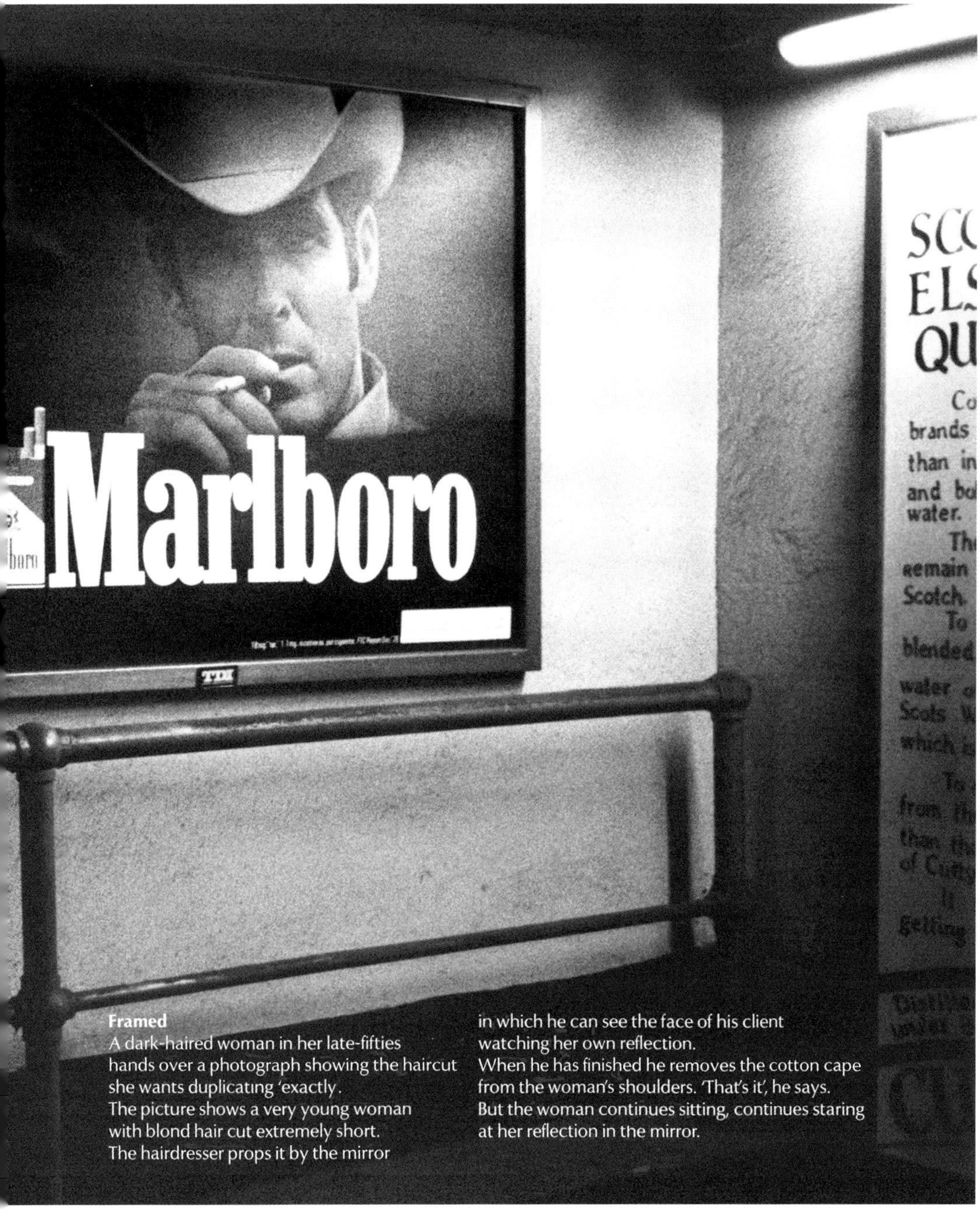

Framed

A dark-haired woman in her late-fifties hands over a photograph showing the haircut she wants duplicating 'exactly'.

The picture shows a very young woman with blond hair cut extremely short.

The hairdresser props it by the mirror in which he can see the face of his client watching her own reflection.

When he has finished he removes the cotton cape from the woman's shoulders. 'That's it', he says.

But the woman continues sitting, continues staring at her reflection in the mirror.

formative for the functioning of the self via the process of identification with one's own specular body image. As he writes:

> For the total form of his body, by which the subject anticipates the maturation of his power in a mirage, is given to him only as a gestalt […]. This gestalt […] symbolizes the *I's* mental permanence, at the same time as it prefigures its alienating destination. This gestalt is also replete with the correspondences that unite the *I* with the statue onto which man projects himself, the phantoms that dominate him, and the automaton with which the world of his own making tends to achieve fruition in an ambiguous relation. (Lacan, 2006: 76-77)

The mirror stage, then, is responsible for both the subject's self-recognition as an autonomous being and a split within the subject's self-image that may lead to forms of psychic distress. This ambiguous relation between identification and alienation is condensed in the account of the woman staring incredulously at her own image in the mirror where identification (with the other woman) passes into a state of self-denial as a result of a longing for the stereotypes of beauty and eternal youth produced by the Western advertising and media industry.

What Burgin states for his 1977 published essay "Looking at Photographs," is also valid for *us 77*: both mark the "transition from a 'semiotics of systems' to a semiotics which takes account of the (psychoanalytic) *subject* inscribed in the system in question." (TP: 14)

2.4.3. Scopophilia and Surveillance

During a six-month stay in Berlin on a DAAD fellowship, Burgin realized the serial piece *Zoo 78*. (Fig. 2.14.) Comprising eight diptychs, the work reflects the artist's encounter with the city, not the "real" city, but the "city of the mind," in which images of the wall, enclosure, and isolation overlap with fantasies of cosmopolitan life, decadence, and sexuality. (Godfrey, 1982: 20) In one diptych, the idea of framing takes a central place again, with the difference that this time, as Burgin explains, "it's a matter of the frame as an aid to *looking*—as a scopophilic device, like a keyhole." (21) The left image shows a dancer of a West Berlin peep show booth situated in the area of the actual Berlin Zoo—Zoologischer Garten—at that time infamous as a gathering place for drug addicts and prostitutes. The text printed on the photograph describes Bentham's Panopticon, a circularly-designed prison, allowing a watchman to observe every move of the inmates in the cells without being seen. (Fig. 2.15.) In Foucault's *Discipline and Punish*, to which

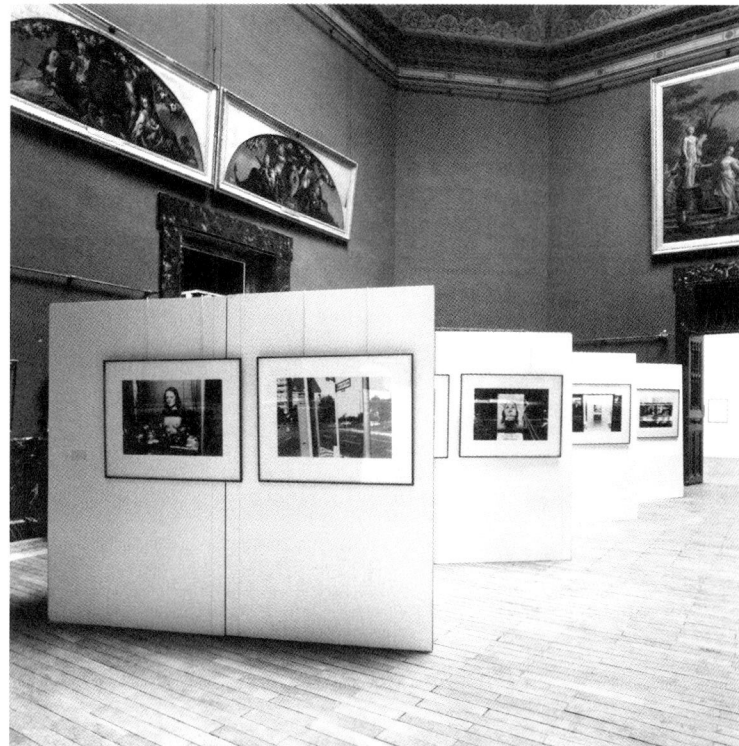

Figure 2.14.

Zoo 78, 1978.

8 diptychs, each panel
50×75 cm. Installation
view, Palais des Beaux-
Arts, Brussels, 1979.

Burgin refers (PT: 104), we can read that the panopticon's purpose is "to induce in the inmate a state of conscious and permanent visibility that assures the automatic function of power." (Foucault, 1977: 201) In accordance with Foucault's stance, Burgin's work alludes to the panopticon as a symptom of the modern surveillance society, albeit putting a particular emphasis on the "oppressive surveillance of woman in our society" subjecting the naked female body to the aggressive, mastering look of man. (Godfrey, 1982: 20) This voyeuristic act of scopophilia is put side by side with a view of a café's wall having a painting on it showing an idyllic view of the Brandenburg Gate before the Second World War. While the photograph's edge defines what can be seen and what is excluded, the frame of the painting opens up onto the glorious past of an undivided Berlin contributing to the "pervasive disavowal of the real situation." (21) The woman as sexual object of desire thus meets its counterpart in the Brandenburg Gate as political object of desire.

This connection between political and sexual displays of observation and control is also stressed in a diptych juxtaposing a view from West Berlin toward the Eastern part of the city with the photograph of a barmaid. (Fig. 2.16.) To some extent, the photograph of the bar counter is an updated version of Edouard Manet's *A Bar at the Folies-Bergère*

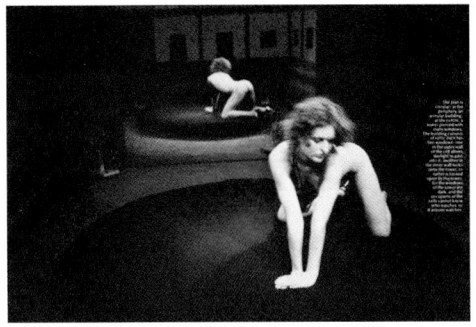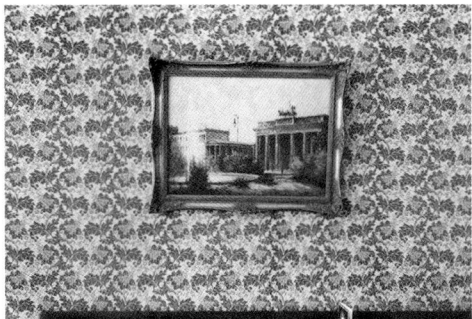

Figure 2.15. *Zoo 78*, 1978.

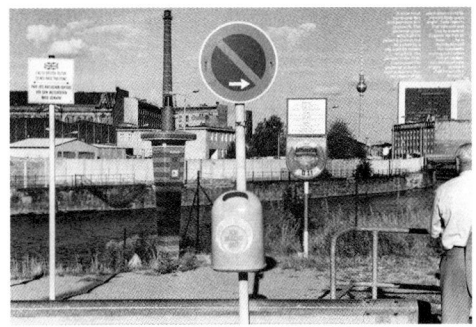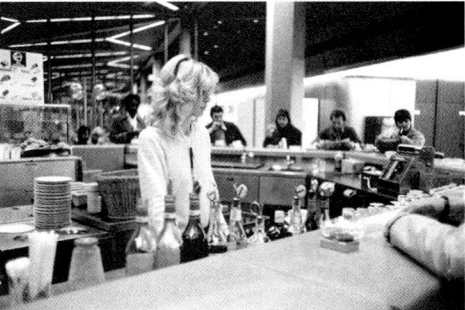

Figure 2.16. *Zoo 78*, 1978.

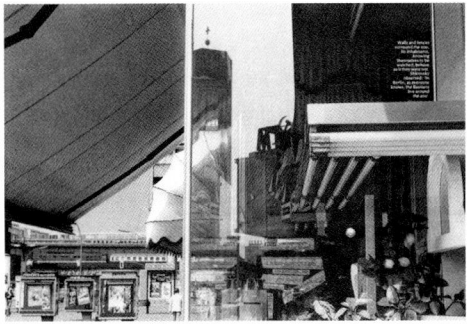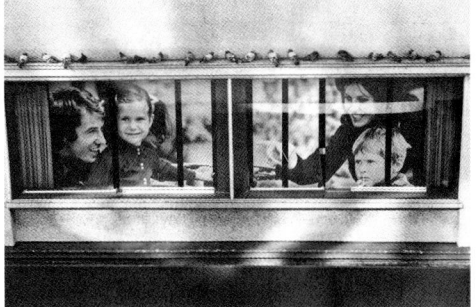

Figure 2.17. *Zoo 78*, 1978.

(1882), a painting in which the woman behind the bar stares vacantly into space while the reflection in the mirror in the background reveals a man situated in front of her. T. J. Clark and others suggest that the woman in Manet's painting represents a prostitute. Indeed, Guy de Maupassant, in his novel *Bel-Ami*, describes the Folies-Bergère as a place where "vendors of drink and of love" are looking out for clients. And he adds: "Behind them, tall mirrors reflected their backs and the faces of the passers-by." (de Maupassant, 2001: 12; Clark, 1986: 245) If we relate the photograph of the blond barmaid to the text printed on the other photograph of the diptych, this allusion to love for sale and sexual desire seems to be confirmed. The text describes a display, imagined by Sade in his 1800 *Eugénie de Franval* as a kind of modern precursor of the peepshow, according to which a woman's naked body would be set on a pedestal separated from the viewer by a channel filled with water. By means of a silk cord, the viewer could revolve the pedestal in order to observe the object of his veneration, transformed into a living statue, from every angle. The image itself shows the barrier that divided East Berlin from West Berlin, while the television tower on the left dominates the background as a symbol of panoramic overview and the achievements of a surveillance regime.

Framing as an act of submission and control runs like a golden thread through the whole series. In another diptych, the right-hand photograph shows an advertising image of a stereotypical family printed on window-blinds and framed by the architecture as if confined within a commercial light box. (Fig. 2.17.) The black stripes separating them from the real world look like prison bars through which the family members look at us in a carefree and cheerful way. The text of the opposite panel, depicting a view of the Zoo district, reads like a comment on the family's situation: "Walls and fences surround the zoo. Its inhabitants, knowing themselves to be watched, behave as if they were not. Shklovsky observed: 'In Berlin, as everyone knows, the Russians live around the zoo.'" (Shklovsky, 2012: 66) Writing in the early 1920s, Viktor Shklovsky of course did not refer to a divided Berlin with the Russians controlling the other side of the wall. But in this context, the historical Berlin of Shklovsky's novel *Zoo or Letters Not about Love* (1923), the actual political and social situation of people living in Berlin around the zoo in the 1970s, and the stereotypical image of the happy family form a narrative exploring the commercial, political, and social effects of visual control.

However, the dedication of Burgin's *Zoo* to Shklovsky's novel is not only of biographical importance (both Victors found their "exile" in Berlin). First of all, the analogy between the animals living behind bars, as in prison, and the Russian writer in exile feeling like "the ape [who] languishes without his forest" takes on additional meaning as a metaphor for the situation of the people living in both parts of Berlin. (Shklovsky, 26) It seems that Shklovsky's use of analogies and the mosaic quality of his writing provide a model for Burgin's own artistic method, according to which the various subjects of the photographs are commented by a fragmentary text mixing personal observations with literary quotations. If Shklovsky praises Remizov's creation of a new "book made from bits and pieces […], a book made from scraps of books" (23), this could be said of Burgin's image-text collage as well. On the one hand, this approach has to be considered in the context of Burgin's interest in techniques of collage and montage in the socio-political work of the Russian avant-garde. On the other hand, the heterogeneous fabric of the text in which references to Shklovksy, De Sade, and Bentham are woven into a formally uniform yet diversely constituted storyline draws on poststructuralist definitions of intertextuality. As we will see in the following chapter, this definition of the work of art as an intertextual complex of meanings moving along an endless chain of references will play a crucial role for the development of a "psychical realism" in Burgin's writing and artistic practice of the 1980s.

Chapter 3
Tales from Freud

What interests me most, in fact, are the ways in which our experience of "real life," the "real world," is mediated by our memories and fantasies—this is what all my work, in one way or another, tries to deal with. (BN: 135)

3.1. Toward a Psychical Realism

With the understanding that ideologies do not exist as things in themselves in society, but must always be thought of in relation to the subject and to the "constitution of the subject in language" (TP: 7), Burgin arrived at a modified concept of realism, ultimately finding expression in a term he coined in the mid-1980s: "psychical realism." (Batchen, 1989: 9) In contrast to those Marxist-oriented artists and intellectuals who define ideology as "false consciousness" and thereby establish truth and falsehood as absolute values, Burgin was interested first and foremost in how representation is perceived in specific contexts: "what is to be interrogated is its *effects*." (TP: 9) Thus, "the constitution of the subject as the locus of meaning" increasingly comes to the foreground. (Burgin, 1976d: 2) This shift from the *semiological* to the *psychological* can be traced in issues of *Screen* published in the course of the 1970s.[23] As of 1975, the journal regularly published essays with a psychoanalytic methodological stamp, and these would prove to be an important influence on Burgin's art and thinking. Thus, Laura Mulvey's above-mentioned "Visual Pleasure and Narrative Cinema" became an important reference for using psychoanalytical theory to uncover how "the unconscious of patriarchal society has structured film form," as well as other visual forms of representation. (Mulvey, 1975: 6)

As mentioned, in the mid-1970s the main focus of Burgin's work shifted from a particular interest in economic relations in UK 76 to questions of the construction of subjectivity, in terms of sexuality, ideology, and psychoanalysis, in US 77. Around 1980, however, psychoanalysis came to be centerstage, "not only for its concepts but also for its form." (Tickner, 1984: 20) In *Tales from Freud*, a series of four related photo-text works exhibited for the first time at the John Weber Gallery, New York, in 1982,[24] Burgin refers to seminal essays of Freud in order to explore the construction of identity by means of unconscious projections and fantasies. Burgin's argumentation goes as follows: if the real world can only be accessed through representations and if representations are projections of culturally and ideologically informed processes, they depend on psychical, unconscious fantasies as much as on conscious, rational thinking. Burgin goes even further when he states: "Consciousness of 'reality' is seamlessly interwoven with unconscious fantasies and projections; consciousness, the basis of rational action, is a set of imaginaries." (Batchen, 1989: 9) Consequently, Burgin's primary concern is not the exterior "real world," but what Freud calls "psychical reality," the unconscious processes at work in the construction of the subject and its representations. According to Stuart Hall, the production of the subject in terms of psychological or psychical processes becomes particularly obvious in Thatcherism, which dominated British politics during the 1980s. Referring to Jacqueline Rose's analysis of Thatcherism as a kind of political paranoia based on profoundly contradictory elements, Hall concludes:

> If you want to understand the "logic" of Thatcherism [...] you will get closer to it by thinking in terms of the logic of a dream rather than the logic of philosophical investigation. It is absurd to say that Thatcherism cannot work because it is internally contradictory. The beauty or the symmetry of the operation lies in its capacity to condense and display contradictory symbolisations in the same space. (Hall, 1995: 64)

Seen from this angle, Burgin's shift, around 1980, toward psychical reality and toward a conception of his work analogue to the logic of a dream may also be understood as a reaction to the political circumstances in Britain at this particular historical juncture. (CP: 58)

It is precisely this connection between the logic of neoliberal politics in a media society and the logic of unconscious processes as described by Freud that led Burgin to the concept of "psychical realism," which he introduced in the essay "Geometry and Abjection," first given as a talk in May 1987 at the Centre for Research in Philosophy and Literature of the University of Warwick. (IDS: 56) The paper retraces the relationship between geometry and representation since Antiquity before suggesting that in the postmodern sphere of the fold-over spaces of global capitalism and information technologies such traditional dichotomies as subject versus object, and inside versus outside, do not hold anymore. According to Burgin, the dominating model of representation in Western society since the Renaissance, the cone of vision, seems to be inadequate within the new social and cultural order where "spaces once conceived of as separated, segregated, now overlap." (44) Burgin therefore introduces Freud's concept of "psychical reality" as a more appropriate concept to describe this postmodern space of overlapping and changing places. He writes: "The spatial qualities of the psychical mise-en-scène are clearly non-Euclidean: different objects may occupy the same space at the same (non)instant, as in condensation in dreams; or subject and object may collapse into each other." (47)

While in the 1970s Burgin described photography in semiological terms as an environment based on a "heterogeneous complex of codes," in the early 1980s his focus shifted to the psychological implications in the perception of photographic images within public space: "We encounter the everyday environment of photographs as if in a waking dream, a daydream: taken collectively they seem to add up to no particular logical whole." (TP: 211) Photography is embedded in what Freud called another locality ("die Idee einer anderen Lokalität"), this other space that Lacan described as the "*between perception and consciousness.*" (BN, 6) The aim was now to address the ways in which the relationship between perception, representation, and identity is negotiated within a society dominated by a capitalist economy and the circulation of images via the mass media. The discovery of psychoanalytical concepts as means to understand processes and developments within a postmodern and postindustrial society went along with an increasingly skeptical attitude vis-à-vis the Marxist position of the left. In regard to the latter, Burgin stated in an interview:

> [They are] facing this present techno-sociological upheaval with the philosophical baggage of aesthetic Realism, including its positivist epistemologies and its Cartesian coordinates. What I was trying to talk about in "Geometry and Abjection" was a feeling of being inside a new space today—socially, politically, technologically, psychically. (Lewis, 1987/88: 63)

In what follows I will discuss Burgin's use of psychoanalytical concepts and theories in his work of the 1980s as an investigation of the unconscious desires and fantasies underlying the ways in which representation is constituted and perceived within the Western media society. In this regard, his psychical realism takes into account the complex imbrication of simultaneously overlapping layers of heterogeneous temporal and spatial realities, which are constituted as much through physical, "real" actions and events as through psychical processes such as fantasies and desires. Since the 1980s, and to this day, Burgin's works have been part of an overarching project of mapping "my sense of the complexity of being in this world at this moment—of this world being in me, in so far as it is a necessary condition of the subject." (63) Burgin's aim is in fact to update Honoré Daumier's motto of realism, "Il faut être de son temps," in reconsidering the relation of subject and object in terms of the psychical and physical experiences within specific social, political and technological conditions. The 1982 exhibition *Tales from Freud* at the John Weber Gallery, New York, and the Yarlow-Salzman Gallery, Toronto, can be seen as a first substantial step toward a "Psychical Realism." While in the exhibition only four works were shown—*In Lyon* (1980), *Grenoble* (1981), *Gradiva*, and *Olympia* (both 1982)—Burgin also included, from a retrospective point of view, *The Bridge* (1984) and *Portia* (1984), for all of these works have in common that they draw on a specific tale in, and essay by, Freud. (mail exchange with the author, August 2018) Issues of sexuality and politics were now linked to the psychical concepts of fetishism and voyeurism, while condensation and displacement as elementary mechanisms of dream-work served as underlying principles of the work's structure. As a response to "the ways in which fantasy functions throughout our everyday perceptions, beliefs, values, and actions" (Batchen, 1989: 9), the *Tales from Freud* address aspects of scopophilia, fetishism, masquerade, and the relationship between woman and man, which situates them within that period's seminal feminist debates on pleasure and sexual difference.

3.2. From Socio-history to Psycho-history

> My work over recent years has been "about" an apprehension of sexual difference—an imaginary relation to the woman. In works like *In Lyon* and *In Grenoble*, the city provided me with the raw materials from which, through a process of projection, I formed metaphors, analogies, and assembled them into a whole—a "work"—which than stood in for the lived experience, but always, as I've said, as a memorial to a previous state of that experience. (Lewis, 1987/88: 64)

Whereas Burgin's pieces of the late 1970s were primarily concerned with socio-political aspects of sexual difference and scopic regimes, *In Lyon* and *In Grenoble* are both tackling these questions explicitly from a psychoanalytical point of view, suggesting thus a psycho-history where the boundaries between historical facts, personal experiences, and analytical discourse dissolve.

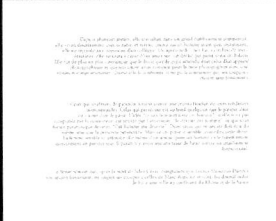 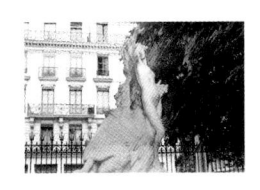 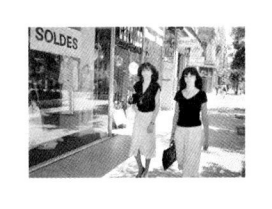

3.2.1. A Socio-historical "Psychodrama"

Commissioned by the Espace Lyonnais d'Art Contemporain, *In Lyon* maps the geographical structure of the city in order to provide "a cartography that is invariably animated by the projections of desire." (Bann, 2002: 59) (Fig. 3.1.) Divided into three parts by the rivers Saône and Rhône, the city's topology is at the origin of a complex layering of various formal and content-related constellations, all of them based on the number three. The work consists of three triptychs, each one composed of two images and a text. The latter confronts three discourses: a historical outline that refers to three distinct moments of the city's history, from its Roman origins via the medieval and Renaissance era to the contemporary urban space; a narrative text that summarizes and condenses a case of paranoia described by Freud in his paper "A Case of Paranoia Running Counter to the Psychoanalytic Theory of the Disease"; and the psychoanalytical commentary of this case, also derived from Freud's text, that reveals the complex psychical structure of the female protagonist comprising a conception of herself as a woman, as a child, and as her own mother all at once. In a letter to a German critic, Burgin describes *In Lyon* as "a condensation of a complex of images/ideas centred around the imbrication of the psychic and the social, of sexuality and politics." (BN, 97)

If we relate *In Lyon* to Freud's paper and to Burgin's own article "Photography, Phantasy, Function," published in *Screen* in the same year as the creation of the work, it becomes clear that photography, rather than referring to the physical reality of the city, is part of a process of projection based on the condensation of historical events, imagined narratives, and analytical descriptions. After all, if, as Burgin suggests, we "encounter the everyday environment of photographs as if in a waking dream" (TP: 211), what is more obvious than using photography as a kind of psychogrammatical component of a condensation process that functions analogous to the dream-work? As we will see below, Burgin

Figure 3.1.

In Lyon, 1980. 3 triptychs, each panel 50×66 cm. Installation View, Espace Lyonnais d'Art Contemporain, Lyon, 1980.

actually refers to the mechanisms of the dream—metaphorical conden-sation and metonymic displacement—as constitutive processes in the way we perceive and experience reality.

According to the narrative text and its commentary, Freud's paper deals with the case of a woman who accused her lover of having ordered a photographer to take an image of them while making love. It turns out, that this paranoiac fear of persecution was triggered by the wom-an's observation of her lover talking with her superior, a grey-haired woman whom she compared with her mother. From this, Freud con-cludes that the woman's paranoia stems from the unconscious phan-tasy of "watching sexual intercourse between the parents," with her lover being her father while "she herself had taken her mother's place." (Freud, 1915/1957: 269) According to Freud, the "click or beat" that the woman identified with the noise of the camera shutter was not there in the outside world, but had its real origin in "a knock or beat in her clitoris. And it was this that she subsequently projected as a perception of an external object. Just the same sort of thing can occur in dreams." (270)

This comparison of the click of the camera with the contraction of the clitoris brings us to the way Burgin uses photography in his photo-textual "psychodrama." (Gintz, 1981: 16) Actually, Freud's case evokes the use of photography as a means to provide an authentic and reliable document, which can be used to bear witness to or against something or somebody, in this case sexual intercourse. Yet, the photo-graphs that accompany the texts of Burgin's work are not there to prove anything. Rather than identifying the depicted elements and persons as parts of an objective external reality, they offer metaphorical and met-onymic associations with the three subtexts confronting the subjective experience of the artist with historical, social, and psycho-sexual dis-courses. Or to paraphrase Freud: the click of the camera as an objective mechanism to represent the world overlaps with the knock or beat of the sexual organ triggered by drives, desires, and phantasies.

In the first triptych a photograph shows a sculpture of an old man and a young woman referring to the male Rhône and the female Saône as the two confluent rivers determining the city's geographical struc-ture. (Fig. 3.2.) While this fluvial couple represents the protagonists of Freud's case, the status of the Saône as female lover can also be linked to the two women in the second image of the triptych. Dressed almost identically, the young woman and her older counterpart stand for the complex relation that the young protagonist has with her superior, sug-gesting "such themes as 'identification' and 'introjection.'" (BN: 98) The "'click' which seemed to come from the balcony" is here trans-posed from Freud's case-study to contemporary Lyon, tracing a trajec-tory from one of the balconies in the background of the first image to the frontal shot of the two women in the second photograph. These associative interrelations between text and image, and between images, can also be observed in the second and the third triptych.

In the images of the second triptych, vestiges of the Roman site at Fourvière offer a sharp contrast with a modern apartment block and the commercial center of Part-Dieu, while the historical part of the text outlines events that occurred during the Middle Ages, when by the 13th century members from the bourgeoisie began to challenge the feudal and religious authorities in order to achieve independence and political rights. (Fig. 3.3.) The text fills the historical void left by the photographic representations of the Roman origins and the contemporary city. In fact, "the birth of a new class, the urban bourgeoisie," to which the text refers, constitutes the historical condition for the development of the modern city with its shopping malls, office buildings, and apartment blocks. Once again, the photographs are not functioning as documents of a clearly definable setting. While the left image brackets the entire history of Lyon by confronting the past—symbolized by the capital's leaves carved in stone—with the present of the real leaves and the contemporary urban architecture, the right photograph reiterates the Freudian theme of the three women in the form of the silhouettes of a sculpture and two women progressing from right to left as well as from the foreground to the background. On a formal level, this process of condensing urban history with psychological story is embodied by the superposition and interpenetration of distinct spatial layers caused by the reflecting surfaces of the commercial center's glass walls.

3.2.2. The Shattered Composite

In Grenoble also originated from a French commission. (Fig. 3.4.) The Museum of Painting and Sculpture of Grenoble asked Burgin to "establish a link between their seventeenth-century collection and the contemporary city." (BN: 100) Once again, Burgin conflated different moments in history: the seventeenth century, represented by a landscape by Claude Gellée, called Lorrain, and the modern satellite town "Villeneuve," situated on the periphery of Grenoble, as an example of a "socialist Utopia" where different classes and cultural interests coexist. While in the French version of the piece, constituted of six panels, the text is descriptive and informative in its tone, the five-partite English version is more associative and open to different interpretations. In the first photograph, a panel with a map, supposedly representing the first settlement in the area, stands out against the bleak façade of a modernist apartment block that appears as if put behind bars by the grid structure in the right part of the image. Alluding to the map on the panel as an "anatomical drawing," the text connects the image with "figures 1

For many years she had worked for a large business concern. She lived quietly with her mother and there had been no man in her life until, recently, she had responded to the attentions of a colleague. One afternoon in his apartment, in the midst of their embraces, she was startled by a sharp sound, a kind of 'click' which seemed to come from the balcony. She became increasingly convinced that the noise she had heard had been the sound of a camera shutter, and that her lover had conspired to have her photographed in a compromising situation. She confronted her lover. He could not convince her that her suspicions were unfounded.

Those suffering from paranoia are struggling against an intensification of their homosexual tendencies. The persecutor is at bottom someone whom the patient loves or has loved in the past. The idea 'I (a man) love that man', if unacceptable to consciousness, is rejected through the inversion, 'I hate that man'; which in its paranoiac form becomes, 'That man hates me.' Thus the persecutor must be of the same sex as the person persecuted. But this present case seems to contradict this thesis. The woman seems to be defending herself against love for a man by directly transforming him into a persecutor. There seems to be no trace of a struggle against a homosexual attachment.

Following the death of Julius Caesar the Roman Senate, fearing that Caesar's former lieutenant Lucius Munatius Plancus might combine his own troops with those of the mutinying Mark Antony, ordered him to build a city at the confluence of the Saône and the Rhône.

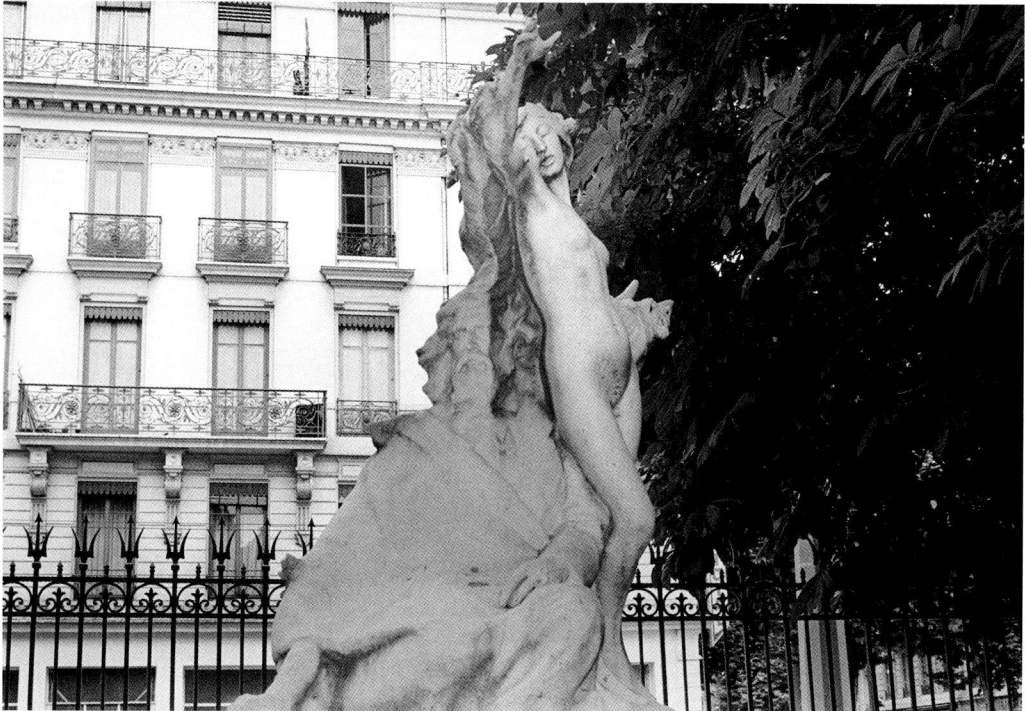

Figure 3.2.
In Lyon, 1980. First triptych.

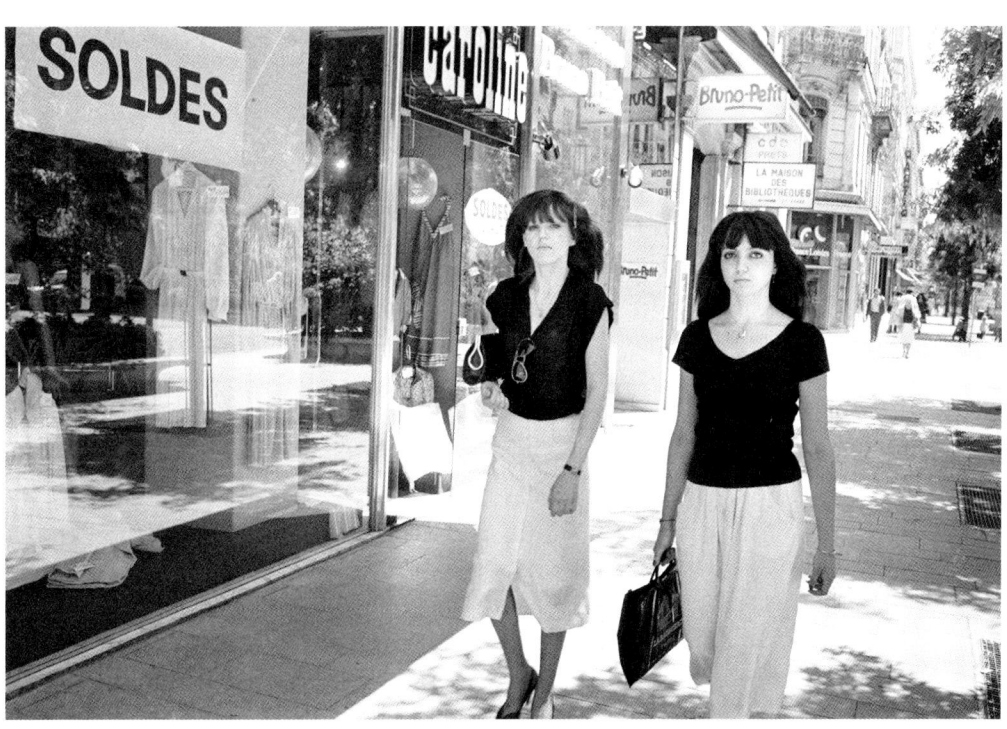

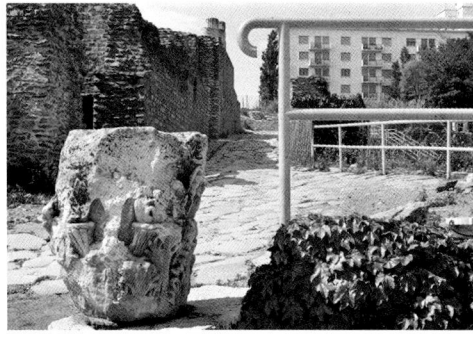
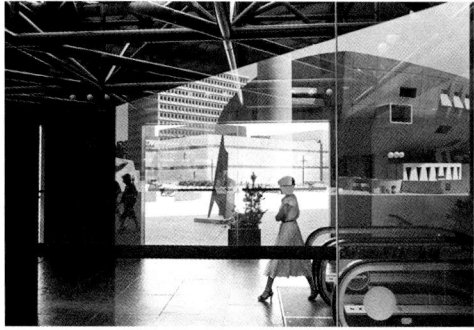

Figure 3.3.

In Lyon, 1980.
Photographs of second
triptych.

and 2," which can be interpreted in several different ways: the two set-
tlements on both sides of the river, the contrast between the first settlement in the region and the contemporary city, or the two distinct forms
of representation of the map and the photograph. The second photograph shows a large-scale historical picture of an older and a younger
woman as part of a museum display. The text panel in the upper part
of the image reads: "On the other hand, in the large factories the seam-
stresses were under surveillance. The forewoman and the noise permit-
ted neither singing nor conversation." (BN: 108) The first two lines of
Burgin's caption seem to comment the museum photograph in the way
of a dream: "The two figures are my mother and sister. They cannot
speak and I am forbidden to shake hands with them." Two other kinds
of interdiction are added here to the social interdiction of the panel *in*
the photograph: institutionally, it is forbidden to touch the women's
image as part of the museum display; on a representational level, the
spectator is also kept at arm's length from the women captured on film
a long time ago.

   Finally, if we relate the identification of them as mother and sister
to the text of the fifth panel, the link to the incest prohibition of the
Oedipus myth as one of Burgin's Freudian inspiration sources becomes
evident. Once again, the photograph depicts an older and a younger
woman while the text comments: "my sister is my daughter." Yet, in the
Oedipus myth the protagonist, after having slayed his father, marries
his mother who gives birth to two sons and two daughters. The conflation of mother/sister and daughter/sister might then, following Freud's
explanations in his *The Interpretation of Dreams*, represent "the fate of
all of us […] to direct our first sexual impulse towards our mother and
our first hatred and our first murderous wish against our father. Our
dreams convince us that that is so." (Freud, 1900/1953: 262) In fact, the
occurrence of repressed wishes and desires in dreams is a crucial issue in the *Tales from Freud* pieces. Arguing that the desire expressed in
a dream is always blurred by psychic censorship, Freud distinguishes

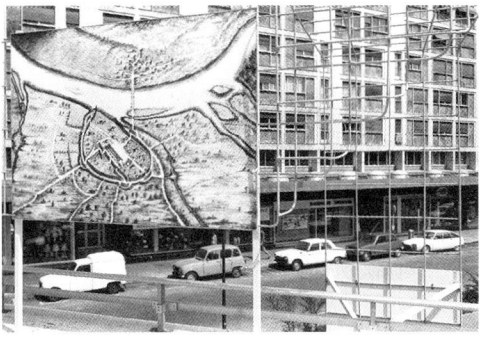

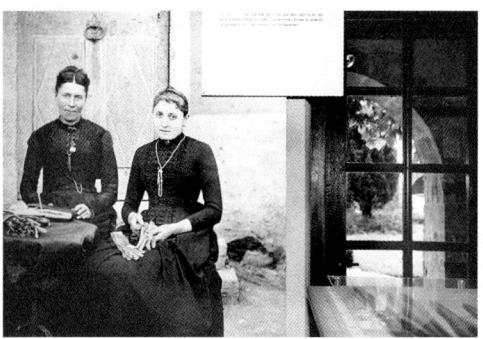

THE PLAN OF THE PLACE
WHERE I GREW UP
IS AN ANATOMICAL DRAWING.
THE THOUGHT OCCURS:
"THEY ARE FIGURES 1 AND 2".

THE TWO FIGURES ARE MY MOTHER AND SISTER.
THEY CANNOT SPEAK AND I AM FORBIDDEN
TO SHAKE HANDS WITH THEM.
THE THOUGHT OCCURS:
"IT IS BECAUSE WE ARE IN THE BANK".

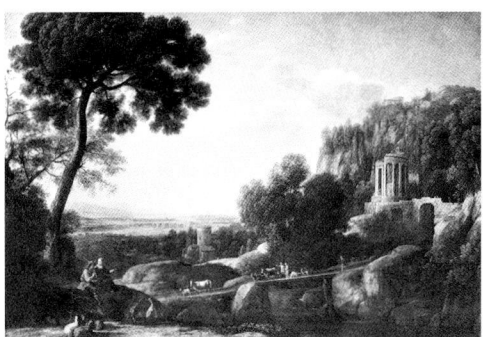

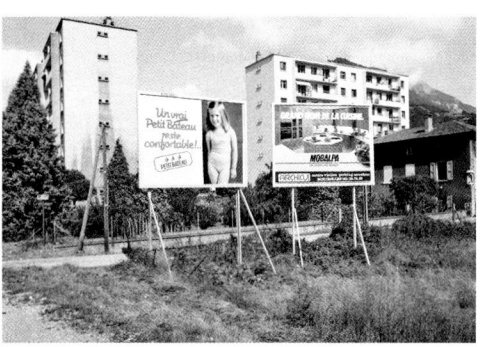

ON THE BANK TWO PEOPLE ARE MAKING MUSIC.
I CAN SEE THE BUILDING WHERE
MY SISTER AND I GREW UP.
THE THOUGHT OCCURS:
"I AM IN THE RIGHT".

ON THE RIGHT THE BUILDING HAS A DISTINCTIVE FORM:
A CIRCLE FROM WHICH A SEGMENT HAS BEEN REMOVED
TO REVEAL AN INTERIOR SPACE CONTAINING SOMETHING.
THE THOUGHT OCCURS:
"IT WILL COME OUT IN MARCH".

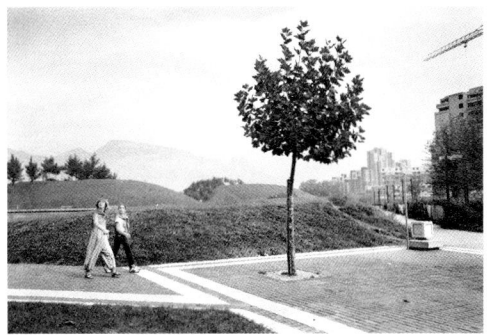

THEY MARCH. A TREE STANDS AGAINST THE SKY.
A BRIDGE SPANS A RIVER. A BUILDING IS IN RUINS.
MY SISTER IS MY DAUGHTER.
THE THOUGHT OCCURS:
"ACCORDING TO PLAN".

Figure 3.4.
In Grenoble, 1981.
5 parts, each 50×61 cm.

two psychic processes that obscure the factual meaning of the dream: condensation and displacement. While condensation compresses the dream-thoughts to a highly incomplete and fragmentary version (278), displacement refers to the fact that the manifest dream is "as it were, differently centered from the dream-thoughts." (305)

As an example of displacement Freud evokes his own dream about his uncle in which the beard as a central component seems to have no connection with the dream-thoughts. (305-306) The structure of this particular dream, composed of a "thought being succeeded by a picture" (137), was adopted in its inverted form by Burgin in the captions. (BN: 108) In Freud, the image of his Uncle Josef represented two colleagues who had not been appointed to professorships. As for his own case, Freud conjectured denominational reasons for the refusal of their promotion, why he projected characteristics attributed to his Uncle on his colleagues, stigmatizing one as a simpleton and the other as a criminal. In a subsequent passage of *The Interpretation of Dreams*, Freud compares this kind of "composite figures" with Galton's family portraits: "namely by projecting two images on to a single plate, so that certain features common to both are emphasized, while those which fail to fit in with one another cancel one another out and are indistinct in the picture." And he deduces from this: "The construction of collective and composite figures is one of the chief methods by which condensation operates in dreams." (293) Although drawing on Freud's understanding of composite photography as a metaphor for psychical mechanisms, Burgin rejects Galton's deterministic model of composites as a means of social classification and surveillance. (Hamilton and Hargreaves, 2001: 4) On the contrary, Burgin shows to what extent such processes of superposition are subjective projections of repressed and unfulfilled desires and therefore cannot be pinned down to a general, objectively describable type. Actually, the photographs of *In Grenoble* are not composite images. They are rather parts of different operations of condensation and displacement analogous to Freud's dream mechanisms. The superposition of the modern city of Grenoble and Lorrain's landscape is thus not a real, physical or photochemical, process, but an imaginary act of association.

By the same token, the process of displacement, according to which a component of the dream refers to something else, is used as a structural means to avoid the fixation of the relation of the individual photo/text-panels and a final closure of the work's meaning in general. Consequently, Burgin plays with the polysemy of words, thus establishing a complex chain of significations where meaning is always deferred without ever coming to an end. The "figures" of the city plan refer in the second image to the mother and sister, the bank as a financial institution becomes the shore of a river in Claude Lorrain's painting, the publicity announcement "to come out in march" is followed by two women marching across a square. The captions not only refer to the images to which they are directly assigned; they further extend their semantic influence to the preceding and the following panels, each time taking on a different meaning. The condensation of the modern city of Grenoble and the Lorrain painting further occurs in the image-text associations across the panels. In the fourth panel, the text "A circle from which a segment has been removed to reveal an interior space containing something" can be related to the built-in kitchen on the advertising panel, but it refers as well to the temple ruin of the painting in the third panel. The tree in the painting reappears in the photograph of the fifth panel on a square of modern-day Villeneuve with the additional words: "A tree stands against the sky."

Burgin's Freud-inspired model of condensation uses processes of cross-reading and associative thinking in order to shatter Galton's composite image of the ideal type across a heterogeneous field of spatial, historical, and socio-psychological phenomena, in which the position of the subject can never be fixed or determined from outside.

3.2.3. Visual Pleasure and the Photographic Fetish

At this point, it is indispensable to remember the historical context in which these works were produced. In fact, Burgin's intense occupation with Freud has to be considered against the backdrop of the ways in which psychoanalytical theory was discussed and applied in feminist circles of the 1970s. In particular Laura Mulvey's "Visual Pleasure and Narrative Cinema" had a major influence on these debates for its use of Freud's theory of scopophilia, as the "pleasure in looking at another person as object." (Mulvey, 1975: 9) Drawing on Freud's *Three Essays on Sexuality*, according to which the gaze at women is always threatened by the anxiety of castration because of woman's lack of the penis, Mulvey identifies two "avenues" in Hollywood cinema allowing the male spectator to escape this dilemma: a sadistic drive to devaluate, punish, control the "guilty object" and the transformation of the represented figure into a fetish. As a beautiful body to be looked at, the woman becomes a fetish for the voyeuristic gaze of man. (Mulvey, 1975: 13-14) In his paper "Photography, Phantasy, Function," Burgin takes up Freud's concepts of scopophilia, voyeurism, and fetishism, and he links them, like Mulvey, to the problem of representation and sexuality.

Burgin's focus, however, is not any longer on cinema, but on the "connection, in photography, between psychology and point-of-view." (TP: 186) He adopts some of Mulvey's reflections concerning fetishism and scopophilia along with Oudart and Dyan's concept of *suture* as "a set of effects in which the subject recognizes the discourse as his own." (TP: 188)[25] But while Oudart/Dyan are interested in the process of identification through specific techniques in film (point-of-view, shot/reverse shot), Burgin seeks to investigate the concept of suture in the field of photography. In photography, he argues, the subject incorporates itself in the image through "identification" with the camera position's shifting between a controlling gaze (voyeurism) and narcissistic identification with the camera and/or the represented figure. (TP: 189) Narcissistic investment, he adds a little later, can also be achieved through the "appreciation of the superficial beauty of the 'fine print'" as a crucial characteristic attributed to connoisseurship in art photography. Photography, unlike cinema, does not only represent the fetish, but functions itself like a fetish:

> The photograph, like the fetish, is the result of a look which has, instantaneously and forever, isolated, "frozen," a fragment of the spatio-temporal continuum. In Freud's account of fetishism something serves in place of the penis with which the shocked male infant would "complete" the woman; the function of the fetish is to deny the very perception it commemorates, a logical absurdity which betrays the operation of the primary processes. This structure of "disavowal" is not confined to cases of fetishism proper, it is so widespread as to be almost inaccessible to critical attention. (TP: 190)

Photography as a fetish, Burgin continues, represents two forms of disavowal according to its two principal ideological functions: the reality function of the document as an objective representation of the world and the aesthetic function of art photography as beautiful print and formal composition:

> Disavowal in respect of photographs shifts polarity to accommodate the nature of the obstruction to desire: on the one hand, "I know that the (pleasurable) reality offered in this photograph is only an illusion, but nevertheless;" on the other hand, "I know that this (unpleasurable) reality exists/existed, but nevertheless *here* there is only the beauty of the print." (TP: 191-192)

Earlier, the distinction of two ideological functions of the photograph was made by Allan Sekula in his 1975 published "On the Invention of Photographic Meaning," which is also included in *Thinking Photography*. As mentioned in Chapter 2, Sekula identifies two myths in photographic discourse: the "realist" folk-myth of documentary photography endorsing the empirical value as witness, and the "symbolist" folk-myth of art photography as expressive value. (Sekula, 1982: 108) Concerning the latter, he refers to Clive Bell's modernist theory of "significant form": "The invention of the photograph as high art was only possible through its transformation into an abstract fetish and 'significant form.'" (103) In "Photography, Phantasy, Function," Burgin takes up this critique of Modernism as fetishization of the photograph with respect to the cult of specificity as developed by Szarkowski and Greenberg but in a quite diverging manner. In contrast to Sekula's Marxist inspired concept of the fetish, Burgin builds on psychoanalytical considerations because in his view the constitution of the subject is based on unconscious fantasies and projections: "consciousness, the basis of rational action, is a set of imaginaries." (Batchen, 1989: 9)

In Lyon and *In Grenoble* can then be understood as responses to the modernist fetishization of the photograph as a psychological form of disavowal emphasizing the fascination of good composition and fine print. The serial structure and the fragmentary character of both works as well as the multilayered use of the text—respectively, the contrasting of diverse discursive practices (narrative, analytic, descriptive) in *In Lyon* and the associative captures and cross-references between text and image in *In Grenoble*—deny the possibility of the photograph's transforming into a fetish. As argued, the complex image-text relations confront the observing subject with "metaphorical and metonymical processes of the unconscious." (BN: 109) Based on condensation and displacement as main achievements of the dream-work, Burgin's *Tales from Freud* unravel the associative and unconscious mechanisms at play in representation while deconstructing fetishistic satisfaction offered by identification with the photographic subject or admiration for the composition.

But it would be wrong to understand these works merely as part of a feminist project of deconstruction destined to refuse voyeuristic and narcissistic pleasures all at once. Burgin rejects a merely intellectual, theoretical approach to his work and emphasizes explicitly its associative, dream-like character when he writes: "You *don't* need a knowledge of psychoanalytical theory to deal with work like this—you simply need to know how to dream." (BN: 109) In contrast to traditional habits of spectatorship, such as aesthetic contemplation and distraction, Burgin invites the beholder to a specific way of "dreaming" in front of the work. She or he takes up the cues given in the images and texts, in order to add thoughts, associations, and considerations of one's own to the processes of transformation and transposition *within* the work. The attitude of this kind of "attentive dreamer" is at once critical and intuitive, as well as receptive and productive.

Retrospectively, Burgin has acknowledged that, after the "semioclasm" of his works of the 1970s, it was with *In Lyon* that he "began to allow the image its power of fascination." (CP: 52) This new attitude has to be seen, once more, against the backdrop of the visual pleasure debate that has its origin in Laura Mulvey's provocative suggestion to use the "destruction of pleasure as a radical weapon" against the reduction of woman to a state of "to-be-looked-at-ness." (Mulvey, 1975: 17) To break down the scopophilic look of the camera, the materiality of the film and the relation between camera, filmic content and spectator must be made explicit in order to interrupt the fetishistic fascination for the image.[26] In *US 77* and *Zoo 78*, Burgin aligned himself with this project involving the destruction of visual pleasure. The grainy, harsh quality of the prints and the covering of parts of the image with text run counter to fine art photography and contribute to spoil the pleasure of looking. Around 1980, however, Burgin changed his perception of the problem of visual pleasure:

> [I]f you deny those visual pleasures [...] they will simply seek gratification somewhere else, in advertising, pornography, and so on. [...] it was no longer a question of how to deny pleasure but rather of how to offer pleasures [...] without perpetuating and reinforcing oppressive social relations. (Batchen, 1989: 8)

And elsewhere he added:

> So the problem Laura Mulvey posed became displaced: it was no longer a question of how to deny visual pleasure, but rather of how to offer pleasures—of how to gratify the desire for pleasure—without perpetuating and reinforcing oppressive social relations. Pleasure, after all, is not singular—that one word contains a universe of possibilities. (Lewis, 1987/88: 57-58)

At the time, Burgin was hardly alone in seeking to reorient the pleasure problem. Artists and writers such as Mary Kelly, Griselda Pollock and Stephen Heath drew on Bertolt Brecht's concept of "distanciation" in order to define visual pleasure in positive terms. As early as 1974, Heath pointed to the fetishistic structure of the photograph for its pleasurable reassurance of the existence of the represented object while being at a safe distance from it. (Heath, 1974: 107) With Brecht's epic theatre, Heath argued, the fetishistic gratification of illusionist theater (and cinema), grounded in a fixed relation of representation and speculation, would be broken down by the interruption of the narrative, creating thus a "new contact between stage and the auditorium and thus giving a new basis to artistic pleasure." (109) Instead of permitting the male spectator to project his voyeuristic fantasies on the woman-as-image from a secured position outside of the picture, the repositioning or depositioning of the spectator includes him "in a critical-multi-perspective" within which the relationship between imaged woman and imagining observer are reshuffled. (109) The strategies detected by Heath in Brecht's multi-perspective approach can all be found in Burgin's work of around 1980. In *In Grenoble*, for example, "presentation-as-quotation" is achieved by the fact that some of the photographs quote Claude Lorrain's painting (the kitchen in the fourth photograph or the tree in the fifth photograph); "ceaseless displacement of identification" appears in the reference to Freud's paper "A Case of Paranoia" (*In Lyon*) and in the shifting roles of mother, daughter, and sister (*In Grenoble*); finally, the "play of contradictions" and the "idea of transformation" occur in *In Grenoble*, as we have seen, in the shifting meanings of the keywords of the captions and some image-text relations.

Brecht's "theatre of pleasure" is based on the idea that the spectator "is no longer a simple consumer, he must also produce." (Brecht quoted by Heath, 1974: 112) Mary Kelly, in the catalogue text of her much-noticed exhibition "Beyond the Purloined Image,"[27] refers to Brecht via Heath, when she describes the difference between American artists, such as Sherrie Levine, Cindy Sherman, and Richard Prince, and recent developments in photographic practice in Britain in terms of an opposition between purely quotational appropriation and a "strategy of *de-propriation*." (Kelly, 1983: 68) Rather than denying pleasure, artists such as Olivier Richon, Karen Knorr, Ray Barrie, Yve Lomax, and Judith Crowle would be "obsessed with pleasure" as the production of meaning in the sense of Brecht, which is to "transform finished works into unfinished works," to interrogate issues of subjectivity and sexuality. In the view of Kelly: "The depropriative text is heterogeneous, disruptive, open, pleasurable *and* political." (Kelly, 1983: 72) Even though Burgin was not part of Kelly's exhibition, his work of this period can be described in terms of depropriation as a *critical* enterprise" highlighting heterogeneity, hybridity, and discontinuity while offering the pleasure of a "constant process of reading." (Heath, 1974: 120) If Griselda Pollock describes Kelly's own work as a way visually to "acknowledge but interrupt the evident pleasure," the same could be said of Burgin's work as well. (Pollock, 1988: 266)

Burgin's position, however, differs from that of most of his contemporaries in one important respect. Whereas most artists concerned with politics and feminism rejected the features of art photography altogether, trying to disconnect pleasure from the fetish, Burgin wondered about the possibility of a "productive" fetishism. As a result, he reintroduced, in *In Lyon*, the aesthetic principles of accurate framing, good quality paper, and fine printing in order to acknowledge that fetishism is an aspect of the subject. (Gintz, 1981: 17) Burgin sought his way out of the conundrum of how to deconstruct fetishism without disavowing the pleasures connected to it in a paradoxical movement similar to what Barthes described as the perverse attitude of the cinema spectator. In his paper "Leaving the Movie Theatre," Barthes overtly rejects the idea of dissociating oneself from cinema's ideological discourse by endorsing the position of a Marxist-inspired radical counter-ideology. Anxious of avoiding purely critical distanciation as just another variant of ideology, he prefers to employ the double strategy of "amorous distance"

> by letting oneself be fascinated twice over, by the image and by its surroundings—as if I had two bodies at the same time: a narcissistic body which gazes, lost, into the engulfing mirror, and a perverse body, ready to fetishize not the image but precisely what exceeds it: the texture of the sound, the hall, the darkness, the obscure mass of the other bodies, the rays of light, entering the theater, leaving the hall; in short, in order to distance, in order to "take off," I complicate a "relation" by a "situation." (Barthes, 1986: 349)

The closing question of the paper, "would there be, in the cinema itself (and taking the word at its etymological suggestion) a possible bliss of *discretion?*," finally suggests that this sort of fetishistic perversion—confronting one's fascination for the image with the conditions of its presentation—can finally give rise to both, the immediate gratification of pleasure and the distance of critical reflection. Borrowed from the Latin *discretio/discerno*, the etymological roots of the word "discretion" refer to discernment as an act of distinction, to the power to decide or judge. This is precisely what Burgin's work is about: by integrating fetishistic forms of pleasure in a constantly shifting formation of heterogeneous discourses and meanings, he creates a dialectical movement between dream and reality, associative intuition and critical reflection. Dreaming as a form of discernment, then, would be the paradoxical attitude of the spectator in front of Burgin's work of this period.

3.3. The Rebus as a Model of "Critical Seeing"

In "Photography, Phantasy, Function," Burgin extensively ponders the relevance of the rebus in order to describe how we encounter photography in our everyday environment. He writes:

> Freud remarks that time does not exist in the unconscious, the dream is not the illogical narrative it may appear to be […], it is a *rebus* which must be examined element by element—from

each element will unfold associative chains leading to a coherent network of unconscious thoughts, thoughts which are extensive by comparison with the dream itself (which is "laconic"). We encounter the everyday environment of photographs as if in a waking dream, a day-dream: taken collectively they seem to add up to no particular logical whole; taken individually their literal content is quickly exhausted—but the photograph, too, is laconic, its meaning goes beyond its manifest elements. (TP: 211-212)

This passage is crucial for a deeper understanding of Burgin's theoretical and artistic positions. On a theoretical level, the increasing psychoanalytical interest in the unconscious is expressed by the way Burgin conceives of the perception of photography in terms of environment. In the 1976 paper "Modernism in the *Work* of Art," Burgin insisted on the fragmentary character of photography, "received as an *environment*" of heterogeneous codes (photojournalism, amateur, advertising, documentary, etc.). (EAT: 20) Several years later, he drew an analogy between the way we perceive photography and the mechanisms of the dream as described by Freud in terms of rebus. To put it another way: the semiotic analysis of the *consciously received* environment of photography finds its extension in the psychoanalytically inspired exploration of the way photography is *perceived unconsciously*, like in a daydream. To Michel Butor's account that "the author of the rebus, from a certain level on, explores the coulisses of our languages, of our consciousness" (Butor, 1980: 75), we might add in regard to Burgin that he employs the rebus to explore the coulisses of photography and its functioning within our everyday environment.

As mentioned above, Burgin himself already acknowledged the analogy between the artwork's structure and the figure of the rebus for *In Lyon*, created in the same year as the publication of "Photography, Phantasy, Function." Asked by Claude Gintz if *In Lyon* could be considered a kind of rebus, Burgin confirmed that the non-linear, synchronic, and fragmentary configuration of his work would be similar to the principles of a dream rebus. (Gintz, 1981: 16)[28] Yet, the extensive captions, written in the form of three short texts echoing the discourses of analysis, narration, and history, jib at the idea of the rebus as a combination of pictorial and verbal fragments that reveal the message only when being translated phonetically in a linear sequence. The fragmentary, heterogeneous, and enigmatic character of the rebus is much better conveyed in the two works that follow *In Lyon* and *In Grenoble* and that are dedicated to well-known pictures of women. Both realized in 1982 in the context of the *Tales from Freud* exhibition, *Gradiva* and *Olympia* combine photographs with lapidary captions in order to trace "the complex and unstable foundations of masculine desire." (Tate Gallery, 1986: 7)

In *The Interpretation of Dreams*, Freud uses the term "rebus" as a metaphor to explain the structure of the dream-content. Obscured by the psychic mechanisms of condensation and displacement, the dream-rebus has to be translated into the language of the dream-thoughts at issue. (Freud, 1900/1953, 277-278) Even if he admits that there is no guarantee of finding an ultimate resolution—for example the degree of condensation is strictly speaking indeterminable—his purpose is to translate the heterogeneous mix of visual and linguistic elements of the dream into the linear structure of phonetic language. As we shall see, *Gradiva* and *Olympia* adopt the psychic structure of the dream-rebus as a process of condensation and displacement in order to explore the "spaces of the 'other scene' of the unconscious" and the ways this "other scene" acts upon us in terms of identification, sexuality, and scopic relations. (TP: 212)

3.3.1. The Suspended Peripeteian Moment[29]

Gradiva consists of a sequence of seven black and white photographs with text. (Fig. 3.5.-3.12.) Burgin leaves no doubt about the rebus-like character of the work when he claims: "This form of visual art practice, to some extent, is analogous to pictographic, hieroglyphic, writing." (BN: 124) In his work he relates Wilhelm Jensen's eponymous novel of 1903 to Freud's famous essay on the text of 1907. The text tells in lapidary words the story of Jensen's novel: a young archaeologist falls in love with an idealized woman in the form of a Roman bas-relief. He names her "Gradiva" because of her particular stride. Having seen this woman in his dreams at the moment of her death, caused by the eruption of Mount Vesuvius in 79 B.C., he travels to the ruins of Pompeii where he encounters his long-forgotten childhood playmate whom he takes to be the ghost of the Roman girl. By gradually disclosing her real identity she finally cures the young man's delusion. Having regained his senses, the man realizes his love for his childhood friend.

The seminal force of Burgin's image-text-sequence lies in the complex displacement structure of the peripeteian moment. In his own words, he wanted to parody the typical "scene from popular film and television romances where the lovers run towards each other from opposite sides of the frame. […] I wanted to represent a situation in which the lovers run towards each other, and miss—like two express trains hurtling by on their separate tracks, towards their individual destinations." (BN: 122) The accompanying text of the first three images tells us the story as experienced by the girl in the usual reading order from

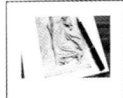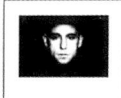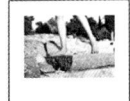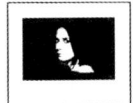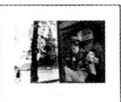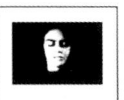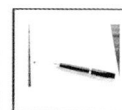

left to right, whereas the three pictures concluding the series take the perspective of the young man in reverse direction, i.e., from right to left. Finally, the sentence of the central image seems to merge the two narratives while describing the moment when the young woman "became aware of the figure of a man watching her." But instead of dissolving the story into a happy end, the challenging gaze of the photographed women deflects the narrative while appealing to the spectator who, henceforth, is engaged in a game of reciprocal observing.

For an understanding of the work it is crucial to know that the woman's picture, like the other portraits of the series, has been taken from a cinema screen. Even though the original films from which the screen shots have been taken remain unknown—Burgin indicates tersely "details of origin forgotten" (BN: 121)—the film still of the woman emerging from a black background acts exactly like the image of another woman appearing in the beginning of Chris Marker's *La Jetée* (1962). In his lucid analysis of the film, Burgin states:

> The image of the woman at the end of the pier is not invested with affective significance after the event; its affect remains constant but it insists. A bright figure upon the shadowy ground of other memories, this image has all the attributes of a *screen memory*. In Freud's account, the screen memory, brilliant and enigmatic, dissimulates another memory, thought, fantasy—one that has had to be repressed. […] The woman in the image, the woman the man subsequently encounters, is indeed a "woman as image." […] Making no demands of her own, compliant signifier of the man's desire, she is pure function: precipitating cause of the narrative. (RF: 99)

Being simultaneously photographic and filmic image, flat surface and deep memory, the film still constitutes a kind of psychic palimpsest where different layers of recollection and repression overlap one another. The paradox of the frozen image as impetus of filmic and psychic narration is reinforced by another possible reading organized in the ouroboros form. The image-sequence starts with a photograph partly representing the reproduction of the ancient relief on the frontispiece preceding the essay on Jensen's *Gradiva* in the Sigmund Freud Standard Edition. The stylograph, lying on the print, reappears in the

Figure 3.5.

Gradiva, 1982.

7 parts, each 50×61 cm. Installation view, John Weber Gallery, New York, 1982.

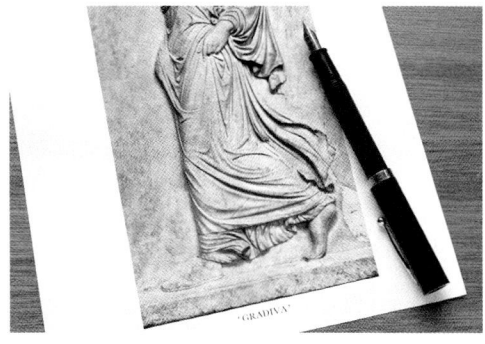

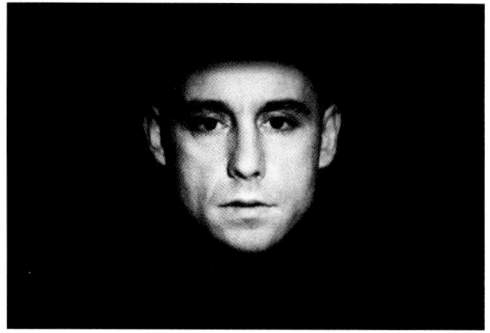

SHE WAS RAISED
BY HER FATHER,
A DISTANT MAN,
FOREVER LOST
IN HIS WORK.

IN CHILDHOOD SHE FOUND COMPANIONSHIP
WITH A NEIGHBOUR'S BOY OF HER OWN AGE.
YEARS LATER, NOW ADULT, SHE ENCOUNTERED HIM AGAIN, BY CHANCE;
HE SHOWED NO SIGN OF HAVING RECOGNISED HER,
WHICH PLUNGED HER INTO DESPAIR.

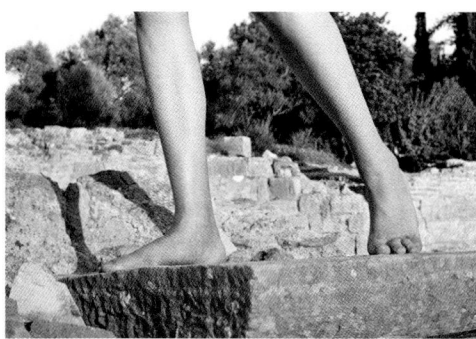

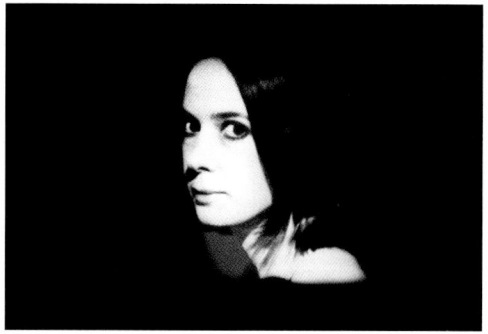

SHE COULD TAKE NO INTEREST IN ANY SUITOR.
SHE RESIGNED HERSELF
TO THE COMPANIONSHIP OF HER FATHER,
ACCOMPANYING HIM
ON HIS TRIPS ABROAD.

IT WAS WHILE SHE WAS VISITING
THE RUINS OF POMPEII
THAT SHE BECAME AWARE OF
THE FIGURE OF A MAN
WATCHING HER.

Figures 3.6 – 3.12.
Gradiva, 1982.

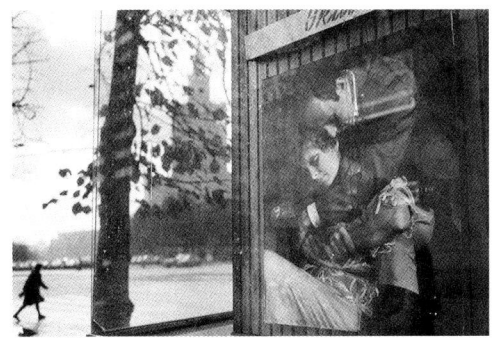

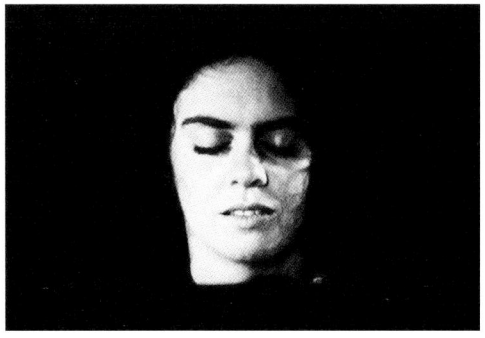

ALONE
IN THE RUINED STREETS
HE WAS STARTLED BY THE SUDDEN APPEARANCE OF
THE FIGURE OF A WOMAN
MOVING WITH GRADIVA'S UNMISTAKEABLE GAIT.

IN A DREAM OF THE DESTRUCTION OF POMPEII
HE BELIEVED HE SAW GRADIVA, AS IF TURNING TO MARBLE.
HE RESOLVED TO TRAVEL TO POMPEII
IN THE HOPE OF FINDING SOME TRACE OF
THE LONG-BURIED GIRL.

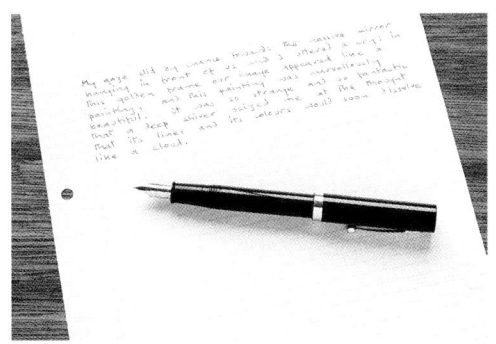

THE RELIEF REPRESENTED A YOUNG WOMAN, STEPPING FORWARD.
ONE FOOT RESTED SQUARELY ON THE GROUND,
THE OTHER TOUCHED THE GROUND ONLY WITH THE TIPS OF THE TOES.
THIS POSTURE CAME TO HAUNT HIS THOUGHTS;
HE GAVE THE GIRL THE NAME 'GRADIVA' – 'SHE WHO STEPS ALONG'.

last image where it has obviously served to transcribe a passage out of Leopold von Sacher-Masoch's *Venus in Furs*. The visual reference to the circular structure by means of the stylograph, which actually resembles the fountain pen used by Freud around 1938, is affirmed on the level of signification. (Engelman, 1976: 140) The text under the last photograph describes the relief represented in the first image. Furthermore, the passage quoted from *Venus in Furs* evokes a phantasm complementary to the delusion of the young archaeologist:

> My gaze slid by chance towards the massive mirror hanging in front of us and I uttered a cry: in this golden frame our image appeared like a painting, and this painting was marvelously beautiful. It was so strange and so fantastic that a deep shiver seized me at the thought that its lines and its colours would soon dissolve like a cloud. (BN: 120; Sacher-Masoch, 1991: 240)

The transformation of the real woman in a mirror image in Sacher-Masoch's novel is the counterpart of the bringing to life of a sculptured image in the imagination of the *Gradiva* protagonist. In both cases the adoration of a woman tips over into fetishism linked with idolatry. In *Venus in Furs* the painted portrait of the idolized woman, realized as a result of the mirror scene, becomes a symbol of the man's servile submission, while Freud concludes his analysis of Jensen's novel by pointing out the passive and masochist nature of one of the protagonist's dreams. (Freud, 1907/1959: 93) Introducing this effect of circularity in the visual order as well as in the psychic structure of his arrangement, Burgin avoids the classic peripeteia as defined by Aristotelian theory of tragedy. Or more precisely, the peripeteian moment is caught in a never-ending movement of displacement. Being simultaneously at the beginning, in the middle, and at the end of the sequence, it is hardly possible to pinpoint one single turning point in the narrative.

Yet the circular movement of shifting and overlapping narratives seems to be suspended by the capacity of photography to arrest time. As Burgin remarks: "Photographs of course are all, in a way, monuments to the past." (BN: 123) The third image of the sequence, a close-up of Gradiva's gait performed by a model set on a plinth, represents a quite literal staging of this idea. Actually, Craig Owens describes *Gradiva* "as an allegory of photography" precisely because it demonstrates what Barthes described, in *Camera Lucida*, as the subject's transformation into an image during the process of "posing" in front of the camera. (Owens, 1984: 10; Barthes, 1982: 10) Relating the idea of "Gradiva, as if turning to marble"—as expressed in the penultimate image's caption—to the death-mask-like close-up of the woman's face with closed eyelids, Owens deduces: "What do I do when I pose for a photograph? I freeze—hence, the masklike, often deathly expressions of so many photographic portraits." (Owens, 1984: 12) Consequently, Owens, following the Lacanian approach of Herman Rapaport, links photography to the question of "mastering events through overcoming time." (Rapaport, 1982: 64) Seen from this angle, the transformation of Gradiva into stone is a metaphor for photography as the "figuration of a gaze which objectifies and masters." (Owens, 1984: 10)

This brings me back to Sacher-Masoch and, in particular, Gilles Deleuze's essay on masochism in which he advocates for an approach to sadism and masochism as two distinct forms of perversion, bearing in mind both "a critical and clinical appraisal […] as well as the artistic originalities." (Deleuze, 1991: 14) Defining masochism in terms of fetishism as a mechanism of disavowal and projection, Deleuze locates the masochist ideal as "suspended in fantasy." The masochistic suspension emerges at the moment when the "woman torturer freezes into postures that identify her with a statue, a painting or a photograph. […] her movement is arrested as she turns to look at herself in a mirror. As we shall see, these "photographic" scenes, these reflected and arrested images are of greatest significance." (33) It is precisely such a fetishistic "photographic" scene that we encounter in the excerpt from Sacher-Masoch's text as well as in the photographed film portraits of *Gradiva*. But while, as in Owens' interpretation, the mastering photographic look condemns the subject to the immobile state of death, the "photographic" scenes of *Gradiva* punctuate the narrative structure of the work, avoiding a final closure which is always deferred.[30] On the one hand, this corresponds to Burgin's use of a filmic analogy when he describes the individual photograph as "the point of origin of a series of psychic 'pans' and 'dissolves,' a succession of metonymies and metaphors which transpose the scene of the photograph to the spaces of the 'other scene' of the unconscious." (TP: 212) On the other hand, this kind of immobile mobility—or mobility through immobility—seems to fit perfectly to Deleuze's account of masochism where "the same scenes are reenacted at various levels in a sort of frozen progression." (Deleuze, 1991: 34) If we define masochism, as Deleuze does, not materially or morally, but as an essentially formal matter (74), we may come to the conclusion that the complex structure of *Gradiva*, holding the constantly displaced peripeteian moment in ceaseless suspension, reveals the "specific constellation of masochism" defined by suspense, waiting (as postponed pleasure), fetishism, and fantasy. (72)

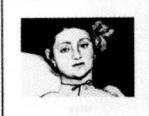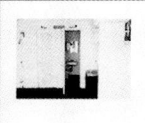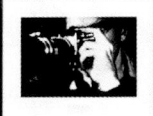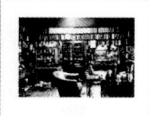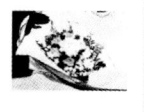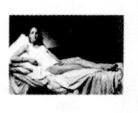

3.3.2. Voyeurism, Masculinity, and the Uncanny Dance of Ideology

In *Olympia* the focus shifts from questions of the fetishist and mas-ochist gaze to the problem of sexual identification and masculinity. (Fig. 3.13.-3.15.) This second work dedicated to a venerated, idealized woman, consists of two triptychs, each of which comprises three photographs with short captures. The first triptych initiates with a de-tail of Manet's famous eponymous painting which stages the face of the concubine looking straight toward the spectator. The caption sum-marizes the intrigue of E.T.A. Hoffmann's *Sandman* in which the male protagonist falls in love with an android named Olimpia. The second picture provides a view into a woman's lavatory in which a mirror is installed reflecting the body of the photographer. The caption—"Oh! (A door opens on a memory)"—refers to both: the doll of Hoffmann's story introduced in the first caption as "O." and, literally, the door of the second photograph that marks the social confine between the body of the male photographer and the woman's restroom as a space prohib-ited for him as a man, a space he simultaneously occupies (as an image) and evades (as a real body). I will return to this issue below. The mem-ory may well be that of a film, watched some time ago and appearing in the third part of the triptych in the form of a screen shot from Alfred Hitchcock's *Rear Window*, taken in a Paris cinémathèque in 1978. (BN: 133) In this movie, Jeff (James Stewart), confined to a wheelchair, uses a camera equipped with a telephoto lens to spy on his neighbors through his apartment window. In Burgin's series, instead, his gaze crosses the lavatory photograph in order to hit the left side of the face of Manet's *Olympia*, while the caption evokes a dreamlike situation in which the act of watching is taking place in a room where everything is petrified, frozen. Yet it remains open whether this room that "returns my gaze, holding me spellbound" refers to the apartment observed by Jeff in Hitchcock's film, the boudoir in which Manet's prostitute waits for her male client, the office where the young student of Hoffmann's novel is enlightened about the delusion concerning the identity of his love ob-ject, or, finally, the woman's lavatory as a place of gender segregation.

The second triptych begins with a documentary photograph of Freud's study in Vienna. The associated text lists the symptoms of Anna O., according to Freud one of the most notable cases of hysteria,

Figure 3.13.

Olympia, 1982.

2 triptychs, each panel 50×61 cm. Installation view, Yarlow-Salzman Gallery, Toronto, 1982.

in order to establish connections with the doll of Hoffmann's *Sandman* ("the people she sees seem like wax figures") and the next image in the sequence, another detail of the Manet painting, this time showing the flower bouquet held by the prostitute's servant ("in a bunch of flowers she can only see one flower at a time"). The laconic caption of the second picture— "O. (A story opens on a memory)"—is a variation of the caption of the lavatory photograph. Like the latter, it multiplies references (O = Olympia, Olimpia, Anna O.) and situates them in the psychical realm of representation and recollection. Associative memory is also at the origin of the third symptom of Anna O.: "she knows she is wearing a brown dress but sees it as a blue one." As we can read in Breuer and Freud's case-study, this confusion follows from the fact that Anne O. conflates the color of her own dress with the memory of the color of her father's dressing-gown made with the same material. (Freud and Breuer, 1893/1955: 33-34) The last picture of the second triptych shows a model posing as Manet's *Olympia*. As a contemporary reenactment of the painting, the photograph circles back to the close-up of the head of the painted Olympia, thus reopening the eternal play of looking at and being looked at. Similar to the final photograph of the first triptych, the text seems to summarize a dream, but this time the petrified, frozen space (which might be related to the photographic image) makes way for the impression of a room where "everything shimmers, nothing is still," or, in brief: the narrative space of "telling stories." However, the story that Burgin tells is not a linear, continuously unfolding narrative confined by a beginning and an end; it is rather a heterogeneous, fragmentary montage based on discontinuities, interruptions, associations, and cross-references.

For a deeper understanding of the work, it has to be situated within a polemical debate about Manet's *Olympia* and Modernism that took place in *Screen* in 1980. In his paper "Preliminaries to a Possible Treatment of 'Olympia' in 1865," Timothy J. Clark argues that Manet's painting would be a failure because of its inconsistent position in relation to the established codes of bourgeois ideologies. Although *Olympia* "refuses to signify" according to the social and aesthetic conventions of the time, the picture would not suggest an alternative reading that sustains a radical critique of these conventions. In other words: Manet failed because, unlike Courbet, he did not place his Olympia "in another classed code—a place in the code of classes. She would have to be given a place in the world which manufactures the Imaginary, and reproduces the relations of dominator/dominated, fantisiser/fantasised. The picture would have to construct itself a position." (Clark, 1980: 39)

In his reply, published in the following *Screen* issue, Peter Wollen accuses Clark of misinterpreting the openness and unfixed character of Manet's *Olympia* as an ineffective and insignificant "play of the

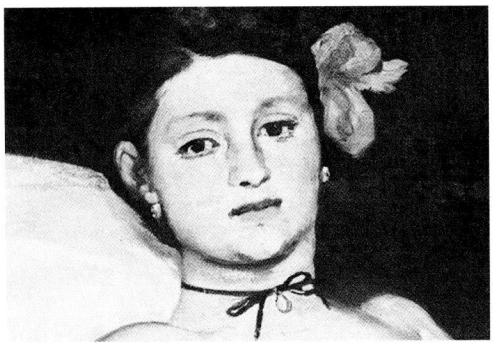

0. is a life-like doll, the creation of a brilliant professor.
Believing her to be real, a young student falls in love with her.
An intruder tries to steal the automaton, but is surprised by the professor.
A fight ensues in which the doll loses her enamelled eyes.
At that moment her admirer, sensing she is in danger,
bursts into the office.

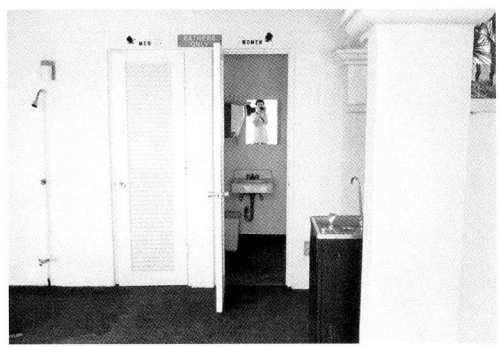

"Oh!"
(A door opens on a memory.)

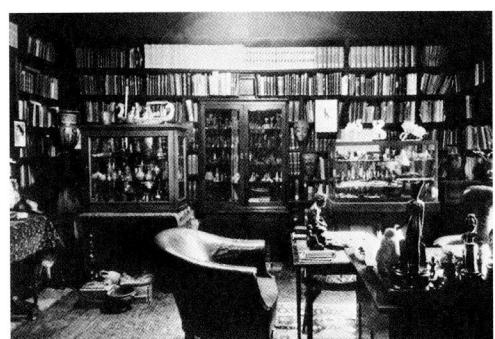

0. is twenty-one, the patient of a brilliant professor.
Amongst her symptoms: all the people she sees seem like wax figures;
she knows she is wearing a brown dress but sees it as a blue one;
in a bunch of flowers she can only see one flower at a time.
A year now has passed since she was separated from her father
and had taken to her bed.

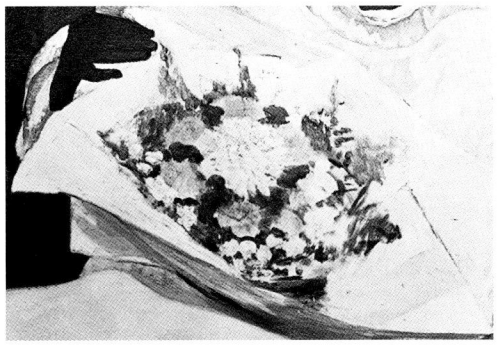

0.
(A story opens on a memory)

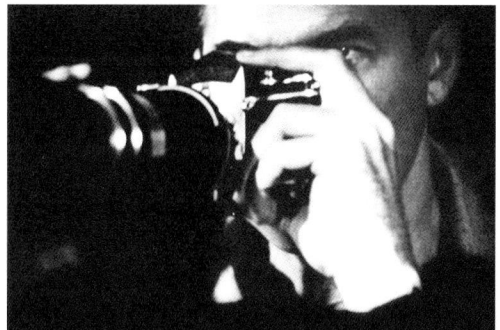

Everything is petrified, frozen for all time, as I watch
the room in which she is to be seen sitting, motionless.
It seems she is staring in my direction,
although I cannot be certain. Sometimes her chair is empty,
but I continue to watch. It is as if the vacant room itself
returns my gaze, holding me spellbound.

Figure 3.14.
Olympia, 1982.
First triptych.

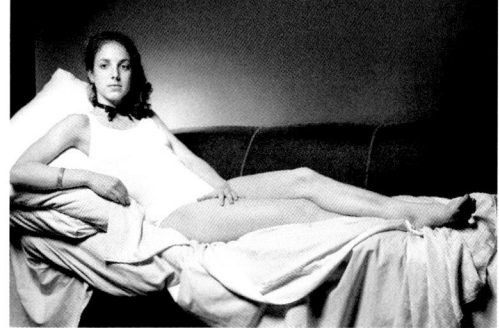

Everything shimmers, nothing is still, as I watch
the room in which my father lies.
It seems men and women are eyes and mouth,
although I cannot be certain; sometimes I cannot speak.
But I continue to tell stories. It is as if the vacant room itself
listens, holding me spellbound.

Figure 3.15.
Olympia, 1982.
Second triptych.

signifier," as tied to his conviction that a painting "should provide a clear, consistent and complete picture, drawn from the public and familiar world of class division and class struggle, able to command unambiguous recognition." (Wollen, 1980: 16) Wollen further argues that Clark would completely ignore feminist and psychoanalytical theories of the gaze and subject positions according to which the representation of woman is not merely a question of class difference but concerns "the production of woman as fetish in a particular conjuncture of capitalism." Rather than identifying woman with a specific oppositional (class) position, Wollen suggests that Manet's painting reveals "the underlying mechanisms which produce the sexual discourse within which women are placed." (Wollen, 1980: 23)[31] In this regard, dis-identificatory practices, based on Brechtian concepts of montage and multiplicity, would be of major importance as a means to resist "the dance of ideology." Seen from this angle, the open, unfixed, shifting meaning of Manet's painting is not a sign of inconsistency but rather marks a caesura in the history of representation substituting concepts of uniformity and homogeneity by strategies of discontinuity and multiplicity on a formal and an identificatory level.

Toward the end of his article, Wollen summarizes his position when he writes:

> "Complex seeing," in this sense, simply involves a multiplicity of semiotic practices, formal devices and points-of-view, distinguishing, for example, the representation of plot from the representation of commentary, or narration of past events from hypotheses about future events, documentary from fiction, and so on. (Wollen, 1980: 25)

Obviously, Wollen's account of Manet's *Olympia* draws on feminist discussions on sexual difference and visual pleasure, as addressed above. He seems to be interested less in situating the painting within its specific historical context than in its virtue to raise general questions about sexuality and difference in the space of representation since modernity. It goes without saying that Burgin was aware of this debate, and Wollen's remarks on "complex seeing" as a multiple semiotic practice shifting constantly between different discursive modes (story and commentary), narrative forms (documentary and fiction), and temporal realities (past, present, and future) certainly apply to *Olympia* as well.

Multiplicity and shifting perspectives are also main characteristics of E. T. A. Hoffmann's novel *The Sandman*, written in 1815, exactly fifty years before Manet exhibited his painting at the Salon. The novel begins with Nathanael's epistolary exchange with his fiancée Clara and her brother Lothar. Before giving the floor to the third person extradiegetic narrator, Hoffmann introduces two intradiegetic narrators who represent two diverging views on reality. While Nathanael believes that man is at the mercy of destiny as an external omnipotent force, as "a dark fatality [that] has actually suspended over my life a gloomy veil of clouds" (Hoffmann, 2008: 10), Clara locates such "dark and hostile power" within one's own self—identifying it as "the phantom of our own selves." (15) But Hoffmann leaves it undecided who is right. He keeps the reader in suspense about the question of whether Nathanael's madness is caused by real, external events or whether it involves a sheer delusion. Actually, throughout the whole novel Hoffmann refuses to draw a clear line between reality and fiction, insisting on the relative character of "truth."

It is precisely this blurring of apparently secured positions that provides fertile ground for the advent of the uncanny. In his famous paper "Das Unheimliche" (1919), Freud endorses Schelling's remark that the term 'uncanny' (unheimlich) *"is the name for everything that ought to have remained … secret and hidden but has come to light."* (Freud, 1919/1955: 224) Concerning Hoffmann's novel, he admits that "the incomparably uncanny effect of the story" to some extent springs from the motif of the seemingly animate doll Olimpia with which Nathanael falls in love, but that the actual motif of the uncanny would involve the Sandman who tears out the eyes of naughty boys and girls as food for his children. Identifying the act of tearing out the eyes with the fear of castration, Freud focuses his attention entirely on the couple Coppelius (the lawyer involved in the death of Nathanael's father) and Coppola (the optician who throws Olimpia's glass-eyes on Nathanael's breast and thereby causes his madness). From this perspective, it is perfectly consistent that Nathanael's final bout of madness, which pushes him to suicide, would have been provoked, according to Freud, by spotting Coppelius through the spyglass bought from Coppola. But Nathanael, in Hoffmann's novel, does not direct the spyglass toward Coppelius but toward the face of Clara, who reactivates his love madness triggered by Olimpia. For the sake of his argument, Freud simply modified the original facts. In Hoffmann's text, the experience of the uncanny is attributed in an equal manner to both, the "the terrible goblin" ("unheimlichen Spuk") of the "dreadful Sandman" and the inanimateness of Olimpia's eyes ("she had no power of sight") that made Nathanael feel "very uncomfortable" ("ganz unheimlich"). (Hoffmann, 2008: 6; 17) And as it is the gaze through the spyglass that, for him, animates Olimpia's fixed eyes and rouses him to passion, it becomes plausible that Clara's magnified face seen through the same optical device drives him into a frenzy.

When returning to Burgin's *Olympia*, it seems now obvious that his interest in the Sandman story lies less in the male castration complex, linked to the loss of the eyes, than in the constantly shifting "power of sight" on which the relationship between Nathanael and Olimpia is based. Nathanael's use of the spyglass to dominate Olimpia corresponds to Jeff's voyeuristic gaze at Olympia by means of the telephoto. But the instauration of a system of domination based on the voyeuristic gaze fails. The photographed face of the painted Olympia is as little real as the automaton in Hoffmann's story. Burgin takes up the apparently unconnected threads of various historical contexts and media (the cinema movie *Rear Window*, the novel *The Sandman*, the painting *Olympia*, his own photographs), not to tell a single overriding story, but to evoke multiple stories. This brings me back one last time to the visual pleasure debate and the picture interposed between Olympia's head and Hitchcock's photographer. In an interview in 1989 Burgin said:

> My own response to feminism in the '70s was to *start* making images of women. It seemed to me that a major problem in theory and practice at that time was that while female sexuality was endlessly problematized, male sexuality was taken for granted as something simple and self-evident. Sexuality, again, was being treated as a "woman's problem." For about 10 years—I'm working on other things now—my work aimed to represent male sexuality as every bit as uncertain and problematical as female sexuality: no essential masculinity—only *masculinities*. (Batchen, 1989: 8)

In *Olympia*, at least three types of "masculinity" occur in relation to the question of the gaze. The photographer's gaze "which objectifies and masters" (Owens, 1984: 10) is represented by the Hitchcock screen shot; Nathanael represents the paranoiac gaze projecting woman as "phantom of our own selves"; and, finally, the second photograph suggests a reflexive gaze that rises "questions of (sexual) identity and relations (here, the relation, 'looking/being looked at')." (BN: 137) These questions have to be related as much to the history of representation, which informs our memory and our ways of seeing, as to the situation in which we inscribe ourselves in the sexual matrix of representation in terms of looking subjects and objects looked at. Burgin's *Olympia*, then, is a multi-perspectival exercise in "complex seeing" (Wollen, 1980: 25), whereby the fixed position of the male gaze is deconstructed and revealed as contradictory and uncertain:

> Although the *male* spectator in the gallery may be identified with the man reflected in the mirror, the reflected self-image is situated, contradictorily, in a place from which the man is excluded; the *female* spectator in the gallery may occupy this place but not, contradictorily, the identity "male photographer." (BN: 136)

3.4. Between: From Intertext to Masquerades in the Gallery

3.4.1. Hetero-optic Writing

The ambiguous mirror self-portrait of *Olympia* also concludes the essay "Tea with Madeleine," which Burgin contributed to the Winter 1984 issue of the journal *Wedge*, published in conjunction with the exhibition *Difference: On Representation and Sexuality* at the New York Museum of Contemporary Art (December 8-February 10, 1985). Designated by Griselda Pollock as "a major feminist event," this exhibition traveled from New York to the Renaissance Society at the University of Chicago and had its final showing at the Institute of Contemporary Arts in London, from July 19 to September 1, 1985. (Pollock, 2003: 213) The show included thirty-one, mainly American and British artists, such as Ray Barrie, Dara Birnbaum, Hans Haacke, Mary Kelly, Barbara Kruger, Sherrie Levine, Martha Rosler, and Jeff Wall. Marcia Tucker, then director of the New York Museum of Contemporary Art, emphasized that the aim was to offer "an intellectual as well as visual exploration of how gender distorts 'reality.'" (Tucker, 1984: 4) Burgin contributed three works to the *Difference* show. In addition to *Gradiva* and *Olympia* he created a new work, *Portia* (1984) which should also be included in *Tales from Freud*, given its reference to a specific tale in Freud's work. (Fig. 3.16.) In his paper "The Theme of the Three Caskets," Freud refers to the famous scene from Shakespeare's *The Merchant of Venice*, in which the suitors of the merchant's daughter have to spot among three caskets the one that contains her portrait. Freud interprets this act of choice as a gesture of command according to which choosing the desired woman compensates the fear of death. (BN: 178; Freud, 1913/1958: 299) In *Portia*, this mechanism of repression

Figure 3.16.
Portia, 1984.
50×129 cm.

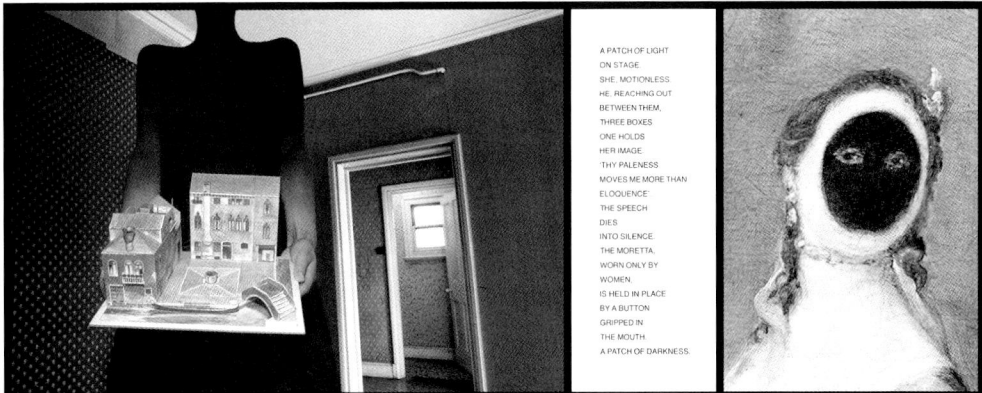

is evoked by different forms of displacement and condensation: while the architectural model of the left picture is a combination of typical features taken from various squares in Venice, thus signifying the psychical process of condensation, the right photograph represents a detail of Pietro Longhi's painting *Exhibition of a Rhinoceros at Venice* (1751) in the National Gallery, London. It shows a woman's face hidden behind a Moretta, a small oval mask worn at carnival in Venice, which was held with the teeth by means of a button attached to its underside. The gesture of command over desire and death in Freud's account is thus related to a triple fantasy of domination: the dream of political and economic power is represented by the person demonstratively showing the Venice model, whereas the detail of the Longhi hints at both, sexual desire awakened by the erotic promise of the mask and fantasies of exhibiting, and thus controlling, wild animals, here represented by a rhinoceros, called Clara, which was toured around Europe in the eighteenth century and was publicly displayed as an exotic attraction. As discussed below, the exhibition display and the mask feature prominently in Burgin's work of the mid-1980s.

But let me first return to Burgin's "Tea with Madeleine." This essay, as the thematic focus of the *Wedge* winter issue suggests, "re/positions" sexuality within a new, experimental discursive field in which various narratives and heterogeneous representations merge. On the visual level, the question of the social and institutional production of sexual difference posed in the mirror portrait is taken up and developed in the illustration at the beginning of the essay. The theatrical representation of Casanova in Federico Fellini's 1976 movie features an "androgynous fantasy" that, in a narcissistic gesture, annihilates the subject's sexual identity. (Pacteau, 1986: 82) On a structural level, the heterogeneous organization of the text corresponds to this insecure position in terms of gender and sexuality. More precisely, the text is not presented as a unity, but unfolds in two parallel columns developing two different narratives—one academic, the other poetic, associative. The third, absent column, finally, would be, as Burgin suggests, the gallery work from this period. (EAT: ix)

Burgin adapts the parallel column system as most prominently known from the synoptic Gospels of the New Testament. But while the visual appearance of "Tea with Madeleine" is in accordance with the etymological roots of the Greek word "synopsis," meaning "seeing together," the essay's complex structure, its intertextual cross-references, and its montage character entangling various literary and visual genres and associations confront the reader rather with a kind of "hetero-opsis"—a form of "seeing differently" or "seeing other."

Consequently, the text of the left column deconstructs, in the wake of the poststructuralist writings by Lacan and Derrida, the difference between "man" and "woman" as socio-psychological terms. Kristeva's thoughts on a feminine language are touched upon before fetishism is defined in terms of the disavowal of difference in the sense of divisions of form from content, the private from the social, the word from the image, the "masculine" from the "feminine," theory from practice, the inside of the institution from its outside. (EAT: 108) The text ends with the optimistic conclusion: "It is in the interest of showing the *meaning* of social difference as, precisely, a *process of production*; as something mutable, something historical, and therefore something we can do *something* about." (108)

In some way, the right-hand text is a poetic demonstration of this process-oriented, ever-shifting conception of meaning according to which nothing is fixed or permanent. Taking the form of an assemblage of fragments of different origins and contexts, which are woven into a heterogeneous, highly associative narrative fabric, the right column text connects in a dreamlike stream of consciousness motifs and figures from cultural productions as different as the 1945 romantic drama film *Brief Encounter* by David Lean, Hoffmann's *Sandman*, Fellini's *Casanova*, Hitchcock's *Vertigo*, the Marx Brothers, Shklovsky's account of his exile, and so forth. Burgin's own account of a stay in Warsaw is intersected by titles of jazz standards and earworms such as Jule Styne's *I Fall in Love Too Easy* (1944), Thelonious Monk's *Round Midnight* (1944), and Cole Porter's *Love for Sale* (1930). These personal memories are followed by some considerations on Virginia Woolf's feminist essay *A Room of One's Own* (1929), arguing for a space for women in the literary tradition, commented by Kristeva's mantra "woman, as such, does not exist!" (EAT: 105) Indeed, as we learn slightly later on with reference to Sacher-Masoch's *Venus in Furs*, woman only exists as image. As we can easily guess, *Gradiva* lurks behind the mirror of the narcissistic construction of identity. The right column text ends with a condensed association of references to Freud's case of Anna O., Shakespeare and Millais' *Ophelia*, and the romantic lovers of soap operas who, after having missed each other, are "closing their respective doors behind them." (109) These final words do not only echo the structure of Burgin's series *Olympia*; they also refer to the concluding image of the mirror self-portrait in which the door is wide open, so that the spectacle of sexual difference can start all over again.

From this follows that sexual identity is constructed, first, within the space of representation and, secondly, on the basis of uncountable intertextual cross-references between multiple visual and verbal elements springing from diverse temporal and spatial origins. Two years before the publication of "Tea with Madeleine," Burgin insists, with Barthes, Derrida and Kristeva, on the definition of text in terms of space rather than in terms of object when he writes in "Re-reading *Camera Lucida*":

Text, as conceived of by Barthes (with the prompting of, notably, Jacques Derrida and Julia Kristeva), is seen not as an "object" but rather as a "space" between the object and the reader/viewer—a space made up of endlessly proliferating meanings which have no stable point of origin, nor of closure. (EAT: 73)

Obviously, Burgin takes up the distinction that Barthes makes between "text" and "work" in his essay "From Work to Text." (Barthes, 1977: 155-164) While the "work," defined as an "object of consumption," (161) is the result of filiation, authorship, and the law of the Father, the text is conceived of as intertext, as "being the text-between of another text." (160) As such the latter constitutes a plural, infinite network of over-crossing meanings demanding the reader's "practical collaboration." (163) Barthes concludes that the text is not subjected to the pleasure of consumption, as is the work, but offers *jouissance* as a kind of pleasure without separation, a pleasure proliferating in "that space where no language has a hold over any other, where languages circulate (keeping the circular sense of the term)." (164) Burgin's *hetero-optic* approach in "Tea with Madeleine," slipping restlessly along endless chains of associations (or, as Derrida and Barthes put it, "signifiers"), could not be described better. Yet in "Diderot, Barthes, *Vertigo*," Burgin leaves no doubt about how such chains are disposed. As he writes: "It is because of the *mise-en-scène* of desire, which is fantasy, that dissemination does not 'centrifugally' dissipate itself but rather 'circles back' on itself to repeat—but *differently*." (EAT: 128) If, as discussed, this circular yet open movement, compared by Burgin with a spiral, can be observed in *Gradiva* and *Olympia*, it is also at play in "Tea with Madeleine," where the doors, after being closed in the final sentence of the essay, are re-opened in the photograph on the next page, inviting the reader "to start again," as the very first words of the text suggest. (EAT: 97)

3.4.2. Between Gallery and Cinema

When Burgin refers to his gallery work from this period as the third, absent column of "Tea with Madeleine," this specifically applies to *Gradiva* and *Olympia* and, first and foremost even, to *The Bridge* (1984). (Fig. 3.17.-3.24.) This extensive photo-text work consists of seven single or composite panels of variable length, each of which measuring 30 inches in height. Conceived as "an extended work which fills a room" (Burgin, 1988a: 7), *The Bridge* ties in with the spatial design of his works from the late 1970s, such as UK 76 and US 77. But whereas the size, appearance, and arrangement of the photographs of US 77 evoke the repetitive occurrence of interior billboards (PT: 57), the tableau-like

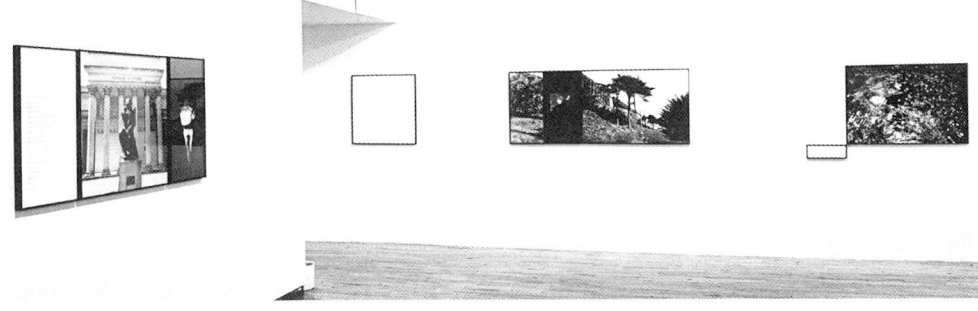

presentation of the black framed panels of *The Bridge* pays tribute to the work's actual setting in the gallery space. It is at this particular moment that Burgin increasingly begins to pay attention to questions of art history, composition, and the expectations of the museum visitor. Although Burgin has explained that he started "to address the 'legitimate expectations' of people who walk into art galleries" (Magnani, 1989: 120), this did not mean that he proffered an uncritical return to painting and art as an easily understandable consumer good. It rather meant that his aim was now to take into account the historical and institutional framework of the production and perception of art, precisely because this is the only way to apprehend its socially and ideologically conditioned institutional boundaries, as well as its relations with representations from other cultural contexts. With this shift of attention to the institutional space of the gallery, the question of specificity becomes a main concern within Burgin's artistic work. This does not pertain, obviously, to Greenberg's notion of specificity as defined in terms of formal independency and autonomy. Specificity, as Burgin understands the term, relates to the particular situation within which the work of art is displayed, as well as the specific conditions in and for which it is produced.

In his 1984 paper "Diderot, Barthes, *Vertigo*," Burgin specifies the phenomenological properties of the gallery, as the institution where art is normally encountered, in contrast to the situation of the cinema:

> the cinema is the "negative" of the gallery [...]: in the cinema we are in darkness; the gallery is light; in the cinema we are immobile before moving images; in the gallery it is we who must move; in the cinema we may interrupt the sequence of images only by leaving; in the gallery we may order the duration of our attention in whatever sequence we wish. (EAT: 136)

Figure 3.17.
The Bridge, 1984.
7 parts,
76/89/92×86/153/155/190.
Installation view, John Weber Gallery, New York 1984.

THE BRIDGE

'i'vegno per menarvi a l'altra riva'
'I come to carry you to the other shore'
Dante Alighieri *Inferno* Canto III, 86

In everyday language it is common to find the word 'bridge' used metaphorically to express such otherwise abstract notions as 'exchange' between two parties and 'transition' from one state to another. In the literature of psychoanalysis the image of the bridge is often cited as figuring in dreams and phantasies as more specifically representing the penis which joins the parents in sexual intercourse and the transitions of birth and death. Water, with which bridges are readily associated, does of course itself have both actual and symbolic associations with sexual intercourse, birth and death. Further, in the history of Western representations, literary and visual, water is strongly associated with the woman, and it would not strain scholarship too far to argue an (admittedly less pronounced) association of the bridge with the man.

The work shown here has a particular bridge – the Golden Gate Bridge – as its 'jumping-off point'. More appositely, switching metaphors, the work is born from a watery theatrical scene for which this bridge serves as proscenium arch – that moment in Hitchcock's *Vertigo* when Madeleine (Kim Novak) throws herself into San Francisco Bay and is rescued by the detective, Scottie (James Stewart).

When I first read a short essay by Freud called 'A Special Type of Choice of Object Made by Men', I was struck by the similarities between the syndrome of male desire Freud describes and the pattern of behaviour Scottie exhibits in Hitchcock's film: the first condition determining the choice of love-object by the type of man discussed in Freud's essay is that the woman should be already attached to some other man – husband, fiancé, or friend; in the film, Scottie falls in love with the woman he is hired to investigate – the wife of an old college friend. The second precondition is that the woman should be seen to be of bad repute sexually; Madeleine, the college-friend's wife, suffers from a fixated identification with a forebear whose illicit love-affair, and illegitimate child, brought her to tragic ruin. The type of man described by Freud is, "invariably moved to rescue the object of his love", and prominent amongst the rescue phantasies of such men is the phantasy of rescue from water; Scottie rescues Madeleine from the Bay. Finally, Freud observes, "The lives of men of this type are characterised by a repetition of passionate attachments of this sort … each an exact replica of the other", and he remarks that it is always the same physical type which is chosen; following Madeleine's death, Scottie becomes obsessed by Judy, who physically resembles Madeleine and who he sets about 'remaking' into an exact replica of Madeleine.

Behind the pattern of repetitious behaviour he describes, Freud identifies a primary scenario of male Oedipal desire for the mother – already attached to the father, her sexual relations with whom bring her into ill-repute in the eyes of the little rival for her love. The ubiquitous phantasy of rescue from water represents a conflation of 'rescue' with 'birth', just as he was, at birth, 'fished from the waters' and given life, so will he now return this gift to his mother in a reciprocal act of recovery from water. Finally, the adult man's love-attachments form an endless series of similar types for the simple reason that, as mother-surrogates, they can never match the irreducibly unique qualities of the original.

As I have already remarked, the history of Western representation is flooded with watery images of women – from the birth of Venus to the Death of Ophelia, with countless bathing scenes in between. If, in the history of representations under patriarchy, water is seen as woman's natural element, it is most likely because, in male phantasy, the woman's body is itself liquid: in its lactation; in its menstruation, matching the movement of the tides; in its wetness in love; in its (socially sanctioned) capacity for tears; and so on. By corresponding token, the over-arching (over-bearing) patriarchal principle readily finds figuration in the image of the bridge. It is by way of such metaphorical tableaux – allegories – that the social order is imprinted in the unconscious. In the way we repeat or recast such tableaux, therefore, there is always more at issue than 'mere metaphor'.

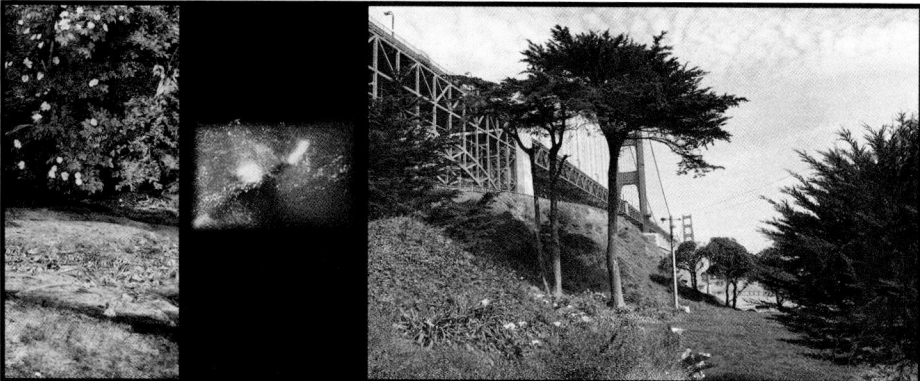

Figures 3.18–21. *The Bridge*, 1984.

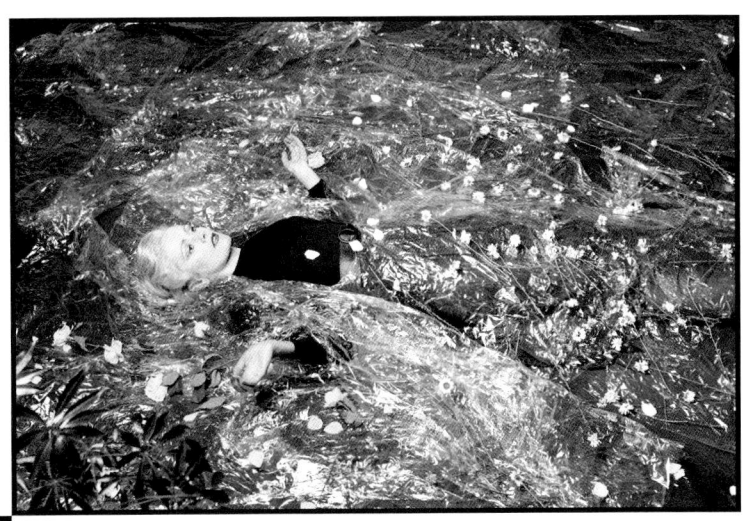

SILENTLY	1/8
VIOLENTLY	ACROSS THE POOL
THE WATERS BREAK	FALLING
AROUND THE EMERGING FORM	UPON THE GLASS WALLS
OF A WOMAN	OF THE CORRIDOR
HER TANNED FLANKS	I TOOK MY LAST CASE
STREAMING WATER	FROM THE ROOM
SHE FOLDS THE TOWEL	AND CLOSED THE DOOR
AROUND HER NEW BORN BODY	LEAVING
LONG SHADOWS OF PALMS	CALIFORNIA

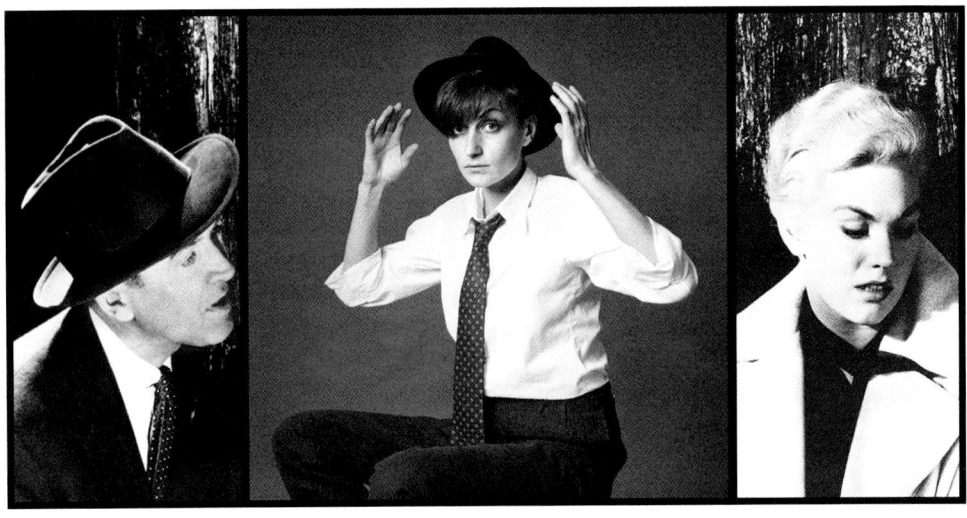

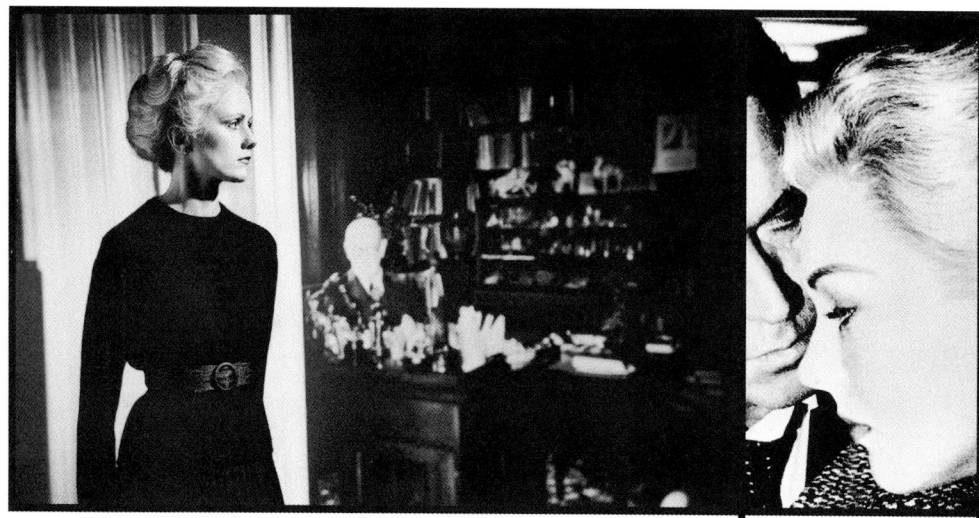

Figures 3.22–24. *The Bridge*, 1984.

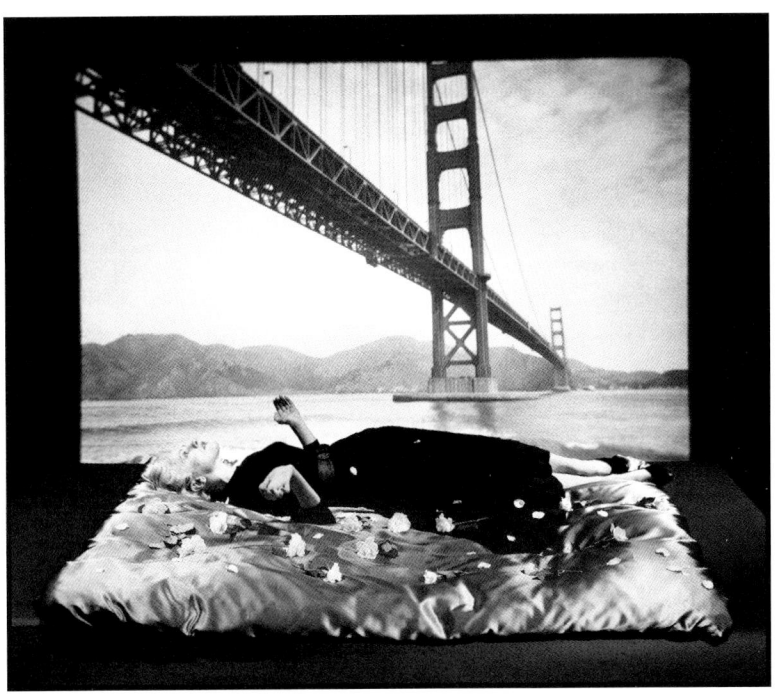

I' VEGNO PER MENARVI A L'ALTRA RIVA

For the first time, Burgin articulates a profound distinction between the ways art and movies are perceived according to their institutional setting and thus lays the foundation for his concept of the "uncinematic," introduced around 2007 as a specific feature of his gallery work. (VBP: 77)[32] But cinema will hardly be excluded from his work. On the contrary, together with the fine arts, cinema becomes the crucial concern in *The Bridge*. Burgin emphasizes in the last lines of his "Diderot, Barthes, Vertigo" that even though attention to specificity is necessary in order to approach "the phenomenologically-given field of representations theoretically" (and their ideologically-given field as well, we might add), such attention becomes unhelpful when "fetishized" for institutional or commercial purposes in terms of substantial specificity of objects and disciplines. By contrast, Burgin's claim is to "take account of the *total* environment of the 'society of the spectacle.'" (EAT: 139) *The Bridge* epitomizes this approach to the concept of specificity. If for its presentational form the work reacts to the phenomenological setting of the gallery, its content refers not only to artistic disciplines but also to practices of popular culture such as cinema, documentary photography, and fashion photography. The photographs confront staged scenes from Hitchcock's *Vertigo* (1958) and details from Millais' *Ophelia* (1851-52) with a historical photograph of Freud in his Vienna office, a recent image of Rodin's *The Thinker* in front of the Fine Arts Museum of San Francisco, and practices of fashion photography. In the first triptych of the work, a contemporary view of the bridge is combined with a still from *Vertigo* showing Madeleine's submerged body and a detail of the dead body of Millais' *Ophelia* floating in the water. In the next image, a model, dressed like Madeleine and bedded on cellophane covered with flowers condenses the two images of women, while the horizontally and vertically readable text offers a chain of associations of water as symbol of woman.[33] Burgin describes this picture as follows:

> This image provides an example of "condensation:" the model has adopted the pose of Millais' *Ophelia*; her clothing, make-up, and wig, however, are styled on the basis of movie-stills from Hitchcock's *Vertigo* [...] the convention of using cellophane to represent water is derived from fashion-photography practices of the 1930s—particularly from the work of Cecil Beaton. (BN: 172)

The photograph merges two well-known motives from painting and cinema—*Ophelia* and *Vertigo*—in order to conflate, or to use Burgin's own word, to "condense," various aesthetic, emotional, historical, and social contexts and uses within one photographic image. This is precisely what Burgin calls an intertext: a broad space of circulating meanings where one text, in the sense of a signifying structure, opens continually onto other texts. (EAT: 73)

Still another triptych consists of two stills of Scottie and Madeleine, framing the picture of a woman who, dressed like the detective, repeats the gesture of the drowning Ophelia. But this time the pose of the standing woman appears to be the reaction of somebody being told to put up one's hands to be arrested. Accordingly, the classical positions in Hollywood cinema of active man and passive woman, as revealed by Laura Mulvey in her "Visual Pleasure" essay, become blurred. As Burgin states: "The position of this figure in terms of power, in terms of sexuality, is unclear." (Burgin, 1988a: 7) In another triptych, a photograph shot by Edmund Engelman of Freud in his office shortly before fleeing Vienna and the Nazis in 1938, is framed by a close-up of the protagonists of *Vertigo* and an image of the female model dressed like Madeleine. The accompanying text links Engelman's photograph to Freud's case-study about Dora, *Fragments of an Analysis of a Case of Hysteria*, in which Dora's mother wants to save her jewel-case from a fire, which Freud reads as the girl's disavowal of her sexual desire for a friend of the family who annoys her. Freud's subsequent remark that representation acts "as a disguise if the wish is a repressed one" (Freud, 1905/1953: 67) might be seen as a key message of *The Bridge*, for it does not merely refer to the female actor disguised as Madeleine, but also to another essay by Freud, "A Special Type of Choice of Object Made by Man," which serves Burgin to reveal that "Scottie's desire is for an image, the truth of which is consistently denied to him." (EAT: 99) Actually, in the contextualizing panel Burgin observes that Scottie's behavior would match perfectly with four preconditions identified by Freud as crucial for a certain type of male desire: first, the woman is attached to another man; secondly, the woman is of bad repute sexually; thirdly, the urge to "rescue" the loved woman; and finally, that all chosen love-objects "turn into easily recognizable mother-surrogates." (Freud, 1910/1957: 169) In *The Bridge* these surrogates take their own lives traveling through a multitude of temporal, representational and psychic-sexual dimensions without coming to a rest.

"I'vegno per menarvi a l'altra riva" ("I come to carry you to the other shore") are the words borrowed from Dante Alighieri's *Inferno Canto III* that serve as a subtitle of the picture in which a female model is lying on satin sheets in front of a projected image of the Golden Gate Bridge, the fabric of her resting place imitating the uneven, scintillating surface of the water behind her. What we are looking at, put briefly, is not an image but the *mise-en-scène* of a fictional situation where diverging spatial and temporal realities collide. Indeed, *The Bridge* invites us to a journey on various levels: from reality to dream, from the single item to the environment around it, from image to text, from photography to film or painting, from cinema to the gallery, from the act of observing to the state of being observed.

Unlike conventional cinema, *The Bridge*, is not a unified temporal object. It is rather a spatial object in which fragments and references are scattered across the various parts of the work in order to form what Burgin will later call a "heterogeneous psychical object." (IDS: 23) In "Diderot, Barthes, *Vertigo*," he compares his fantasy of the scattered pieces of Giotto's Scrovegni Chapel fresco, raining down on the city of Padua, with the way in which a film is perceived outside the cinema in the modern media environment: in form of posters, film stills, magazine images, forming a metaphorical and metonymical web of references. (EAT: 137) Concerning his own approach to cinema, Burgin writes elsewhere: "I take in a lot of films this way, in the form of synopses and stills, and also in the form of film theory, with its photograms and fragments of significant dialogue. This explains why I enjoy Godard, but not why I like Hitchcock." (BN: 154) Burgin's decision to situate his work in the uncertain location of "between" (6) can in fact be linked to Godard's method which, according to Deleuze, is based on the interstice between one image and another:

> It is the method of BETWEEN, "between two images," which dies away with all cinema of the One. It is the method of AND, "this and then that," which does away with all the cinema of Being = is. Between two actions, between two affections, between two perceptions, between two visual images, between two sound images, between the sound and the visual: make the indiscernible, that is the frontier, visible. (Deleuze, 1997: 180)

The Bridge then may be understood as an aesthetic response to both, Burgin's conceptualization of the way in which film is encountered within the media environment, and his personal approach to cinema, oscillating BETWEEN theory AND practice, fragmentary still images AND verbal elements. Yet the heterogeneous object of cinema is not only the result of an encounter with the actual environment of the medias. It is also the result of processes of memory and recollection. As Burgin said in an interview:

> I'm more interested in the movie we remember than the one we see on the screen. I'm also interested in the way we may "remember" a film we never saw except through such things as reviews, posters, trailers and television clips, synopses, illustrated books and so on. My interest in actual films shows in the element of sequentiality and *mise-en-scène* in my work. (PT: 97-98)

In "Diderot, Barthes, *Vertigo*," Burgin draws on Barthes when he correlates the film still as a "material entity" and the "mnemic-image" as "a psychic entity," being both "fragments abstracted from the whole." (EAT: 113) *The Bridge* is all about this relationship between the material and the psychical components of film and representation in general. As the contextualizing text-panel suggests, the work unfolds along chains of associations in which the symbolic link, established in Western representation, between water, woman, birth, and death is invoked by the references to *Vertigo*'s rescued woman: drowned Ophelia and foam-born Venus. (BN: 173; Lewis, 1987/88: 56; EAT: 133)

3.4.3. Between the Masks

If traditionally the bridge may represent the male symbolic counterpart of woman's association with water, the quotation of Dante's inferno offers, together with the staged photographs, another avenue. With regard to the sexual masquerade, performed by the female model, the phrase "I come to carry you to the other shore" may also be understood as an invitation to leave the secure position of the socially sanctioned roles for men and women. Burgin reduplicates Scottie and Madeleine in terms of a "*composite* figure" represented by a female actor who returns the spectator's look. As he points out, clothing functions here as a kind of masquerade: "The identity is 'slippery;' and if the identity receiving our look is so uncertain, then perhaps the same uncertainty may now have invaded the position from which *our* look is given." (BN: 174)

The staging and reenacting of different sexual roles and behaviors in *The Bridge* correlates with feminism's engagement with masquerade. In the late 1970s, feminist thinkers such as Michèle Montrelay, Mary Ann Doane, Luce Irigaray, and Laura Mulvey began to theorize the term in order to reject the existence of a genuine femininity, arguing that feminine identity is nothing but a psycho-social construction. Most of them draw on Joan Riviere's seminal essay "Womanliness as a masquerade" (1929), in which the British psychoanalyst and translator of Freud gives a psychoanalytical explanation of the phenomenon that women have to wear masks of "womanliness" if they want to succeed in a patriarchal society.

> Womanliness therefore could be assumed and worn as a mask, both to hide the possession of masculinity and to avert the reprisals expected if she was found to possess it. [...] The reader may now ask how I define womanliness or where I draw the line

between genuine womanliness and the "masquerade." My suggestion is not, however, that there is any such difference, whether radical or superficial, they are the same thing. (Riviere, 1986: 38)

From this follows that there is no "authentic womanliness" beyond the mask that mimics it, for womanliness is always already a form of staging, of "gender play-acting." (Apter, 1992: 243) The question of role-playing is a crucial issue in Riviere's essay, in which she describes the behavior of a female university lecturer who, when lecturing to colleagues, choses particularly feminine clothes while peppering her talk with caustic remarks and jokes completely inappropriate to the occasion. As Riviere proposes: "She has to treat the situation of displaying her masculinity to men as a 'game,' as something not real, as a 'joke.'" (Riviere, 1986: 39) The conclusion that Stephen Heath draws from Riviere's definition of the masquerade as a game is decisive for a deeper understanding of *The Bridge*: "she puts on a show of the femininity they demand, but inappropriately, keeping her distance, and returns masculinity to them as equally unreal, another act, a charade of power." (Heath, 1986: 56)[34]

Mimicking both the feminine passive attitude of Madeleine/Ophelia and the active male couple of Detective/Criminal, the female actor of *The Bridge* performs exactly this ambivalent game on which the constitution of gender is based. But the detective is under arrest. His/her gesture is suspended between the investigating detective Scottie and the passively re-acting figure of Madeleine. As Laura Mulvey states for trans-sex identification of women, the disguised actor "shifts restlessly in its borrowed transvestite clothes," implying that masculine behavior is as uncertain and constructed as feminine behavior. (Mulvey, 2009: 35) Although Mary Ann Doane and Stephen Heath insist on the "effectivity" of masquerade to create "a distance from the image" in order to destabilize old positions from within representation, they neglect the performative aspects of masquerade as a staged event within the socio-psychical game of gender construction. (Doane, 1982: 87; Heath, 1986: 59)

This performative dimension of role-playing is fully assumed in *The Bridge* where the movie actors' rehearsal of conventional sexual behavior is parroted and parodied at once by the photo model's reenactments. Certainly, the doubling of the masquerade in cinema by the masquerade in the staged photographs recalls Barthes' considerations on the film still as an image "doubled by another text, the film." (Barthes, 1977: 66, note 1) Yet in Burgin's theoretical and practical work of the 1980s this particular interest in the relation between still images and film is embedded in the attempt to outline a "psychopathology of everyday representations" within which masquerade appears as both a symptom and a destabilizing artifice of the ways gender roles are performed in a patriarchal society. (EAT: 113) Judith Butler describes gender as "an act that one performs, […] an act which has been rehearsed, much as a script survives the particular actors who make use of it, but which requires individual actors in order to be actualized and reproduced as reality once again." (Butler, 1988: 526) The way in which *The Bridge* performs gender differences through alternating masquerades exposes gender constitution as such a dynamic process of reenactment. But while the rehearsal of conventional gender roles reiterates and legitimates socially established meanings and identities, the ever-shifting masquerades of *The Bridge* deconstruct the very concept of a stable, fixed identity and invite the spectators to rethink their own role as actors within the theater of representation.

Chapter 4
Psychotopologies

4.1. The Discursive Spaces of Postmodernism

With its concerns of intertextuality, masquerade, shifting identities, and blending of vernacular culture and art history, *The Bridge* articulates Burgin's overarching project of a psychical realism in terms of critical theory *and* artistic practice. It is precisely in this period that Burgin intervenes in the controversial debates about postmodernism, feminism, and representation that emerged in the Western discourse on art around 1980. When Craig Owens, in his 1983 essay "The Discourse of Others: Feminists and Postmodernism," claimed to explore the "crossing of the feminist critique of patriarchy and the postmodernist critique of representation," this effort was perfectly in line with Burgin's work at the time. (Owens, 1983: 59) What Owens discerned as the "blind spot in our discussions of postmodernism in general: our failure to address the issue of sexual difference" (61), Burgin in fact addressed in his theoretical work as of 1982.[35] To this day, it is commonly held that Owens was one of the first to suggest the close affinities between postmodernism and feminism. (Wolff, 1990: 187)[36] Burgin's highly original and relevant considerations on the topic passed relatively unnoticed. But many of the characteristics and attitudes shared by feminism and critical postmodernism according to Owens are found in Burgin's theoretical and artistic work of the 1980s: the "simultaneous activity on multiple fronts" (i.e., art, critical writing and theory), the replacement of the *grand récits* of modernity by a multitude of discourses, the "deliberate *refusal* of mastery," and the investigation of "the social construction of masculinity." (Owens, 1983: 63-64; 68)

Beyond the significance of feminism, Burgin's multifaceted and critical stance toward postmodernism must be considered against the backdrop of a specific postmodernist discourse dating back to the late 1970s and informed by discourse analysis and poststructuralist criticism (Foucault, Barthes), as well as theories of the delegitimization of the master narratives (Lyotard) and simulacrum within late capitalism's media society of consumerism and the spectacle (Baudrillard, Jameson, Debord). Regarding his own artistic practice, Burgin adopted principles of pastiche, fragmentation, and reproduction in order to challenge Modernism's basic claims of autonomy and originality. At the same time, he kept back from so-called postmodernist art, in particular appropriationism (i.e., the work of Richard Prince, Sherrie Levine, and Cindy Sherman) and, in a more definite way, neo-expressionism and neo-geo as new tendencies in painting emerging in the early 1980s. Burgin took a decidedly critical stance vis-à-vis postmodernism. In various texts of the 1980s and 1990s, gathered in *The End of Art Theory. Criticism and Postmodernity* and *In/Different Spaces. Place and Memory in Visual Culture*, he cautions against the "trivialization of the idea of the 'postmodern'" while embracing Fredric Jameson's definition of the "postmodern" as an aesthetic and political *problematic* referring to heterogeneous contexts and discourses set against the historical and theoretical conditions of the "modern". (EAT: 163-164)

On the one hand, some major issues of postmodernist discourse—such as Lyotard's claims about the absence of master narratives of legitimation and the refusal of totality—are the critical bedrock on which Burgin built his conception of artistic practice as a continuous "*process of writing and revision*," foregrounding its own embeddedness within the social formation. (EAT: 180) Consequently, Burgin rejected radical left artists' claims of working outside the art institutions as romantic humanism, based on the values of autonomy and expressive individuality, precisely because the heterogeneity and the complexity of the art institution "offers no *singularity* which may be confronted from an unproblematic 'outside.'" (192) On the other hand, he strongly condemned the reaffirmation of conservative values of masculine mastery and the cult of the artist as genius, which he detected in the neo-expressionist large-scale painting promoted since around 1980 by the art market and blockbuster exhibitions such as *A New Spirit in Painting* (Royal Academy of London, 1981) and *Zeitgeist* (Martin Gropius Bau, Berlin, 1982).[37] Celebrated by its proponents as a massive counter-attack against abstract art, conceptualism, minimalism, and photographic empiricism (Rosenblum, 1982: 12), neo-expressionism was, in turn, denounced by left art historians and critics, such as Benjamin H. D. Buchloh, as a sign of growing authoritarianism in the Western world. (Buchloh, 1981: 40) In a similar way, Burgin linked this return of figurative representation to the reaffirmation of conservative values within the cultural and political situation in England, embodied—economically—by Saatchi and Saatchi and—politically—by Thatcherism. (EAT: 46) As we will see, Burgin's artistic practice of the mid-1980s reacted to this revival of painting by reintroducing painting not as absolute expressive value but as a signifier of a given historical and socio-cultural discursive situation. (EAT: 184) But unlike Buchloh, Burgin did not identify the return to representation within postmodernism as mere "pluralism of meanings and aesthetic masquerade." (Buchloh, 1981: 41) Postmodernism as an aesthetic, cultural, political phenomenon, he suggested, "comprises both tendencies for change and conservative tendencies." (EAT: 47)

In line with Hal Foster, Douglas Crimp and others (Foster, 1983: xii; Crimp, 1980: 91; Hopkins, 2000: 203), Burgin distinguished an apolitical, reactionary tendency of an anything-goes postmodernism, which transforms everything into pure signifiers of the spectacle of the capitalist commodity society, from a position which recognizes the ideological conditions of art at a particular historical conjuncture and provides a critical perspective on its underpinning socio-political processes and values. (EAT: 201-202) For a postmodern society, in which, according to Fredric Jameson, technologies of reproduction have replaced technologies of production (Jameson, 1984: 79), and in which representations circulate as pure simulacra "in an uninterrupted circuit without reference or circumference" (Baudrillard, 1994: 6; see also EAT: 170), this means that painting, as much as any form of art, cannot be confined to a supposedly specific aesthetic or institutional discourse. It rather has to be approached, as Burgin suggests in the final lines of *The End of Art Theory*, "across the broader spectrum of what I have called elsewhere the 'integrated specular regime' of our 'mass-media' society." (EAT: 204)

If Burgin denounced neo-expressionism's regressive return to romantic values of autonomy, authorship, and individuality (EAT: 35), he did not reject painting all at once (as Burgin himself and other conceptual and post-conceptualist artists did in the late 1960s and the 1970s). His answer to neo-expressionism rather consisted of the reintegration of painting in his art since the mid-1980s. As we have seen, this is already the case in *Olympia*, *The Bridge* and *Portia*, where fragments of paintings are woven into a heterogeneous network of verbal and visual signs in order to constitute a dream-like intertext of associations and cross-references. In terms of an engagement with the discursive formation and the artistic tendencies of postmodernism, *Office at Night* certainly marks a turning point in Burgin's work of the mid-1980s. For this reason, this chapter will start with an analysis of *Office at Night* as a reaction to the heterogeneous and often controversial discourses of painting, feminism, and postmodernism.

Around 1986, "space" became the fundamental category in Burgin's writing and artistic practice. Drawing on Jameson's idea that in postmodern times daily life would be "dominated by categories of space rather than by categories of time" (Jameson, 1984: 64), Burgin increasingly focused on the relation between "Psychical Space and Postmodernism"—as is the title of a paper published in 1987[38]—in its multiple dimensions including historical, geometrical, socio-political, and urban aspects, as well as the hyperspace of television and other media. Space and technology became the crucial issues right when he was about to leave the UK for the United States, first to do a residency at the Massachusetts Institute of Technology in 1986 and next, more definitively, in 1988 when he was appointed a professor of Art History at the University of California, Santa Cruz. (Magnani, 1989: 121) For Burgin, the development of cable and satellite television in the 1970s and the introduction of the personal computer in the early 1980s did not pass unnoticed. During his residency at MIT in 1986, he began to use computer-generated images to reflect on the social, perceptual, and psychological consequences of the new global time-space of television. (PT: 109)[39] The main part of this chapter will discuss how Burgin explored the new social, political, and psychological implications and dynamics of the postmodern "fold-over spaces of information technologies." (IDS: 44) Springing from a feeling of "being inside a new space today" (Lewis, 1987/88: 63), he started focusing his psychical realism on refashioning Daumier's demand for contemporaneity ("Il faut être de son temps"), described by Linda Nochlin as "one of the central issues, if not the very crux, of nineteenth-century Realism." (Nochlin, 1971: 103)

4.2. Epistemophilia

Conceived by Burgin as a "*re*-viewing of art through a prism of contemporary concerns" (BN: 182), *Office at Night* (1985-86) subscribes to Daumier's imperative by engaging with postmodern concerns and discourses in many ways, including feminist deconstruction of gender roles, questions of communication and technology, and recent debates on the revival of painting. (Fig. 4.1.-4.2. and Plates 3 + 4) Constituted of seven parts and a context panel, the series takes its departure from Edward Hopper's famous eponymous painting of 1940. In the Hopper, we see a secretary standing at a file cabinet while dropping her gaze toward an indeterminable point somewhere between the sheet of paper lying on the ground and her boss sitting at his desk. Her body is twisted into an anatomically impossible torsion. She turns both chest and buttocks to the spectator provoking thus an erotic and voyeuristic tension that seems to be completely ignored by the man apparently absorbed by the document he is holding in his hands. While *she* represents sexual desire, *he* stands for the law. In a feminist reading of the painting, the scene expresses the patriarchal order according to which woman is defined by her erotic, seductive body: *she* becomes an object of voyeurism, while *he* is associated with intellectual activity and moral superiority.

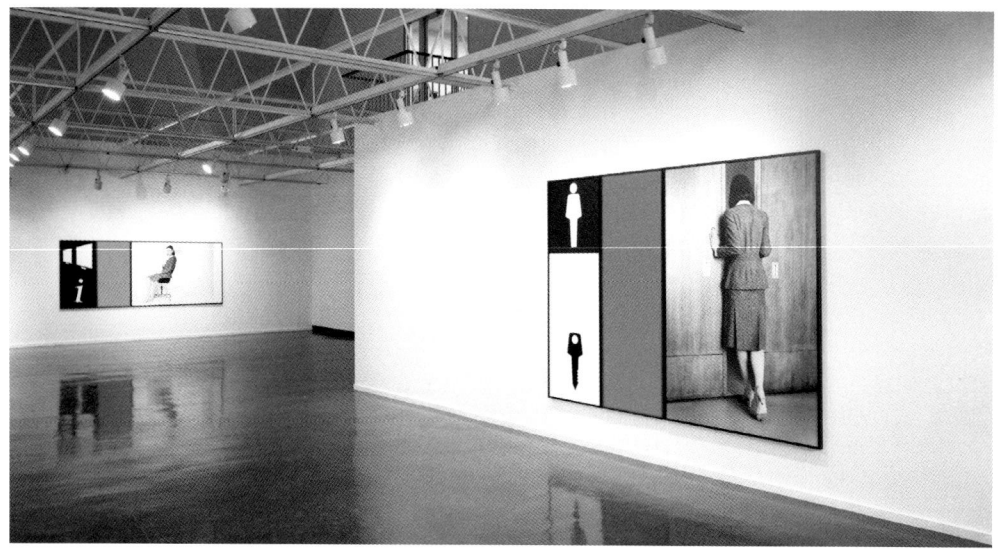

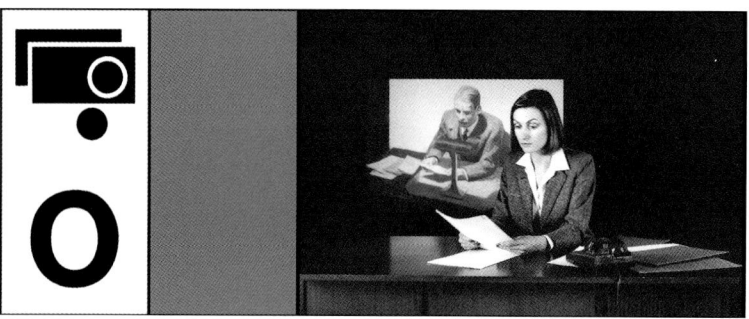

Figure 4.1.
Office at Night, 1985–86.
7 parts, each
183/122×244/305 cm,
+ text panel. Installation
view, The Renaissance
Society, Chicago, 1986.

Figure 4.2.
Office at Night, 1985–86.
122x305 cm.

In Burgin's series, this "mise-en-scène of the conflict of 'Desire' and the 'Law'" (BN: 182) is visually commented and deconstructed by a female model, who appears across the seven panels in different positions, once posing as the secretary, once imitating the activity of the boss. Neither her clothing nor her behavior and gaze are seductive. She rather seems to rehearse these different gestures as if they would belong to a conventional system of signs which determines human behaviors, actions, and perceptions. Borrowing Judith Butler's idea of gender as performance, Nicolas Mirzoeff recently described the postmodern artist as someone who replaces the modern propensity for the once-for-all of the event by the logic of the performance that can be done over and over again. (Mirzoeff, 2016: 49) But instead of endlessly performing the same exercise of gender roles as suggested in the Hopper, the woman introduces variations and changes roles, thus marking the traditional social roles of woman *and* man as unsteady.

The pictograms on the left part seem to confirm this interpretation. As may be deduced from the text panel, they refer to Otto Neurath's Isotype, a set of standardized pictorial signs designed to facilitate education and international communication. While Neurath's utopian aim was to achieve social betterment by direct, unambiguous communication beyond class and national borders, it is undeniable that the very principles on which the Isotype is based—standardization, repetition, and efficiency—are also those of industrialized capitalism.[40] The context panel's laconic remark that the Isotype movement failed to solve the problem of how to "design a pictogram which says neither 'man' nor 'woman' but simply *person*" reveals the Isotype's failure to address "the particular problem of the organization of sexuality *within* capitalism [...][and] *for* capitalism" precisely because it is part of that problem. (BN: 183) As a consequence, the pictograms in *Office at Night* deny easy comprehension, they have no fixed meanings but constantly shift from one semantic level to another: from a cinema visitor watching his likeness on the screen to a box which connects the visual symbols with the filing cabinet drawer opened by the woman in the photograph; from the sign for "man" to a key that might have served the photographed woman to open a sliding door; or, finally, from an eye which could also be interpreted as the telephone mouthpiece—together representing "vision and audition, voyeurism and eavesdropping" —to void brackets referring, in the photograph, to the woman's gesture "of 'bracketing out' the person on the other end of the line." (Burgin, 2005)

As the pictograms are relieved from their semantic confinement, so is the woman in the photographs who leaves the fixed position of the painting and begins to walk around in the virtual space of the office. These processes of semantic and physical displacement are analogous to the psychological conception of the work as a daydream in which the woman, instead of being a passive bearer of the look becomes an active performer of visual re-presentation:

> In terms of working with this image, I decided to adopt a methodology derived from reading Freud, to daydream [...] and my daydream was that this woman becomes freed from the paint which pins her in place, and she progressively occupies the space of the office: she is free to move; she is no longer simply there to be looked at, but she also acts. (Burgin, 1988a, 8)

Burgin aims to overcome the division into male activity and female passivity by attributing both characteristics—active and passive—to the woman. Retrospectively Burgin states: "My aim was to transform the role of the woman from *object* of curiosity to that of *subject* of curiosity—to transform showing into knowing, *exhibitionism* into *epistemophilia*." (Burgin, 2005) Consequently, the woman's gestures are not directed at the spectator but perform self-conscious acts of knowledge, recognition, communication, and emancipation (writing a note, reading the papers in place of her boss, pointing at herself, holding a telephone receiver while covering the mouthpiece, leaving by passing through a door, turning her back to the spectator).

This *epistemophilic* act of deconstructing the image-of-woman-as-fetish goes hand in hand with another attempt at demystification concerned with the fetishistic status of the artwork in the course of the "massive *revivalism* of painting." (EAT: 45) While the quotation of the Hopper painting refers to a historical stance of realism in modern art, the color panels occupying the center of the three-part tableaux are more ambiguous. On an emotional level, they add an expressive value to the two black and white panels, the photographs and the pictograms. On a formal level, they quote both the modernist tradition of monochrome painting and neo-geo, a neo-conceptualist tendency *en vogue* at the time in New York's intellectual art scene. Inspired by postmodern theories of the simulacrum, artists such as Peter Halley quoted modern geometric abstraction in order to criticize the standardization of modern life. Halley's *Two Cells with Conduit and Underground Chamber* (1983) represents, in the artist's own words, "the simulated space of the videogame, of the microchip, and of the office tower." (Halley, 1984: 114) Burgin's problem with this kind of postmodern simulationalism is that the paintings, when hung on the gallery wall, would be indistinguishable from self-contained modernist abstraction. Highly decorative and disconnected from their theoretical discourse, they just would become another commodity fetish of the art market. (Burgin, 1988b: 111) As in Freud's description of the fetish, Burgin argues, the value of this kind of paintings reposes on their "*pure presence*" as irreducible, unique objects inscribing themselves in the patriarchal symbolic order of capitalism. (EAT: 43-44)

Still, Burgin's own huge tableau-like framed images, destined to be displayed in the gallery, are hardly immune to the art market mechanisms. To address the expectations of the gallery visitor, then, one also has to pay tribute, to some extent, to the gallery itself as an institutional and commercial structure that is subject to the laws of capitalism. Burgin's way of dealing with this conundrum is not to withdraw from the art system, but to integrate reflexivity and hybridity into his art as critical means to avoid easy appropriation. For this reason, he contrasts the monochrome surface—as the ultimate incarnation of modernism—with an alternative modern painting style in the guise of Hopper's cool figurative realism, while also confronting both with other means of representation such as photographs and pictograms. Included in a larger constellation of different media and symbol systems (verbal language, pictogram, photography, projection, cinema, etc.) the monochrome panels become, as Tony Godfrey put it, "part of an investigation into the nature of coding." (Godfrey, 1986: 17) As for the pictograms, they operate as a kind of hieroglyphs, lingering on the threshold between verbal and visual signs, suggesting thus that a critical reflection on the image of women can never be confined to a specific medium such as cinema, advertising, or painting. As different as the intentional and the institutional conditions of these images might be, they all belong to the same cultural and ideological formation: "The relation to the woman […] is inescapably a relation to the image—and one overdetermined by a cultural history." (Lewis, 1987/88: 65)

In this respect, Burgin's approach has also to be distinguished from appropriation art and the accompanying discourse of the "photographic activity of postmodernism." (Crimp, 1980) In his widely noticed 1979 essay "Pictures," Douglas Crimp discussed works of artists such as Jack Goldstein, Sherrie Levine, Cindy Sherman, and Robert Longo, who later became generally known as Pictures Generation, in terms of a radical break with modernist ideas of medium specificity and formal autonomy. In contrast to the self-referential formalism of modernist art, Crimp defines postmodernist art—echoing Barthes' idea of the text as "a tissue of signs" (Barthes, 1977: 147)—as "stratigraphic activity" in which "processes of quotation, excerptation, framing, and staging" are employed to uncover the character of representation as a layering of pictures referring always to another picture without coming to rest at an alleged origin. (Crimp, 1979: 87) If Crimp further describes Sherman's *Untitled Film Stills* (1977-1980) as staged photographs unfolding a "fictional narrative" (80), this seems perfectly in accordance with Burgin's definition of representation:

> [O]ur self-image, and the images we have of others, are always to some degree *fictional*. The word "fiction" here may bring with it such notions as "narrative" and "staging," a vocabulary of *representation* which is entirely appropriate to the field of human actions. (EAT: 40)

In his essay "The Photographic Activity of Postmodernism," Crimp argues that Sherrie Levine's and Richard Prince's re-photographed photographs and Cindy Sherman's staged film scenes are based on a "discontinuous series of representations, copies, fakes […] severed from an origin, from an originator, from authenticity." (Crimp, 1980: 99-100) These artists would thus subvert the recuperation of an aura for photography undertaken in the course of the medium's discovery by modernist art history and museology, concerned with connoisseurship and the uniqueness of the art object. (97) Like Crimp, Rosalind Krauss insists on the fact that the notions of copy and mechanical reproducibility are essential features of photography, highlighted by these postmodernist artists in order to "explode the unities of art." (Krauss, 1984: 63) In Sherman's work, Krauss argues, the concatenation of stereotypes derived from Hollywood cinema, TV soap operas, and advertising coincides with the medium's position as simulacrum, as false copy, which, instead of constituting an essential connection to the represented object, endlessly reproduces and multiplies itself. Krauss concludes that in Sherman's work the photographic discourse of the simulacrum operates as a critic of the "myths of creativity and artistic vision." (68)

Although Burgin concurs with Crimp and Krauss concerning photography's important role for the articulation of an artistic project that resists the ideas of originality and connoisseurship, his interest in the medium lies less in its ontological status, as means of reproduction and multiplication, than in its function within the contemporary "specular regime" in which it constitutes, together with other media, a phantasmagoric, hallucinatory space of representation. (EAT: 37) Insisting early on that the meaning of a photograph emerges only in interaction with other media, and never in isolation, Burgin's position is, in this concern, more in accordance with Martha Rosler's critique of Sherrie Levine's photographs of well-known photographs. (Rosler, 2004: 140) Simple quotation without contextualization, Rosler suggests, is insufficient for a critical strategy, precisely because "there is no production than the production of images." Consequently, the photograph is nothing but a surface of projections without offering an alternative critical position. (Rosler, 2004: 142)[41]

Considering finally the way in which the panels are hung, it becomes clear that *Office at Night* is anything but an accumulation of individual paintings or photographs. Arranged panoramically across the four walls of the gallery space, the seven parts constitute "a single visual field" with the text at the entrance being "a caption to that totality." (Lewis, 1987/88: 57) Yet, the installed work does not offer the illusion of a coherent, immersive space into which the spectator can plunge. Similar to *The Bridge*, the elements of *Office at Night* are scattered through the space, inviting the spectator to establish connections between the fictional content of the staged photographs and "the literal space in which the viewer confronts the image." (65) This is precisely what psychical realism is about: exploring the boundaries between physical and psychical space within contemporary time-space where different forms of representation clash and are renegotiated simultaneously: the discourse on art, feminism, and the media environment. Against the fetishism of presence, a critical postmodernism would then consist in recognizing, intervening within, realigning, reorganizing, these networks of differences in which the very definition of "art" and what it *represents* is constituted: the glimpse it allowed us of the possibility of the absence of "presence," and the possibility of *change*. (EAT: 48)

4.3. Psychical Space and Postmodernism

In the second half of the 1980s space became *the* crucial issue in Burgin's theoretical and artistic work. The three panel piece *Danaïdes/Dames*, produced in 1986 during a residency at the Massachusetts Institute of Technology, may be understood as a reflection on the radical change from a Euclidean perspective to the "fold-over spaces of information technology." (IDS: 44) In "Geometry and Abjection," of which a first draft was published under the title "Psychical Space and Postmodernism" in the catalogue of the exhibition *The British Edge* in the summer of 1987, Burgin explores the role of psychical reality within the fluctuating spaces of postmodernism. But before addressing the question of how these shifts from the "modern" to the "postmodern" are articulated in the light of the concept of "psychical space," it is useful to begin with a description of the piece.

Danaïdes/Dames is composed of three components, including text, pictograms, a photograph, and colors. (Plate 5) The text of the context panel provides a brief and condensed summary of the images and contexts to which the piece refers: as a local reference, the work is inspired by the mural by John Singer Sargent, *The Danaïdes* (1916-1924), in the Boston Museum of Fine Arts. The blue and yellow color panel hints at the basic colors which Sargent used for the background of his grisaille painting. The women in the painting, pouring water from their urns into a huge amphora placed in the center, are ascending and descending the steps in an endless procession resembling, as the context panel states, "each other so closely they might be considered the same woman at successive moments in time." Obviously, Burgin here alludes to Muybridge's photographic studies of motion. Burgin further links the performance of the Danaids to Busby Berkeley's movies of the 1930s, in which the women of the chorus line "circulate in the kaleidoscopic image of one woman become many." When choosing the women for his films, the context panel reveals, Berkeley selected them "'like pearls'; measuring each against a grid where each body must inscribe itself perfectly. With Vitruvian precision, the men fit their women into compositions in grisaille." In fact, the central panel represents a reenactment of Leonardo da Vinci's Vitruvian man. But while Leonardo depicts a male body, solidly anchored within the geometrical coordinates of a circle and a square, as the principal source of architectural order, Burgin's female version falls out of the frame. Reminiscent of Berkeley's chorus lines, the woman seems to rehearse gymnastic exercises in order to prepare for a performance. But she is not one of many, nor is she performing for an audience as erotic spectacle; turning away from the spectator, she is rather acting in her own right. Even though her spread-out arms remind one of Vitruvian man, the woman resists further integration into the perfect harmony of geometrical space. Within the circular and rectangular frames of the picture her body is decentered, and, if we acknowledge the fact that her position is slightly distanced from the foreground, she would not even fit into the frame according to the law of perspective. The isotypes on the left side of the panel also challenge perspective and geometrical space. As pointed out by Burgin in an interview with Jon Bird, the wave is inspired by a contemporary Japanese warning sign from a beach. Moreover, as added by Bird, in an art context it also evokes, of course, Hokusai's famous print. (Bird, 1988: 27) In this regard, it is not irrelevant that Hokusai's delineation of space with color and line defied classical perspective, and, consequently, was highly influential for Modernism's path toward abstraction. If Vitruvian man and the wave respectively stand for early modern one-point perspective and the flat space of Modernism, the triangular shape below, echoing the Greek initial Delta, hints at the name of the Danaids. It further constitutes an ambivalent form, endlessly turning the inside out and the outside in, like a Möbius strip or a torus. (29)

The reference to Muybridge is here of particular interest. As Tom Gunning put it, Muybridge's photographic studies on animal and human locomotion rely on a concept of space and time as "unified, standardized and measurable" entities, which underpins modern scientific, economic, and industrial mastery and efficiency. (Gunning, 2007: 21) In "Geometry and Abjection," Burgin situates the origin of this calculated modern space in the invention of perspective in the Renaissance, when Euclidian geometry and optics were combined in order to objectify and dominate space by a sovereign gaze, which places the observer at the center of the world. This gaze, Burgin argues, is also that of mercantile capitalism and entrepreneurship, which subjects the world to the perspective of the economically and politically acting subject. (IDS: 42) While the Vitruvian man epitomizes this new homocentric order, Muybridge's chronophotography, in turn, stands for the way how, in the modern era of industrialization and scientific management, the human body navigates within a space of calculation determined by mechanical repetition and technological apparatuses:

> His images of the nude human body framed within a geometrically regular grid capture the transformations of modern

life brought on by technological change and the new space/time they inaugurated, as naked flesh moves within a hard-edged, rational framework. (Gunning, 2007: 21)

In the "postmodern space of our 'changing places'" (IDS: 56) both frames of reference involving a calculated space are out of synch. The cover image of *In/Different Spaces* gives a perfect illustration of the falling apart of fixed spatial coordinates and references. Against the backdrop of a square grid, a man, suspended in space, is falling seemingly without end or ground. The image stems from the series *The Four Seasons* (1994), consisting of four diptychs, each of which juxtaposes a photograph of a modern concrete highway bridge with a male or female body inscribed in a regular grid. (Plate 6) While the human figures and the background color of the right panels change, the left panels are identical, except the German word printed on the photograph, indicating each time a different season. The cyclical time of the seasons, representing nature, is here washed away by the monotone, ever-same repetition of modern space, which, in turn, has ceased to provide a stable framework for human agency and interaction.

In *Danaïdes/Dames*, the debris of the modern universe of calculation are differently rearranged. The woman does not fit into the geometrical space of perspective, nor does she integrate the abstract grid of Muybridge's calculated space. Instead, she is acting for herself within an indefinable place where different representational signs and spaces collide and coexist. In "Geometry and Abjection," Burgin describes this kind of multi-representational space as a postmodern process of spatial and temporal disintegration induced by technologies of electronic communication and, economically, the tendency of multinational capitalism. The visual heterogeneity, encountered within the public and the private sphere, due to new media technologies such as electronic billboards and satellite television, entails that, phenomenologically, space is "apprehended as 'folding back' upon itself. Spaces once conceived of as separated, segregated, now overlap." (IDS: 44) This is precisely what happens in *Danaïdes/Dames*, in which such "fold-over spaces" are the result of digital image processing. As pointed out by Burgin on various occasions, the decision to replace the camera by the computer for the image production is directly related to the capacity of digitalization to bring "everything onto a common ground"—actually perceived and remembered images, visual and verbal signs:

> At any moment during the day, what I'm actually seeing can be overlaid by recollection and anticipation of other images, from other moments. The computer allows me to construct analogues of the way these image-fragments—Freud used the expression

> "the day's residues"—work together in the mind. The virtual
> space of the computer screen comes to represent the psychical
> space of mental processes such as fantasy and memory. (PT: 106)

The computer, then, is not just a means to create images *of* the world;
it is rather both a technology of image production and a metaphor for
the complex process of image formation in the mind, including fantasies, memories, and actual perceptions of the physical world. The
parallel between this intertwining of physical "real" space and "virtual"
psychical space in perception and the way in which digital technologies re-structure the postmodern space of representation is at the very
heart of Burgin's concept of a psychical realism. In this respect, it is
of utmost significance that the Delta-initial in the lower right corner
of the central panel resembles a Möbius strip because of its self-contained shape and the undecidedness of its surfaces, oscillating between
inside and outside. In "Geometry and Abjection," Burgin refers to the
topological models of the Möbius strip, the Klein bottle and the torus,
which Jacques Lacan used in the *Séminaire IX, L'indentification* (1961-
1962) in order to illustrate how in the postmodern media environment
modern binaries such as inside/outside, representation/reality, subject/
object, private/public, and interior/exterior increasingly get blurred.

According to Lacan, the lack of an origin and the interchangeability
of outside and inside in such topological models represent the inter-
connectedness of "exterior" conscious speech and "interior" unconscious wishes. (Arrigo, 2004: 159) The torus further illustrates the
function of the desiring subject: As the torus' center of gravity lies outside of its volume in its central void, as it were, it is decentered, like the
subject incapable of satisfying desire within the self and has to search
for it elsewhere. Comparable to the continuous, endless circling along
the surface of a torus, the subject responds to repeated demands of
the self by accomplishing successive rotations around its axis of desire.
Just as the empty center of the torus can only be filled by another torus, the desire of the subject depends dialectically on the demand of
the Other, and vice versa. (Dor, 1996: 110-113) Relating these ideas of
a space without boundaries and clear separations to the challenge of
the postmodern fold-over spaces of electronic media and global financial capitalism, Burgin insists on the urgency of considering psychical
reality as a determining factor for a critical reflection of the ways in
which representations are disseminated and perceived today. Beyond
a critical analysis of the given situation, he further stresses the importance to understand "the changing geometries of our changing places"
(IDS: 56) as an opportunity to overcome the dominant modern model
of representation of the cone of vision, which, based on the subject/
object division, lies at the political and economic bottom of patriarchal

Western societies. Instead of embracing the unreflecting pluralist attitude of anything goes-postmodernism and unfettered economic liberalism, a critical postmodernist position would then be to reconsider what has been repressed or foreclosed from the modern space of representation: the pre-Oedipal "borderless space of the body in fragments," the "abject body," which threatens the clean and proper space of Euclidian geometry and therefore makes it susceptible for all kinds of repressions against what does not fit into it, such as minorities and immigrants. (IDS: 129-131)

4.4. The Paranoiac Space of the City

The idea of defining the subject in terms of its dialectical concatenation with the Other resurfaces in the works *Park Edge* (1987) and *Minnesota Abstract* (1989), in which Burgin addresses the conflicting relationship between the city and the body within postmodern geographies. (Fig. 4.3.) About *Park Edge*, a commission for the Bicentennial of Adelaide, Burgin said: "I wanted to articulate two ideas: the idea of the city as formed in relation to its other, and the idea of the city as a projection of the body." (Batchen, 1989: 9) In this remark, of course, we can easily identify the crucial ideas of "Geometry and Abjection," which Burgin recently finished when he made the work. This time, however, the focus lies less on the general relations between body, geometry, and

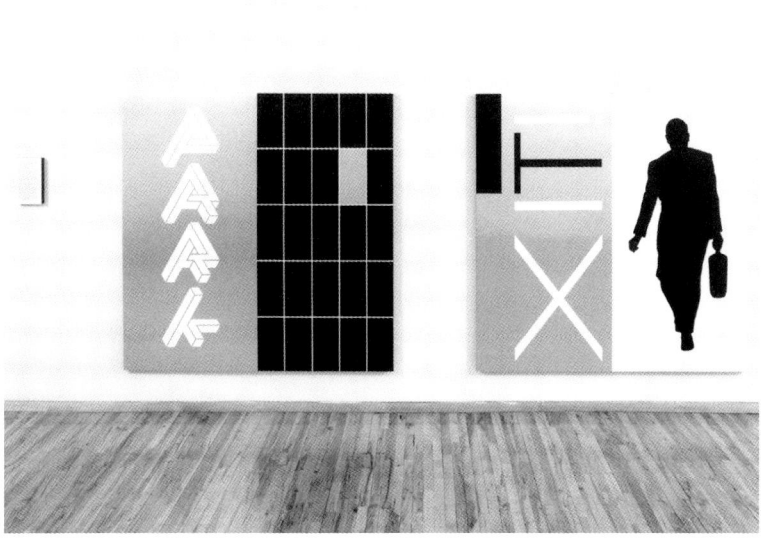

Figure 4.3.

Park Edge, 1987.

Diptych and text panel. Each 180×180 cm. Installation view, John Weber Gallery, New York, 1989.

postmodern space, but on the city as a sort of "psych-architecture" in which "psychic structures and urban structures are continuous." (9) Burgin borrows this idea from the comic figure "Captain Light," who shares his name with the man who designed Adelaide two hundred years ago as a square grid bounded by a park. The text panel, as the first part of a triptych, relates this "Metropolis in Arcadia" to complex histories and discourses of boundaries: Freud's psychanalytic account of the paranoiac subject caught in his delusions, the geographical boundaries of Australia, the frames of landscape painting, various techniques and applications of profile-tracing, and, finally, the walled city-state as projection of an imaginary body. These different principles of separating the inside from the outside, the subject from the Other, are scattered across the two visual panels where they appear as discontinuous fragments which—literally and symbolically—have lost their frames of reference. They become ambiguous. In the second panel, the letters of the word "park" consist of white stripes which progressively evolve into tridimensional reversible figures. Like the Möbius strip or the torus, they are irresolutely suspended between inside and outside, foreground and background. Adjunct to the rectangular field containing the word "park," a regular grid composed of black rectangles represents the abstract schema of the city of Adelaide. But instead of bounding the walled city-state as its arcadian counterpart, it intrudes into the urban fabric. Rosalind Krauss suggested that the very basis of modern art is the "flattened, geometricized, ordered" structure of the grid, which categorically declines all naturalist, mimetic and realist tendencies alike. (Krauss, 1979: 50) Here the rational of the grid, as founding structure of both modern urbanism and modernist painting, is threatened from inside.

The third panel is also split in two parts, the left one of which contains the letters "xit," vertically arranged, followed by an exclamation mark. Reading "exit," the word may be related to the silhouette of a business man on the righthand side. But because of the flattening effect of the cutout technique, it remains unclear if he is turning his back to the spectator (in this case the picture would be the exit *from* reality), or if he's about to leave the pictorial space, heading toward the exit *to* reality. In either case he is lingering on the threshold between pictorial and real space, undecided on where to put his business suitcase. If we interpret the white rectangle in the grid of the second panel as a void to be filled with the business man as an underwriter of the flowering economy of Western capitalism, a double conclusion can be drawn: on the one hand, the silhouette refers to the anonymous, faceless menace of global capitalism; on the other hand, it may also be encountered as a go-between operating at the interstice between pictorial and real space, thus serving as a mirror for the spectator.

The "X" of the panel's left part sustains this interpretation if we read it as a cross. In the accompanying text, Burgin refers to the biological term "chiasm" as "crossing over of two physiological structures" before highlighting that the cross as a figure composed of two reflecting right-angles also evokes "chiasmus"—"the rhetorical term for the trope of 'mirroring.'" This passage can also be found in "Geometry and Abjection," where it appears in the context of Lacan's discussion of the constitution of the subject during the mirror stage when the infant recognizes "its own image as such in a mirror." (Lacan, 2006: 94) Burgin is most interested in the ambivalence of this process of identification with the reflected image, which also implies self-alienation, for in the mirror the infant recognizes itself as other. (IDS: 49) Lacan further describes the mirror stage as a drama, during which the "subject caught up in the lure of spatial identification, turns out fantasies that proceed from a fragmented image of the body to […] its totality." (Lacan, 2006: 78) This idea of a formerly "borderless space of the body in fragments" is taken up by Burgin in a later essay, "Paranoiac Space," where he argues that paranoiacs fail to differentiate themselves from others and hence experience external objects as if they "had invaded the subject." (IDS: 129) On a more general scale, this menace of a psychotic space of failing boundaries can be found in the paranoid nationalist and racist subject which, fearing being invaded by others, seeks "to take its place on the 'clean and proper' side of abjection." (131) Against this backdrop, "Park Edge" can be read as an allegory of paranoiac space because its visual and verbal fragments, rather than forming a totality, symbolize the disintegration of cultural, geographic, psychical, and economic boundaries within a society that is based on the paradox between globalization's free flowing capital across borders and the adherence to ideas of the national state and cultural supremacy.

Minnesota Abstract (1989) addresses more explicitly the problem of the oppression of ethnic and cultural minorities. (Plate 7) Following an invitation to make a work for the cities Minneapolis and St. Paul, Burgin wondered how, from a psychoanalytical stance, the repressed fact that both cities were founded on the expropriation of the indigenous peoples returns in the national and cultural imaginary. In the central panel of the work, the face of an Indian chief with the words "MUTUAL TRUST" printed across his eyes, is derived from logotypes of the *Mutual of Omaha*, the *Detroit Bank and Trust*, and *Continental Airlines*. (Burgin, 1990: 64) Condensing these three logos to one single image, Burgin reveals the contradiction that consists in the association of the deprived indigenous peoples with the fundamental values of a postindustrial, capitalist society: insurances, financial services, and unrestricted mobility. Burgin mentions two different, albeit related, local stories that largely influenced the making of the work. An article in the *Star Tribune* of Sunday July 23, headed "Historian finds names of Minnesota's forgotten Indians," relates the story of the relocation of the Chippewa Indians in the White Earth Reservation, created in 1867. As soon as agriculture began to prosper in this region, white settlers demanded to open it up to people from outside, with as a result that by 1982 only a small fraction of the land remained in trust. A similar destiny was about to be shared by the mainly native residents of a federally sponsored housing development project in the Twin Cities, which as a result of mismanagement was threatened to be transformed into a profitable investment opportunity. In this context, the words "mutual trust" take on quite an ambiguous undertone. Blinded by the financial trusts of the Western world (such as insurances and banks), the Indian is, quite literally, foreclosed from a relation of mutual trust and confidence.

Each of the two flanking panels depicts citations of distinctive buildings in the two cities. The word printed on the red panel evokes the more "colonial" style of the architecture of St. Paul, whereas the modernist shapes of the buildings in the blue Minneapolis panel are associated with "cubism." Taken together, the words "Colonial Cubism" constitute the title of a work by American artist Stuart Davis that hangs in the Walker Art Center in Minneapolis. In 1954, the year he painted *Colonial Cubism*, Davis wrote to his dealer Edith Halpert: "I am strictly a European (French, that is) man myself, although forced by birth and circumstances to live in the American Art Desert as exile." (Wilson, 1993: xii) If we add that the three colors of the panels evoke the French tricolor, and thus commemorate the Bicentennial of the Declaration of the Rights of Man, we get a dense net of references presenting the city as an aggregation or, in psychoanalytical terms, a condensation of unresolved and repressed political, social, and economic problems in American (and European) history related to issues of exile, colonialism, exclusion, oppression, and dispossession. This is the borderless paranoiac space of the city in fragments.

4.5. Third Space. The Interstitial Location of Culture

In this period, the connection of the construction of identity with postcolonial issues of nation, ethnicity, and race became increasingly important in Burgin's thinking. In a public conversation at the Institute of Contemporary Arts, London, in April 1991, Homi Bhabha defined Burgin's work as a "third space," an interstitial in-between space, which triggers a moment of surprise capable to interrupt and displace the established ideological order. While the ordinary function of representation consists in suturing the spectator's gaze into the narrative of the image, Burgin's intermediate spaces would interrupt that gaze, thus questioning "the notion of the private and the public." (PT: 96-97) The work from which Bhabha and Burgin departed in the discussion that followed was *Family Romance* of 1989. (Fig. 4.4.) The theme of family is all but new in Burgin's work. As discussed in Chapter 2, Burgin addressed the nuclear Western family as early as 1973, in his photo-text series *VI*, where he reveals that the values commonly associated with the family are not naturally given, but the ideological product of specific historical, social, and political conditions. In a similar vein, the small book *Family* of 1977 presents a short Marx-inspired history of the dissociation of the private from the public in the wake of industrialization and the concomitant transformation of the family into a support structure of the consumerist capitalist society. (Wollen, 2001: 24) (Fig. 4.5.)

While the private is outsourced from the production process, so the book ends, the family still reproduces the latter's very principals, most notably individual property and authoritarian hierarchies. Some of the pictures support this anti-ideological materialist discourse as they allude in a quite straightforward way to economic and national symbols and communication systems of capitalist societies (advertising poster, television, American flag, house as property). But although these textual and visual components, including the design in the form of an alphabet exercise book, seem to convey a didactical orientation, some pictures are intriguingly enigmatic. In particular the last photograph, showing the reflex of the artist's silhouette in a glass panel or a

Figure 4.4.

Family Romance, 1990.

5 Diptychs, Each panel 213,4 (91,4) x 91,4 (213,4). Installation view, John Weber Gallery, New York, 1990.

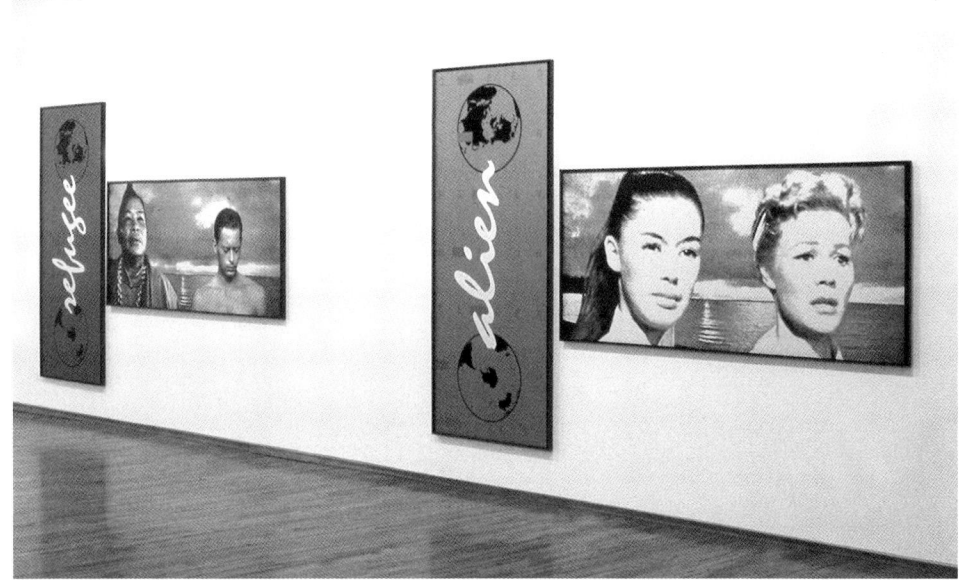

store window, troubles clear subject-object relations by superimposing the position of the artist/spectator outside the image with the photographed object inside the image. If we remind that Burgin, around this period, rejects Marxist-oriented theories of false consciousness as just another form of ideological positioning, it becomes clear that this photograph appears as a warning. Even though a critique of the existing ideological apparatuses (in the Althusserian sense) with the family as one of its most prominent expressions is urgently required, one should always remember that there is no outside of representation, and that it is from within representation—the photographer and the spectator being literally included in the image—that we have to operate if we want to overcome the vicious cycle of ideology and counter-ideology.

The "interrupted gaze" that Bhabha claims for Burgin's work can already be detected in this book from 1977, in which the interruption concerns both the ideological (capitalist) trained view and the counter-ideological (Marxist) one. *Family Romance* addresses this "interrupted gaze" at the family from a different angle. A first difference resides in the addition of a psychoanalytical stance. As the title suggests, Burgin's work is inspired by a 1909 published eponymous paper by Freud, which deals with the fantasy of children that their father and mother are not their actual parents. A second difference lies in the introduction of a postcolonial perspective, pertaining to questions of national identity, race, and sexuality within our contemporary media society. As will be argued, Burgin's work opens up onto what Bhabha described, in his book *Location of Culture*, as the hybrid and interstitial space of the postcolonial and the postmodern.

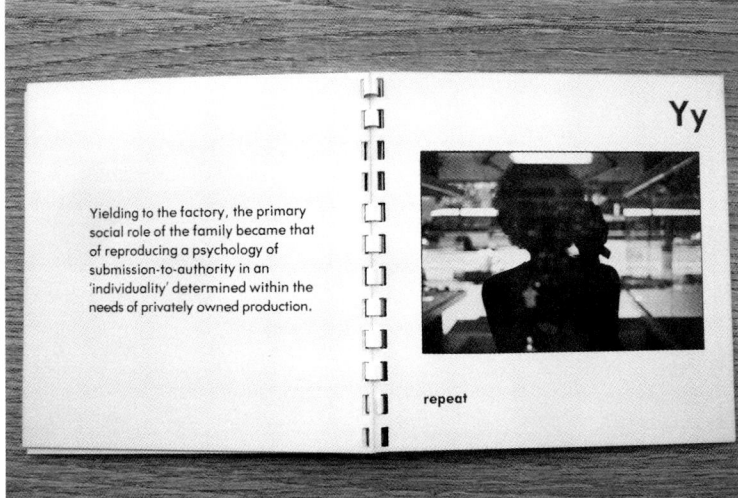

Figure 4.5.
Family, 1977.

The Work of Victor Burgin

Family Romance consists of five diptychs, each composed of two panels of equal dimension, a vertically arranged text panel and a horizontal panel showing two or three people in front of a sunset seascape. (Fig. 4.6.-4.7.) In the text panel, the words "Family Romance" appear vertically written, each letter corresponding to the initial letter of one of seven paragraphs which provide a complementary discourse in parallel with the work. To the right of the text, the same number of iconic symbols relate to concepts that are addressed, more or less explicitly, in the text: religion, education, globalization, industry, metropolis, military, justice. The sentence formed by the words intercalated between the paragraphs leaves no doubt about the reality degree of the images: "virtual scenes played between virtual characters in virtual spaces." Actually, the depicted scenes do not refer to situations as they happened in the real world but represent characters of the Hollywood movie *South Pacific*, which are removed from their narrative setting in the film before being reassembled on the computer. Neither photographic nor filmic recordings of reality, they are electronic revenants gathered in constellations as they never appear in the film and put in front of ever the same exotic background: a seascape with a sunrise or sunset, which is the very first image of *South Pacific*. This procedure entails a second fictionalization of the already fictional characters of the film who are now part of a completely virtual environment. But this new, virtual setting is not just a celebration of the Baudrillardian simulacrum as a free play of the sign detached from its referent. It encompasses rather the tacit space of the film's unconscious concerned with sexual, racial, and ethnic differences in the process of identity formation.

> What I've done, watching *South Pacific* unroll on the screen of my computer rather than on the cinema screen, is I've been able to disarticulate the film, inspired by the notion that the film has a manifest content, a manifest face—the public face of the film, turned towards us—but that there is always, escaping in that fleeting afterimage, the sense of something *which might* have taken place in the film. There is a "latent content," another film, other films, inscribed in the manifest film. (PT: 99)

The romantic musical film from 1958 presents two love stories on a South Pacific island during World War Two: one between an American nurse and an expatriate French plantation owner whom the woman rejects when she learns that his children are from a native Polynesian woman; and another between a girl of Vietnamese origin and a young Navy lieutenant who refuses marriage fearing the reaction of his conservative Philadelphia family. In both cases, the American protagonists overcome their racial prejudices and finally adhere to their feelings for

F reud's essay 'Family Romances' is about the fantasy that one's family is not one's real family. 'The commonest of these imaginative romances', he writes, is 'the replacement of both parents or of the father alone by grander people'. The family romance however is almost infinitely various: 'its many-sidedness and its great range of applicability enable it to meet every sort of requirement.'

virtual

A 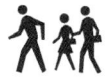 nostalgia for the relational world of earliest childhood is at the root of family romances. In the eyes of the child its parents are all-powerful. The 'grander people' apparently substituted for the father or mother in later fantasies are merely these same parents as they originally appeared to the child.

scenes

M aturity brings the knowledge that one's parents are not omnipotent. Their idealised images however are not abandoned but displaced. National leaders and other figures in positions of authority or caring may be unconsciously identified with the ideal parents. As such expressions as 'motherland' and 'fatherland' imply, nationalism itself is a beneficiary of feelings originally directed towards the parents.

I dentification with the perfect parents in an international arena underlies the 1955 photographic exhibition *The Family of Man*. Prevalent opinion in the US during the immediate post-war years saw the country as being in a tutelary position of benevolent authority towards the rest of the world. Appropriately, the particular version of 'the family' which this exhibition projected into every part of the globe was the domestic ideal of the Eisenhower years.

played

L overs (heterosexual), marriage-ceremonies, pregnancies and birth are the subjects of the large black-and-white photographs in the entrance to *The Family of Man* exhibit, and at the beginning of the exhibition catalogue. (The very first image, with a caption from the bible, is of a sunrise—or sunset—over an ocean.) A common biology is offered as guaranteeing what the curator's introduction calls 'the essential oneness of mankind throughout the world'.

between

Y  et another variation on the family romance might be seen in *The Family of Man* exhibition, one rooted in earliest experience. The infant does not initially distinguish itself from its (m)other, the difference has to be learned. Failure to adequately separate self from other may result in others being seen merely as a more or less disguised reflection of oneself. In the ensuing misrecognition an erroneous 'understanding' takes the place of *tolerance* of an unbridgeable difference.

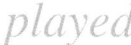

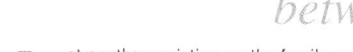

Figure 4.6. *Family Romance*, 1990. Text panel.

Rodgers and Hammerstein based their Broadway musical *South Pacific* on two romantic episodes from James Michener's book *Tales of the South Pacific*, in turn founded on Michener's experiences as a US officer on a 'French' Pacific island during World War II. Publicity for the 1958 20th Century Fox screen version of *South Pacific* emphasised its dual virtues as spectacle (it was shot using the TODD-AO wide-screen process) and as 'family entertainment'.

virtual

One story tells of the love between a young Navy nurse and a middle-aged French plantation-owner. She fears that her lack of sophistication will disqualify her from entry into his world, while he is afraid that she will prefer younger men to him. She rejects his proposal of marriage however only when she learns of his previous marriage to a native Polynesian woman. She subsequently overcomes her racial prejudice and accepts him and his children.

characters

Much the same problems of race and class differences within sexual relations trouble the other romance in *South Pacific*, that between a young Navy lieutenant and a native Polynesian girl. He—WASPy, wealthy and Ivy League—first rejects marriage to her, worrying how it would be received by his Philadelphia family. He later resolves to follow his heart, but dies in the course of a combat mission before he is able to tell her.

As was normal in the 1950s, *South Pacific*—like the *The Family of Man* exhibition—depicts sexual relations as purely biologically determined. Love is assumed to be exclusively heterosexual and to ineluctably issue in marriage and children. Historian John Diggins records, 'By 1957 an incredible 97 percent of Americans "of marriageable age" had taken the vows'. When Allen Ginsberg turned up in San Jose to continue a homosexual affair with Neal Cassady he was shown the door by Cassady's wife.

in

Nellie, the Navy nurse, says to Emile, the planter: 'I'll show you a picture of a Little Rock fugitive… I got this clipping from my mother today'. Emile reads aloud, 'Ensign Nellie Forbush, Arkansas' own Florence Nightingale…' The film of *South Pacific* appeared shortly after an actual image from Little Rock had appeared in newspapers world-wide. It shows fifteen-year old Elizabeth Eckford trying to enter Little Rock's Central High School. She is prevented from doing so by the Arkansas National Guard and a mob of jeering Whites.

virtual

Class identifications were never strong in the US. No history of feudalism had drawn clear distinctions between the masses and a ruling elite. Little of the US Socialism which had nevertheless developed into the1930s survived the Soviet invasion of Hungary in 1956. The Korean war—ostensibly a UN intervention but fought mainly at the instigation of, and by, the US—was a war against communism. Unsurprisingly, *South Pacific* was able to represent class conflict only in ethnic terms.

spaces

Ethnic, sexual and other forms of 'identity politics' were becoming the alternative to national party politics in the disunited states at the same time that ethnic rivalries were proving stronger than proletarian union in the soviet socialist republics. Throughout the world ethnic conflicts and solidarities alike nevertheless remained subordinate to nationalism. In spite of mutating distributions of ethnic populations within nations, increasing displacements of populations between nations, and space-contracting technologies, the fantasy of 'nation' remained the most powerful form of the family romance.

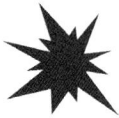

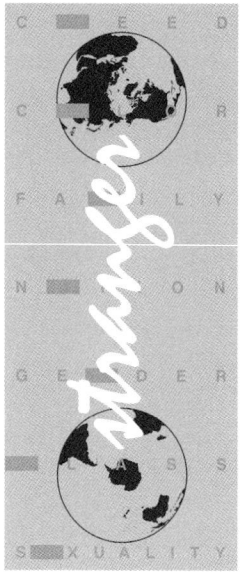
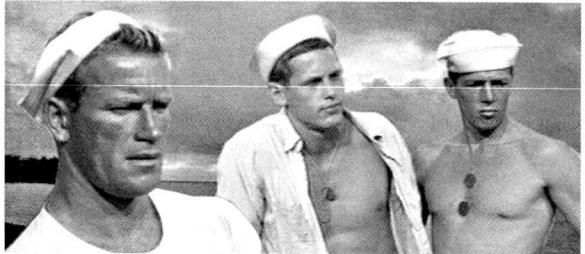

Figure 4.7.
Family Romance, 1990.

their beloved, even though the second love affair ends dramatically with the lieutenant's death. It is worth noting that the film is based on Rodgers and Hammerstein's homonymous musical from 1949, which has been celebrated for its tolerance and its universalist humanism in a time when State Representative David C. Jones declared that interracial marriage was a threat to the American way of life. (Most, 2000: 307) But while the film overtly addresses the problem of ethnic and racial difference, it fully acknowledges the role of the concepts of nation and family as fundamental issues in the constitution of identity. As Burgin observes in the context panel, *South Pacific* "depicts sexual relations as purely biologically determined" with marriage as its ultimate goal. In contrast, homosexuality is completely banned from the film, even though it returns as the repressed in the shape of the homoerotic cliché of the muscular sailor. (PT: 100) In Burgin's work, this homosexual subtext is emphasized by the penetrant appearance of half-naked Navy guys who, disconnected from their original environment in the musical, seem to pose like models in an erotic magazine.

In the vertical panels, the words "creed," "color," "family," "nation," "gender," "class," and "sexuality" indicate essential components of a "politics of identity" in sexual, ethnic, social, and religious terms. But as the blanked-out letters in the words suggest, forming together the "latent" word "romance," these concepts are unstable and incomplete. Finally, the idea of a unified identity is a fantasy, an illusion or a fiction that conceals the "postcolonial problematics" evoked in the vertically written words "refugee," stranger," "alien," "migrant," and "exile" (101). Of particular interest in this regard is Burgin's comparison of *South Pacific* with the exhibition *The Family of Man*, as well as his use of Freud's essay *Family Romance*, which gave the piece its title. Edward Steichen's photography exhibition *The Family of Man* was first shown in 1955 at the New York Museum of Modern Art, after which it travelled to countless locations throughout the world with the aim of celebrating the universal aspects of human life. As Steichen claims in his introduction to the catalogue, the exhibition "was conceived as a mirror of the universal elements and emotions in the everydayness of life—as a mirror of the essential oneness of mankind throughout the world." (Steichen, 2013: 3) This liberal humanist agenda was heavily criticized by left-wing intellectuals, most prominently by Roland Barthes who, as soon as 1957, cautioned against the myth of the human condition as a way to naturalize and to sentimentalize the institution of the family. (Barthes, 1991: 100-102) It is certainly no accident that a second wave of critique of *The Family of Man* emerged soon after Ronald Reagan became president of the US in January 1981, heralding the start of a new politics of neoliberalism and military strength. In early 1981 Allan Sekula wrote:

> Clearly both, the sexual and international politics of *The Family of Man* are especially interesting today, in light of the headlong return of American politics to the familialism and interventionism of a new cold war, both domestic and international in scope. *The Family of Man* is a virtual guidebook to the collapse of the political into the familial that so characterizes the dominant ideological discourse of the contemporary United States. (Sekula, 1981: 21)

And in 1982 Christopher Phillips added that the forms of the exhibition would reflect "the familiar mass-cultural mingling of popular entertainment and moral edification" in order to emphasize the "global patriarchical family proposed as utopia." (Phillips 1982: 46-48) Burgin shares this discomfort in the view of political developments in the 1980s when he situates the work, retrospectively, in "the horizon of expectations within which I was working at that time, some nine months before the Gulf War broke out." (PT: 98) In fact, two iconograms of the introduction panel, one representing a jet fighter and the other an explosion, seem to announce the US military intervention in Iraq starting in August 1990 under the codename *Operation Desert Shield*. In this particular political context, Burgin observes a new wave of conservative politics, coming along with a nostalgic return to traditional familial and national values of the 1950s, the period in which the US achieved cultural and political hegemony on a global scale. Consequently, Burgin conceived of *Family Romance* as "a restaging of some current issues in terms of fragments from the fifties." (Cottingham, 1991) *The Family of Man* and *South Pacific* are two major cultural spectacles of the 1950s in which the ideological and religious premises of Western society are celebrated, melting all kinds of racial, sexual, social, and cultural differences into one global humanism. In this regard, it is important to know that the sunset background, taken from *South Pacific*, refers to the first image of the *The Family of Man* catalogue, which represents a sunset captioned "U.S.A. Wynn Bullock" and is accompanied by the biblical words "And God said, let there be light (Genesis 1:3)." The sun, which is at the origin of the creation of the world, shines here for the glory of both, the US as the dominant nation bringing light to the civilized world, and photography as the medium using light for the constitution of Steichen's "mirror of the essential oneness of mankind throughout the world." (Steichen, 2013: 3)

In *Family Romance*, this blending of the supposedly universal nature of photography and the imaginary utopia of a global humanism is deconstructed by drawing on Freud's eponymous essay. According to Freud, the child or adolescent frequently develops the fantasy that his or her parents are not the real parents but that he or she is descended from grander people. This replacement of the parents by superior ones is rooted in the child's nostalgia for an earlier moment of his or her childhood when the parents were perceived as the most perfect and most noble people. (Freud, 1909/1959: 241) In his commentary on the work, Burgin compares this process of family romance with the idealization of the patriarchal authority within nationalism. According to him, *The Family of Man* exhibition projects the "identification with the perfect parents in an international arena," for it imposes a universal humanism that levels out all cultural and social differences in the name of Western liberalism.[42] In the image panels of *Family Romance*, this dream of a unified world under American supremacy is disintegrated in space and time.

The first panel, for example, unites Tokinese trader Bloody Mary and the young American lieutenant Cable, who has a love affair with Bloody Mary's daughter Liat before being killed in combat. (Plate 8) These two images are taken from two different scenes of the film, however. The Bloody Mary portrait is an inverted image of the scene in which Liat and Cable meet for the first time and fall in love, while the bust of the lieutenant stems from a scene some thirty minutes later when Cable meets Liat for the last time, confessing her that a marriage is impossible. The sun ray on the ocean marks not only the demarcation line between two different spatial locations and temporal moments in the film, but also the difference between love's bliss and separation, and, related to it, the ethnic and racial divide in American society. If in this context the word "refugee," written across the accompanying text panel, may well be associated with Bloody Mary's civil status because of her Tokinese origins, it may also suggest that, as long as our belief system is based on myths of the nation, there will always be those who are marginalized or excluded and who therefore have to seek refuge somewhere else.

Burgin himself links this problematic of exile and foreignness to the conditions of the work's production—its "site specificity." Initially created for an exhibition in Los Angeles, *Family Romance* reflects his own position as a "resident alien" in the US, as well as the sort of debates he was involved in at the University of California, Santa Cruz—situated on a hill overlooking the Pacific. This "psychogeographical" condition of exile is also addressed in Burgin's theoretical writing of that time. In "Paranoiac Space," Burgin denounces the commonly made opposition of "exile" / "nation" as a logic of exclusion/inclusion, subsequently embracing Julia Kristeva's definition of the "foreigner" as someone who confronts us with "the possibility […] of *being an other* […] of *being in his or her place.*" The foreigner, Kristeva continues, prefigures "the art of living in a modern era, the cosmopolitanism of the excoriated." (IDS: 119; Kristeva, 1988: 25) This violent image of the loss of one's skin as protective barrier between the self and the other reveals the painful insecurity in which the exiled, the alien, the refugee is living, being rejected as the other on one occasion and next being assimilated into the universal family of man by the humanizing discourse of neocolonialism. (Sekula, 1981: 21)

Burgin's suggestion is neither to build barriers between one's own space and the space of the other, nor to ignore the existence of differences, but to acknowledge the arduous process of coming to terms with these differences and renegotiating them in a constant dialogue: "to encounter the other in one's own space is to confront one's own alterity to that other's space." (PT: 119) This is the "in-between" space, the "interstice" position of the postcolonial perspective which, according to Homi Bhabha, articulates cultural difference as "overlap and displacement of domains of difference." (Bhabha, 2004: 2) In *Family Romance*, the in-between space of overlapping cultural (not biological) differences between man and woman, homosexuality and heterosexuality, Asian and Western societies and ethnicities, appears in the horizontal panels in the juxtaposition of various characters from *South Pacific*. In this way the present situation in the US is examined through the prism of historical events and images (American postwar society and 1950s' Hollywood cinema), which are reworked by means of recent computer technology. This corresponds to Bhabha's claim for an in-between art that "does not merely recall the past as a social cause or aesthetic precedent," but creates a "disjunctive temporality" that "innovates and interrupts the performance of the present." (Bhabha, 2004: 10) Bhabha further suggests that the spatial and temporal displacements within postcolonial culture can be described in terms of translation, for the location of cultural difference is never stable or definite but always involved in a constant process of negotiation and communication due to the fact that, as Walter Benjamin writes, in translation there is always an element that resists, that is not completely transferable or resoluble. (Bhabha, 2004: 321) What Bhabha writes about the time of translation applies also to Burgin's work:

> The "time" of translation consists in that *movement* of meaning, the principle and practice of a communication that, in the words of de Man "puts the original in motion to decanonise it, giving it the movement of fragmentation, a wandering of errance, a kind of permanent exile." (2004: 326)

Based on verbal and visual fragments which permanently respond, contradict, and redefine each other, *Family Romance* comments on and undermines hegemonic familial ideologies as they are represented in the visual culture of the 1950s, while also confronting them with a more recent nostalgia for the greatness of America as dominant political power in the world. Aside from the abovementioned temporal disjunction in the horizontal images and the tensions between the words of the vertical panels, the color adds another contradictory dimension. In *South Pacific*, Burgin remarks, the application of color gels on the camera lens served the cameraman, Leon Shamroy, to bathe an entire scene in an atmospheric color space, thus emphasizing the film's drama. Further, he observes that these colors would be typical of the color design of the 1950s as one can find it, for example, in advertising for domestic products. (PT: 107) By covering the vertical panels with similar hues, Burgin confronts a color palette of Western consumer society with a vocabulary of otherness, thus insisting on the disjunctive moments within postcolonial culture. If, as Marianne Hirsch put it, the family album and exhibits like *The Family of Man* foster "a conventional and monolithic familial gaze" that glosses over apparent contradictions and differences in order to situate "human subjects in the ideology, the mythology, of the family as institution" (Hirsch, 2012: 11), Victor Burgin counters this "familial gaze" with an "interrupted gaze," a gaze that disrupts the ideological narrative of the universal human family. In fact, the gazes of the disintegrated and then reassembled figures of the horizontal panels neither meet each other nor the gaze of the spectator: they look into the virtual void of the digital limbo of that era's globalizing media society.

4.6. Fiction Films

In 1991, during a stay in Paris, Burgin produced two works which, like *Family Romance*, are based on fragments of classical movies reassembled in the virtual space of the computer. Yet, other than *Family Romance*, *Portrait of Waldo Lydecker* and *Fiction Film* are concerned less with postcolonial discourse than with the situationist and surrealist concepts of *dérive*, chance, and *errance*. Burgin's involvement with Surrealism coincides with his increasing interest in the development of the postmodern city and the psychological implications of its experience. In his 1988 essay "Seiburealism," he describes the Seibu department store of Tokyo as "a work of surrealism in its postmodern phase."[43] As an assemblage of a variety of boutiques, restaurants, video game sales areas, travel agencies, and book departments, distributed across several floors without a visible, coherent logic, the Seibu *departo* would be, similar to the collective writing practices of the surrealists, "a work whose inexhaustible permutations are written 'automatically' by the flaneur," who navigates through this heteroclite consumerist environment in a state of distraction. (IDS: 115) In addition to defining the Seibu store as a conglomeration of different functional spaces, Burgin observes that the numerous projection screens and ambient videos, installed throughout the entire building, provoke an overlapping, or even a collapse, of virtual and real spaces, inside and outside, fiction and fact, present experience and past memories.[44] To describe how such a temple of consummation is experienced, he takes recourse to the Japanese concept of the act of reading—*tachiyomi*. As an opportunistic, desultory, and fragmentary way of reading "while on the move," *tachiyomi* would be comparable to André Breton's and Jacques Vaché's cinema-hopping in Nantes in which the two surrealists intended to visit as many movies as possible during a day without respecting the films' duration or paying attention to their narrative content. Burgin establishes an analogy between this Surrealist practice of *dérive* and the postmodern neo-capitalist space of consumerism and media technology when he argues that this is precisely how "today we switch TV channels" or how we perceive "cinema" outside the movie theatre (through advertising, magazines, television): "in a state of distraction." (IDS: 110; 165)

Like the daydream, this "state of distraction" is situated between conscious activity and unconscious processes. And it is exactly this borderline on which the Surrealists operated in order to develop their aesthetics of the marvelous and the enigmatic. As Burgin writes:

> The surrealists could not see what was "hidden in the forest" until they closed their eyes in order to imagine it; even then they could

not be sure, for there are other forests to negotiate, not least amongst these the "forest of signs" which is the unconscious. (IDS: 76)

Of course, Burgin alludes here to René Magritte's famous painting *La femme cachée* as it was reproduced in the twelfth and last issue of the surrealist journal *La Révolution surréaliste* (1929). The painting represents a female nude in the pose of a classical *Venus pudica*, framed by the sentence fragments "je ne vois pas la" (above) and "cachée dans la forêt" (below), becoming thus part of the minimal rebus "je ne vois pas la femme cachée dans la forêt." In the journal's reproduction, Magritte's painting is surrounded by the portraits of sixteen surrealists with their eyes closed (including Aragon, Breton, Buñuel, Dali, Éluard, Ernst, and Magritte himself). (*La Révolution surréaliste*, 1929: 73) This collage is inserted in an inquiry about love as the sole irreducible idea capable of reconciling all human beings with the idea of life. (65) In the same inquiry, Breton defines love as the only indispensable object which, normally hidden from the mind, should be approached with a child's sense of wonder to reveal itself as the great mystery it is. (71)

In "Chance Encounters," Burgin draws on psychoanalytical theories by Melanie Klein, Sándor Ferenczi, Sigmund Freud, and Paul Schilder in order to explain how the small child learns to differentiate between its inner world of affects and feelings and the symbolic order of the exterior world. According to Schilder, it is the space of the perception ego that determines our actions and orientations in the real world. As he argues: "We live our personal lives in relation to love objects, in our personal conflicts, and this is the space which is less systematized, in which the relations change, in which the emotions pull objects nearer and push them further away." (IDS: 98; Schilder 1935: 278) If this regressive space prevails, Schilder concludes, one enters the "space of magic," a schizophrenic space in which the identification of the self with object images suspends the capacity to distinguish between fantasy and external reality. Breton's exaltation of love's mystery may be understood as a longing for this fusional space of magic, which, for the "normal" adult, remains unfulfilled. In fact, in his novel *Nadja* (to which I will return below), Breton perhaps refers to Magritte's painting when he writes: "I have always, beyond belief, hoped to meet, at night and in a woods, a beautiful naked woman or rather, since such a wish once expressed means nothing, I regret, beyond belief, not having met her." (Breton, 1977: 39) Breton's failure to meet this woman is tied to the fact that she was a pure fantasy and to the fact that Breton, who was neither a small child nor a psychotic case, just could not identify with his object of desire. The same is true of his surrealist colleagues, one might add, given that all of them close their eyes in order to *dream* of this woman, which means, in turn, that they are not able to *see* her. The danger of this introspective adventure may well be comparable to what Melanie Klein described as the experience of the infant before he or she enters the symbolic order: "The early ego largely lacks cohesion, and a tendency towards integration alternates with a tendency towards disintegration, a falling in bits." (IDS: 99; Klein, 1986: 179) There could not be a better description of the collage reproduced in *Révolution surréaliste*. In fact, while the female nude is completely incorporated into the circle of the surrealists, the different elements of the collage blatantly lack cohesion: there is no dialog, no exchange of glances, each of the surrealists seems to be encapsulated in his own world while the woman directs her gaze into the void.

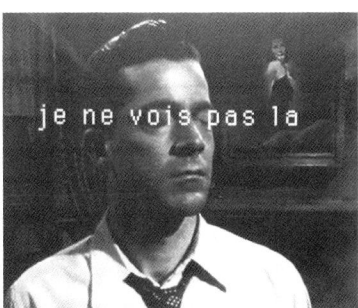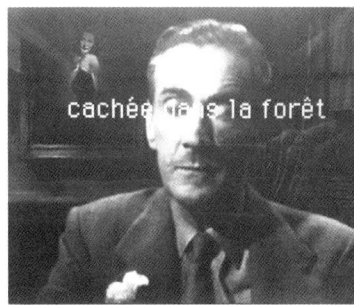

Figure 4.8.

Portrait of Waldo Lydecker, 1991.

2 panels.
Each 120×150 cm.

The diptych *Portrait of Waldo Lydecker* can be understood as a comment on these surrealist fantasies within the postmodern age of simulation and computer technology. (Fig. 4.8.) Burgin produced the work in 1991 for the opening of the new spaces of the Durand-Dessert gallery in rue de Lappe, Paris. The work is inspired by two events that took place at the same moment: the large exhibition *André Breton, La beauté convulsive* at Centre Pompidou and, on the other bank of the Seine, a Gene Tierney Festival. (PS: 170) The panels show the two male main characters of the film, police detective Mark McPherson on the left hand and newspaper columnist Waldo Lydecker on the right hand. Both are framed in medium close-up, eyes closed, standing in front of the same background representing the living room of the female protagonist, Laura Hunt. But while in the right panel Laura's painted portrait is located on Lydecker's left, it appears in the left panel mirror-inverted on the detective's right. The yellow words "je ne vois pas la … cachée dans la forêt," running at eye level across the two panels, are written in a pixelized computer typography. In the left panel, the last word of the first part of the sentence cloaks Laura's body exactly at the level of her womb, as does the first word of the second part in the right panel.

As in Magritte's painting there is no doubt about what is hidden in the woods: the woman whose physical body is absent while her image haunts the dreams and fantasies of the two men.

The plot of the story goes as follows: A woman, supposedly Laura Hunt, has been killed in her apartment through a gunshot in her face. Police detective Mark McPherson, who conducts the investigation, interrogates the main suspects: Laura's fiancé, her wealthy aunt, and her elderly friend and mentor Waldo Lydecker. In the course of the investigation, McPherson, who reads Laura's letters and her diary, begins to fall in love with the absent Laura to the point that he wants to purchase her portrait. When Laura, presumed dead, suddenly reappears, it turns out that the victim was a model who had a love affair with Laura's fiancé and erroneously was killed because of her fatal resemblance with Laura. In the dramatic final scene, the actual murderer, Lydecker, who attempted to murder Laura because he could not bear to share her with other men, tries to kill her once again but is finally shot dead by one of McPherson's colleagues. In Burgin's work, the portrait of Lydecker is taken from the scene in which the columnist and McPherson have diner in the restaurant where Laura and her mentor frequently went before her supposed death. On this occasion, Lydecker tells the detective their whole story, from the moment they first met to their last telephone call a couple of days preceding her disappearance. When Lydecker, who supported Laura to become a successful advertising executive, explains that "she deferred to my judgement and taste," including headdress, clothing, and comportment, it becomes clear that he tried to form her according to his own desires and dreams. In Burgin's work, Lydecker's eyes have been closed by means of computer manipulation, suggesting that the painting—similar to a thought bubble in comics—is not the representation of a real woman, but the emulation of the columnist's mind. Like Breton and the surrealists, Lydecker cannot see the woman because he only sees in her the mirrored image of his own fantasies— what is emphasized in the fact, that his portrait is a mirror-inverted version of the original image in the film. Analogously, McPherson's eyes in the left portrait are closed as well. In this case, it is not the police detective but the background with Laura's portrait that is mirror-inverted. This can be related of course to Lacan's mirror stage in which the infant, confronted with the reflection of his own body, begins to differentiate between the I and the other. Here this differentiation fails. Neither of the two men is capable of acknowledging Laura as the other, as an autonomous counterpart. Instead, they are falling in love with their own desires and fantasies: Lydecker by transforming the real woman into an ideal image and McPherson the other way around, by fabulating a living person on the basis of visual and verbal forms of representation. What is more, the two panels unite disparate elements from different cultural, historical, and technological horizons: the electronically created images and the typography represent digital technology; the sentence and the portraits evoke the surrealist movement; finally, the figures and the painting refer to different moments in the Hollywood movie. Whereas the surrealists juxtaposed the distinct components of the image—the portraits and the painting—, Burgin's digitally generated space is based on techniques of layering and mirroring, which makes it nearly impossible to keep things separate. It seems that in the "age of electrobricolage" (Mitchell, 1992: 7), the psychological state of the early ego, as described by Melanie Klein, has found its technological counterpart in a new virtual space oscillating between total integration and a "tendency towards disintegration, a falling in bits." (Klein, 1986: 179)

Fiction Film expands on this analogy between the psychological space of desire and the technological space of postmodernism. (Fig. 4.9.) In "The City in Pieces," Burgin refers to Walter Benjamin's metaphor of the

Figure 4.9.
Fiction Film, 1991.
Portfolio of nine photographs.
Each 75,5×95,2 cm.

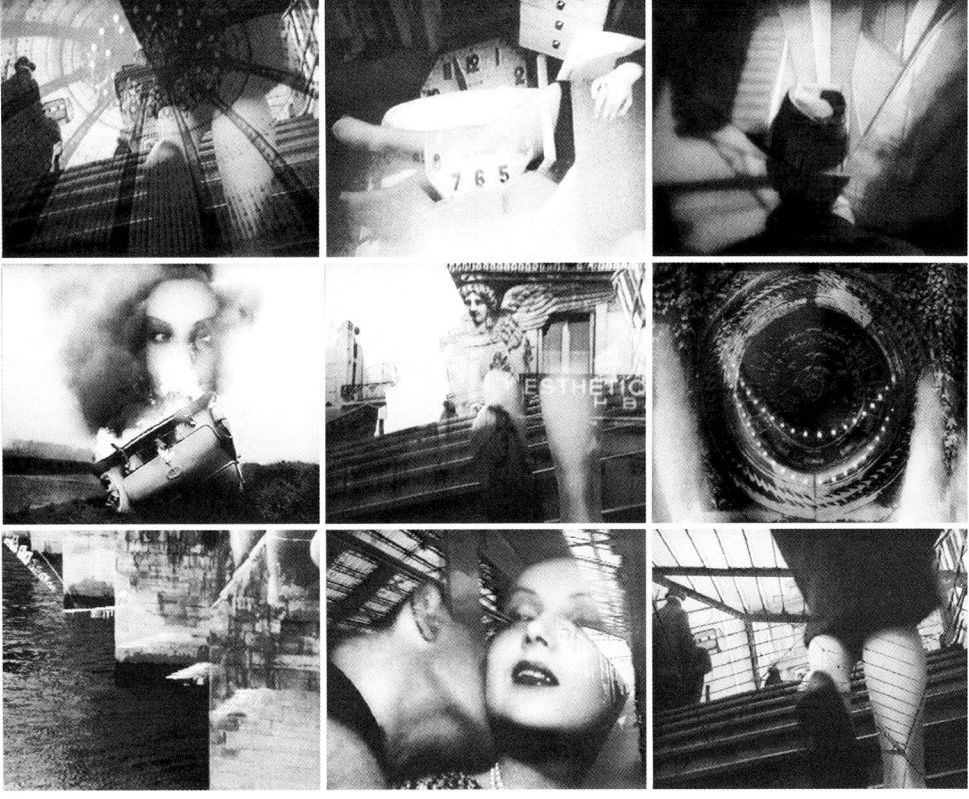

porosity of Naples as an example of how ever since Modernism a dialectic of interior and exterior spaces has emerged that culminates in the palimpsest spaces of the contemporary environment of mass media. Burgin compares this "fusion of spaces" with "an arrested filmic lap-dissolve, which refuses to decide either origin or destination, the image forms through condensation." (IDS: 145) This is precisely what the nine computer-generated screen-prints of *Fiction Film* are: composites that layer two images of different origin, thus suspending their signification between two competing, incongruous realities. Each image superposes a still of a classic movie with a photograph the artist took in Paris at locations where André Breton and Nadja passed on their rambles through the streets of the French metropole. Burgin actually suggests that these composite images are the rejected lap dissolves of a purportedly lost film, "perhaps gathered by some infatuated assistant editor from the cutting-room floor, and which are themselves fictions." (PS: 170) Dating from 1928, Breton's novel *Nadja* is a semi-autobiographical account of his love affair with a young woman, Nadja, which describes the couple's interactions and strolls through the streets of Paris over the course of ten days. Their random wandering in fact defines the novel's storyline, because this activity opens the door for surprise and the accidental, allowing the author to evoke the enigmatic in the everyday. (Nachtergael, 2005: 166) In "Chance Encounters," Burgin remarks that "Nadja, for Breton—for a time—is to be the locus of the transformation of everyday life, as if the social revolution absent from the France of 1928 could be acted out on the stage of sexuality." (IDS: 102) Too much occupied with the acting out of his Surrealist program of the encounter with the marvelous, Breton would finally misrecognize Nadja's illness. While she has no distance to her experiences in the street where she finds "those scattered objects she cannot contain when alone," he plays the role of an "actor-director" who always keeps control over his actions and experiences, eager to transform them into an aesthetic object. (IDS: 103; 105) In *Fiction Film*, these conflicting interests and tempers are represented in the confrontation of the photographs of the actual places of the novel with fragments of a fictional love story composed of movie stills, including romance (kissing couple), drama (burning car), and luxury (pearl necklace). The burning car lying upside down at the side of the road hints to a specific passage in a footnote of Breton's novel, in which the author describes how Nadja, during a nocturnal car ride, "pressed her foot down on mine on the accelerator, tried to cover my eyes with her hands in the oblivion of an interminable kiss, desiring to extinguish us, doubtless forever […]." (Breton, 1977: 152) Needless to add that Breton resisted the temptation of a final union in death.

The motive of walking the urban streets in Breton's novel was a crucial inspiration for Burgin: "I wanted a sense of the repetitious street-walking in all this finding, losing, pursuing and refinding of Nadja, as she herself wanders aimlessly the streets of Paris."[45] On another occasion, he further explained: "I researched the various bits of Paris where he [Breton] went and I shot them and included them."[46] The nine panels of *Fiction Film*, then, are the condensation of three different modes of "psychogeographic" exploration: the compulsive, aimless wandering of Nadja in which the geographical experience is subjected to psychic drives or forces; Breton's aestheticization of these walks in the name of the encounter with the marvelous; and Burgin's quest of the traces they left in the city as a kind of pilgrimage in which the experience of the actual, present space mingles with memories of this other, fictional and historical space of the novel. The term "psychogeography" was defined in 1958 by Guy Debord as "the study of the precise laws and specific effects of the geographical environment, whether consciously organized or not, on the emotions and behavior of individuals." (Knabb, 2006: 8) The act of *dérive* as fundamental psychogeographic procedure consists of an unplanned roaming through urban space with the aim to discover new ambiances and sensations beyond the calculated boredom of the city planning in advanced capitalism. Burgin embraces the concepts of psychogeography and *dérive*, even though his interest lies less in urbanism and city planning than in the relations between the physical and psychical experience of the city and its representations. (IDS: 32-33) Actually, Burgin's journey is not retraceable on maps, as is the case for Debord's *The Naked City* (1957), which this author conceived as an illustration of his concept of psychogeography.[47] Leaving aside the fact that the images, organized to a regular grid, do not indicate specific directions in which the story might advance, the layering of the urban shots and the film stills generates a semi-fictional space in which time and space are condensed to what Michel De Certeau called a "lieu palimpseste" ("place that is a palimpsest"). (De Certeau, 1988: 109) In "Change Encounters," Burgin refers to this author's distinction between the "concept city" and the city as lived space in terms of spatial practices. (IDS: 94) According to De Certeau, the first is the city of the urbanist planner, the cartographer and the linear perspective of Western painting since the Renaissance. It is the theoretical projection of a "panorama-city" which offers a maximum of control and overview. The second mode of mapping urban space is defined by the operation of walking. Using a literary metaphor, De Certeau describes the walkers as practitioners whose paths constitute a network of "moving, intersecting writings […] shaped out of fragments of trajectories and alternations of spaces." (De Certeau, 1988: 93) From this, he concludes that a place is not just a portion of space or a particular position or location, but a stratification of varying operations, stories, and memories composed by a series of displacements of "accumulated times that can be unfolded but like stories held in reserve, remaining in an enigmatic state, symbolizations encysted in the pain or pleasure of the body." (De Certeau, 1988: 108) Without any doubt, De Certeau pursues here a psychogeographic definition of the city inspired by Freud. This becomes obvious when he describes, in analogy with Freud's analysis of the dream, the experience of place as a rebus based on a series of condensation and displacement processes.[48] The places of *Fiction Film* are, in fact, quite literally "encysted in the pain or pleasure of the body," insofar as they not only allude to Nadja's and Breton's sentimental experience of the city, but also merge with cinema's images of pain and pleasure (love, luxury, accident, death). Burgin's exploration of the city, then, is neither a Situationist *dérive* in terms of a "rapid passage through varied ambiences" of urban landscapes, nor a surrealist *errance* through the city to expose its erotic and unconscious aspects. (Knabb, 2006: 52; Nachtergael, 2005: 167) It rather reveals the city as a "lieu palimpseste" consisting of intertwining fragments of memories and stories oscillating between past and present, history and fiction. In this regard, *Fiction Film* perfectly agrees with De Certeau's characterization of travel as a "walking exile": "it is a fiction, which moreover has the double characteristic, like dreams or pedestrian rhetoric, of being the effect of displacements and condensations." (De Certeau, 1988: 107)

4.7. The Teletopological Puzzle[49]

In April 1992, Burgin participated in a conference at Wayne State University, organized to commemorate the centenary of the birth of Walter Benjamin.[50] In his contribution "The City in Pieces," he suggests a re-reading of two essays by Benjamin, "One-Way Street" and "Naples," in which he borrows the Benjaminian concepts of porosity and penetration to describe the fragmentary and kaleidoscopic experience of the city in the "global space-time of television." (IDS: 34) In the same period, the relationship between the city, mass media, and the construction of identity became increasingly important in Burgin's artistic work and writing, particularly in his first video, *Venise* (1993), and the book *Some Cities* (1996), which the author conceived as "an autobiographical travelogue—an evocation in text and images of the traces certain cities have left in my memory." (CP: 75) (Fig. 4.10.) For a deeper understanding of these two works, it will be necessary to make a detour into the way Burgin relates Benjamin's ideas to the teletopological experience of the city in the age of mass media.

   As has been recurrently noted in the literature on Benjamin, the concept of "porosity" has a large array of significations including topological, sociological, anthropological, architectural, and epistemological aspects.[51] In fact, in the essay "Naples," which appeared in August 1925 in the German journal *Frankfurter Zeitung*, Benjamin and his then lover Asja Lacis understand the porosity of the city's buildings as both a feature of the actual urban fabric, or a principle of action and social life, and a mode of representation. In Naples, Benjamin and Lacis write, "building and action interpenetrate [...] to become a theatre of new, unforeseen constellations." (Benjamin and Lacis, 1978: 169) In this porous city, nothing is definitive, for the boundaries between private space and public space, between observing and being observed, between real space and narrated space are constantly shifting. In Benjamin's "One-Way Street," the porosity of the city has its equivalent in the porosity of the text, which consists of a montage of verbal fragments alternating observations of daily life with dream accounts. If Burgin writes

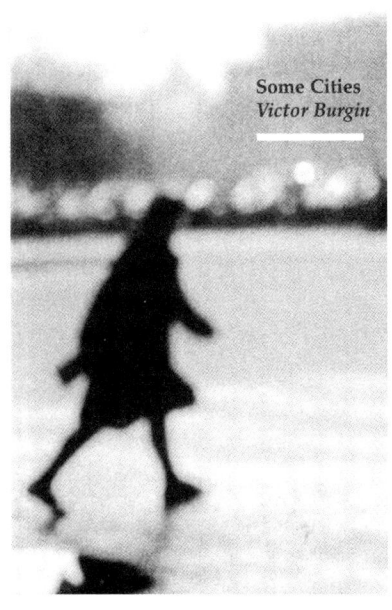

Figure 4.10.

Some Cities, Berkeley and Los Angeles, University of California Press, and London, Reaktion Books, 1996.

Cover.

that "One-Way Street" has "the appearance of a city plan: avenues of open space cross its pages, between compact and irregular blocks of text" (IDS: 139), he stands in a tradition of interpretations that begins with Ernst Bloch and is taken on by Susan Buck-Morss and, more recently, Benjamin Fellmann. Insisting on Benjamin's surrealist way of thinking as the underlying principle of "One-Way Street," Bloch, in *Heritage of Our Times*, writes that "Benjamin's experiment offers photos of this journey, or rather at once: photomontage." (Bloch, 1991: 335) Since then, it has been frequently remarked that the chapter titles of "One-Way Street" correspond to words or sentences as they appear in the streets of a city in the form of street signs, billboards, and advertising signs. As Buck-Morss suggests, "the outside world of gas stations, metros, traffic noises, and neon lights, which threatens to disrupt intellectual concentration, is incorporated into the text." (Buck-Morss, 1989: 17) Fellmann adds to this that Benjamin conceived of his text as a montage of different points of view in order to mimic the "local mediality" ("örtliche Medialität") of the metropole defined by porosity and multiperspectivity. (Fellmann, 2014: 56) Concerning "Naples," Fellmann finally comes to the conclusion that the text would be based on the principles of filmic montage, which Benjamin defined in his essay "The Work of Art in the Age of Mechanical Reproduction" as "successive changes of scene and focus which have a percussive effect on the spectator." (Benjamin, 2003: 267; Fellmann, 2014: 58)

In his introduction to *In/Different Spaces*, Burgin writes that this Benjaminian shift from architecture to cinema can be observed in postmodern discourses on the media society in which the object becomes, as Fredric Jameson put it, a mere "media phenomenon." (Jameson, 1992: 169; IDS: 34) Burgin agrees with Jameson when he suggests we consider the city less in urbanistic or sociometric terms than in terms of decentered and multinational communication entailing the dispersion of the subject across the hybrid and heterogeneous sites of representation. But in contrast to Jameson's account, Burgin argues that the fragmented global space-time of postmodernity is no longer that of cinema but rather that of television with its almost unlimited possibilities of zapping through multiple channels accessible 24 hours a day. As early as 1934, in his preface to *The Heritage of Our Times*, Ernst Bloch described modernity as a "kaleidoscopic period" of which the basic principle would be montage, for it "breaks off parts from the collapsed context and the various relativisms of the times in order to combine them into new figures." (Bloch, 1991: 3) In postmodern media society, Burgin observes, the kaleidoscopic fragments of modernity have been integrated in the discontinuous and fragmentary representational space of television. Unlike Bloch's kaleidoscopic space, the new media environment offers a purely virtual space of ever-changing and overlapping representations, and this makes it impossible to assemble the fragments in a limited temporal or spatial frame or continuum, as is the case with avant-garde collage and montage. In the disintegrated space-time of the mediatic environment, categories that used to be strictly distinct, such as exterior/interior, object/image, and private/public become permeable, being "simultaneously confirmed and confused." (IDS: 154)

At this point, Burgin refers to Henri Lefebvre's image of the membrane as "a boundary whose degree of permeability may vary." (Lefebvre, 1991: 176) Even though (private) property and one's position in a town or a nation are defined by closed frontiers, Lefebvre argues, the barriers between inside and outside are always relative and permeable. As an example of this permeability, he mentions the house "as permeated from every direction by streams of energy which run in and out of it by every imaginable route: water, gas, electricity, telephone lines, radio and television signals, and so on." (93) Burgin takes up Lefebvre's idea of the permeated architecture when describing the transmission and reception of television images as a process of perforation in which the electrons that encode the image successively pierce the walls of the building, the television screen, and the body of the spectator, thus dissolving the difference between exterior and interior realities. (IDS: 154-155) Consequently, the metropole is not the fugitive, fragmentary, and transitional urban space of Baudelaire's flaneur anymore, ultimately based as it is on the actual experience of the flux of the city; it rather has been incorporated into what Paul Virilio described as the teletopological puzzle of television: a superimposed vision of surfaces and images "that never turns off, that always gives and receives […]." (Virilio, 1991: 71) Wondering about the consequences of this mode of teletopological perception for the subject, Burgin discerns two extreme psychocorporeal attitudes toward the world: schizophrenia, as a scattering of the body throughout the world, and autism, as an absolute form of closing down one's relation to the world. (IDS: 152-153) In the postmodern era, Burgin concludes, these two pathological states would find their analogy in the paradoxical nature of television, which allows us both total isolation from the real world and extensive travelling through the most varying and dispersed places in the world: "Today, the autistic response of total withdrawal, and the schizophrenic anxiety of the body in pieces, belong to our psychocorporeal forms of identification with the teletopological puzzle of the city in pieces." (IDS: 158)

In the summer of 1993, Burgin was invited to Marseille for a residency at the Institut Méditerranéen de Recherche et de Création (I.ME. RE.C). (SCR: 32) During his stay in Marseille, Burgin made a 30-minute single-channel video that he described as a "psycho-documentary" addressing the question of "the production of an identity in relation to places, the history of those places, personal memory, and other people." (VB: 192) The video is conceived as a dialogue between San Francisco and Marseille, which are both cosmopolitan port cities in which different cultures and histories clash and overlap. Oscillating between fact and fiction, the video alternates images made by Burgin in these two cities with film excerpts from Hitchcock's *Vertigo* (1958) and Julien Duvivier's *Pépé le Moko* (1937). A female narrator with an Arabian accent and a male narrator with an English accent read passages in French from the novel by Pierre Boileau and Thomas Narcejac, *D'entre les morts* (1954), that served as basis for Hitchcock's movie.

The factual circumstances of the commission's local conditions and Burgin's life as a US resident, teaching at the University of California in Santa Cruz, some seventy miles to the South of San Francisco, thus have their counterparts in the settings of the fictional stories of *D'entre les morts* (Marseille) and *Vertigo* (San Francisco). The movie's plot centers on a man who falls in love with the woman he should follow as a detective and who becomes clinically depressed when his beloved purportedly commits suicide. After his release from the sanatorium, he encounters a girl who reminds him of his beloved, and he gradually transforms her into the woman's exact likeness. This relationship between the construction of (female) identity and (male) desire also featured in my discussion of *The Bridge* (in Chapter 3). What is new here is the way Burgin links the problem of identity to the question of the city as a melting pot of various cultures and histories. While the two voices relate the parable of the construction and reconstruction of sexual identity that underly both the novel and the movie, the intertitles evoke historical and political aspects of exile, immigration, and memory. The four volumes of *Migrance. Histoire des migrations à Marseille*, edited by Émile Temine and others, are cited, as well as a letter by Walter Benjamin, revealing his intention to embark to Marseille or America, and the names of Buchenwald, Mauthausen, Sobibor, and Sachsenhausen-Oranienburg—the Nazi concentration camps to which Marseille residents were deported after the January 1943 raffle in the Vieux Port.

The musical backdrop for this assemblage of heterogeneous verbal and visual materials is an eclectic mix of chansons, classical music, jazz, and oriental sounds reflecting the oppositions and amalgamations of American, European, and Oriental cultures. The extensive use of cross dissolves, fade-ins, fade-outs, and text/image transitions represent, on a formal and technical level, the „dissolving of differences between cities and identities," and contribute thus to Burgin's attempt to "'deconstruct' the binarism of centre and margin, of self and other." (Burgin, 1996: 66) Raymond Bellour defines the videographic medium as a "passageway," which, deprived of a proper identity because of its hybrid status between cinema, music, and pictorial arts, constitutes "a system of transformations of images interpenetrating each other." (Bellour, 2012: 20) With its cross-references of visual, verbal, and musical components, *Venise* employs the medium's hybrid position *Between-the-Images* (to quote the title of Bellour's book) and blends it with the idea of cultural hybridity that, according to Homi Bhabha, affords the "borderline conditions to 'translate,' and therefore reinscribe, the social imaginary of both metropolis and modernity." (Bhabha, 2004: 9)

Interestingly, Burgin's shift from photography to video doesn't serve him—as might be assumed—to sacrifice the spatial dimension of the city for the sake of its temporal exploration. Even though *Venise* can be understood as a journey through the cities of Marseille and San Francisco, this journey cannot be compared with a successive, chronological way of travelling. For this particular journey traverses various geographic, historical, urban, and psychical regions which intertwine and overlap in time and in space:

> Marseille as an aggregate of village societies [...] [is] a spatial picture... But, of course, the other thing that you have to bear in mind with the spatial picture is that the histories and the memories which pass through those points are different. So we are passing not only from a spatial picture which included the model of the centre and the periphery, but also passing into a different picture of time in which it is no longer a question of history as a single linear story—and neither his-story nor her-story—but rather a picture of a multiplicity of simultaneously existing histories and memories. (Burgin, 1996: 66)

The freeze frame is a crucial element in order to evoke this spatial picture of the aggregate city. A lot has been said about the freeze frame's capacity to stop time, to transform the filmic narration into a pictorial composition, to mark the irruption of the (photographic) past in the (filmic) present, or to make the film "transparent to itself." (Bellour, 2007: 122; Stewart, 1987: 19) In his essay "Death, Photography and Film Narrative," Garrett Stewart emphasizes the suggestive power of the freeze frame when it comes to figure death scenes: "Into the (metonymic) chain of contiguity, of continuous motion, of sequence, of plot, breaks the radical equation *stasis equals death*, the axis of substitution, the advent of metaphor." (Stewart, 1987: 22)

This is precisely what happens near the beginning of the video, where a car ride through San Francisco that re-stages a scene in *Vertigo* is suddenly interrupted by a freeze frame exactly at the moment when the narrator mentions the death of Madeleine, the female main character of the film. Toward the end of the video, in contrast, a stop-motion sequence shows Madeleine entering the bell tower from which she will plunge to her death. Tinted in a deep blue, this stop-motion sequence, which signifies the woman's suspension between life and death, is preceded by a sequence in which a historical photograph of the transporter bridge in the port of Marseille, destroyed by the German army in 1944, dissolves into the contemporary filmic images of a destroyed bridge in San Francisco. (Plate 9) Past and present, life and death, memory and lived experience are suspended between the photographic and filmic representations of the two seaport towns. It becomes clear that this is neither the chronological time of historical progression nor the physical urban space of the city. It rather drafts a "fantasmatic geography" that also comprises the teletopological puzzle of the mediatic environment. (SCR, 33) As such, its disintegrated, overlapping spatio-temporal structure might be compared, as Burgin suggests, with psychoanalytical processes, proceeding, as Shoshana Felman writes "not through linear progression but through breakthroughs, leaps, discontinuities, regressions, and deferred action." (IDS: 35-36; Felman, 1987: 76) *Venise* is full of leaps, discontinuities, displacements, and breaks. In this regard, it is worth mentioning that the title—as the quotation that follows the stop-motion sequence reveals—refers to Italo Calvino's novel *Invisible Cities*. The intertitle quotes the famous passage in which Marco Polo replies to Kublai Khan's question why he never speaks of Venice, his hometown: "Every time I describe a city I am saying something about Venice." (Calvino, 1974: 86) This passage is crucial because it situates the city within the subject's psychical space of memories and recollections. But there is another passage that is even more in line with Burgin's conception of the city as a psycho-topological construct of memories, fantasy, desires, and anxieties:

With cities, it is as with dreams: everything imaginable can be dreamed, but even the most unexpected dream is a rebus that conceals a desire or, its reverse, a fear. Cities, like dreams, are made of desires and fears, even if the thread of their discourse is secret, their rules are absurd, their perspective deceitful, and everything conceals something else. (Calvino, 1974: 44)

It is hardly possible to give a more appropriate account of *Some Cities*, a psychogeographic travelogue that was published at the same time as *In/Different Spaces*, in 1996. Rejecting a linear autobiographical narrative, the book follows a "stream of consciousness" in which Burgin recalls the cities that he visited during his life. (PT: 111) As Norman Bryson eloquently observes in the blurb of the book, *Some Cities* is "a meditation on cities that is at the same time an autobiography, a work of cultural criticism, an essay on the history of industrialized culture, and a dramatic enactment of the functions of irony, humor and political analysis in a world irrevocably altered by the mobility of people, things and ideas in our time." Like *Venise*, the associative and fragmentary narrative reflects the idea of the city as a spatial picture composed of a multitude of histories and memories. In fact, the linear biographical structure, taking as its starting-point Burgin's hometown of Sheffield and ending with his present city of residence, San Francisco, is constantly interrupted by flashbacks, and visual associations that reveal the heterochronic and multidimensional character of the narrative. Already on the first pages of the book a "shock of recognition" is triggered by a 1936 Bill Brandt photograph of Halifax, a city Burgin had never visited, but which he chose because of its resemblance with a situation experienced when he was a young schoolboy in Sheffield. (SC: 10) (Fig. 4.11.)

On the following pages, reflections on migration, class, and capitalism are accompanied by photographs of the social life in London and Coventry, represented by workers, punks, and families. Yet, the photographs are not just illustrations of the text or documents of the exterior world. Beyond their function as credible eyewitnesses of street life, some of them are also components of artworks and thus refer to Burgin's gallery work. (19-23) Others, like the photograph of a sculpture taken in the garden of the church of Saint-Germain-des-Prés in Paris, are not intended to reproduce a place or an event, but they rather respond to the author's recollection of other images. (34-35) (Fig. 4.12.) The idea that a photograph not only depicts the physical world but is also part of an imaginary memory space can be transferred to the experience of a city. As Burgin writes: "At the same time that the city is experienced as a physically factual built environment, it is also, in the perception of its inhabitants, a city in a novel, a film, a photograph a television programme, a comic strip, and so on." (SC: 175)

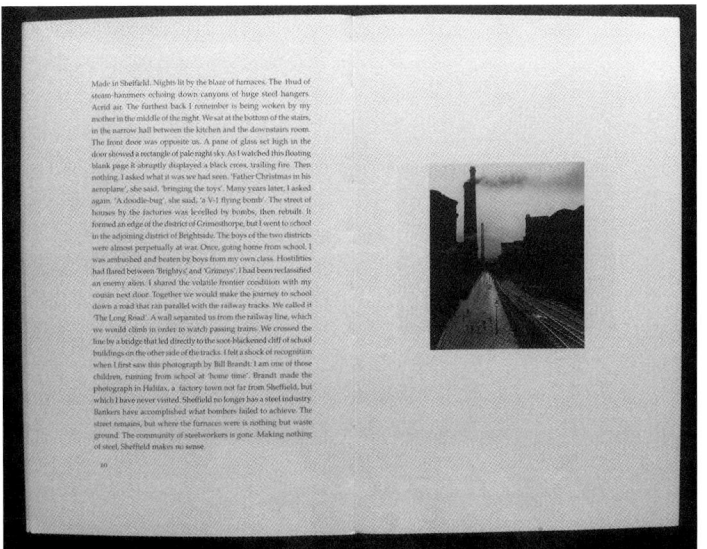

Figure 4.11.

Some Cities, 1996 (Halifax, 1936. Photograph: Bill Brandt), 10–11.

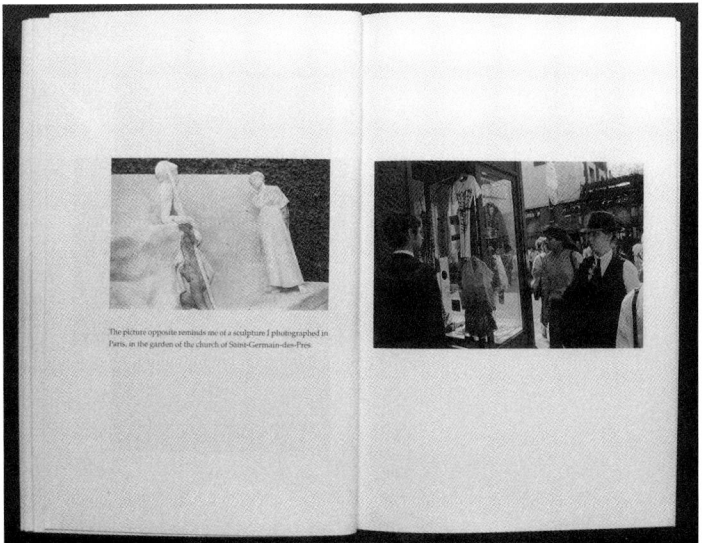

Figure 4.12.

Some Cities, 1996 (Paris, 1984; Kings Road, London, 1984), 34–35.

This concept of the hybrid city, oscillating between lived experience and remembered representations, is at the origin of an unrealized work that the City of Blois commissioned from Burgin in 1992. (Fig. 4.13.) Described by the artist as a "fantasmatic *mise-en-scène*," the project consists of a series of posters spread throughout the historical center and the Nord *quartiers* in order to create a metaphor for the social division of the city in two distinct spaces. (SC, 176) In *Some Cities*, Burgin quotes the submission text, according to which the city of the project is "undecidedly both factual and fictional," mingling impressions of the actual Blois with possible associations from movies, novels, and magazine and television representations of other places and times. The title *Loin d'Ici* (*Far From Here*) refers to the idea that the experience of a city is always connected to the memories of other cities, experienced at other moments. On a more political level, the project explores the blatant contradictions between the organization of urban space, which is always determined by social segregation between different neighborhoods, and the fantasy of the permeable, fluctuant city without limits as it is transmitted by the media:

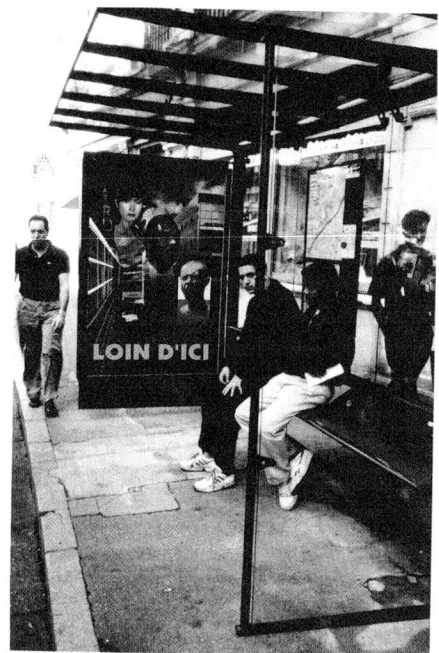

Figure 4.13.

Some Cities, 1996 (*Loin d'Ici* (*Far From Here*), Project for the city of Blois, 1992), 177.

> Heterogeneous and hybrid, in its spatial and temporal condensations and displacements, in its self-citations and rapid and random alternations of ideal, mundane, and violent images, the media-imaginary environment increasingly resembles the interior space of subjective fantasy turned inside out. (PS: 186)

Another artistic project described in *Some Cities* is the installation that Burgin created in 1994 for the multi-media library of Orléans. (Fig. 4.14.) The question of the city's porosity in times of satellite television is here linked to the book as potential object of resistance to electronic communication: "The work was prompted by the simultaneous presence, in our daily lives, of the printed word and the electronic image: the book and television." (SC: 178) It follows a description of the video projection which, suspended at a place of transit between the space with the real books and the multimedia space, shows an endless stream of live television images commented on through quotations from books out of the library. Burgin concludes: "Favouring the perpetually instantaneous, television tends to efface the continuity of memory and history necessary to stable identities. (In this respect, the library has become a 'counter institution' to television.)" (178) This might be read as a commentary to the double function of *Some Cities* itself: As a stable object of the library, the book resists the telecommunicational flux of images shattering the city in thousands of pieces. In contrast, the interaction between image and text, as well as the hybridity of the content, constitute a psycho-topographic adventure in the course of which the urban environment and the imaginary city overlap to a point that it becomes nearly impossible to discern the difference between fiction and fact. In *In/Different Spaces* Burgin quotes an image taken from Freud's *Introductory Lectures on Psycho-Analysis* in which the psychanalyst compares the dream with "a piece of breccia, composed of various fragments of rock held together by a binding medium, so that the designs that appear on it do not belong to the original rocks imbedded in it." (IDS: 178) By analogy, one might deduce that *Some Cities* is such a piece of breccia, with the pag-

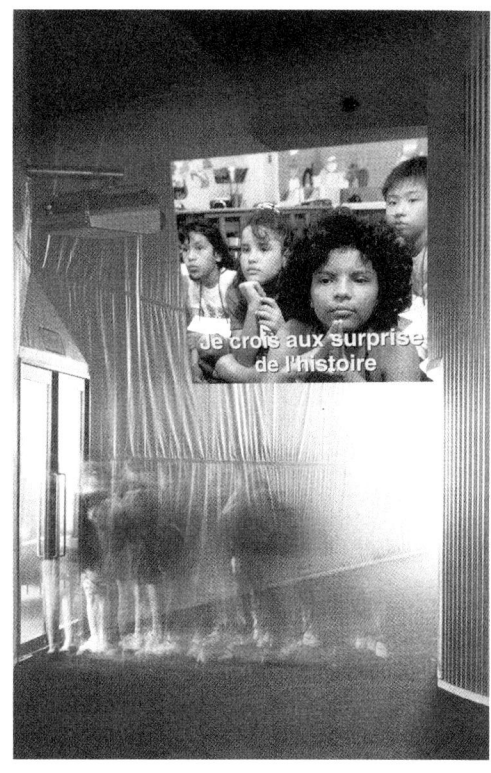

Figure 4.14.
Some Cities, 1996
(Installation at the
Médiathèque d'Orléans,
1994), 179.

es serving as binding medium for a heterogeneous mix of visual and textual elements including impressions of visited cities, descriptions of artistic projects, and critical reflections on the perception and the experience of the city in the era of the postmodern media environment.

As mentioned, the porous city of postmodernity is pierced by the incessant stream of visual and verbal information generated by the mass media. On the one hand, *Some Cities* provides a critical account of the psychological effects of the teletopological puzzle on the perception of the city. On the other hand, the book offers a very personal rendering of Burgin's experiences in cities around the world. The first lines leave no doubt about the emotional and human aspect of encounters with and in the city:

> Our relations with cities are like our relations with people. We love them, hate them, or are indifferent toward them. On our first day in a city that is new to us, we go looking for the city. We go down this street, around that corner. We are aware of the faces of passers-by. But the city eludes us, and we become uncertain whether we are looking for a city, or for a person. (SC: 7)

This is why the experience of the city will always involve a quest for human interaction as well, perhaps even a love affair, which pierces the body of the urban flaneur, just as Asja Lacis cut "One-way Street" through the body of Walter Benjamin. In his dedication to his book, Benjamin writes:

> This street is named
> Asja Lacis Street
> after she who
> like an engineer
> cut it through the author.

Some Cities is traversed at irregular intervals by seven film stills taken from Hitchcock's *Vertigo*. (Fig. 4.15.) Three shots of a woman walking down a corridor appear in such a way that the scene is repeated twice before the sequence ends with the initial image. The reader who is familiar with Hitchcock's movie might remember that the woman in the corridor is Midge, the main character's ex-fiancée, who visits the detective in the sanatorium where he has been interned after his nervous breakdown caused by the alleged suicide of the woman he loves. In *Some Cities*, however, each still marks a transition, a passageway, from one city to another or from one discursive mode to another.

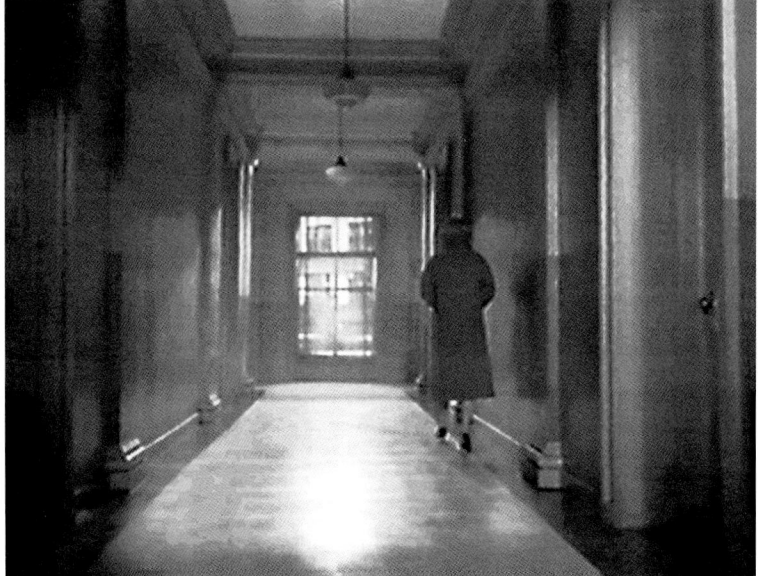

Figure 4.15.

Some Cities, 1996 (still from Hitchcock's Vertigo, 1958), 13, 121, 173.

The book ends with a photograph taken in 1994 by Burgin at Le Corbusier's *Cité Radieuse* in Marseille. (Fig. 4.16.) It shows a woman walking down a corridor. Turning the page, the reader learns that it is the woman to whom the book is dedicated. (SC: 219) Just as the phantasmagoric body of Midge, removed from Hitchcock's Hollywood movie, cuts her way through Burgin's psycho-topological travelogue, it seems that the real body of the woman of the last photograph extends this journey, beyond the limits of the book, into the future. As the dedication suggests, it is she who cut *Some Cities* through the author in order to renegotiate the permeable boundaries between the body and the teletopological city in pieces.

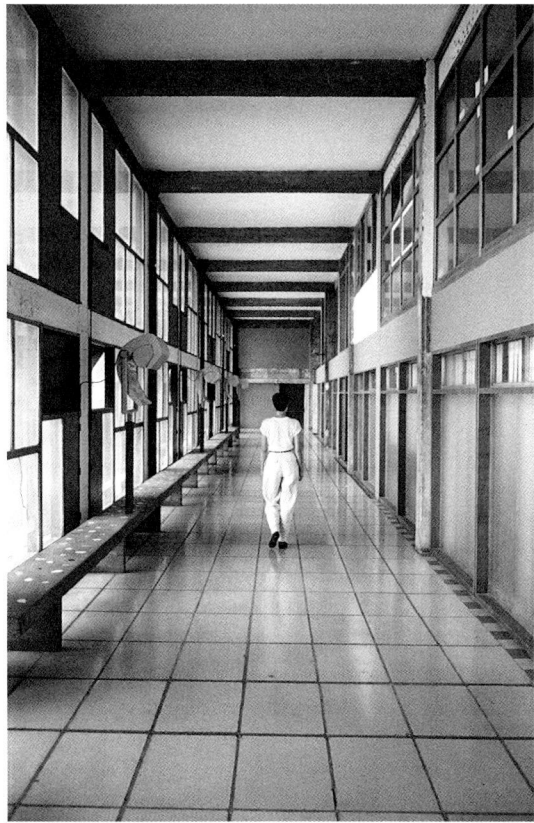

Figure 4.16.

Some Cities, 1996
(Marseille, Cité Radieuse,
1994), 217.

Chapter 5
The Psychomediatic

After *Venise*, most of Burgin's works are videos or projection pieces. But while *Venise*—despite its complex assemblage and layering of fragmentary, heterogeneous images—still conforms with the conventions of traditional film, determined by a beginning and an end, the following works are organized as relatively short loops that offer neither a linearly evolving story nor a coherent narrative. Instead, they consist of disparate still and moving images, as well as verbal elements and sound fragments, all of which are arranged as elements of a non-hierarchical, associative constellation. In various essays and papers, Burgin describes this kind of "moving image practice" as "uncinematic." (PT: 200; TC: 2018: 224) As discussed in more depth below, the concept of the "uncinematic" is crucial for a better understanding of both the specificity of Burgin's artistic practice and the way he conceives of the production and the perception of art within the institutional setting of the gallery and the global context of the environment of media images. That many other terms have been suggested to describe Burgin's artistic practice since the 1990s—such as "paratactical" (PT: 200), *da capo* (Massin, 2007: 143), "cybernetic" (Bishop, 2019: 140), or "lectographic" (King, 2014: 73)—is probably tied to the ex negativo facet of his "uncinematic" concept and the ambivalence of the term "cinematic." Most of these other concepts may be useful to understand significant structural, formal, and phenomenological aspects of Burgin's work, but they are less appropriate when it comes to understanding the projection works as a response to the psychical and perceptual conditions of contemporary digital culture of which they explore the underlying principle while constituting at the same time an aesthetic counter-environment.[52] To put it with a question posed by Nicholas Mirzoeff in his *Counterhistory of Visuality*: "How we can think with and against visuality?" (Mirzoeff, 2011: 2) In Burgin's projection pieces, this balancing act of thinking with *and* against contemporary visuality takes shape in the work's relationship with unconscious processes and the manner in which images nowadays circulate and are perceived. After a discussion of the concept of the "uncinematic," I will therefore introduce the "psychomediatic" as a concept, which in my view better fits the way the projection works in-scribe themselves in Burgin's overarching project of a psychical realism.

As outlined in the preceding chapter, the spatial and psychological consequences for the perception and recollection of images in the era shaped by mass media has been a major concern in Burgin's theoret-ical writing and artistic practice at least since the mid-1980s. Yet, in 1996, in *In/Different Spaces*, Burgin draws on Virilio's term of the "tele-topological puzzle" as a key concept to analyze the impact of the media (photography, cinema, advertising and television) on the changing per-ception of the world and the concomitant construction of identity and subjectivity. Eight years later, in his book *The Remembered Film* (2004), Burgin refers to the environment of media images as the "cinematic heterotopia." At first glance, this shift in focus from television to film and cinema may appear astonishing if we remember that Burgin, in *In/Different Spaces*, precisely argued that the medium which embodies most symptomatically the psychotypological condition of the postmodern time would be television, not cinema. But at that point already he re-vised his own former definition of film as an object that depends upon a specific institutional setting—the movie theater—when he wrote[53]:

> a "film" might be encountered through posters, "blurbs," and other advertisements, such as trailers and television clips; it may be encountered through newspaper reviews, reference work syn-opses and theoretical articles (with their "film-strip" assemblag-es of still images); … Collecting such metonymic fragments in memory, we may come to feel familiar with a film we have not actually seen. Clearly this "film"—a heterogeneous psychical ob-ject, constructed from image scraps scattered in space and time—is a very different object from that encountered in the context of "film studies." (IDS: 22-23)

In this passage, a fragmentary, heterogeneous character is attributed to film, because of its dissemination via a multiplicity of codes and media systems which require us to also consider film *as* "environment." In the introduction to *The Remembered Film*, Burgin quotes this same pas-sage, yet the reference medium for a volatile, fluctuating environment of visual representations is now the Internet:

> As a delivery system, the Internet offers video *bricoleurs* and ar-tisans of *détournement* with a source of clips from both old and new film releases; as an environment, it has become the site of modes of telling that owe little to traditional narrative practices. [italics in original] (RF: 13)

As it appears from this quotation, the cinematic heterotopia has nothing to do with films viewed in a movie theater, but is rather concerned with a new mode of perceiving, accessing, appropriating, and creating films. The Internet becomes the cinematic heterotopia, the "other place"— "heterotopia"—of the film as heterogeneous psychical object. However, in contrast to Foucault, from whom Burgin borrows the term "heterotopia," the cinematic heterotopia is not a hermetic microstructure designating real, concrete social places such as prisons, cemeteries, or hospitals. (Foucault, 1986: 22-27) Burgin's cinematic heterotopia suggests that we are dealing with a construct bursting forth from different virtual media spaces and subjective mental spaces. Consequently, the photographic, cinematic, and textual fragments conjured up by the virtual spaces of the media are mixed together in the mental space of the beholder with personal memories and fantasies, through which the "film," in any single moment, may be newly (re)constructed in the mind of any individual.[54]

In addition to the Internet as a new way to distribute, share, and use images, new digital technologies and their capacity to create new forms of hybrid images between stillness and movement increasingly gain terrain in the work of Burgin. In his works of the 1980s, already produced on the computer (*Danaïdes/Dames*, *Park Edge*, *Minnesota Abstract*, *Family Romance*), he assembles visual, graphic, and textual elements within the confined immobile space of the tableau. In the following projection works, fragments of movies, photographs, intertitles, sound, and panoramic images constitute a hybrid constellation in which temporal and spatial components, and still and moving images, mingle and overlap. This new approach to produce images *between* stasis and movement goes hand in hand with the theoretical rejection of an ontological difference between photography and film in the digital era.[55] Since the late 1990s, the boundaries between photographic and filmic images have become increasingly blurred: technically, in drawing on the same software and hardware engineering, as well as perceptually, in leaving the viewer in doubt of the (photographic or filmic) nature of the image. As a consequence, hybrid images emerge throughout all fields of visual culture. In cinema, techniques such as morphing and bullet-time are used to intensify the experience of a scene. Various multimedia frameworks and applications such as QuickTime, Photosynth, iMovie AutoStich, and FantaMorph animate photographic images or transform them into navigable virtual environments. And artists such as David Claerbout, Nancy Davenport, Shelly Silver, and Akram Zaatari merge photographic and filmic processes in order to reflect on issues of time, memory, and perception.[56] Burgin takes account of this technological and phenomenological revolution both as an artist and as a theorist. For him, the advent of digital technology has two consequences.

First, as these new hybrid images permeate all areas of image production, they destabilize the distinction between the cinema screen and the gallery wall, engendering "hybrid forms of attention, narration and time." (SDZ: 2019: 240) As a result, Burgin returns to the question of specificity, which he addresses through the idea of the "uncinematic" as a key term for his production of and reflections on art. Secondly, this new technology once again raises the issue of the medium. Including the hybridization of traditional media—such as photography and film—as much as the creation of purely computer-generated environments, the projection works hint at the fact that images are not based on material substrates any longer, but on algorithmically driven processes, which finally amounts to the obsolescence of photography:

> Because the distinction between still and moving images is no longer definitive, because cameras are nodes in the Internet, because the camera has dematerialised, for these and no doubt other reasons there is no longer any singular objective basis to serve as material ground for the attribution "photography." (SDZ: 164)

On this point, Burgin agrees with Rosalind Krauss's remark that photography today "can only be viewed through the undeniable fact of its own obsolescence." (Krauss, 1999: 289; SA: 307) Yet he disagrees with her insistence on the redemptive force of the outmoded as a means to reinvent the medium in the post-medium age. (PT: 133-134) Drawing on Brecht's remark that in certain times it would be necessary to turn away from the "good old things" and to start from the "bad new things," Burgin's theoretical and artistic interest shifts toward computer generated images and their place in the actuality of everyday representations. (Chiocchetti, 2019: 23) In the projection pieces, this shift of focus can be observed as a successive integration of software technology into the production process of the work. While the video works from the late 1990s are exclusively produced on the basis of photographic and filmic materials taken from archives, films, or shot by Burgin himself (*Love Letters*, 1997, *Lichtung*, 1998-1999, *Another Case History*, 1999), the "panoramic" works of the early 2000s—from *Nietzsche's Paris* (1999-2000) to *Hôtel D* (2009)—introduce virtual camera pans which disconnect the production of movement from the action of a body. Henceforth, it is the algorithm that determines the experience of the image. Since 2010, Burgin has been creating virtual models by means of 3D imaging software in order to reconstruct actual architectures (*A Place to Read*, 2010) before he started, with *Parzival* (2013), to design environments entirely computer-generated from scratch. This technological evolution is significant for more than one reason. First, it conforms with Burgin's demand for a psychical realism, postulating that art should always take into account the means of image production of its time. Secondly, it also connects with what D. N. Rodowick called the "naming crisis" of the moving image in contemporary art. (Rodowick, 2014: 17) The images of the earlier video projections are produced by lens-based cameras and, accordingly, they can still be identified with discourses on video art and film, but the computer-generated images produced by 3D-modelling and game-making software are harder to associate with a specific field or domain of image production. Burgin therefore prefers the neutral term "projection work" to describe his recent pieces.[57] (VBP: 16) As Rodowick points out, such works challenge "our confidence in knowing what these images are, or what they are becoming—as images and in movement." (Rodowick, 2014: 18) In what follows below, it is not my primary aim to present a way out of this aporia of the "naming crisis." By posing the question of what a psychical realism might mean in the age of the "cinematic heterotopia," this chapter investigates major themes, such as the uncinematic, the panorama, the sequence-image, melancholia, and spectatorship, which mark the specificity of Burgin's projection works and, furthermore, permit us to situate them within the chronological perspective of his own work since the 1960s.

5.1. The Uncinematic

Burgin coined the term "uncinematic" in 2007 in a paper given on the occasion of an event to mark the publication of David Campany's reader *The Cinematic*. (VBP: 77 and 154, note 40) In his introduction, Campany clarifies right from the beginning that the essays gathered in this volume are concerned less with the definition of cinema or the "cinematic" as aesthetic categories than with the relationships of film and photography and their significance "for each other not just technically but aesthetically and artistically." (Campany, 2007: 10) In the light of this orientation, it is not surprising that the anthology also includes one of Burgin's essays, "Possessive, Pensive and Possessed" (2006), in which the abovementioned concept of "cinematic heterotopia" is linked to the concept of the sequence-image as a perceptual category of memory images between stillness and movement.[58] If the purpose of the book, according to its blurb, is to give a survey of the "manifestations of the cinematic in photography and of the photographic in cinema," the exclusive emphasis on the "cinematic" in the title is perhaps somewhat surprising—all the more so because the introduction does not provide any definition of what the term actually means. Burgin develops his reflections on the "uncinematic" as a response to this omission. During the following years, this concept evolves into a generic term for the relationship between his own artistic practice and the cinematic heterotopia of the environment of media images.

Burgin's reflections on the uncinematic take their departure from the American Oxford dictionary's definition of the adjective "cinematic" as relating to or having the quality of motion pictures. His own projection works, in turn, would be uncinematic, in at least three respects: the space of spectatorship, the "characteristics of the image," and the "nature of the soundtrack." (CP: 90) Concerning the first, Burgin ties in with considerations on specificity and the difference between cinema and art that he had developed already two decades before. As addressed in Chapter 3, series like *The Bridge* or *Office at Night* are conceived of and arranged according to the specific setting of the gallery and the expectations of the gallery visitor. When Burgin takes up this discussion in regard to his projection works, he insists on the usefulness of the concept of specificity as it has been developed by Greenberg and others.[59] But in contrast to the modernist claim that the specificity of a work lies in its material substrate, Burgin defines it as a "set of conditions" of the gallery. (VBP: 60) For the projection works, this means that their difference from motion pictures as encountered in cinema is linked to the specific phenomenological mode of their reception. (SDZ: 240) Contrary to the movie theater, the spectator can enter and leave the gallery space whenever he wants. For this reason, Burgin's projection works are designed as loops with no particular beginning and end, so that the viewer is not obliged to enter the room at a particular moment. Other than cinema, the projection works have a dual temporal structure, for the material duration—the "length" of the film—does not coincide with the viewing time—the time the viewer actually spends with the work. (VBP: 77) Concerning the voice-over or intertitle text, in the view of Burgin, "any sentence may occupy the position of 'first' sentence, just as any image may be the first image." (TC, 2018: 204) Further the images and the soundtrack are uncinematic in that they do not connect to a linear narrative; rather than assembled to tell a singular story, their spatio-temporal structure is associative, repetitive, discontinuous, and indeterminate. Burgin compares this method of juxtaposing disparate elements of which the relations "are not given but must be inferred" with the rhetorical figure of *parataxis*. (PT: 200) He draws on Adorno's poetics of critique, according to which "the book must […] be written in equally weighted, paratactical parts that are arranged around a midpoint that they express through their constellation." (TC: 225; Adorno, 2013: 481) Although the spatial structure of the projection works may be considered as a constellation of heterogeneous elements, the temporal organization of these elements in a loop and their repetitive occurrence are closer to Benjamin's remarks on the treatise as a process of thinking that tirelessly "makes new beginnings, returning in a roundabout way to its original object." (Benjamin, 1992: 28) In view of his own projection works, Burgin identifies this spiraling process of thought as "the return of the same," a process of "repetition, reprise, recapitulation" in which—analogous to the *da capo* or the *ritornello* in music—a formal element returns at a later moment, being transfigured by the memory of its first occurrence and the new context of its second appearance. (CP: 93; Massin, 2007: 143)

One of the first works to take the form of such a paratactical loop is *Lichtung* (1998), a video produced on the occasion of the *Weimar 99* cultural festival and installed in a room of Schloss Ettersberg. (VB: 216) (Plate 10) The work is inspired by a simple architectural gesture with which Walther Grunwald, the architect commissioned with the restauration of Schloss Ettersberg, connected the building, formerly Goethe's "Court of the Muses," with the site of the Buchenwald concentration camp by clearing a long-concealed hunting path. The video consists of various fragments of text, music, and different types of images: the opening bars of the overture of Mozart's opera *The Magic Flute* (*Die Zauberflöte*) played against a screen of pure red color; video footage showing the castle of Ettersberg and introducing a woman dressed as in the times of Goethe; a close-up of a pomegranate gently swinging in the wind; once again red color filling the screen while a female voice reads some lines from Goethe's *Elective Affinities*; the historically dressed woman shown in different positions on her way through the corridor in the forest that connects Schloss Ettersberg with the site of Buchenwald; archival film material depicting a crowd and a girl waving a swastika pennon; the sound of a train engine that can be heard while the archival images are replaced by a black-and-white film still of Buchenwald as viewed from the hunting path; and, in the end, this arrested image turning into a colored moving image. But does the work really end here? As the video loops, with no title or closing credits interrupting the flow of images, it is difficult to spot either a beginning or an ending. The structure of the work confirms its anti-linear character. Although a minimal narrative can be detected—the woman's stroll through specific locations (from Schloss Ettersberg to Buchenwald) and times (from Goethe's days to the horror regime of the Nazis)—the components of the work appear in a non-hierarchical, repetitive, and fragmentary order denying all kind of dramatic suspense or storytelling. Reflecting the antagonism of the humanist ideal of the Enlightenment symbolized in Goethe's works and the barbarism of National Socialism, the work is based on contrasts, breaks, interruptions, and oppositions, which are comprised in almost every sequence and may be interpreted differently according to the moment of their viewing. Commonly regarded as a symbol of love and prosperity, the pomegranate, when viewed a second time after the Buchenwald image, may rather be related to its other significations as "fruit of the dead" or human blood. (Seeram, Schulman, Heber, 2006: 168) The same ambivalence resides in the musical citation of Mozart's *Magic Flute*, which opposes the enlightened sovereign Sarastro to the obscure and revenge-driven Queen of the Night. The documentary sequence taken from footage shot by Marie Bonaparte on the occasion of Hitler's parade through Vienna on first May 1938, finally, represents this antagonism in a most uncanny way.[60] It shows a cheering crowd of adherents of the Nazi regime, while the underlying sound of a railway train and the subsequent shot of the Buchenwald building link these images to the deportation of the victims of the Final Solution. Finally, the quotation from Goethe's *Elective Affinities*, in which Ottilie, one of the female protagonists, suggests they build the park pavilion at a place on a hill from which it would be impossible to see the mansion but where "you would find yourself in a new and different world," can be seen, to recall Adorno's words, as the midpoint around which "equally weighted, paratactical parts [...] are arranged." (Adorno, 2013: 481) In fact, this "new and different world," which, in a first moment, invokes the utopia of Schloss Ettersberg as "the Court of the Muses," turns into the dystopian nightmare of Buchenwald when the repetition of the phrase is followed by the documentary sequence and the shot of the concentration camp. The circular, recurrent character of the work's constellation and the semantic ambivalence of its elements make it eventually impossible to embrace its meaning after one single viewing if it. Burgin describes the ideal viewer of his projection pieces as one who "accumulates his or her knowledge of the work" by a process of layering during which the repeated encounter with an image may entail different meanings and interpretations. (CP: 91) Henceforth, Homay King suggests that Burgin's projection works "are less cinematic than lectographic." (King, 2014: 73) Drawing on Gilles Deleuze's concept of the lectosign, King emphasizes the stratigraphic character of the images, which have to be read "the way a geologist might read strata of rock." (87)

The anachronistically dressed woman who traverses the literal space of the forest plays the role of an intermediary figure connecting and interrelating the video's different spatial, temporal, and symbolic strata.[61] Always seen from behind, she appears in different postures and in different spots between Schloss Ettersberg and Buchenwald, connecting the different kinds of images and indicating thus an imaginary trajectory through the actual and imaginary spaces depicted. As Norman Bryson has observed, this female figure can be related to paintings of Caspar David Friedrich, in which the "vistas of the Sublime are always blocked by another, by figures who turn their back, by a *Rückenfigur*." (Bryson, 2001: 50) Burgin confirms this interpretation when he writes that "[t]he 'retro' figure [...] helps to create an added distance" on a personal and cultural level. (PT: 156) Yet, this understanding of the *Rückenfigur* as a critical means of distancing should not hide the fact that the main function of this compositional device consists in weaving the spectator into the image by means of doubling the attitude of contemplation. In fact, the female figure embodies both Goethe's Ottilie, who dreams of a "new and different world," and the critical attitude of the contemplative spectator who, in keeping with the etymological meaning of the verb "contemplare," is encouraged "to look attentively, thoughtfully." (201) As Burgin noted on various occasions, layering and contemplation are processes and attitudes closer to painting than to cinema.[62] In fact, the shots of the woman in a certain sense *are* paintings, not only in that they allude to a particular pictorial trope, the *Rückenfigur*, but also because in most of these shots the female figure remains immobile resembling thus a specific type of painting—a *tableau vivant*. As re-enactment of a well-known artwork, performed by actors in appropriate historical costumes, the *tableau vivant* is a hybrid image that oscillates between the past and the present, between stasis and movement, between real space and fictional space, between collective memory and individual perception. As such, the *tableau vivant* functions exactly like *Lichtung*, which, as Burgin states, "selectively incorporating fragments from the image environment […] also branch[es] out to weave private and public into a unitary network of meanings." (RF: 72) I would argue that it is precisely for their ambivalent nature that Goethe included two long descriptions of *tableaux vivants* in the second part of his *Elective Affinities*. As a heterogeneous structure combining the competing art-forms of painting, theater, and sculpture, the *tableau vivant* offers an aesthetic model of the polarities on which the novel is based: attraction and repulsion, passion and conjugal life, wild and domesticated nature. But there is another aspect of Goethe's fascination with the *tableau vivant* that makes it even more relevant to Burgin's projection pieces. In *Italian Journey*, Goethe describes the "attitudes" of Lady Hamilton, performed as a living gallery of statues and paintings, as follows:

> He [Sir William Hamilton] has had a Greek gown made for her, which suits her finely, and she loosens her hair, takes a pair of shawls, and makes such an alternation of stance, gesture, and countenance, that one finally thinks one is dreaming. (Goethe, 1994: 170)

This adequation of the aesthetic experience with the state of dreaming comes very close to Burgin's conception of his work as a chain of associations closer to the spatio-temporal structure of unconscious discourse than to the narrative logic of a film. (PT: 198)

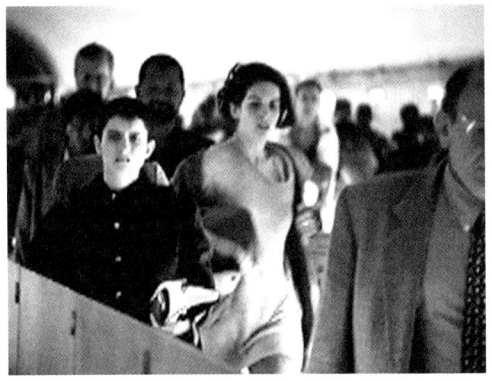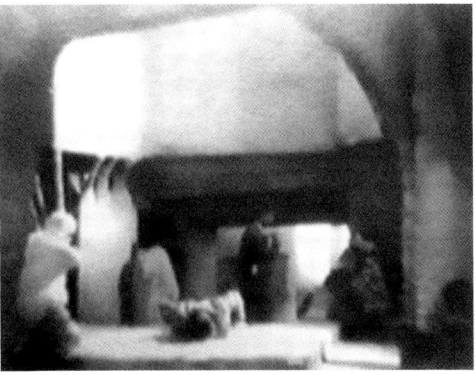

5.2. The Psychomediatic: Remembering, Repeating, and Working Through

Figure 5.1.

Stills from *Remembering, Repeating*, 1995.

Two-screen video projection. Two DVDs, 3-minute programme loops, colour, NTSC, stereo.

Burgin identifies, as the very principle of his audio-visual gallery work, that which Freud, in the title of one of his essays, defines as the fundamental stages of psychoanalytical therapy: "Remembering, Repeating and Working Through." (vbp: 78) In his essay of 1914, Freud states that in analytic treatment, the patient tends to replace the remembering of an unpleasant, forgotten, or repressed past experience by repeating it, more exactly: by transferring it to the doctor or a current situation: "He reproduces it not as a memory but as an action." (Freud, 1914/1958: 150) In the analytic treatment, the compulsive act of repeating as a form of resistance has to be brought to consciousness, to be *worked through*, in order to awaken the repressed memories. (155) Although Burgin's projection works are not to be confused with a psychoanalytic session, they function, on a structural level, in a similar way. Rather than merely reproducing identical and identifiable images or memories, repetition is part of a dynamic act of displacement in which the relation to memories is established through an active process of working-through, as an activity of bringing to consciousness, of re-constructing memory, that has to been done by both sides: on the side of the artist who connects the repeated elements to a loop of heterogeneous fragments and on the side of the viewer who has to make sense of these repeated memory fragments by an act of interpretation and confrontation with his own memories and recollections.[63]

Predating *Lichtung* by three years, the two-screen video projection *Remembering, Repeating* (1995) is the first audiovisual work that, quoting Freud's essay in its title, definitely replaces a linear narrative by a repetitive structure. (Fig. 5.1.) Created on the occasion of the inaugural exhibition of the Museum of Contemporary Art in Lyon, the work was a reaction to the 1995 bombing attacks carried out by Islamist terrorists on public transport systems in Paris and Lyon. The installation consists of two three-minute loops, one showing people of different color and ethnic backgrounds passing on an underground moving walkway at Montparnasse metro station, the other presenting a short extract from Julien Duvivier's film *Pépé le Moko* (1937) in which Jean Gabin runs through the Casbah

Figure 5.2.

Still from *Szerelmes Levelek (Love Letters)*, 1997.

Three-screen video projection. DVD, 10-minute programme loops, colour, NTSC, stereo.

of Algiers following the woman he loves. (Burgin, 2000: 34) In a certain way, the confrontation of these two repeated sequences—one from a fiction film set in Algiers before the Algerian War of independence, the other documenting a banal scene of everyday life at a moment of postcolonial violence—suggests a working-through of the political unconscious of French colonial history and its fraught memories. The eternal return of oppression, violence, and threat is evoked on various levels. The moment when a woman in purdah rises straight after Jean Gabin's fall seems to presage the Algerian revolution beginning not even two decades after the film's release. The repetitive, monotonous movement of a multi-ethnic crowd of people in the underground of Montparnasse, as a symbol of capitalist values of mobility and economic development, stands for both: the integration of the people from the former colonies into French society and the threats produced by the unresolved problems in dealing with the colonial history and its legacies.

Produced two years later for the Mücsarnok Museum in Budapest, *Szerelmes Levelek (Love Letters)* reflects the analytical principle of "Remembering, Repeating and Working Through" not only in its structure but also in its content. (Fig. 5.2.-5.3.) The voice-over is composed of two distinct texts. The first is a condensed version of the Hungarian

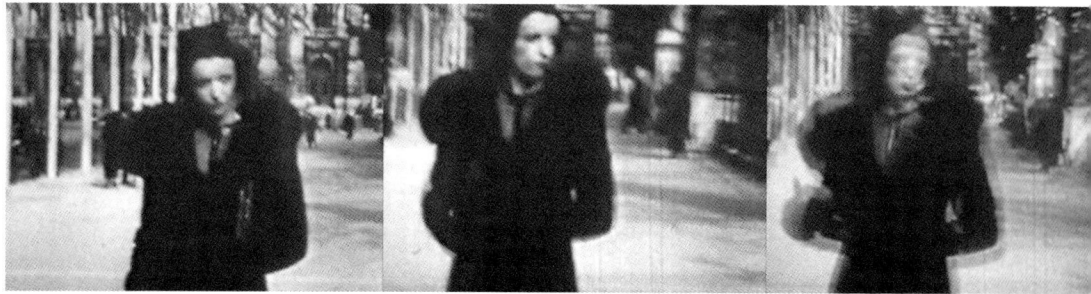

psychologist Sàndor Ferenczi's letters to Freud in which he writes to his elder colleague and friend about his love affair with his patient Elma Pálos, the daughter of his then lover Gizella Pálos. The second is based on Freud's paper "Observations on Transference-love," which follows "Remembering, Repeating and Working Through" as the third part of a series of writings on the technique of psychoanalysis, and can be understood as a theoretical comment on Ferenczi's problematic professional and emotional entanglement. The ten-minute loop of the video projection consists of views of a moving landscape, seen from the train between Budapest and Vienna, the hometowns of the two psychologists. These images are intercalated with footage from a short movie made by the Princess Marie Bonaparte in the streets of Vienna close to Freud's domicile in Berggasse 19, three months after the Anschluss. (Burgin, 1997: 9) Filming the crowd attending Hitler's parade through the streets of the Austrian capital on the 1st of May 1938, Bonaparte, toward the end of the film, frames an isolated young woman who hesitates in front of the camera before disappearing. Digitally reworked, on a frame by frame basis, these four seconds of film are expanded into "dreamlike" sequences that punctuate the landscape and the two narratives. (9)

Deformed, stretched, saccadic, displaced, superposed, these sequences transform the woman into a ghostly revenant from the past while symbolizing, at the same time, Ferenczi's conflict in having to choose between the two women, the mother and the daughter. The fragment from the third act of Richard Strauss's opera *Der Rosenkavalier*, in which the Marschallin, the mature lover of Octavian, yields her place to the younger Sophie, echoes this intricate love constellation in musical form. And when Octavian, in a final duet, proclaims: "We are together. All else is like a dream," he simply inverts the commonly made distinction between love ("dream") and ordinary life ("reality"). In other words, the dream *is* reality. This blurring of the distinction between reality and dream in relation to love is also at the heart of the concept of transference-love as discussed in Freud's essay and summarized by the second voice of *Love Letters*. In transference-love, repressed feelings or

Figure 5.3.

Stills from *Szerelmes Levelek (Love Letters)*, 1997.

Three-screen video projection. DVD, 10-minute programme loops, colour, NTSC, stereo.

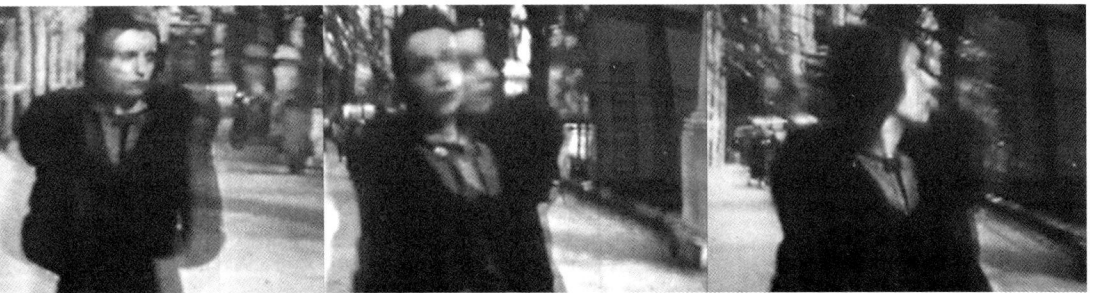

impulses of the past are unconsciously redirected to the analyst. It is thus a form of repetition that hinders the patient from remembering the origin of her or his problem. As a response to the first voice's account of Ferenczi's illicit love relationship with Elma Pálos, the second voice relates Freud's comments on transference-love, emphasizing the danger of returning the patient's feelings by the analyst:

> If the patient's love were to be returned it would be a great triumph for her, but a complete defeat for the treatment. She would have succeeded in acting out, in repeating in real life, what she ought only to have remembered. [...] He (the analyst) must treat the love as something unreal, as a situation which has to be worked through in the treatment and traced back to its unconscious origins. (Burgin, 1997: 27-31)

If there is something in this passage about the abovementioned confusion between reality and dream or fantasy, it seems more important that the problem of transference-love can be resolved not by acting it out but only by tracing it back to its unconscious origins. As Burgin notes by drawing on Freud's book *Group Psychology and the Analysis of the Ego* (1921), the process of transferring an idealized form of love to the analyst, as embodiment of authority, can also be observed in a group's adulation of a political leader, a phenomenon that found its most appalling expression in the unconditional devotion to Hitler during the mass rallies organized by the NSDAP. (Burgin, 1997: 9) In *Love Letters*, the political unconscious interferes in the person of the woman who haunts the streets of Hitler's Vienna as much as she punctuates the narrative of the video in form of a refracted, blurred, deferred specter, which reminds us that in the process of working-through we cannot circumvent the traumas of history if at least we do not want them to return to us as ominous ghosts.

If the analogy with the psychoanalytic session as a process of working-through is an important aspect of Burgin's "uncinematic" projection works, their spatio-temporal structure has more in common with the objects of psychoanalysis: dreams and unconscious fantasies. Referring to the *ritornello* and the psychical mechanism of deferred action, Burgin compares the structure of his work with Jean Laplanche and Serge Leclaire's characterization of the way fantasies and daydreams manifest themselves in the form of "short sequences, most often fragmentary, circular and repetitive." (VBP: 78; Laplanche and Leclaire, 1972: 162-163) In the three works discussed above, these three principles of fragmentation, circularity, and repetition successively come to the fore: *Remembering, Repeating* still focuses almost exclusively on the repetition of two shots that loop on two distinct screens.

Fragmentation becomes a crucial issue in *Love Letters*, where different elements—moving and still images, archive material, monochrome red screens and music extracts—are assembled in a continuous loop. Yet the linear narrative of the two texts and the projection of the same video in three adjacent rooms, each time accompanied by a different voice-over,[64] attenuates the circular character of the loop. *Lichtung* is the first audiovisual piece in which all three structural features are integrated in one continuously looping sequence of repeating image fragments.

As in the works of the 1980s, the projection works are constructed like a dream, "not as a unitary narrative but as a fragmentary rebus." (PT: 199) In view of this double psychoanalytic focus, Burgin's "uncinematic" projection works might be better described as "psychomatic" or, as Anthony Vidler suggests, in terms of "psycho-(pan)optics." (Vidler, 2014: 129) Burgin moreover notes that this particular spatio-temporality of the "uncinematic" would also have "much in common with that of the Internet." (TC: 205) In fact, as addressed above, Burgin compares the way we perceive films today with the psychical structure of unconscious discourse. The *cinematic* heterotopia is finally an *uncinematic* setting, for it dispenses with linear narration in favor of fragmentation and heterogeneity. To demonstrate the coincidences between his uncinematic projection work, the realm of the unconscious, and the environment of media images, Burgin returns to the concept of parataxis:

> In classical rhetoric, *parataxis* is the name given to the juxtaposition of disparate elements, the relations between which are not given but must be inferred. The organization of the cinematic heterotopia is paratactical, as is that of the Internet; the presentation of elements in a psychoanalytic session is paratactical, as is a dream. The form of organization of materials in the type of work I have called 'uncinematic' is also paratactical. (PT: 200)

At this point, the term of the "uncinematic" stretches its limits. First, because the implication that the organization of the "uncinematic" projection loops is analogue to the "cinematic" heterotopia's new mode of reception of cinema leads to the conceptual paradox of the "uncinematic cinematic." More importantly, in defining the work only in terms of what it is *not* (not *traditional* cinema, not motion pictures), the concept lacks a positive approach to what these works eventually *are*. In view of their paratactical organization, which they share with both psychoanalysis and the environment of media images, the projection pieces might be better described as "psychomediatic."

Yet the relationship between the paratactical projection works and the paratactical Internet is dialectical and critical rather than affirmative. Although both have a similar spatio-temporal structure, Burgin's work is all but a mere illustration of the way in which digital media platforms operate. In a certain sense, the paratactical organization of his work is diametrically opposed to the way images are distributed and perceived in contemporary media society. The overall purpose of social media is the unfettered flux of communication, maximal efficiency, and illimited disposability in order to serve a transparence society that, according to the philosopher Byung-Chul Han, tolerates neither gaps of information nor gaps of vision. But it is precisely silence and emptiness that are necessary for thinking and inspiration. (Han, 2012: 11) In opposition to the cinematic heterotopia, however, Burgin integrates gaps, absences, and silences in his paratactical works as an offer to the viewer to close his eyes and to "follow individual trains of associations." (PT, 2011: 200) While our media society seeks to close gaps by burying them under a ceaseless flood of images, Burgin accentuates these "places where nothing happens" by means of blanks between two sequences or moments of stillness. In *Love Letters* and *Lichtung*, for example, the red monochrome surfaces which are inserted into the flow of images function as such gaps which open a space of reflection. Another way to create such moments of stillness is through the interruption of motion by the integration of still images or fixed-camera shots of immobile objects (the *tableaux vivants* of *Lichtung*). Without any doubt, this kind of "pausing" the flow of images must be understood as an invitation to become what Raymond Bellour called the pensive spectator. Similar to a photo that interrupts the movement of a movie, these moments of stillness subtract the viewer from the fictional narrative. "Creating a distance, another time," they permit the viewer "to invest more freely in what [she or he] is seeing." (Bellour, 2007: 120) Burgin compares such "places where nothing happens" with the Japanese concept of *ma* which, according to Augustin Berque, marks "the interval that necessarily […] exists between two successive things; hence the idea of pause." (VBP: 81; Berque, 2004: 29-30) Burgin further states that this kind of understanding of space "emphasizes relations—intervals, gaps, distances—and attenuates objects." (VBP: 83) If we relate this train of thought to the concepts of the pensive spectator (Bellour) and the contemplative spectator (Burgin), it becomes clear that the relational character of Burgin's projection pieces does not only concern the organization of the work itself but also the way it interacts with its viewer. It is precisely the *ma* in the projection works—the gaps, silences, pauses—that counters the pervasive, uninterrupted flow of images across disparate screens and media platforms, thus contributing to a critical reflection "of the media saturated environment of global market capitalism." (VBP: 85)

5.3. Photofilmic Psycho-panoramics[65]

Since the turn of the millennium, Burgin has regularly included pan-oramic images in his work. Historically, he situates these panoramic projection pieces in both the tradition of the panorama of the nine-teenth century and the context of his own work since the late 1960s. In *Components of a Practice* he writes:

> The implied space of my work has its origins not in the history of cinema, but in its prehistory, and in the historical moment of Conceptual Art. […] in retrospect I can see that, whether by co-incidence or unconscious design, all of my work since then (the late 1960s) has taken the form either of frames laid along a track, or of frames panoramically deployed around a room. (CP: 91)

This association of conceptual art and the panorama can also be ob-served in the work of other conceptual artists such as Dennis Oppenheim, Robert Morris, Ed Ruscha, and Dan Graham, who used panoramic for-mats and gestures in order to counter Modernism and to open up new perspectives concerning the aesthetic and cultural status of art, includ-ing its relationship with space, time, representation, and perception. For Burgin, one of the most interesting features of the panorama is that it "produces a frame that is 'acompositional.'" Limited only in height but not horizontally, 360-degree panoramic photography exceeds framing, which is "the very basis of 'art photography.'" (CP: 92) As discussed in Chapter 2, the institutionalization of photography as "fine art" in the 1960s, as it was embedded in a modernist discourse that assesses the detail, the vantage point, and the frame as key standards of the medium (Szarkowski, 2007), was harshly critiqued by Victor Burgin and others. Contrary to Szarkowski's hermetic frame that organizes the lines and forms of the photograph in an independent, autonomous composition, the panorama offered a means to move beyond the limitation of the frame and to conceive of the work as a dynamic process unfolding in time and space.[66] As argued in Chapter 1, *Photopath* (1967) is also based on a panoramic logic, insofar as the work, instead of encasing reality into a single composition, duplicates the real floor by an elongated photo-graphic trace meant to invite the spectator's critical reflection on modes of perception. (Roberts, 1997: 82)

Whereas in conceptual art, panoramic forms and strategies were mostly used to explode the frame of Modernism, the panoramic images of Burgin's projection works are directly linked to recent technological shifts in contemporary visual culture. Made of computer-animated still photographs, they simultaneously evoke silence *and* flow by producing the paradox of moving stillness or still motion. They are "photofilmic"

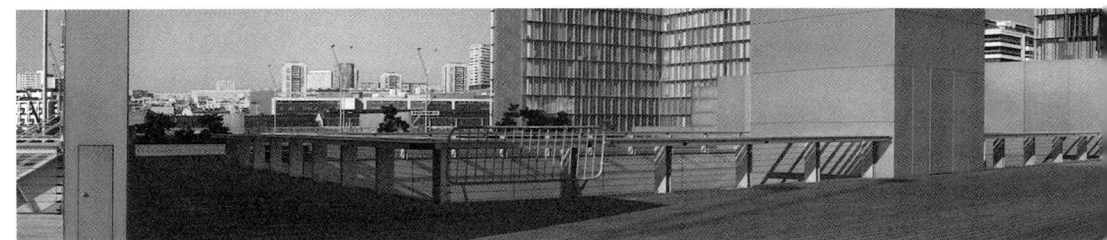

images insofar as they are neither photographs nor films but something in-between, combining photographic stillness with one of cinema's most popular and powerful camera moves, the pan shot, produced by swiveling a camera horizontally while its base is fixed on a point. The term "pan" actually is derived from panorama. Rather than photographs or films, these images are "photographic" *and* "filmic" (that is, "photofilmic"), for they imitate or simulate main characteristics of both media. Computer graphics, Lev Manovich observes, do not so much achieve realism, but "*photorealism*," or "the ability to fake not our perceptual and bodily experience of reality but only its photographic image." (Manovich, 1997: 63) The photofilmic panoramas of Burgin's projection pieces work in a similar manner, except that they do not fake reality but reflect on their own status as images. They are theoretical images. Rather than aiming at an illusionary representation of the real world, they layer, as it were, contradictory principles of photography and film, thus revealing their photographic and filmic conditions. Their theoretical status also concerns the question of specificity. On the one hand, the hybrid character of these photofilmic panoramas acknowledges the fact that, in digital culture, the boundaries between photography and film increasingly get blurred. Produced with the same cameras, relying on similar algorithmic processes, and diffused via the same media platforms, photographic and filmic images cannot be conceived any longer as ontologically and technologically clearly distinct media. (Cohen and Streitberger, 2016: 11) On the other hand, the panoramic sequences in Burgin's projection pieces highlight the specificity of the projection works in general, for they reflect, as a kind of *mise-en-abyme*, the circular structure of the loop. (VBP: 68) In *Components of a Practice*, Burgin points out that the panoramas produce a *theoretical* vision. (CP: 92) Beyond the decision where to place the camera, the production steps are largely automatized: basic principles of subjective photography, such as composition and framing, are reduced to a minimum as the position of the camera is entirely determined by the nodal point of the lens, which must coincide exactly with the axis of rotation to avoid that the effect of parallax "will prevent the software from successfully combining the separate images into a single seamless panorama."

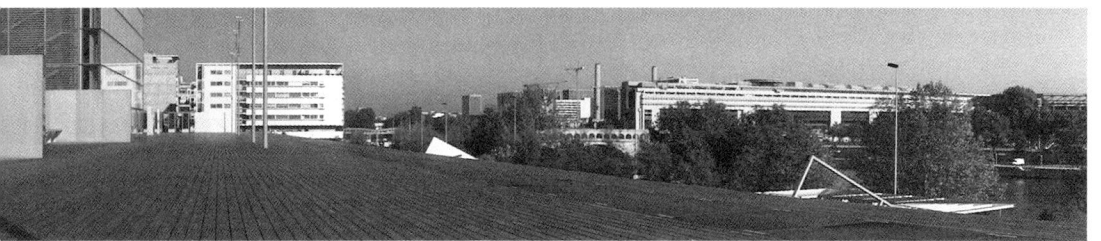

(92) The virtual, computer-generated camera pan, finally, generates an "incorporeal form of vision" based rather on mathematical calculations than on subjective decision-making. As such a-compositional, incorporeal, hybrid theoretical images, these panoramas are not only uncinematic but also unphotographic. Phenomenologically, they have their origin rather in the historical panorama of the nineteenth century. At the same time, they respond to the return of the panorama toward the end of the twentieth century, as animated photographic 360-degree-views that swamp the Internet in the form of software applications and multimedia services such as QuickTime VR, Pano2VR, Photosynth, and Google Street View.

Figure 5.4.

Stills from *Nietzsche's Paris*, 1999–2000.

Single screen video projection, DVD, 8 minute programme loop, colour, NTSC, stereo.

The first projection work to be based on panoramas is *Nietzsche's Paris* (1999-2000). (Fig. 5.4.-5.5.) After having completed *Lichtung* for Schloss Ettersberg, Burgin was encouraged to produce a work to commemorate the centenary of Friedrich Nietzsche's death in Weimar in 1900. This original project did not come to fruition, however. When later on Burgin was asked by the Architectural Association in London to make a video for an exhibition, he returned to Nietzsche, combining him as a topic with the concept of architecture and the site of Paris, where Burgin was living at the time. (Burgin, 2000: 149) Although Nietzsche never visited Paris, the French metropole was part of his im-

Figure 5.5.

Still from *Nietzsche's Paris*, 1999–2000.

Single screen video projection, DVD, 8 minute programme loop, colour, NTSC, stereo.

aginary as a European intellectual, and it was also the place that he chose as the future residence for his intellectual *ménage à trois* with Lou Salomé and Paul Rée. (150) After some intimate weeks Nietzsche spent with Salomé in the forest of Tautenberg in August 1882, the plans of the three friends came abruptly to an end in November when Rée and Salomé unexpectedly left Nietzsche during a common stay in Leipzig. In the video, two elements refer to this romantic triangle relationship: the image of a historically dressed woman, sitting on a

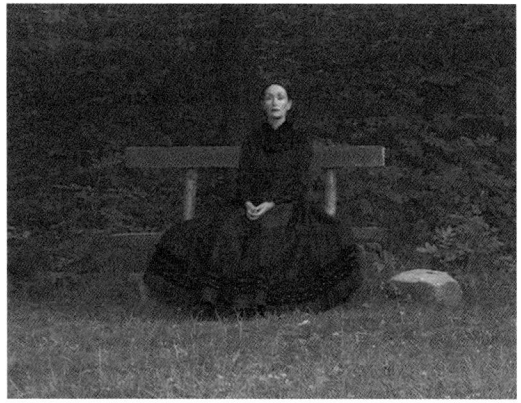

bench in front of a forest, evoking Nietzsche's romance with Salomé in the forest of Tautenberg, and a female voice that quotes, in German, Salomé's dream of an ideal intellectual living community:

> I saw a pleasant study filled with books and flowers, between two bedrooms, and, coming and going amongst us, comrades in thought forming an intellectual circle at once serious and gay. (Burgin, 2000: 150; Andreas-Salomé, 1995: 45)

Both images are related to dreams that do not represent reality but are the result of fantasies and wishes. While Salomé's image of an intellectual circle *is* a dream of an ideal community, the immobile woman, transformed into a *tableau vivant*, becomes an image perceived *like* a dream, an image that—to recall Goethe's words—makes us think that we are dreaming. The image of the woman returns four times in the video, each time following a photofilmic panorama taken on the esplanade of the National library of France (BNF) in Paris. As Burgin explains in an email exchange, the panorama is the result of a complex process of transformation from moving images to still images and vice versa:

> I used a video camera mounted on a still photo panoramic tripod head. This head provides "click stops" in equal increments around 360 degrees. I shot a few seconds of video from each position. I then chose one frame from each of the short video clips. I then "stitched" the frames together in software to create a long panoramic still image. I then retouched the image to remove all human beings. I then animated the image in another program to create a "moving" panorama.

The frozenness of the images and the absence of all human life in these moving still panoramas create an uncanny effect, conjuring up the spirits of modernist urbanism that haunt Dominique Perrault's architecture. (Parfait, 2002: 115) Harking back to the monumental diagrammatic towers of Le Corbusier's 1925 proposal Ville Voisin, Perrault's four huge glass towers found inspiration in modernist concepts of rationality and transparency. But, as Anthony Vidler eloquently argues, Perrault's building "multiplies architectural contradictions," for it blocks the transparency of the glass façades in order to protect the books stored in the towers and further includes a sunken garden that "constitutes a blocked center." (Vidler, 2000: 14) While Burgin's panoramas scrutinize almost every angle and view of the library's esplanade, this "untouchable Eden" from which the public is banned, is completely absent. Or, put another way, Perrault's sunken garden is replaced by a garden of another kind: Salomé's dream of an ideal space where learning, enjoyment, and nature come together—an intellectual circle proposed as an alternative to the ossified panoramic circle of the modernist panoptic view.

At first glance, the four panoramic views seem to be identical, but a closer look reveals that they are not. They are taken from the center of each side of the rectangular site of the esplanade. The soundtrack intensifies the uncanny feel of these "different repetitions." (CP: 94) After a sustained silence throughout most of its duration, the panoramic pan ends each time with a different sound-fragment: two extracts from George Frederick Handel's operas *Alcina* and *Ariodante*, conceivably evoking Nietzsche's love deception (Massin, 2007: 146), alternate with Salomé's dream vision, once spoken in German by a female voice and once in condensed written form. Burgin describes this structure of "different repetitions" in terms of layering and spiraling when he writes: "The work is structured so that each turn of the spiral of reprise will 'thicken' the semantic texture of the piece through a process of layering of knowledges and associations." (CP: 94) On the one hand, this description recalls, once again, the structure of a dream based on the processes of condensation (layering) and displacement (association). On the other hand, Burgin compares this kind of reprise with the psychical mechanism of deferred action, in which an unconscious traumatic event of the past may retroactively acquire a meaning when recalled in different circumstances. (VBP: 78) The loop then takes the form of "an uncanny rondo," (Vidler, 2000: 15) in which both, Nietzsche's and Salomé's romantic vison of an intimate circle of intellectual friendship and the belief in transparency and visual control, as epitomized in Corbusian architecture and the panorama, return as repressed antagonistic—yet complementary—symbols of the conflict of affect and rationality in modern society.[67]

5.4. Panorama and Sequence-Image

In his cultural history of virtual reality, Oliver Grau describes the panorama as a forerunner of digitally-produced, 360-degree immersive imagery. According to him, the panorama, both as a nineteenth-century architectural setting and as a virtual environment within a contemporary digital space, constitutes a "homogeneous images space" that "integrate[s] the observer in a 360-degree space of illusion, or immersion, with unity of time and place." (Grau, 2003: 127, 13) Not heterogeneity, but the totalized space of the *Gesamtkunstwerk*. (126) Anne Friedberg endorses the same position when she opposes the media window's multiple, fractured perspective to QuickTime panoramas as "digital simulacra of perspectival space." (Friedberg, 2006: 3) Yet both accounts neglect the temporal complexity of the panorama, albeit with contrasting conclusions. Grau declares the "360-degree image concept" as the underlying principle of a paradigmatic change toward the immersive, "polysensual virtual *hypermedium*," (Grau, 2001: 136-137 [my translation]),[68] and Friedberg sets the virtual window against panoramic, continuous imaging as "a new logic of visuality," a fractured and multiplied "time-architecture." (Friedberg, 2006: 18)

Yet the panorama has rarely been a merely totalizing, homogeneous time-space simulation. Apart from the ideal case of some city panoramas offering a detailed one-to-one depiction of a 360-degree view from a well-chosen, elevated position, the panorama typically condenses and compresses several different locations and events. Beginning in the early nineteenth century, so-called "moving-panoramas" of picturesque landscapes were rolled out before the eyes of astonished spectators sitting in railway carriages or boats. A sort of virtual tourism, these trips to famous places around the world—from Manchester to Liverpool, along the Bay of Naples, or down the Mississippi from the St. Antony Falls to New Orleans—compressed time-consuming travel to the acceptable timespan of one hour, sometimes even simulating changing day/night effects and seasonal or climatic changes. (Comment, 1999: 64) In fact, this way of compressing time is not specific to moving panoramas, but can also be observed in numerous static, circular panoramas with battle scenes or landscapes. Particularly toward the end of the nineteenth century, in attempting to compete with the moving images of cinema, various strategies were put in place in order to introduce temporal dynamics and narrative properties into the static image, for example by condensing different moments of an event, presenting them simultaneously on the same canvas. A visitor's description of the *Battle at Aboukir* panorama from 1799 clearly points to this temporal incoherence:

> It is night (and what a terrible night it must have been, if the scene reproduced here is accurate). Although the painter had to choose only one moment to portray, nothing prevented him from condensing the most interesting parts of the battle and depicting two different encounters. (Oettermann, 1997: 107)

In his 2005 essay "The Time of the Panorama," Burgin decisively rejects the idea of the panorama as a coherent time-space. "The time of the panorama," he writes,

> was never simply that of simultaneity. Panoramic scenes of battle, for example, tended to display the temporality of their antecedents in the genre of history painting, where the before and after of an historic moment may appear alongside the moment itself, projecting the diachronic onto the plane of the synchronic. (SA: 303)

The temporal perception of the viewer, who is obliged to traverse an apparently frozen moment in time, corresponds with this heterogeneity in represented temporality. "Even cityscape and landscape panoramas," Burgin continues, "inevitably entail the time of viewing, as it is not possible to take in the entire image at a glance." (303) Rather than constituting a spatio-temporal continuum or unity, the panorama contains imbricated representational and perceptual temporalities, which are concealed by the simulation of an overwhelming, totalized experience in the service of ideological, political, and economic aims. This ambiguity in the coexistence of spatial and temporal experience, or, in other words, of instantaneous overview and *durée*, links the panorama to the concept of the sequence-image.

As has been stressed, Burgin compares the way we perceive films within the cinematic heterotopia with psychical processes of inner speech or dreams. In the cinematic heterotopia, Burgin argues, "films" are not viewed in one piece, but emerge in the form of trailers, photographs, reviews, short videoclips, scattered through space and time, which can take on a shape only within the psychical space of memory. Phenomenologically, then, the experience of a film does not depend solely on direct experience but is always permeated by memory images. This leads Burgin to Henri Bergson who becomes a continual frame of reference for his writing and, as I would argue, for his artistic practice as well. In "The Time of the Panorama," Burgin quotes Bergson from *Matière et mémoire* (1939): "Perception is never a simple contact of the mind with the object present; it is completely impregnated with memory-images which complete and interpret it." (SA: 304; Bergson, 1999: 146) From this, it follows that the visible and the remembered, the real and the virtual, are not two opposing or separate categories. They enter, as Deleuze notes, "into a narrow circuit that takes us constantly from one to the other." (SA: 304; Deleuze and Parnet, 2002: 184) Describing the projection loops as anti-narrative loops consisting of recurrent elements "shadowed by a stream of prior and future images," Homay King insists on the importance of Bergson's concept of the virtual in Burgin's work. (King, 2014: 73) As King points out, Bergson understands the virtual not merely in terms of memory images belonging to the past, but also highlights their relevance in the present and their potential for the future. (74) What seems most relevant for Burgin's photofilmic projection loops is the connection Bergson establishes between stillness/movement and past/present. In order to prove that the distinction between movement and immobility is not natural but based on a mental operation, Bergson presents the images of two trains that simultaneously begin to move. In this case, he observes, the impression of immobility is the product of the adjustment of one movement to the other. (Bergson, 1985: 175) He next concludes that immobility is nothing but the effect of a perceptual operation that is necessary to make things one's own by isolating them from the perpetual flux of indivisible movements. According to the philosopher, the same is true for time, because real duration implies the "persistence of the past in the present." (163) This entanglement of movement and stillness, past and present, is crucial to Burgin's projection works, for in them he constantly juxtaposes, confronts, and mingles different times and categories of images. In *Nietzsche's Paris*, for example, Handel's baroque music, Nietzsche's fin de siècle-romance, and Perrault's (post)modernist architecture contrast with and comment on each other, while the panoramas' virtual movements across the immobilized esplanade of the Parisian national library blur the distinction between stillness and motion.

In 2004, Burgin introduced the idea of the sequence-image as a concept apt to think about the way images act in a space *between* memory and perception, past and present, stillness and movement. Even though he is reluctant to apply this term—which he introduced as a "purely theoretical entity"—to his artistic work, I would argue that the idea of the sequence-image is fundamental for a closer understanding of Burgin's projection loops, in particular those in which he refers to cinema, such as *Another Case History* (1999), *Listen to Britain* (2002), *Voyage to Italy* (2005), *Solito Posto* (2008), *Parzival* (2013), and *The Ideal City* (2013). (PT: 215) In the introduction to *The Remembered Film*, Burgin describes his earliest memory of a film as "a sequence of such brevity that I might almost be describing a still image." (RF: 16) The sequence-image refers here to a very specific act of remembering a film that, like a flash of lightning, illumines some features of the movies while most of the film's content remains blurred or obscure. Burgin's account of this memory reads like a condensed description of a dream: "A dark night, someone is walking down a narrow stream. I see only feet splashing through water, and broken reflections of light from somewhere ahead, where something mysterious and dreadful waits." (16) Next, he defines the sequence-image as a train of associations that may emerge spontaneously like "a rapidly arpeggiated musical chord, the individual notes of which, although sounded successively, vibrate together simultaneously." (21) Unlike an image sequence, which is solely a linear arrangement of still images, the sequence-image is a complex, heterogeneous mixture of different kinds of moving and still images based on memories and impressions of the real world: "the 'sequence-image' is both the elemental unit from which chains of signifiers are formed and the hinge between movement and stasis, the motionless point of turning between unconscious fantasy and the real." (SA: 268) Drawing on Bergson's definition of perception as engendered by the encounter between the present object and memory images, Burgin defines the sequence-image as a hybrid constellation situated between past and present, temporal and spatial logics, imagination and reality. In its capacity as a "folding of the diachronic into the synchronic" (RF: 26), the sequence-image has a temporal structure similar to that of the panorama. As argued, the panorama, like the sequence-image, has never been a question of mere sequential narration or of simple, simultaneous presence. Burgin's projection work may be understood, then, as a visual exploration of the relation between panoramic vision and the logic of the sequence-image, opening up a space where different kinds of images coexist in a fragmentary, non-teleological way.

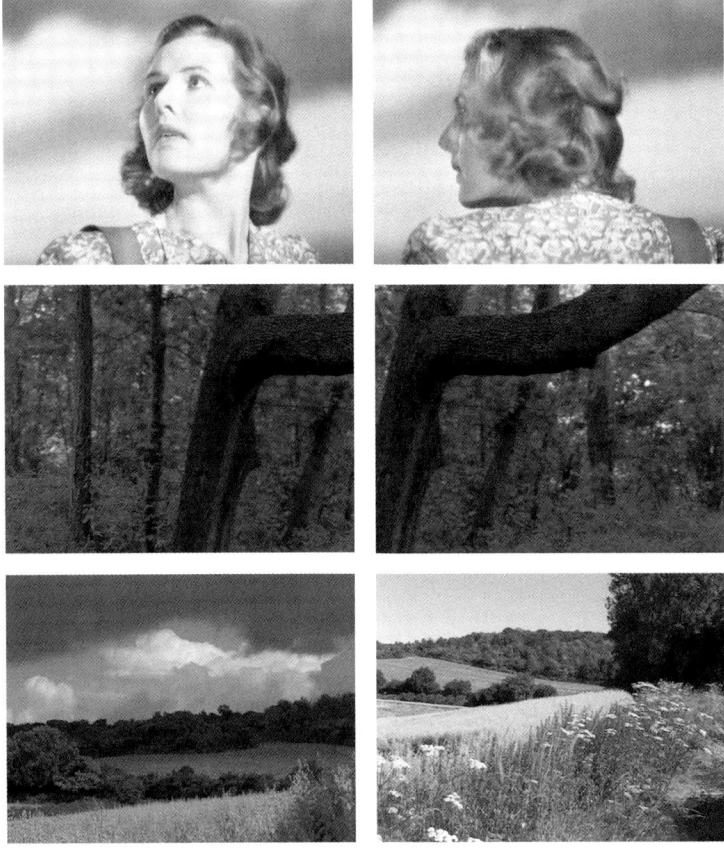

Figure 5.6.

Stills from *Listen to Britain*, 2002.

Single screen video projection, DVD, 7 minute programme loop, colour, NTSC, stereo.

Listen to Britain is inspired by a railway journey Burgin made in 2001 to Bristol, where he was invited to produce a new video for an arts center. (SCR: 51) (Fig. 5.6.) Traveling through a peaceful countryside shortly after *September 11*, he found that the tense situation in Britain led him to think of the documentary *Listen to Britain* (1942), produced during World War Two when the country was threatened by German invasion.

The recollection of this film led him to a scene from *A Canterbury Tale* (1944), a fiction film by Michael Powell and Emeric Pressburger in which the female protagonist, played by Sheila Sim, suddenly turns her head around, thus connecting the view of Canterbury cathedral with a sound that seems to reach her from long ago: "she experiences the unexpected return of an image from a common national history and hears sounds from a shared past that haunts the hill." (SCR: 51) In the video, these film impressions are represented by an edited dialogue from *A Canterbury Tale* and intertitles that resume the film's intrigue, landscape shots that Burgin took of the film's original setting, an extract from Benjamin Britten's composition *A Midsummer Night's Dream* (1960), and, finally, four 90-degree sections of a photofilmic forest panorama based on still video frames stitched together and (re)animated on the computer. Like the sequence-image, the video is a concatenation of disparate components that present themselves in a chain of free associations triggered by "a trace of the trace left in my memory by a film." (53) The "traces" of *A Canterbury Tale* are themselves short sequence-images, in particular the brief film clip of the woman turning her head and the intertitles which are comparable in form to Burgin's recollections (cited above) of his first film:

> American servicemen | in the village | cannot find | local girls | who will go out with them | At night | the Glue Man | emerges from shadows | pours glue on a girl's hair | then disappears (SCR: 47)

The pivotal moment of the video involves the clip from *A Canterbury Tale*, in which Sheila Sim suddenly turns around as if she heard something behind her. But in the video there is no sound. Her "panoramic" gesture occasions a cut, followed by a section of the black-and-white forest panorama. In the subsequent sequence, composed of five different shots, Burgin reconstructs the moment in *A Canterbury Tale* when the camera follows the woman climbing up a hill—but this time the landscape is seen from the climber's point of view. (CP: 131) Now music is playing. It is the original soundtrack of the film, linking the fictional past of the film to the present of the documentary shots. The sequence of shots, tracking through a landscape and accompanied by music, may remind one of another kind of panoramic experience: that of the abovementioned simulation of a train or boat journey. In his book, *The Railway Journey*, Wolfgang Schivelbusch associated panoramic perception with the railroad and "the accelerated circulation of commodities." (Schivelbusch, 1986: 193) Burgin's concept of the panorama is also linked to the railway journey, but not (only) as a symptom of capitalist commodity culture, but (also) as the trigger of a rebus-like concatenation of images: "visual images, word-images and sound-images, perceptions, recollections and fantasies, [which] emerge successively but not teleologically." (SA: 297) In this perspective, *Listen to Britain* comes close to what Burgin describes as a sequence-image and, as such, may be defined as a model for how we perceive a film or other narrative forms within today's mass media environment—as "a heterogeneous psychical object, constructed from image scraps scattered in space and time." (IDS: 22-23; RF: 9)

5.5. Paths through the Virtual Sphere

From around 2010, Burgin became increasingly interested in applications and technologies, such as Photosynth and Google Street View, which ground the claim to totality on the concealment of actual spatial and temporal discontinuities, in order to allow users to "visit" places around the world with 360-degree panoramic imagery. Stitched together with hundreds and thousands of images, these virtual spaces cannot be experienced physically, as was the case with the panorama rotunda. What is promoted as a means of offering direct and constant access to the world and of guaranteeing a "visceral sense of presence" (Snavely, Seitz, Szeliski, 2006: 835), is, in fact, a highly artificial, virtual space, which, rather than depicting reality, coordinates images taken from different perspectives and different times. Developed by Microsoft Live Labs, Photosynth, for instance, automatically reconstructs overlapping photographs into an immersive 3D model. In his account of the 2014 version of Photosynth, Sebastian Anthony wrote enthusiastically: "the new one, Photosynth 3D, is even more guaranteed to blow your mind and redefine how you think about the limitations—and possibilities— of photography in 2014." (Anthony, 2014: 9) Such 360-degree environments can be re-created on the basis of both private photographs taken on the spot or images selected in image hosting websites such as Flickr. In the latter case, the software recognizes automatically different camera positions and orientations within the photographs in order to assemble them into a coherent, navigable 3D-environment. More precisely, the software application "analyses digital images for sites of uniqueness, generates a three-dimensional point cloud of the represented space and reassembles the images into a near-seamless composite." (Uricchio, 2011: 28) The Internet user can move through this virtual space passing outside to inside, zooming in and out, turning around in a 360-degree circle, in order to explore this assembled three-dimensional photographic space in almost any direction. According to Burgin, such technologies merge the cinematic heterotopia "with the endless process of becoming of a perpetual infinite film, the frames of which are the totality of all recorded images, reduplicating the real world in the virtual." (PT: 187) In their article "Finding Paths through the World's Photos," the research team of Washington University and Microsoft Research, which developed the software, indicate that their ultimate aim is "to recreate a compelling experience of 'being there'—virtually traveling to a remote place or interacting with a virtual object." (Snavely, Garg, Seitz and Szeliski, 2006: 11) This is precisely how the historical panorama was conceived right from its invention.

But in contrast with the handmade panoramic paintings, it is now the algorithm that controls the selection of images and the ways in which we experience the 3D-environment. As William Uricchio observed, "it is this algorithmic layer that stands between the calculating subject and the object calculated," and, as he specifies:

> It is a program layer that changes, that is redefined, that offers different affordances—in addition to being the single conduit through which we can access the image—while being completely outside the control of the user. (Uricchio, 2011: 31)

The spooky aspect of this sensation of moving freely around while every movement, every view is made possible and controlled by the algorithm, further lies in the fact that the images selected by the program may come from different sources and may have been taken at different moments. It is imaginable that a Photosynth user, during her or his virtual visit to a building or another location, would discover herself or himself (or another person) depicted in the same space at different ages.

The feeling of total overview and control of a place and of how to move in this place are two features that relate these virtual panoramas to another aspect of the historical panorama: surveillance. Various authors such as Stephen Oettermann, Victor Burgin, and Bernard Comment have related the panorama's tendency toward absolute control within panoramic vision to Jeremy Bentham's panopticon, a circularly-designed prison, allowing a watchman to observe everything that happens in the cells without himself being seen. As argued by Oettermann, the panorama and the panopticon "are at the same time identical and antithetical: in the panorama the observer is schooled in a way of seeing that is taught to prisoners in the panopticon." (Oettermann, 1997: 41) It is well-known that Michel Foucault, in *Discipline and Punish* (1975), discussed the panopticon as a metaphor of modern "disciplinary" societies and their pervasive inclination to observe and normalize. When he writes that the panopticon's aim was to induce in the inmate a specific consciousness, an awareness of permanent visibility that assures the automatic function of power (Foucault, 1977: 201), this reflects pretty well the situation in which we find ourselves today due to omnipresent CCTV-security cameras in real public space and mechanisms of tacking, tracking, and mapping in the digital space of the Internet.

But, while the panopticon of the nineteenth century was part of a disciplinary system aiming at the isolation of marginalized people, such as criminals, from normal life, today's surveillance culture applies to everyone all the time. The panopticon as prison has all but disappeared indeed, it having become integrated into everyday life by means of surveillance cameras or Internet monitoring and tracking software. Drawing on Zygmunt Bauman's concept of "liquid modernity," surveillance theorist David Lyon named this new form of surveillance liquid surveillance. According to Lyon, today's surveillance regimes are not solid, architectural, and isolated. They are mutating, mobile, fragmentary, data-flowing, protocol-governed, "responsibilized." (Lyon, 2010: 330) As we have seen, this is precisely how virtual panoramas such as photosynth—but also Google Street view—may be described. This connection is clearly made by Louise Wolthers when she regards the cameras mounted onto Google cars in order to provide the images for the panoramic environments of Google Street View as advanced, mobile variations of stationary CCTV cameras. The result is an archive of images with precise locations accessible to everyone as part of Google's goal to "organize the world's information and make it universally accessible and useful." (Wolthers, 2016: 16) Burgin's observations on Photosynth and Google Street View go into the same direction: "Today, we move through an environment of virtual images in which the processes of association have become increasingly automated." (PT: 191)

Burgin's projection works around 2010, such as *Hôtel D* (2009), *A Place to Read* (2010), and *The Ideal City* (2013), may be understood as a response to these kinds of heterotopic computer spaces conceived to "replicate the real world in the virtual." (TC: 234) In 2009, Burgin was invited to make a work for Le Printemps de Septembre at the Hôtel-Dieu Saint-Jacques in Toulouse. (Fig. 5.7.) The resulting piece, *Hôtel D*, occupied two rooms of the hospital, the Salle des Pèlerins and the adjoining chapel. (SCR: 100) The work consisted of a loop of digital images played in a projection box that was placed in the center of the pilgrims' hall and a soundtrack, or *voix-off*, diffused by speakers in the space of the chapel and the actual spaces in the Hôtel-Dieu. The juxtaposition of the portraits of Princess Marie-Thérèse de Bourbon and Marguerite Bonnelasvals, a simple orderly (a "fille de service"), featured as the work's "point of anchorage." (PT: 217) While the painting of Marie-Thérèse is inscribed perfectly into the tradition of honoring benefactors by hanging their portraits in the spaces of the hospital, the picture of the maid appears at least unexpected in this context. (SCR: 100) In other words, the image of a person of lower rank appears to be out of place in

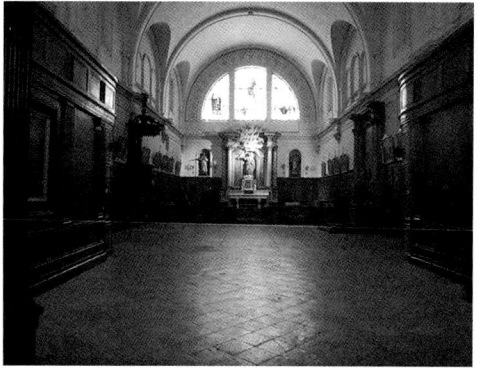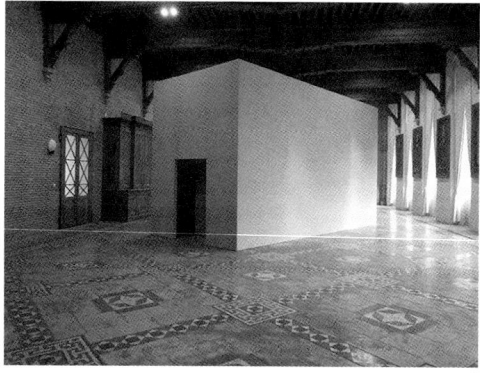

the gallery of wealthy and noble women, thus introducing a dimension
of social and political conflict that, for the distracted visitor, may pass
unremarked. In this sense, "[t]he coincidence of the portraits is a trace
of the political in the overlooked." Burgin calls this kind of unintended,
implicit, almost incidental occurrence of social differences in everyday
life the "granular-perceptual manifestation of the political." (PT: 217-
218) The daily routine of an orderly's work in a hospital or a hotel is described by a woman's voice heard in the chapel, as if the eighteenth-cen-
tury maid would have quit the illustrious circle of benefactors in order
to elucidate the visitor of the chapel about her work. But the technical,
sterile explanations of bed-making are intersected with a dream-like
narrative that intertwines scenes of a hotel room, encounters with pilgrims and the image of kneeling nuns, seemingly praying but turning
out to be cleaning. The projection loop in the box of the pilgrim's hall
also interweaves images from different spatial, historical, and cultural
contexts. The interior of a hotel room in Chicago and a view from the
hotel's façade alternate with different views of the pilgrim's hall, including images of parts of the floor, the wooden ceiling, the lateral walls, and
the entrance doors. The two portraits of the princess and the maid are
cropped in such a way that only a small section of the paintings' lower
part is visible. It is finally only through symbols and signs that the two
women can be identified according to their social rank: the Bourbon
fleur-de-lys carved into the frame of Marie-Thérèse's portrait and the
inscription "Marguerite Bonnelasvals. Fille de service. † 1783" at the
bottom of the other painting. (Plate 11)

When the exhibition visitor enters the projection box, she or he
leaves the "real" space of the pilgrim's hall only to find herself or himself immersed in its virtual photo-realistic reproduction. As Burgin
notes: "The room represented in the box is therefore a mise-en-abyme
of the room that contains the box." (SCR: 100) Although it is possible
to move back and forth between the virtual space and the actual space,

Figure 5.7.

Hôtel D, 2009.

Installation, Hôtel-Dieu
Saint-Jacques, Toulouse.
Chapelle (soundtrack) and
Salle des Pèlerins (image
track).

it is impossible to experience both at once. As argued in Chapter 1, this perceptual problem of the incompatibility between the real world and its representation has already been addressed in *Photopath*. And, as in *Photopath*, the question of "perceptual reality" is linked to a panoramic view. But this is where the parallels end. *Photopath* lacks the historical, social, and political dimensions of *Hôtel D*, but also the production of the work and the image regime to which it refers are completely different. While *Photopath* displays analogue photographs on the floor in order to overcome the traditional artforms of painting and sculpture, the animated spherical panoramas of *Hôtel D* can be understood as a critical reaction to the way the world is experienced in the age of Photosynth and Google Street View. Using a panoramic tripod head, Burgin took countless photographs of the pilgrim's hall. On the computer he then stitched them together to create a sphere in which he could move and track around: "I take a sphere of phenomenal appearances and I take it home, and then I can study it, think about it, live with it and I can start to extract from it, I can extract stills, I can extract camera movements."[69] This way of appropriating a real space by means of computer imagery is not very different from the virtual worlds created by Google Street View and Photosynth. But while the latter promise immediate access, overall control, and unrestricted mobility within an apparently homogeneous and total reduplication of the real world, Burgin reintegrates the panoramic sphere in a historical, social, and physical space, which, rather than pretending to present everything of the world, is an "attempt to represent some unrepresentable 'thing'." This unrepresentable "thing" can be found neither in the real world nor in its virtual replication. It rather has to do with the awareness of the physical presence in a place that is at the same time a historical space, filled with remnants of the past, and a psychical space, in which these physical and historical realities are connected with personal knowledge, perceptions, and fantasies. (PT: 215-216)

Jonathan Crary, in *Techniques of the Observer*, discerns two decisive moments in the history of vision and the reconfiguration of the relations between an observing subject and modes of representation. Whereas in the nineteenth century, the arrival of the age of mechanical reproduction entailed the invention of subjective vision by obscuring the boundaries between interior sensation and exterior signal, the digital revolution since the end of the twentieth century brings along with it a redefinition of perception and vision, detached from the human observer because its "visual images no longer have any reference to the position of an observer in a 'real,' optically perceived world." (Crary, 1992: 2) According to Crary, the optical devices and machines of the nineteenth century, such as the stereoscope, the phenakistiscope, the thaumatrope, and the diorama, constitute the prehistory of recent mutations of vision caused by new technologies as well as the social, institutional, and economic changes that have been linked to them. The discovery of the subjective and temporal character of vision, based on the inseparability of body and observation, announces the precarious position of the contemporary observer. Immerged in a virtual environment where real space and the dematerialized data of digital images mingle inextricably, it becomes increasingly difficult to define the precise, physical position of one's body. In *Hôtel D*, Burgin precisely explores this conundrum. Rejecting the fantasy of the developers of Photosynth to recreate the world in virtual space as an interactive object, Burgin insists on the fact that in these kinds of virtual environments "my part in the theatre of desire has already been written, and I can do no more than play it." (TC: 238) *Hôtel D*, in contrast, inscribes the panoramic sphere in a hybrid environment suspended between the physical/real and the psychical/virtual. The viewer, who cannot experience one without simultaneously being confronted with the other, travels constantly between these two worlds: "The 'work of art' here is in good part a work of the visitor in coming and going between the experience of the actual rooms and their representations." (SCR: 100) This sort of "peripatetic spectatorship" I will further elaborate below in relation to Burgin's works *Parzival* (2013) and *Dear Urania* (2016-2017).

5.6. Monuments of Melancholia[70]

In several projection works of the new millennium, such as *Voyage to Italy* (2006), *Hotel Berlin* (2009), *The Ideal City* and *Parzival* (both 2013), the concepts of panorama and sequence-image are linked to the theme of the ruin. As argued below, the conception of the projection works in terms of ruins closely relates them to the "monument of melancholia," a term Victor Burgin coined in 2008. (SA: 315-329) This "monument of melancholia" points to a theoretical and aesthetic concept that contributes to a deeper understanding of the underlying logic of Burgin's projection works. I will focus in particular on *Parzival* (2013), for the conditions of its creation were similar to those of ordinary monuments. Commissioned by the Musée d'Art Moderne et Contemporain, Geneva, for the Geneva Wagner Festival on the occasion of Richard Wagner's bicentennial year of birth, Burgin's *Parzival* serves as a monument that commemorates a person or an important event: in this case both the composer Richard Wagner and his last opera, *Parsifal*. Furthermore, it may be understood as a monument of *melancholia*, given the fact that Wagner himself, in a letter to Ludwig II on January 10, 1883, considered *Parsifal* his *Weltabschiedswerk* ("world farewell work") and his *Lebens-Abschieds-Werk* ("life-farewell-work")—a work of "escape" (*Flucht*) from the imperialist and militarist world in which he lived. (Borchmeyer, 2013: 349) In the end, this view is confirmed by the central role that Burgin's *Parzival* attributes to the ruin, as perhaps the most prominent emblem of the melancholic worldview. Yet, *Parzival* is neither a monument, in the sense of an official act or place of collective remembering, nor a work on, or about, melancholia in the pathological sense of the word. I rather understand it as a work where the composite concept of a "monument of melancholia" is used in order to constitute a "psychical object," a heterogeneous complex of words, sounds, and images, which invites us to an alternative approach to Wagner's work, diametrically opposed to the pomp and the triumphalism of the conventional monument. (IDS, 1996: 22-23) I will argue that Burgin's concept of the "monument of melancholia" permits one to situate *Parzival* within a longer history of Burgin's work and thinking in the last forty years and provides one with a different way of imagining the monument: as a critical form of monument, as a ruin of the future, a monument of melancholia.

Parzival is composed of a projection loop and eight text panels, the latter consisting of a prelude and seven contemplations related to the months Wagner spent in Venice from September 1858 to March 1859. Rather than commenting on, or explaining the images, these brief wall texts connect biographical elements of Wagner's life and his work on *Parsifal* with Burgin's own references to authors and film directors such as Milan Kundera, W.G. Sebald, Phillip K. Dick, Roberto Rossellini, and Leni Riefenstahl. In the installation, images and texts are presented in separate spaces, which makes it impossible to read the texts and to watch the video simultaneously. In the projection loop, short photographic and filmic sequences alternate with text and sound in order to create a kind of audiovisual collage or chain of associations. A dissolving sequence of idyllic landscape images accompanied by the prelude of Wagner's *Parsifal* is followed by a medium close-up of the boy who, at the end of Roberto Rossellini's *Germany Year Zero* (1947), jumps from a ruined building to find death. Next, a traveling shot through a ruined cityscape echoes the film's opening sequence. This is followed by an underwater scene with sunrays penetrating the surface of the water, evoking the shimmering gold of the Nibelung from *Rheingold*, the first part of Wagner's *Der Ring des Nibelungen*. The intertitle "For eternities I've waited for you. My Saviour, who comes so late!" may refer to Parsifal as both the redeemer of the world and the savior who did not arrive—or who came too late—to save the boy in Rossellini's film from certain death. In fact, the boy's face reappears later, in a slightly different sequence, just before we find ourselves returned to the ruined cityscape though this time viewing a 360-degree panorama of the desolate environment. Another text sequence is an edited extract from Milan Kundera's novel *L'Identité*, where a woman standing at the grave of her dead son confesses that only his death has set her free from the world that she dislikes. Then once again, Rossellini's boy looks into a void, and this is followed by a color still of the ruin and another scene from *Germany Year Zero*, in which the boy's elder sister gives him a kiss on his forehead. Of course, the latter scene reminds us of the ambivalent mother-lover relationship between Parsifal and the mysterious seductress Kundry—which brings us back to Wagner. Additionally, in the following scene, the digital reconstruction of a Venice palazzo, appearing isolated on the high sea, reminds viewers of the two places where Wagner lived briefly in Venice: the Palazzo Giustiniani, where he stayed in 1858 and continued the composition of *Tristan und Isolde*, and the Palazzo Vendramin-Calergi, where he died in 1883. A mesmerizing image of the sea solemnly rolling to the melody of the Parsifal prelude completes the circle. (Plate 12)

To be sure, there is no doubt that this complex, dense, and suggestive concatenation of heterogeneous images, sounds, and texts is everything but an illustration or an interpretation of Wagner's opera. In a note that accompanies the work, Victor Burgin states:

> My work *Parzival* is a representation of a psychological object: an assembly of images, associations, anecdotes, auditory fragments, and so on, loosely turning around those seven months that Wagner spent in Venice, a time when *Parzival* was no longer a medieval romance nor yet an opera, but was itself an unresolved intuition entangled in the residues of Wagner's personal, professional, political and aesthetic everyday life—an indistinct figure in a landscape, within the ruined horizon of the future *Götterdämmerung*. (VBP: 92)

This paradox of "the ruined horizon of the future," the yet-to-be-built future that is already in ruins before it has been constructed, is a crucial idea of the work. The ruin already occurs in Burgin's work around 1980, when he became increasingly interested in psychoanalysis and the question of how our experience of the world—and of the work of art—is influenced by psychological associative processes. In *In Lyon* (1980), as stressed in Chapter 3, the architectural ruins of antiquity are related to social, political, and psychological conflicts that leave the subject in ruins. Three years later, in 1983, Burgin published his book *Hôtel Latône*, in which he combines photographs with short texts in order to form a chain of associations similar to the experience of a daydream. (BN: 142) The book begins with a man and a woman watching television in a hotel room on a weekday. Across the pages, the relationship between text and image becomes increasingly associative and then, from page twenty-five onward, we find ourselves in the ruins of ancient

Greece, where impressions of traditional mythology and modern tourism are condensed and displaced. The ruin becomes a kind of symbolic marker within a reverie, a fragment, laden with memory and history, which occurs like a ghost returning to haunt us at the most unexpected moments. (Fig. 5.8.-5.9.)

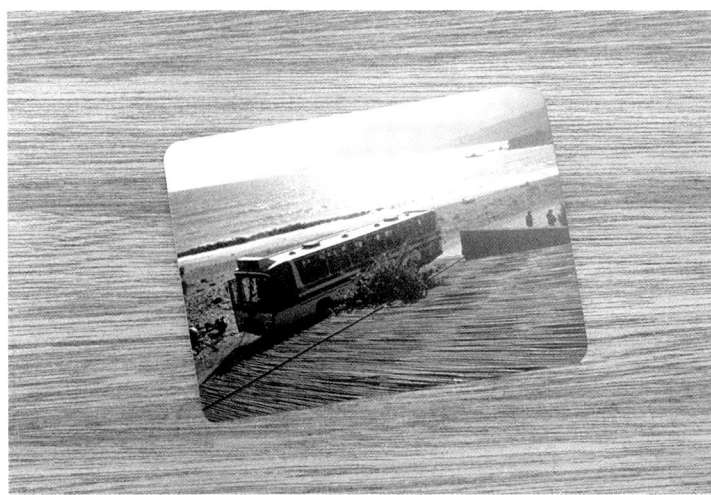

Figures 5.8–5.9.
From Hôtel Latône, 1983

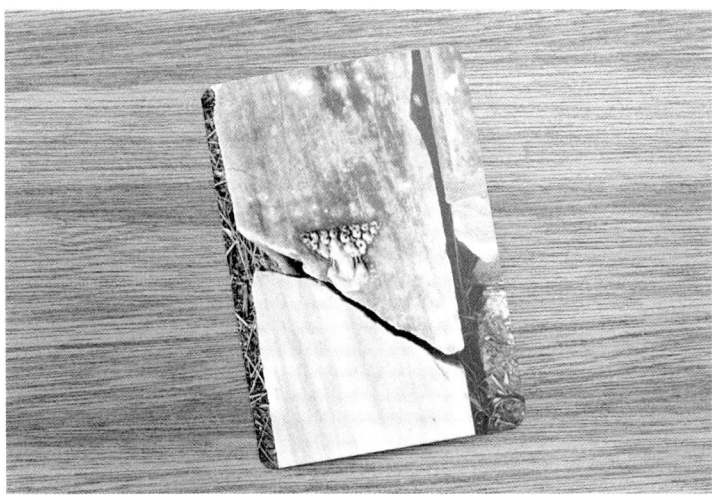

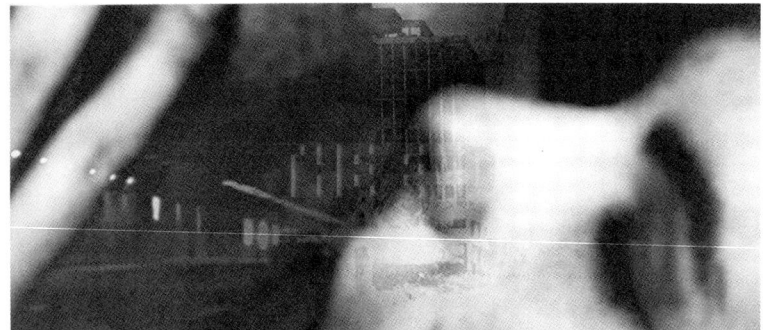

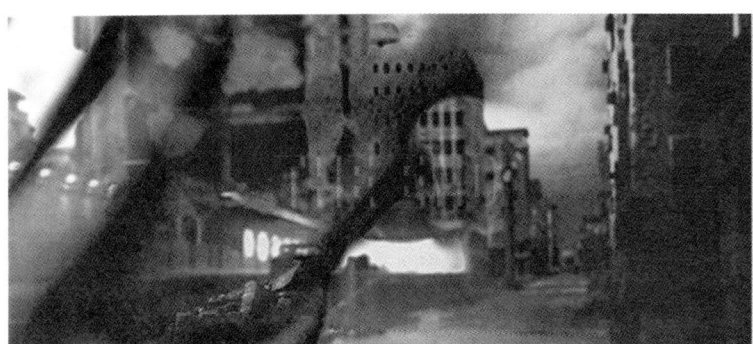

Figure 5.10–5.11.

The End, 1994.

Computer-manipulated photographs. Two of six panels, each 91×213 cm.

In a more apocalyptic scenario, the ruin reemerges in the mid-1990s in Burgin's computer-manipulated photographic works, *The End* (1994) and *Angelus Novus* (1995). Published in a book entitled *History Painting*, these works contrast, as Al Harris F. observes, "the idealism of that genre with the skepticism of the present." (Harris F., 1995: 8) In *The End*, a street-view of a ruined city and a close-up of a kissing couple are combined into a single image together with the title of the series, which gradually changes color and its degree of transparency. (Fig. 5.10.-5.11.) Even the photographic surface seems to be ruined by blurring, and grainy or material defects. These are the ruins of the modern world and of technological progress, which brought us both cinema's illusion of a romantic end as well as weapons of mass destruction, also heralding the end of the world. *Angelus Novus* is a triptych where a woman, walking down a street, is framed by two identical but mirrored photographs, each showing an aerial view of the bombing of a city. (Fig. 5.12.) Clearly, the title refers to the ninth thesis in Walter Benjamin's "Theses on the Philosophy of History," where Benjamin interprets Klee's painting *Angelus Novus* as a tragic allegory of history, turned to the past and watching the historical process as "one single catastrophe which keeps piling wreckage upon wreckage" while a "storm blowing from Paradise" prevents him from repairing the damage. Benjamin ends: "This storm irresistibly propels him into the future to which his back is turned, while the pile of debris before him grows skyward. This storm is what we call progress." (Benjamin, 2007: 258) In Burgin's *The End* and *Angelus Novus*, photography not only illustrates this storm that transforms everything into ruins, but it is also part of that storm. In contrast to analogue photography's insistence on the memorial and historical character of the ruin, the digitally manipulated images project the past vestiges into the present of computer technology. They represent the destruction of the past and offer the promise of ruins yet-to-come, which have been proclaimed by the logic of technological progress already.

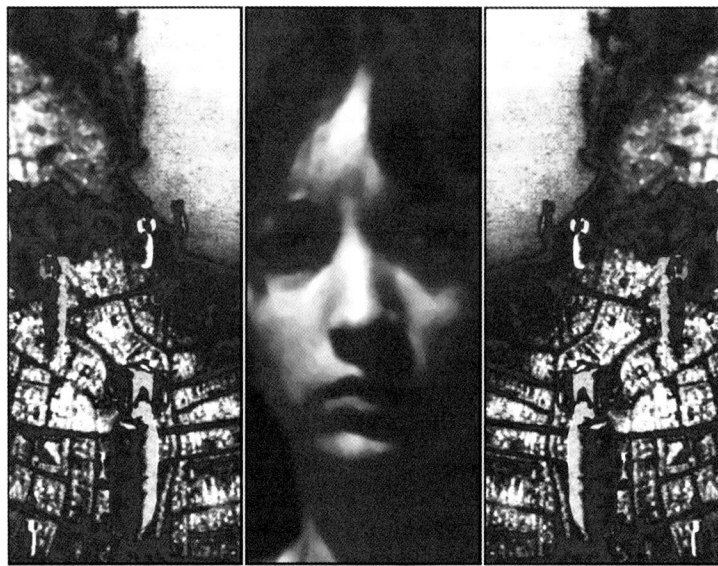

Figure 5.12.

Angelus Novus, 1995.

Computer-manipulated photographs. Three panels, each 213×91 cm.

As a cultural and technological process, rather than as the remains of an object in a state of decay, the ruin is now an allegory of the destructive potential of modern society. But the photographic tableau still provides merely a fixed image of this process. In the video *Voyage to Italy* (2006), the ruin becomes part of the dynamic structure of a rebus-like loop, in which textual and visual elements, and still and moving images, collide. (Fig. 5.13.) Originating with a photograph from the 1860s, depicting a women in the midst of a Pompeian edifice in ruins, the video *Voyage to Italy* is composed of several different elements: two sequences from Rossellini's eponymous film, textual fragments narrating the story of a couple's road trip, and two photofilmic panoramas with 360-degree views of the ruins, one taking the position of the

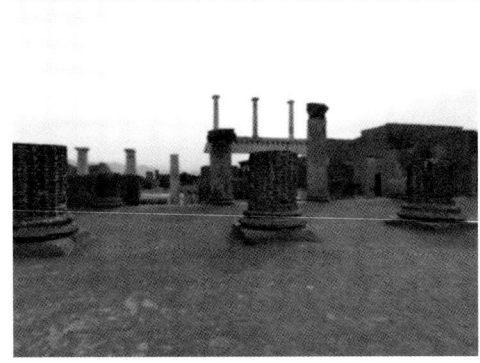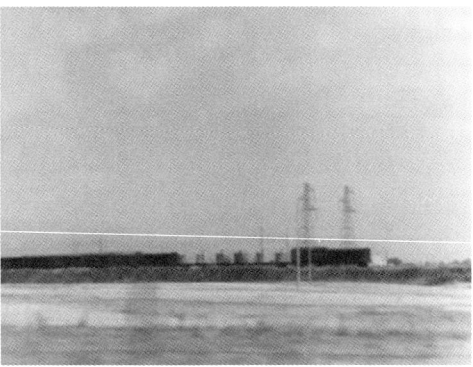

photographer and the other the viewpoint of the woman—all of which create a paradoxical impression of moving stillness or still movement, whereby the past situation of the photograph and the present movement of film overlap. The uncanny effect produced by this regular, mechanic pan through the deserted ruins of the temple is, in fact, comparable to the opening sequence of Rosselini's *Germany Year Zero*: a ghost-like, traveling shot through the streets of Berlin, bombed to ruins.

In his essay "The Shadow and the Ruin," which, in many ways, functions as a parallel text to the video, Burgin writes: "The camera offers the spectator a feeling of gliding through the debris without touching the ground, the kind of motion conventionally ascribed to ghosts." (Burgin, 2006: 81) Shortly afterward, he suggests that the essence of the photograph is a ruin, a "trace of a previous state of the world, a vestige of how things were." Of course, this could be also said of film, being nothing else than a ruin twenty-four times a second—to paraphrase the title of Laura Mulvey's famous book *Death 24x a Second* (2006). Rossellini's film would be, from this point of view, not only a film *about* ruins, but also a film constituted *by* ruins. In his essay, Burgin concludes that "the sum of all photographs is the ruin of the world." (Burgin, 2006: 86) This applies quite literally to the panoramic montage of the Pompeian vestiges in *Voyage to Italy*. Yet not only the panoramas are comments on, or representations of, ruins. In his essay "The Time of the Panorama," Burgin writes about the sequence-image:

> I might compare it to a building site, or ruin, where although it is clear that a building will be, or was, its completed form and function is unclear, and its boundaries ambiguous. In its relation to memory the sequence-image represents, in Lacan's phrase: "the metonymic ruins of the repressed." (SA: 305)

Figure 5.13.

Stills from *Voyage to Italy*, 2006.

Single screen digital video projection with sound.

Exhibited in the gallery, the projected image loop is accompanied by two series of photographic prints. *Basilica I* and *II* show the ruined columns of the Pompeian Basilica from different viewpoints. (Fig. 5.14.) These are the photographic ruins of the past, each photograph referring to a specific fragmentary object disintegrated long ago. In the projection piece, these remnants of the past are revived by digital technology and integrated in a complex network of references within which they become part of a hybrid, heterogeneous object layering multiple times and spaces. These are the photographic ruins of the sequence-image, which, in a first operation, projects the contingent fragments into the continuous space-time of the infinite panorama's presentness, and, in a second operation, weaves them into a dreamlike rebus where different times and varying contexts become entangled with each other. Analogous to the sequence-image, *Voyage to Italy* consists of "metonymic ruins," chains of association where past and present, moving images and still images, reality and fiction, and, finally, memory and experience intermingle without offering a coherent narrative or a definitive signification. *Voyage to Italy* and other works such as *Hotel Berlin* (2009) and *The Ideal City* and *Parzival* (both 2013) do not only represent ruins—they *are* ruins in the sense of Hartmut Böhme's definition of the ruin as "a kind of externalized memory space." (Böhme, 1989: 300 [my translation])

Figure 5.14.

Voyage to Italy, 2006.

Installation view with Basilica I (24 black and white photographs in superposed horizontal rows of 12, and one text. Each image 12×8 cm. Each frame 30×20 cm), Canadian Centre for Architecture, Montreal, 2006.

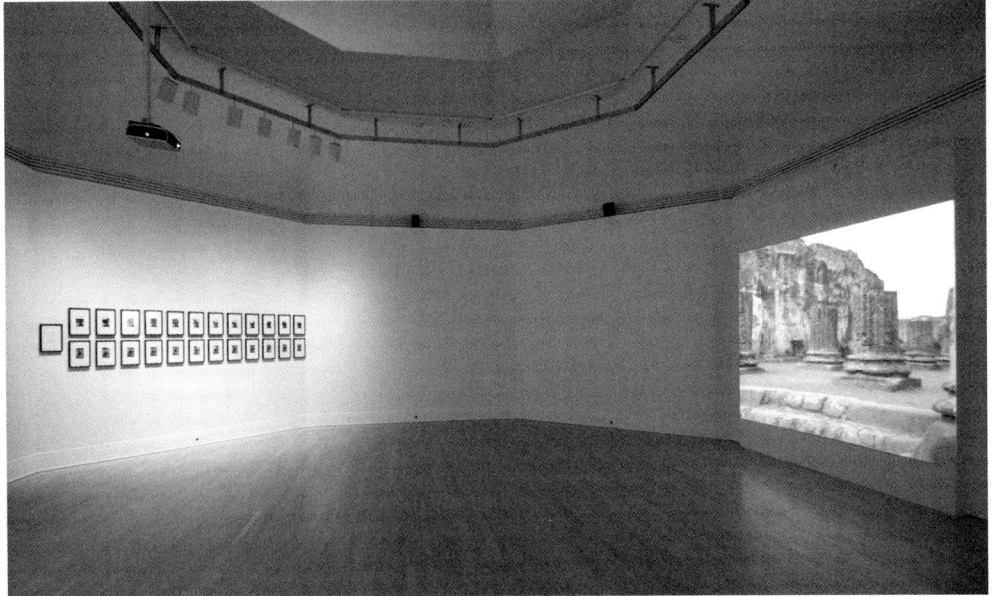

Parzival's panorama refers to both Rossellini's traveling shot in *Germany Year Zero* and the panoramic view in *Voyage to Italy*. Similar to the latter, it offers a 360-degree view of deserted architectural ruins frozen in time, whereas the decor and the atmosphere of the setting are obviously inspired by Rossellini's opening sequence. However, the ghostly atmosphere of the traveling shot is even more intense in Burgin's *Parzival*: there is no sound; the scene is shrouded in mist; and the steady, mechanical movement of the camera provides a view onto a completely deserted, synthetic landscape of ruins and debris. A closer look urges us to recognize that these desolate streets are quite different from both the filmed ruins of real Berlin in *Germany Year Zero*, and the photographed ruins of real Pompeii in *Voyage to Italy*. In fact, the panorama of *Parzival* is the first one made entirely in the virtual space of 3D simulation. (Bishop and Burgin, 2016: 113) The result is a reversal of the relationship between reality and fiction concerning the image of Rossellini's boy: "Rossellini puts a fictional character, the small boy, in a real environment. I put Rossellini's real boy in a fictional environment." (111) Completely independent from any law of physics that applies in the real world, this space is, like a dream, at the same time both perfectly familiar and totally unreal. Rather than vestiges of the past, the computer-generated panoramas represent the future ruins of Venice. Past and future are thus inextricably intertwined.

In the wall texts, this dialectical relationship occurs twice. The ruin's adherence to the past is expressed in a quotation from W. G. Sebald's *The Rings of Saturn*, where the protagonist, Michael Hamburger, walks "like a sleepwalker" through the ruins of Berlin, attempting to rediscover the traces of his youth from there. (Sebald, 2002: 178) The imbrication of present and future manifests itself in the form of a reference to Philip K. Dick's novel *Martian Time-Slip*, where a boy ends up in a psychiatric hospital because of his particular relationship to time and space. The wall text also quotes a passage from the essay, "Monument and Melancholia," in which Burgin states: "We eventually learn that the space-time he inhabits is different from that occupied by those around him on the Red Planet: where they see the present, he sees a palimpsest of present and future. What they are busy constructing, he sees as already in ruins." (SA: 316) The ruins of history—eloquently described by Benjamin as a "pile of debris" owing to "a storm blowing from Paradise" called progress—are here catapulted into the future of a world already in ruins before having been constructed. In his essay "Visible Cities," dating from the same year as *Parzival*, Burgin refers to Walter Benjamin's famous remarks about film that burst our built environment "asunder by the dynamite of the tenth of a second, so that now, in the midst of its far-flung ruins and debris, we calmly and adventurously go traveling." (TC: 240; Benjamin, 2007: 236) Burgin adds, that this is precisely how satellite television and the Internet confront us today with every-day life, and even with cinema itself: as a heterogeneous assemblage of fragments scattered through time and space. "Today, Benjamin's imaginary flanerie through a universe of exploded cities has its counterpart in Internet searches through navigable computer simulations of global urban space." (TC: 240) Under these conditions, the photograph has partly lost its significance as a "trace of a previous state of the world." Constantly reworked, reshuffled and recombined, the photographic image never forms a completed, clearly identifiable object but is part of an endless process of condensations and displacements, which never come to a rest and thus signify "the ruined horizon of the future."

As Hartmut Böhme observes, this complex overlapping of past, present, and future is proper to the aesthetics of the ruin and its particular experience of time: "The view that synthesizes an expanse of rubble to a landscape of ruins is the paused moment between a not already gone past and an already present future. The ruin constitutes itself in all three modes of time, more precisely: not the ruin but the reflexive view which gives shape to the ruin as an aesthetic object." (Böhme, 1989: 288 [my translation]) In this sense, Victor Burgin's *Parzival* echoes the functions of a ruin as a condensation of past, present, and future, where fragments of different periods and cultural conditions and uses overlap. This concept of the ruin as an aesthetic object may be linked to what Burgin calls the "monument of melancholia." Most notably, the abovementioned novels by Sebald (*Rings of Saturn*) and Dick (*Martian Time-Slip*), as well as Rossellini's *Germany Year Zero*, are prominently mentioned and related to Freud's essay "Mourning and Melancholia." The main difference that Freud observes between mourning and melancholia is that mourning is a reaction to the loss of a real object—a loved person, for example—whereas melancholia is a more general "cessation of interest in the outside of the world," with the loss of an unconscious object that cannot be traced back to something in real life. (Freud, 1917/1957: 244) In this context, Julia Kristeva, in her book *Black Sun*, has described the romantic renewal with late antiquity's "perception of melancholia as an extreme state and as an exceptionality that reveals the true nature of Being." (Kristeva, 1992: 7-8) She qualifies melancholia as the "experience of *object loss* and of a *modification of signifying bonds*" (10), and, with reference to Melanie Klein's concept of "parcellary splitting," defines the melancholic self as one that "literally 'falls into pieces,'" (18) due to the operations of non-integration and disintegration. This is not the place to go deeper into psychoanalytical accounts and definitions of melancholia as a pathological state of mind, but three features of melancholia as described by Freud and Kristeva are noteworthy, concerning the concept of the "monument of melancholia" as both an aesthetic category and a psychological object: a) its disinterest in a precise, real object with its specific function and use; b) its critical agenda as an exceptional state of clairvoyance; and c) its tendency to fragmentation and disintegration in contrast to a homogeneous, integrative perception of the world.

In his essay "Monument and Melancholia," Burgin distinguishes between two kinds of monuments. The first, monuments of mourning, are "official sites of remembrance." (SA: 323) They are what Pierre Nora calls *lieux de mémoire*, that is "the places in which the collective heritage […] was crystallized." (Nora, 1996: xv) These conventional monuments provide loci for national memory in order to affirm the significance and indispensability of national identity. All kinds of built monuments, memorials, or museums fall under this category. Monuments of melancholia, in contrast, are *non-lieux de mémoire* in the juridical sense of the expression *non-lieu*, because, as Burgin puts it, "they fail to make their case. The documentation is incomplete, witnesses are missing or unreliable, it is not always clear what is to be proved, and there is so much that has been forgotten." (SA: 323) In his same essay, Burgin addresses how the monument of melancholia functions within psychoanalysis, where the success of a session depends more on the patient's ability to associate freely than on his or her capacity to remember. This would imply, Burgin specifies, in quoting Pontalis, dissociating "existing, well established, liaisons in order to make others emerge, which are often dangerous liaisons." Moreover, he adds, "Dangerous […] to official memory, which relies on a seamless network of associative links." (325) Consequently, the "monument of melancholia" is not only an aesthetic and psychological object, but it also has a political agenda, for it is supposed to resist official representations of memory/history, diffused by means of physical monuments in the streets and various channels of the mass media. Whereas the conventional monument refers to the past as a confined, accomplished container of frozen memory, the monument of melancholia, Burgin suggests, "remains to be completed." "Indistinguishable from a ruin," it provides "the hieroglyphic keys to a lost knowledge, the enigmatic fragments of a rebus." (326) As Norbert Bolz writes, "In the light of melancholia the power of the ruin expands." (Bolz, 1996: 17)

5.7. The Peripatetic Mode of Spectatorship

In the view of Dieter Borchmeyer, Wagner's way of thinking is deeply mythical on a structural level. According to him, the cyclic repetition of prototypical narrative patterns finds its musical equivalent in the recurrence of the leitmotiv. (Borchmeyer, 2013: 185) In his essay "Opera and Drama," Wagner writes about the myth that "its content, how close so ever its compression [*dichtester Gedrängtheit*], is inexhaustible [*unerschöpflich*] throughout the ages." (Wagner, 1995: 191) Analogous with dreams, two major features of the myth are openness and condensation. That Wagner conceived of his opera as a mythical event close to the dream experience becomes evident in his essay "The Stage Festival Theatre in Bayreuth" (1873). In hiding the orchestra from the auditorium, he intended to create "a shimmering sense of distance […] in which the remote picture takes on the mysterious quality of a dream-like apparition." (Spotts, 1994: 52) To be sure, this affinity with the dream's form—with a structure based on circularity, repetition, and condensation—is a feature that Burgin's work shares with Wagner's conception of the opera. Yet there is also a fundamental difference between the two approaches. Whereas Wagner's conception requires total immersion within the dream in order to transport the audience "into that inspired state of clairvoyance" similar to "religious seeing," (52) Burgin's aim is to interpellate the spectator as an individual who "is invited to follow her or his own associative paths through and beyond it." (VBP: 93) In contrast to Burgin's position, Wagner's aim is to fuse the work with the audience. In the end, Wagner's mythical dream is supposed to become that of the audience. For this purpose, Wagner introduced, in his essay "The Art-Work of the Future" (1849), the concept of the synthesis of the arts—the *Gesamtkunstwerk*. Intended as a way to overcome the social and artistic tendency towards isolation, fragmentation, and egoism, the *Gesamtkunstwerk* aims to bring a new kind of art-work of "the people" [*Volkskunstwerk*], the "perfect" artwork that, according to Wagner, "is none other than the *Drama*." (Wagner, 1994: 139) In this sense, Wagner's synthesis of the arts is not an invitation to the audience to participate actively with their own individual thoughts and ideas, but an overwhelming, messianic spectacle that envelops the individual subject within a greater, universal vision of an ideal community. Unity and fusion are thus the very principles of the *Gesamtkunstwerk*.

Victor Burgin addresses a completely different spectator. Through a combination of different artforms such as film, photography, architecture, literature, and music, Burgin's *Parzival* denies both a unified structure and an integrative synthesis of the arts. In this regard, the installation of the work is of utmost importance, for it is impossible to view the work at once. (Fig. 5.15.) Text and image are displayed in

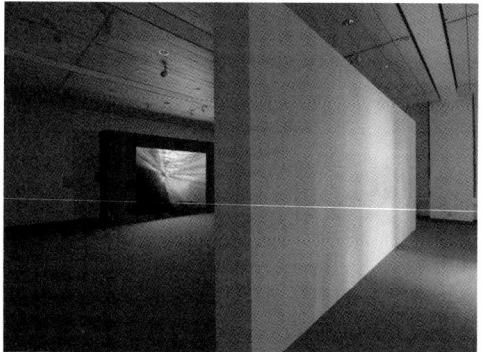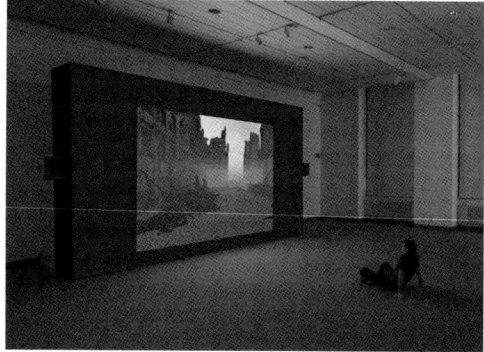

separate spaces, which means that the spectator is obliged to move from one place to the other if she or he wants to apprehend the whole work. It is impossible to read the text and to watch the video at the same time. On the one hand, this means that the text panels do not provide the subtitles to, or an interpretation of, the projection loop. They are part of the work, which, as Burgin states, "is structured in a literal and figurative coming and going between the optical and verbal registers of the image." (Unpublished note to *Parzival*) On the other hand, this play with absence and presence in the structure of the work ties in with ideas that Burgin has developed since the late 1960s, most prominently in his essay "Situational Aesthetics" (1969), where he notes that an object, rather than being a thing-as-such, constitutes itself solely within a situation, or in other words, the encounter of the object with the environment and the perception of it by a subject. (SA: 10) As argued in Chapter 1, *Memory Piece* (1967) illustrates this idea of situational aesthetics in an exemplary way, making it relevant to return once more to Burgin's essay "Monument and Melancholia." In this text, Burgin describes the architect Walther Grunwald's intervention in the forest of Schloss Ettersberg for the Weimar 99 cultural festival as follows:

> He commissioned the clearing of the long-concealed hunting path that connects the site of Goethe's Court of the Muses to the site of the Buchenwald camp. Visitors to Weimar are now able to walk from one place to the other, through the same trees that sheltered them both. The walk is physically arduous; no less difficult is the task of covering the emotional and intellectual ground between the two sites. The woods are now much as they were then: the space is the same, as one moves down the path the knowledge of where one is in time is subject to an irrational

and dreadful doubt. Certainly this "empty" space between provides more effective an occasion for remembrance than the inert monuments that border it. (SA: 323)

The German title of Grunwald's memorial, *Zeitschneise*, means both a "time lane" or "time corridor" and a cutting through time. In an unpublished paper, Grunwald writes, "The forest of Buchenwald at the Ettersberg renders both places—the castle and the concentration camp—invisible for each other. But in the mind both places and what happened there co-exist." Burgin's interest in Grunwald's Buchenwald memorial might be explained by its obvious affinity with his own concept of situational aesthetics. In fact, as discussed above, in *Lichtung* (1998-99) a woman explores the same hunting path that leads from Schloss Ettersberg to the Buchenwald camp, the latter being characterized with the words taken from Goethe's *Elective Affinities* announcing "a new and different world." Viewed in this light, the monument of melancholia is not an immobile object to be venerated and contemplated, but a dynamic environment that necessarily includes the spectator as a physically *and* psychically active person who assimilates the work's ruins into her or his own horizon of experiences and expectations.

As noted above, the 2009 installation *Hôtel D* at Hôtel-Dieu in Toulouse also presumes a spectator who engages with the work in an active, corporeal and mental way. I have also pointed out that Burgin designs his projection works as repetitive, short loops in order to accommodate the expectations of the gallery visitors who may enter and leave the room whenever they wish to do so. In a talk given on 22 May 2010 at Jeu de Paume, Paris, in the context of the *Hôtel D* exhibition produced by the museum, Burgin coined the term "peripatetic viewer" for this kind of itinerant spectator:

> Most works made for the gallery are therefore designed to loop, with a seamless transition between the first and last frames of the material. With a peripatetic viewer and an indeterminate viewing time the conditions of spectatorship of a projected image in an art gallery are closer to those of painting than to cinema. (PT: 197)

Most of the earlier projection works, however, take account of the "peripatetic mode of spectatorship" of the gallery visitor only by means of their inner structure as non-teleological loops. (SDZ: 159) The way they are shown in a dimmed room as single-screen projections comes closer to the cinema experience than to the situation of the museum where the visitor has to move along the walls and through the consecutive rooms if she or he wants to discover the displayed art objects. The "ideal" peripatetic viewer becomes an actual itinerant spectator only at the moment when the setting makes it inevitable to walk around in order to get a complete experience of the work.[71] Works such as *Hôtel D* and, to a lesser extent, *Parzival* engage more explicitly with a peripatetic viewing subject, for they are spatial installations that spread soundtrack, image, and text through various actual and virtual spaces. Building on these installation works, *Dear Urania*, displayed at Galleria Lia Rumma in Naples from October 16 2016 to January 21 2017, was conceived as an exhibition through which the visitor has to move if she or he wants to unravel the multiple layers of which the work is composed. Burgin emphasized this shift from an "ideal" peripatetic viewer to a factual peripatetic mode of spectatorship when writing:

> The present exhibition distributes heterogeneous interrelated elements throughout the gallery. […] The peripatetic form of reading—in which the viewer moves between different components of an exhibition—is a projection into space (in a relation of mise-en-abyme) of the way sense is to be made of my single-screen works. (Burgin, *A Note on Dear Urania*)

The exhibition comprised two photo-text works from 2006, *Basilica I and II*, two digital projection loops, *Dear Urania (Moon)* and *Dear Urania (Letter)*, and *Pages from the Sketchbook of Ernestina Capocci* (six framed inkjet prints which refer to the other parts of the work). The projection loops and other elements of the exhibition—as their spatial extension—functioned as a mise-en-scène of the permanently changing perception of identical formal elements: the ruins of the Basilica in Pompeii encountered in the photographs of the first room reappear in the sketchbook of Ernestina Capocci, exposed in the second room. The loft interior, represented in one of the sketchbook's drawings, could be experienced as a 3D modeled animation in the projection loop in room three, and so on. (Fig. 5.16.) In view of the complex, open structure of the exhibition and the specific topographic context in which it was shown, it is almost inevitable to call to mind Walter Benjamin and Asja Lacis's already quoted images of Naples as "a theater of new, unforeseen, constellations" where "the stamp of the definitive is avoided." (Benjamin and Lacis, 1978: 165)

Dear Urania was inspired by Ernesto Capocci's *Report on the First Voyage to the Moon Made by a Woman in the Year 2057*. In his novella the Italian mathematician and astronomer narrates a fictional voyage to the moon in the form of a letter written by the protagonist, Urania, to her friend Ernestina who remained in Naples. Fascinated by the fact that Capocci chose a woman to relate his speculations on the geological features of the moon, Burgin based the work on an imagined reply letter written by Ernestina from Earth. While the loop projected on the

STANZA N°1/FIRST ROOM

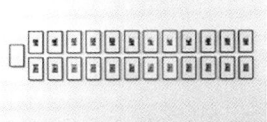
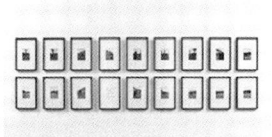
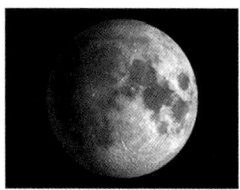

Basilica I, 2006
24 black and white photographs in
superposed horizontal rows of 12 and 1
text panel
Overall dimensions 68x345; image
size 12x8 cm each; frame size 31x21
cm each
Edition of 3

Basilica I, 2006
24 black and white photographs in
superposed horizontal rows of 12 and
1 text panel
Overall dimensions 68x345; image
size 12x8 cm each; frame size 31x21
cm each
Edition of 3

Dear Urania (Moon), 2016
projected image loop, silent
1 minute
Edition of 3

STANZA N°2/SECOND ROOM

STANZA N°3/THIRD ROOM

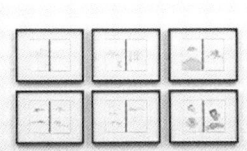
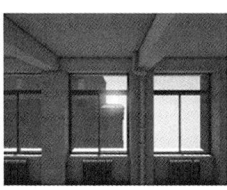

Pages from the sketchbook of Ernestina Capocci, 2016
6 archival inkjet prints mounted on
archival board
Overall dimensions 67x133 cm; image
size 30x40 cm each; frame size 37x41
cm
Edition of 3

Dear Urania (Letter), 2016
Projected text/image loop, silent
Duration 11 minutes 59 seconds
Edition of 3

wall opposite to the gallery's entrance shows the different phases of the
moon, the projection piece in the third room is based on Burgin's fantasies of what Ernestina might have replied. As the wall text explains,
this double fiction (a fictional response to a fictive person) condenses
past, present and future to a paradoxical time-space in which different temporalities are interwoven: "Urania wrote to Ernestina in 2057,
her friend received the letter in 1857, Ernestina replied in 2017." The
projected images, created by software used to make video games, further condense and juxtapose disparate spatial, aesthetic and geographic realities. The virtual "dolly out" along a building obviously evokes
the opening scene of the science fiction opera Star Wars, showing a
spaceship entering the frame. The following images of the interior of
a loft are interrupted by intertitles referring to Urania's report, written
by Capocci, where she enthusiastically describes the moon craters as
gigantic versions of the Vesuvius volcano. (Capocci, 2015: 42) A brief
clip from Fritz Lang's film of 1929 Frau im Mond (Woman in the Moon)

Figure 5.16.

Dear Urania, 2016.

Components of the exhibi-
tion, Galleria Lia Rumma,
Naples, October 16, 2016
to January 21, 2017.

evokes another fictional voyage made by a woman to the moon, Frieda, who represents "an ideal or ironic incarnation of Ernestina's imaginary of Urania, or merely an in-joke between friends." (Note on *Dear Urania*) Next, after Ernestina signed her letter, the camera orbits above the rumpled bedclothes before approaching the bed's surface and metamorphosing into a sparse, moon-like landscape that reveals itself as the bay of Naples with Vesuvius at its center. Continuing its descent toward Vesuvius, the volcano's orifice finally dissolves into the sun that shines on the spaceship-like building and the loop restarts its course.

This kind of layering and interweaving of different historical and fictional temporal strata differs from most fictional narrative forms of cinema, literature, or game playing. It comes closer to Borges' conception of labyrinthic writing as outlined in the short story "The Garden of Forking Paths":

> In all fictional works, each time a man is confronted with several alternatives, he chooses one and eliminates the others; in the fiction of Ts'ui Pên, he chooses—simultaneously—all of them. *He creates*, in this way, diverse futures, diverse times which themselves also proliferate and fork. […] In contrast to Newton and Schopenhauer, your ancestor did not believe in a uniform, absolute time. He believed in an infinite series of times, in a growing, dizzying net of divergent, convergent and parallel times. This network of times which approached one another, forked, broke off, or were unaware of one another for centuries, embraces all possibilities of time. (Borges, 1964: 26-28)

But this "plurality of times" is also a "plurality of worlds," as one of the intertitles calls to mind. Real Naples encounters the fictionalized moon, the protagonist of an avant-garde silent movie meets the fictional character of Capocci's novel, and finally the science fiction saga of Hollywood cinema dissolves into Burgin's fantasy of a fictional Ernestina living as an artist in the loft of an undefined American city. Opening up an imaginary, psychical space where heterogeneous temporal and spatial layers are condensed and scattered across the virtual space of the computer-generated projections and the real space of the gallery, the exhibition reminds us of the way we experience the cinematic heterotopia, oscillating constantly between fiction and fact, fantasy and the real.

In comparison to Burgin's earlier work of the 1980s, the period when he began to use the term "psychical realism," we can observe some major shifts which may be understood as responses to recent cultural and technological developments. With the use of game software for the creation of the entirely computer-generated projection images,

Burgin reacts to the film and videogame industries. More precisely, *Dear Urania* can be understood as a critical commentary to discourses on "interactivity" and "immersion" that all too often pass over the fact that supposedly interactive features in videogames and computer art are based on algorithms and programs that leave little choice to move freely within predetermined environments. (PT: 191-195) Burgin prefers to think of "interactivity" as the activity of a peripatetic viewer who assembles and structures the encountered image fragments in his mind. It is precisely because of its physical and peripatetic character that *Dear Urania* offers a critical reflection on recent developments in virtual reality. As Marie-Laure Ryan suggests:

> It is only when interactivity is conceived as action-upon-a-world that it involves mind and body. What is at stake in the synthesis of immersion and interactivity is therefore nothing less than the participation of the whole of the individual in the artistic experience. (Ryan, 2015: 13)

Distributing images produced by game engines, simulations of sketchbook drawings, and conventional photographs across different rooms of the gallery, *Dear Urania* invites the viewer to "act upon the world" by accumulating layers of associations and meanings while walking through a fragmentary text-image environment. If the spectator is not supposed to intervene directly in the physical texture of the work, the corporeal experience is nevertheless decisive to becoming aware of the specific conditions of being in this world at this moment: physically in the spatial and institutional setting of the gallery, and, psychologically, in the "imbricated time of our global lived space," where many different kinds of images collide and coalesce in our mind. (IDS: 184)

Although *Dear Urania* refers to technologies (game engine) and techniques (bricolage, mashup) of the contemporary media environment, its heterogeneous psycho-physical configuration runs counter to the forms and practices of the global media imaginary. In a talk at the National Institute of Art History in Paris, Burgin cited Félix Guattari and Bernard Stiegler in cautioning against the tendency of the global media industries (including film, television, advertising, videogames, and popular music) to produce an "ecology of the mind" that reduces the audience to "bodies of consumers" with an unconsciousness colonized by the "media-based imaginary." (CP: 82-83) Elsewhere, Burgin quotes Andrew Darley from his book *Visual Digital Culture*, in which the author assesses the mode of spectatorship of media-based digital images as "sensuously rich and dynamic in terms of perceptual activity, yet semantically compromised and relatively quiescent in terms of interpretive activity." (TC: 201; Darley, 2000: 173) *Dear Urania* offers, in point of fact, the exact opposite of this mode of experience. While the layering of various temporal, spatial and narrative registers and the multiple cross-references constitute an extremely dense and complex net of meanings that demands a high level of interpretive activity, the experience of the individual elements of the exhibition, and the exhibition as such, is rather contemplative due to the reduced number of works per room and the slow rhythm of the projected images. In this light, *Dear Urania* corresponds to what Jacques Rancière called an aesthetic politics: a "recasting of the distribution of the sensible, a reconfiguration of the given perceptual forms." (Rancière, 2011: 63) If Burgin, drawing on Rancière, imagines a "project for a museum of the living," this is precisely how the aesthetic politics of *Dear Urania* might be described:

> as a passage into praxis of aesthetic politics in the era of globalized media, a reformatting of reality in which alterity and locality are perpetually reasserted against the globalizing "media-based imaginary" of corporate commodity culture. (CP: 83)

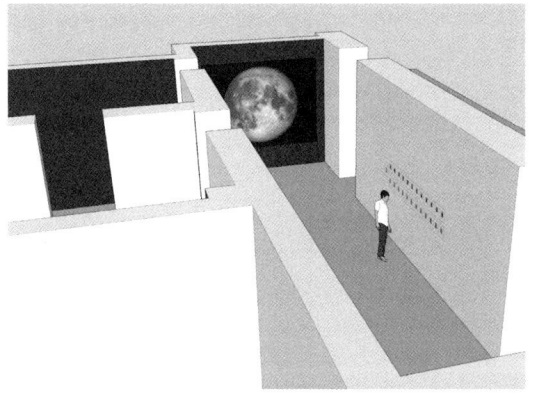
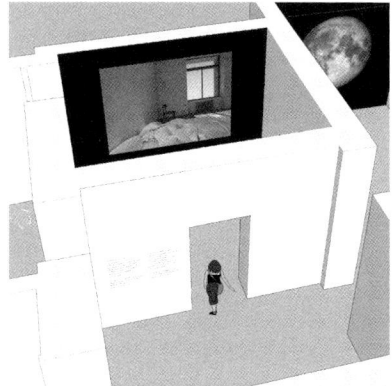

5.8. Afterlife

In preparing his presentation of *Dear Urania* at Galleria Lia Rumma, Burgin made a 3D-model of the exhibition spaces. (Fig. 5.17.) Different views of the model from a high-angle vantage point offer a preview of the way the works are displayed across the three rooms. Occasionally, two figures, a man and a woman, are inserted in the virtual spaces as if taking a tour of the exhibition. No doubt Burgin included these figures to lend a sense of scale to the model. But their resemblance to figures in such 3D virtual worlds as videogames, *Second Life*, or Machinima adds a supplementary signification to the functional aspect of these exhibition views. In this perspective, the woman and the man might also be avatars of some real visitors to the gallery in the immersive virtual metaverse *Second Life*, where they interact with places, objects, and other fantasy characters. Indeed, avatars are not foreign to Burgin's recent projection works based on 3D imaging software.

In *A Place to Read* (2010), the panoramic camera flight over the computer-modeled reconstruction of architect Sedad Hakki Eldem's now mutilated *Taslik Coffee House*, erected in Istanbul between 1947 and 1948 on the top of a hill overlooking the Bosporus, is accompanied by a fictional narrative about capitalist corruption and environmental devastation, both in the real world and in cyberspace. (Fig. 5.18.) The story is told in three sections of intertitles, which describe two acts of reading and an act of writing. It begins with a woman sitting in an idyllic coffeehouse, resembling Eldem's building before its transformation. She reads a book about conspiracy and corruption, where the same coffeehouse in which she sits has been mutilated and integrated within a luxury hotel. The second part focuses on another, a Turkish woman in exile, who is writing on the terrace of a coffeehouse in Geneva. The story she is writing takes place in a virtual reconstruction of the original coffeehouse

Figure 5.17.

Views of a 3D-model of the exhibition *Dear Urania*, 2016.

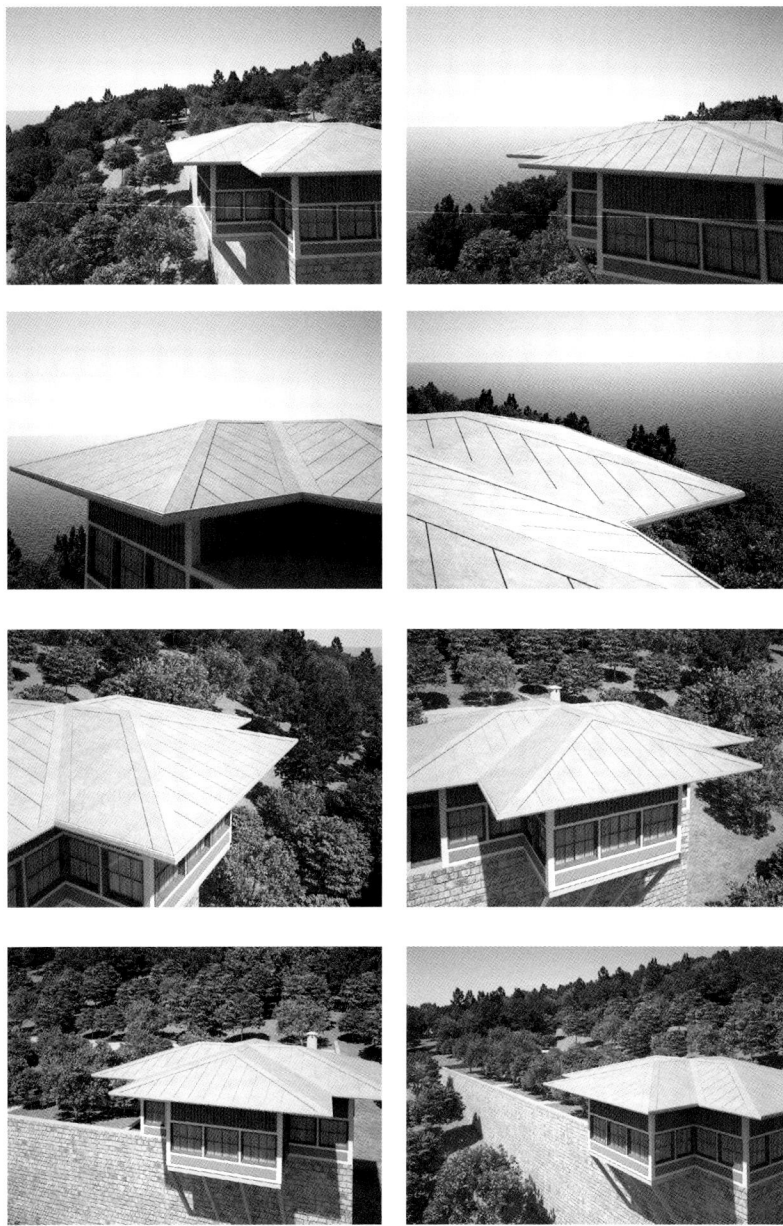

Figure 5.18.

A Place to Read, 2010.

Projected text/image loop, silent, 10 min. 29 sec.

in Istanbul, where the avatars of a man and a woman meet. In the final section of intertitles, a man is trying to read, in spite of the noise, in a coffeehouse on Istanbul's busy *İstiklal Caddesi*. We learn that this is the man who has built the digital replica of the coffeehouse overlooking the Bosporus, which may now disappear as a result of speculation in virtual land. His avatar is walking in the garden of the virtual coffeehouse, accompanied by a woman. Only at the end do we understand that the woman in the first part might not be real but rather the avatar of the man's companion, and that the book she reads is, in fact, about the real world she wants to escape, in frequenting a virtual place. This "allegory of modern Turkey" (PT: 226-227) becomes an allegory of divided memory, because reader and writer, embodied person and avatar, are living simultaneously in different, and paradoxical, spatial and temporal realities.[72] Memories of the real coffeehouse, conjuring up Ottoman and modern traditions, are projected onto a virtual, future space of real estate speculation, bridging a present moment of the building's decay. The ironic punchline is, of course, that the same forces of economic exploitation that caused the mutilation of the real coffeehouse now threaten even its idyllic reconstruction in the virtual world.

In *A Place to Read*, the figure of the avatar emerges in the intertitles while the virtual image environment remains devoid of people. It is only in *The Ideal City* (2013) that Burgin creates a fictive character that ambulates through the debris of a composite urban landscape merging the ideal city of Quattrocento perspective painting with the building of the fascist Casa del Fascio in Como (1930) and a succession of façades inspired by the streets of Milan in Michelangelo Antonioni's film of 1961 *La Notte*. (Plate 13) Actually, the woman, wearing "a light jacket over a summer dress with a pattern of leaves," turns out to be the avatar of Jeanne Moreau, the female protagonist of *La Notte*, as she walks through the streets of Milan. The virtual representation of a fictional character featured as an issue in the Second Life community in 2007 already, when detective Mac Taylor in the CBS series *CSI: NY* enters the virtual world of *Second Life* in order to chase an avatar. As *The New York Times* put it concisely: "Fictional characters get virtual lives, too." (Carter, 2007) The "cyberspace science fiction fantasy" of *Second Life*, which, as Samuel Axon observes, is a profitable business based on the transaction of virtual goods within the community (Axon, 2017), is here integrated into the fiction of broadcast television with its own strategies of storytelling, commercial structure, and fan community. It is further notable that the computer animators who created the *Second Life* environment of the *CSI: NY* episode used machinima to animate the virtual world in which Taylor now could walk and fly around. (Carter 2007) Machinima is, generally speaking, a technique that appropriates the real-time graphic engines of game technology to create new narratives in the form of "animated movies in a 3D virtual environment in real time." (Marino, 2004: 2; Lowood, 2005: 15) Erik Champion emphasizes the hybrid and reflexive character of machinima when he writes:

> Machinima is fascinating because it combines different interactive and prerendered media in a way that causes us to question who we are, what we have experienced, and how we may have taken our past experiences for granted. For the paradox of machinima, that it uses real-time game engines to create prerendered content, may be leveraged creatively to challenge our preconceptions and behavioral triggers. Machinima could be a new hybrid form of reflection-provoking media. (Champion, 2011: 221)

Drawing on Jay David Bolter and Richard Grusin's concept of remediation as a constant refashioning and rivalry between one medium and another, Martin Picard moreover highlights that "re-appropriation and re-using of media content by another media or platform" are fundamental aspects of machinima. (Picard, 2006; Bolter and Grusin, 2000: 65) Operating at the "convergence of filmmaking, animation and game development," machinima are apt to "create a friction, a strategy of resistance between the game creators and game consumers." (Picard, 2006) In his writings around 2010, Burgin repeatedly assesses machinima as a digital technology that provides the conditions for new demotic forms of cinema, which are technically easy to use and economically accessible because of their low costs of production. (TC: 203) However, Burgin sees at least two problems with this new kind of cinematic storytelling. The first encompasses the fairly limited operational flexibility of the filmmaker, whose performance largely depends on the game engine he uses to realize his movie. (222) The second concerns the fact that most machinima films do not "depart significantly from contents and forms of mainstream media productions." (227) The production of *The Ideal City* has to be seen within the context of this fascination for machinima and *Second Life*. Like machinima films, the projection work is a hybrid work based on various media and artforms such as videogames, painting, cinema, and words. Also, as in machinima productions, an avatar walks through a virtual environment, which simulates the real world while being completely independent from the laws of gravity and nature. But instead of including the female avatar in a conventional narrative taking place within a preconstructed homogeneous architectural setting, Burgin puts her in a heterogeneous landscape of different architectural styles, periods, and ideologies which all finally end up as the ruins of past and future histories turning thus the dream of the ideal city into a Babylonian nightmare. Further, the female avatar is not merely the protagonist of a virtual movie but she is a reflexive (or even a theoretical) figure. In the broken smartphone that she picked up from a pile of debris she watches a short clip showing Antonioni's female protagonist, the very person upon whom she was modeled. This inversion of roles according to which the avatar becomes an active agent that controls its counterpart in the real world reveals to what point the relationship between reality and fiction has become problematic in the era of virtual reality and artificial intelligence. Burgin's critical work of unveiling the contradictions and incoherencies of the apparently perfect 3D-simulated realities comes to the fore in an intertitle that draws attention to the artificial, eerie character of such virtual spaces: "Incoherent, incomplete the street forms itself around her as she walks."[73] Once again, viewers find themselves in a dream consisting of incomplete, fragmented, and uncanny ruins through which they travel, as Benjamin thought his contemporaries traveled through the "far-flung ruins and debris" of cinema, with the difference that the persons that appear in this "universe of exploded cities" are not anymore real people (Jeanne Moreau) who play fictive characters (the protagonist of *La Notte*), but fictions of fictions. The avatar is living in a parallel world that increasingly gets disconnected from the physical world and that, such is the fantasy of Burgin's most recent work, *Afterlife* (2018), will survive it in an uncertain future. (Plate 14)

Afterlife exists in two versions, as a website to be navigated on the Internet and as a classic paper book. With the exception of one real photograph, it contains only computer-generated images of different kinds of landscapes and interiors, which, as we learn on one of the first pages, are part of a multiverse called "Afterlife" that "contains an infinity of possible worlds. In one of these the afterlife is not a matter of faith, it is a fact." The text that accompanies the images develops variations of the idea of the possibility to make a "perfect digital copy of the mind," which then leads a life independently of the body permitting the individual to survive his own physical death. This fantasy of achieving immortality by transcending the material human body evokes the transhumanist tenet of mind uploading as propagated by neuroscientists Anders Sandberg and Nick Boström. As they argue:

> The basic idea is to take a particular brain, scan its structure in detail and construct a software that is so faithful to the original that, when run on appropriate hardware, it will behave in essentially the same way as the original brain. (Sandberg and Boström, 2008: 7)

Needless to say that this idea of mind copying or mind transfer has a long history in science fiction literature (from Walter M. Miller's 1951 novella *Izzard and the Membrane* to Hannu Rajaniemi's *Quantum Thief* series of 2010-2014) and in science fiction films such as, most recently, *Transcendence* (2014) or *Self/less* (2015).[74] In *Afterlife*, Burgin actually subverts such futurist fantasies of a disembodied future by creating frictions and contradictions in the virtual worlds represented by the images and the text. The first and most obvious paradox resides in the conception of the work as a classic book. As a material object that has to be manipulated physically by turning the pages, *Afterlife* in fact contradicts the dream of immateriality addressed in the book's content, thus contesting both the conventions of the book and the promise of a being beyond physical reality. As Burgin observed in an interview with Federica Chiocchetti: "My first thought is that, as a photobook, *Afterlife* looks wrong. Perhaps it has something of an uncanny air about it." (Chiocchetti, 2019: 23) This "uncanny air" is also conveyed by the images. Confronted with a series of sinister views of deserted foggy industrial areas, decayed cityscapes and burning cars, which alternate with sublime landscapes and mysterious interiors, the spectator is caught between a dystopian nightmare and the utopian dream of magnificent untouched nature.

Toward the middle of the book suddenly an image appears that marks a caesura on two accounts. As the only real photograph in the book, it interrupts the stream of synthetic images, thus opening an escape route that leads back to the material world. As the only image of a person—a woman leaning against the windowpane of a train—it further introduces human life, which is completely absent from the deserted environments of the computer-generated images. Concerning this photograph, Burgin explains:

> The woman in that photograph stands in for the pivotal object around which my "narrative" turns. The train might also be seen as figuring "passage" in the Orphic myth: first into the Underworld, then out. Where Eurydice follows Orpheus, here she is ahead. Where Eurydice is dead, here the photograph of the woman is the only living thing in a dead world of digital images. (Chiocchetti, 2019: 23)

This structuring device of a pivotal image different from all the others is, of course, a *clin d'œil* to the formal construction of Chris Marker's science fiction film *La Jetée* (1962). As commonly known, Marker's film is composed entirely of photographs except for one filmed sequence showing the female protagonist waking up and blinking. In his essay "Marker Marked," Burgin refers to Marker's observation that *La Jetée* would be a "remake" of Hitchcock's *Vertigo* reminding us thus that "the making of a story is always a remaking of it." (RF: 93) Seen from this angle, *Afterlife* may be understood as a remake or an update of *La Jetée*, a travel through time and memory in the age of digital technology and artificial intelligence. Burgin moreover draws on Donald Winnicott's concept of the "transitional object," when he identifies "transitional time"—that is the time "that transforms the actual absence of the object-mother into a time of potential reunion"—as a state between sleep and waking or daydreaming, "where real objects and internal objects mingle." (101) It is, however, the photo dissolve preceding the blinking-eye sequence, in which the woman slightly opens her mouth with her eyes still closed, that "the dream has prepared for waking into a world in which the most significant object is the one that has already been dreamt." (105) Likewise, the photograph in *Afterlife* is prepared by the image of Michelangelo's *La Notte*, which, as the computer-generated simulation of a commercial replica of the sculpture, appears like a dream within the dream of the *Afterlife* metaverse of which the woman might have dreamt before waking up in the real world. This circling movement oscillating between real space and psychical space is the very structural model of the narrative of *Afterlife* that Burgin describes as a "conscious fantasy: you never quite get where you're aiming, you circle back and begin again, but never arrive." (Chiocchetti, 2019: 23)

But this conscious fantasy does not only spiral along the axis of virtual reality and material world, dream, and waking state; it also interweaves elements from the history of science fiction with references to Burgin's own works, thus creating an intertextual and intermediatic environment in which the finally ahistorical fantasy of eternal life within a perfect space is put to the test. Already the first text lines evoke Tarkovsky's famous science fiction film *Solaris* (1972), to which Burgin referred earlier, in his travelogue *Some Cities*. In Tarkovsky's film a mysterious ocean, capable of copying the thoughts of people, reproduces the protagonist's late wife. But when he tries to unfasten her dress, the fact that he finds lace-holes, but no laces, makes him aware of the deception. In *Some Cities*, Burgin concludes: "We perpetually commute between Earth and Solaris. The signs that tell us where we are are rarely as eloquent as the woman in the unfinished dress." (SC: 181) Made in 1996, this comment refers to the teletopological puzzle of the mediatic environment in which fantasies, memories, and actual perceptions of the physical world overlap (see Chapter 4). Some twenty years later, in *Afterlife*, circumstances are different. While in the teletopological media environment perceptions of the physical world are mingled with images of the mind, "in Afterlife there is no reality other than memories and fantasies." While the teletopological puzzle is constituted of interior *and* exterior image fragments, each duplicate of Afterlife "is its own memory puzzle." In a recent unpublished paper, Burgin draws on Yuk Hui's definition of digital objects as immaterial objects "that take shape on a screen or hide in the back end of a computer program, composed of data and metadata regulated by structures or schemas." (Hui, 2016: 1)[75] Yet Burgin reminds us of the fact that there is another immaterial object—the psychical object—which, together with the digital object, would constitute the virtual object. In *Afterlife*, these two aspects of the virtual object—the digital and the psychical—are constantly related to each other in the form of fragments of anecdotes, remembered stories, and memory images of transient and ephemeral content that Burgin called "*story images*." (email exchange October 2, 2019) Some of these story images summarize entire novels, such as William Golding's *Pincher Martin* (1956):

> There is a story that begins with the sinking of a ship. A sailor is washed up on a large rock, which he sets about exploring for the means of his survival. Throughout the tale the man is troubled by something uncannily familiar about the place where he is stranded. The story ends with his realisation that the rock has the form of a broken tooth he had been in the habit of probing with his tongue. He had summoned the memory as a refuge at the moment of his death.

Another example is the story of a man who meets a woman of whom he realizes in the end that she is a recording of someone long dead. This is, of course, the plot of *The Invention of Morel* (1940), a science fiction novel by Adolfo Bioy Casares, in which a fugitive from the world encounters a woman on a remote island and falls in love with her. Learning that she is a duplicate produced by a recording machine capable of reproducing reality, he finally tries to move beyond the recording to merge with the consciousness of his beloved. Burgin's video *The Fifth Promenade* (2008) is actually based on Casares' novel. But while in the video the fiction is brought back to reality by including a real woman in the natural environment of Île Saint-Pierre, Rousseau's place of exile, the woman of *Afterlife*, being "a recording faithful in every detail of someone long dead," cannot escape anymore from the metaverse.

In view of these historical and biographical cross-references, "afterlife," in terms of the English translation of Warburg's "Nachleben," might take an additional meaning. According to Warburg, the afterlife of images is a specific expression in antiquity surviving through the centuries. As Georges Didi-Huberman writes:

> In Warburg's work, the term *Nachleben* refers to the survival (the continuity or afterlife and metamorphosis) of images and motifs—as opposed to their renascence after extinction or, conversely, their replacement by innovations in image and motif. (Didi-Huberman, 2003: 273)

Continuity and metamorphosis are, in fact, the very principles of Burgin's *Afterlife*. Although technological progress substantially and irrevocably changes the life and being of humans and images alike, there is, to quote the famous words with which Marker concludes *La Jetée*, "no way to escape Time." But the time of *Afterlife* is neither purely backward-looking nor does it seek its salvation in the future. Closely analogous to Benjamin's definition of the present, *Afterlife*, and the projection works discussed above, "[polarize] the event into fore- and after-history." (Benjamin, 1999: 471) If Gerhard Richter deduces from Benjamin's concept of history that "Nachleben therefore is the figure of a repetition that does not repeat, a living on and after that both remains attached to what came before and [...] departs from it in ever-new directions (Richter, 2011: 4)," this also applies to the spiraling, repetitive, and layering structure of Burgin's recent works. Confronting the virtual multiverse with a multitude of forking paths interlacing facts, fictions and fantasies from past, present, and future, Burgin opens up a critical space to reflect upon—to refer one last time to Benjamin's concept of history—"the afterlife of that which is understood; and what has been recognized in the analysis of the 'afterlife of works.'" (Benjamin, 1999: 460) To which we can add that now, in the age of artificial intelligence, this analysis also comprises the afterlife of entire worlds and brains.

Dear Urania

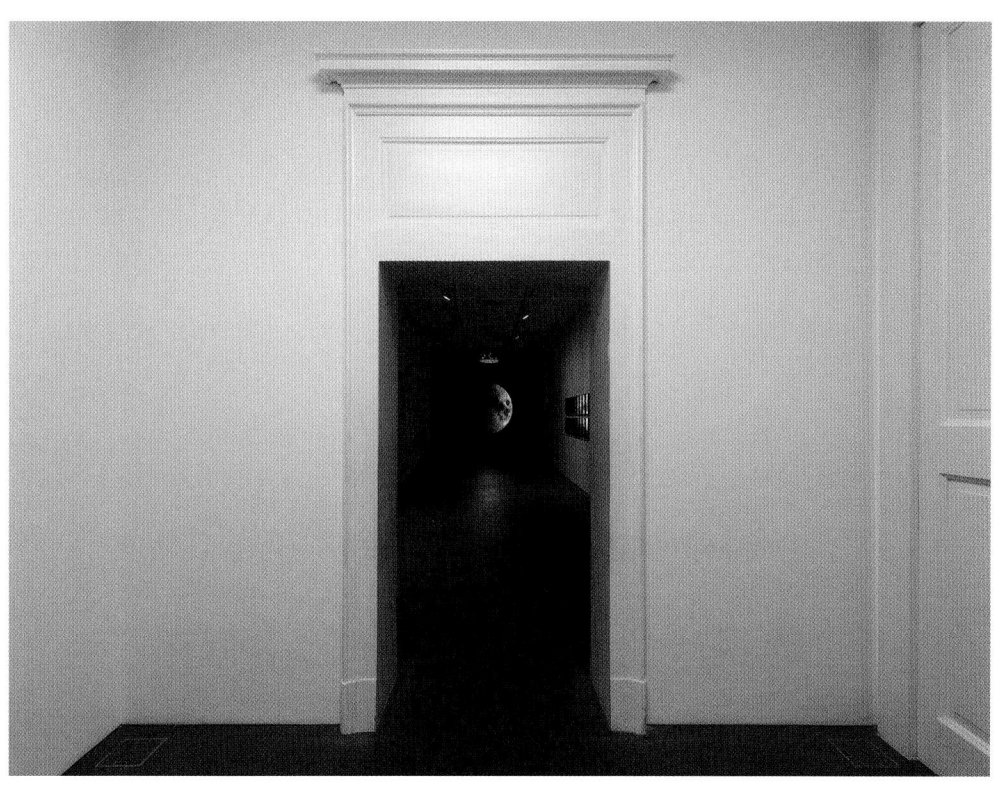

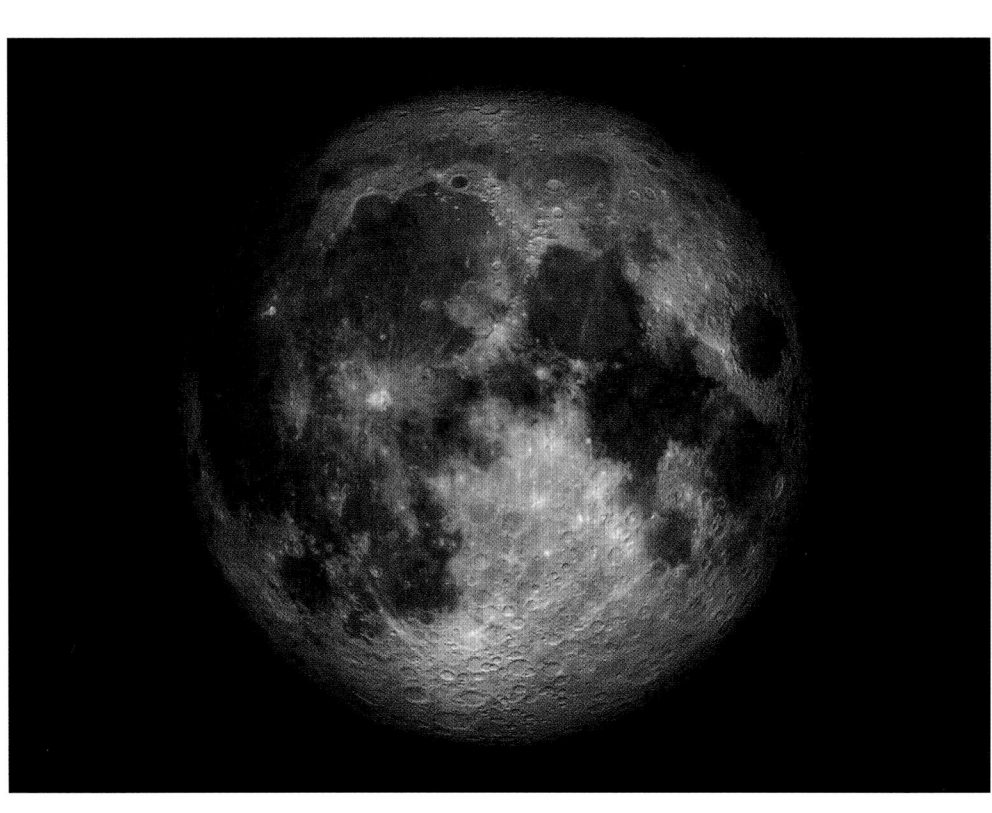

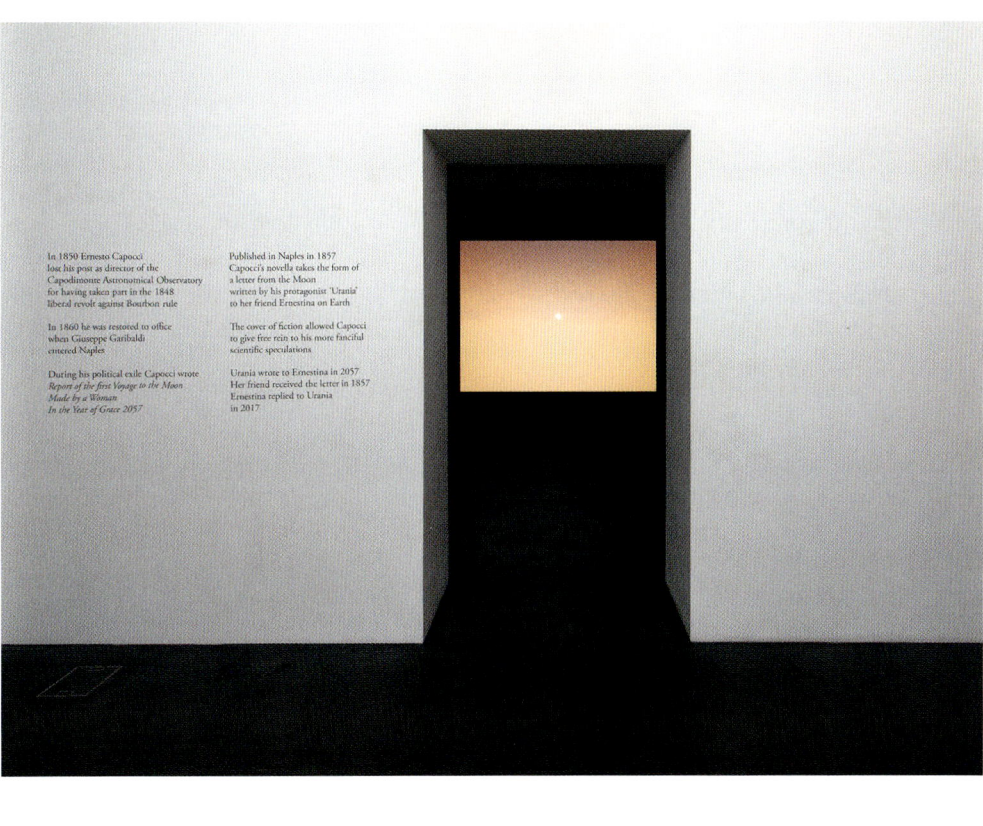

In 1850 Ernesto Capocci
lost his post as director of the
Capodimonte Astronomical Observatory
for having taken part in the 1848
liberal revolt against Bourbon rule

In 1860 he was restored to office
when Giuseppe Garibaldi
entered Naples

During his political exile Capocci wrote
*Report of the first Voyage to the Moon
Made by a Woman
In the Year of Grace 2057*

Published in Naples in 1857
Capocci's novella takes the form of
a letter from the Moon
written by his protagonist 'Urania'
to her friend Ernestina on Earth

The cover of fiction allowed Capocci
to give free rein to his more fanciful
scientific speculations

Urania wrote to Ernestina in 2057
Her friend received the letter in 1857
Ernestina replied to Urania
in 2017

In 1850 Ernesto Capocci
lost his post as director of the
Capodimonte Astronomical Observatory
for having taken part in the 1848
liberal revolt against Bourbon rule

In 1860 he was restored to office
when Giuseppe Garibaldi
entered Naples

During his political exile Capocci wrote
Report of the first Voyage to the Moon
Made by a Woman
In the Year of Grace 2057

Published in Naples in 1857
Capocci's novella takes the form c
a letter from the Moon
written by his protagonist Urania
to her friend Ernestina on Earth

The cover of fiction allowed Capo
to give free rein to his more fancif
scientific speculations

Urania wrote to Ernestina in 2057
Her friend received the letter in 18
Ernestina replied to Urania
in 2017

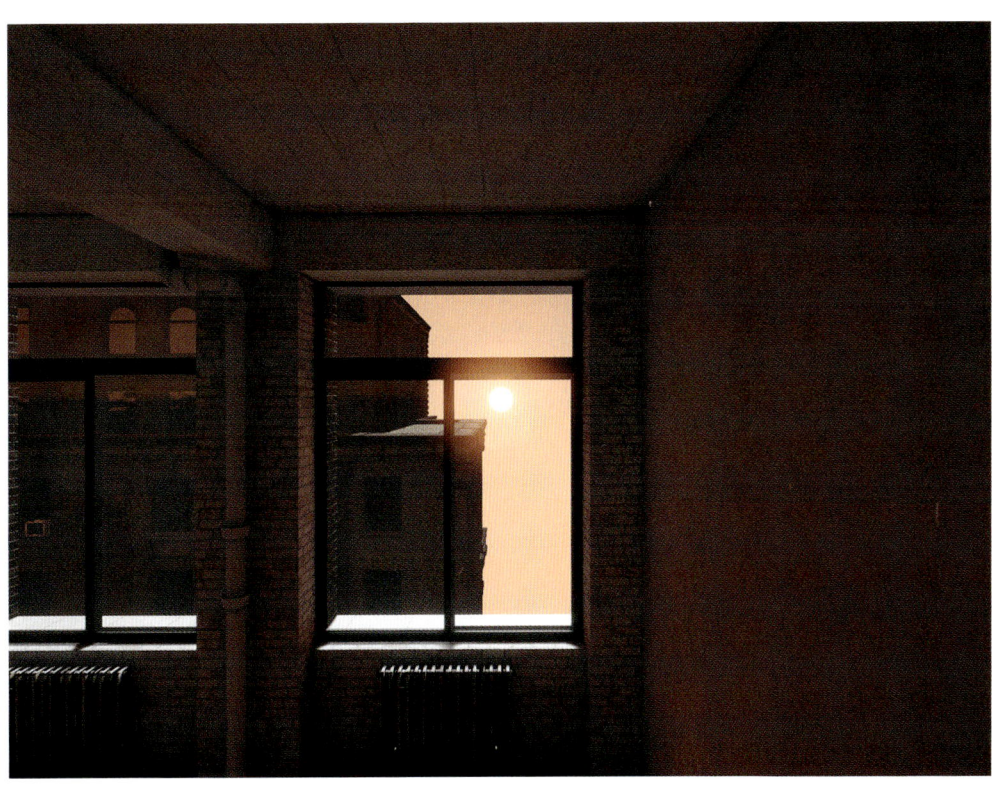

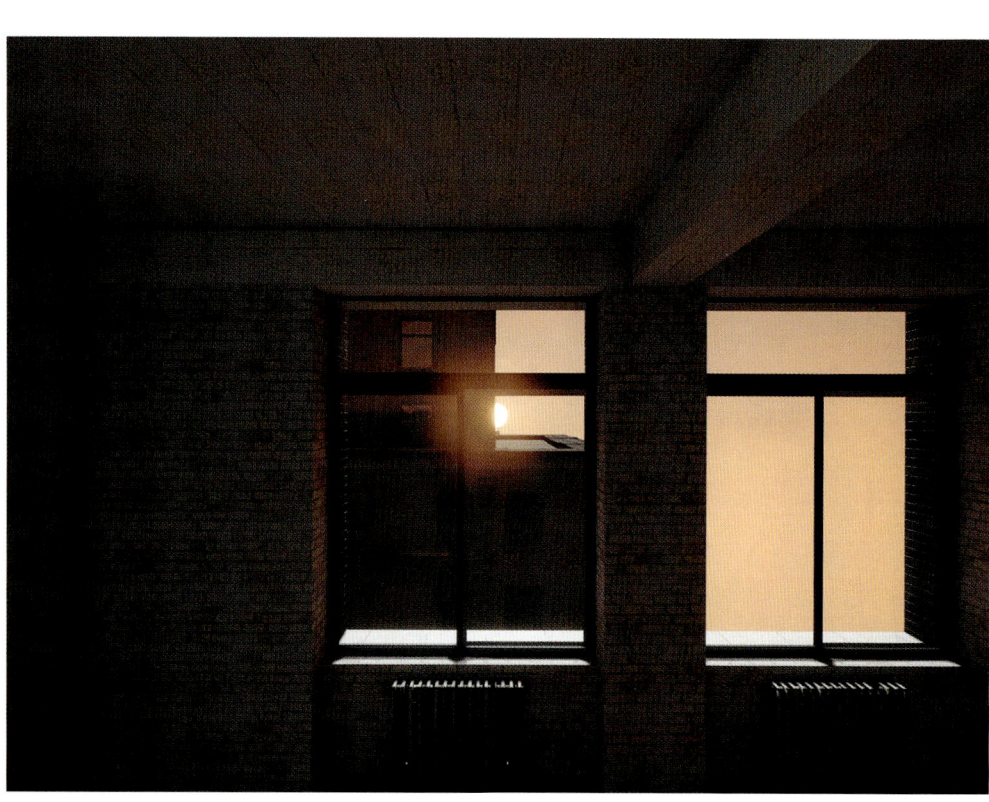

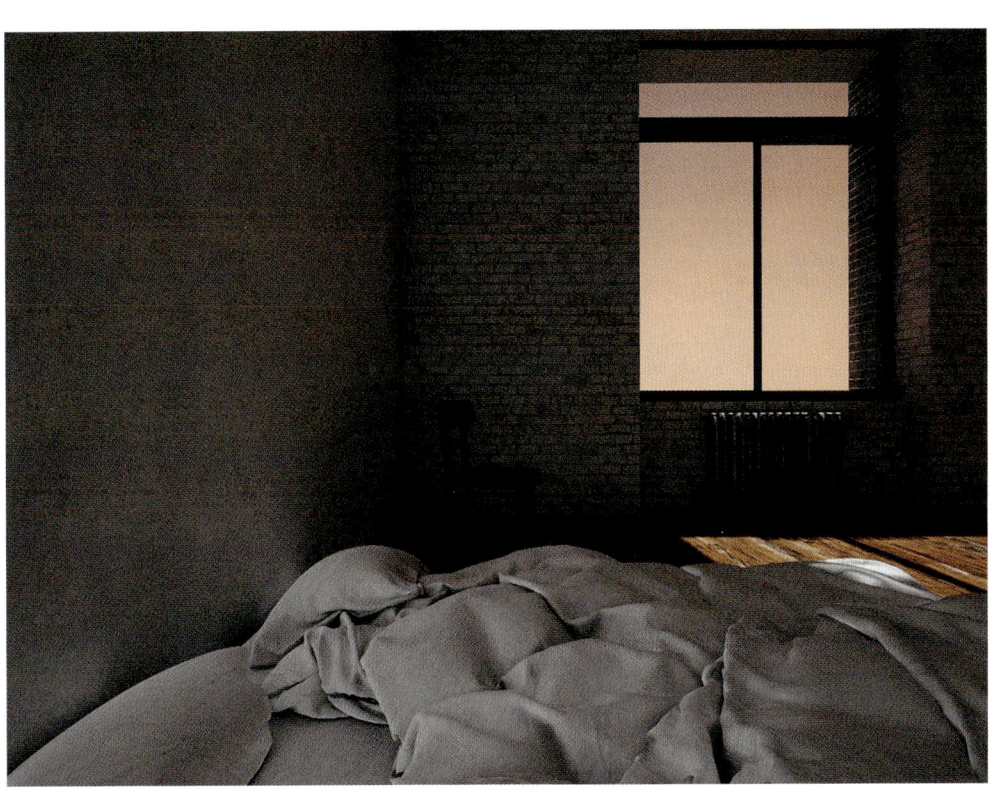

Dear Urania

A night of the full moon
On a night like this Cyrano said
he believed the Moon is
a world like ours

to which our own world appears as a
moon

From here your world appears familiar
to a woman from the Campi Flegrei
accustomed to a world of craters
Mare Morto, Lago Fusaro,
Lago Averno…

…and Pozzuoli, Napoli, Pompeii
Are these not cities of the Moon?

You tell me that the Plato crater
alone of the features
seen from Earth
is endowed with water
air and vegetation

From there you
will set out for
the hidden face of the Moon
which you say will be
a promised land

If I were in your world
I would say
to you

"– not without me – !"

„– und nicht
ohne mich –!"

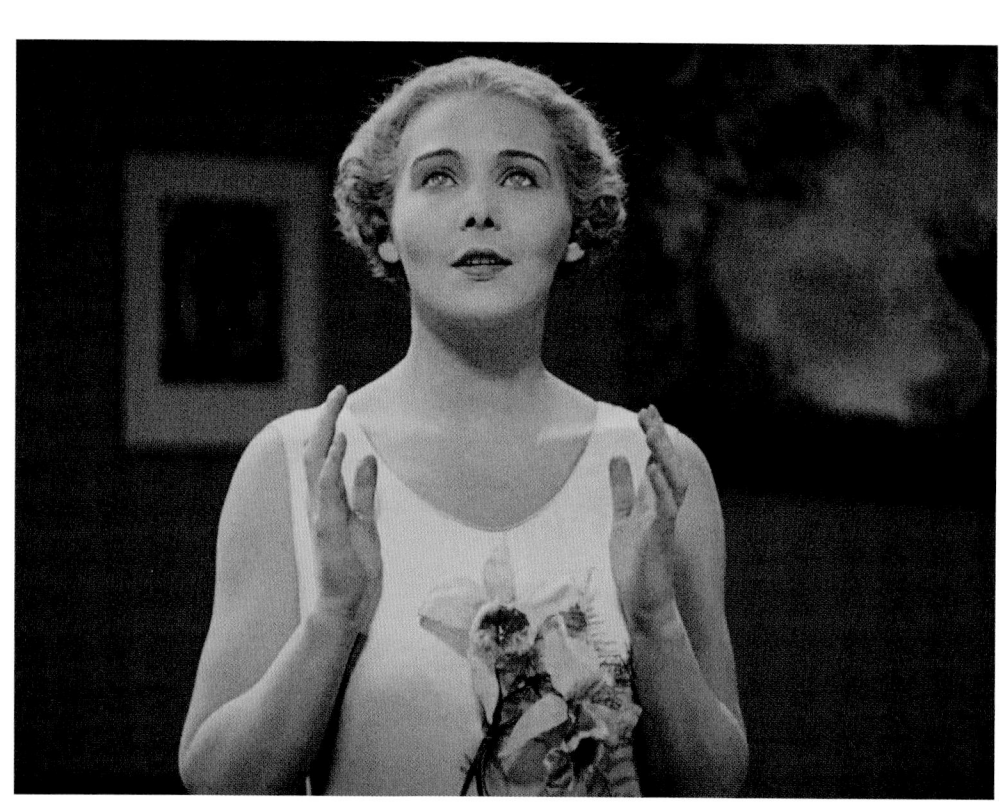

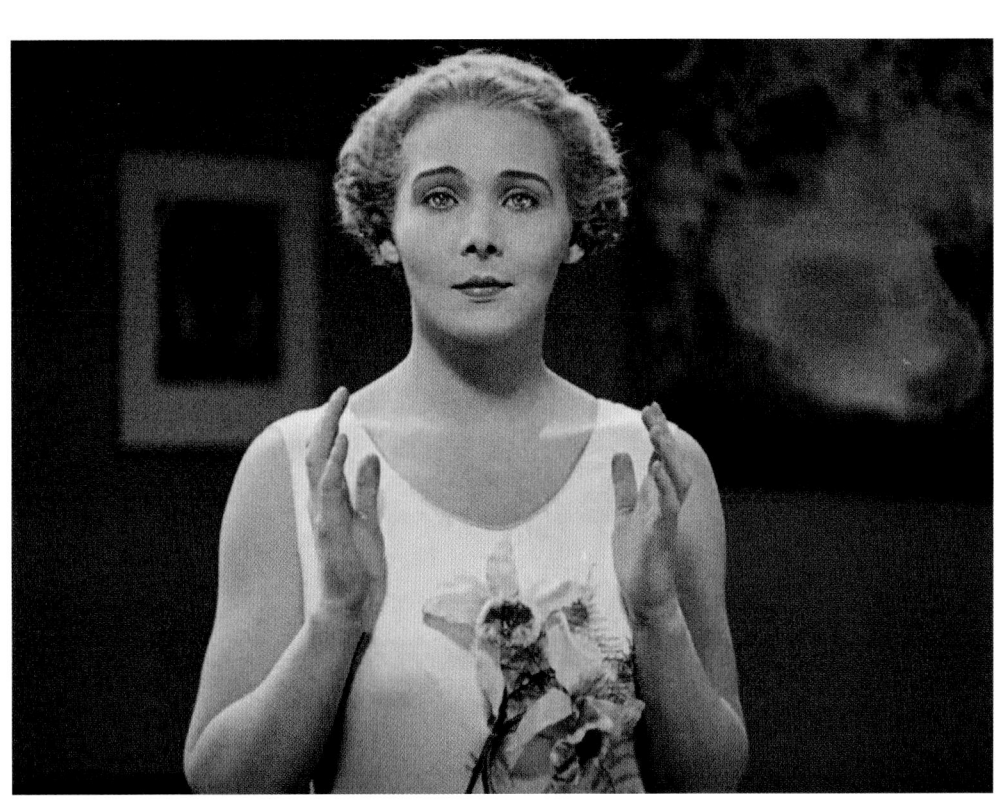

Our twentieth century
exhausted its imagination
fulfilling
a nineteenth century dream

It could not imagine
the nightmare of
the century to come

The lunar surface
has been mapped
exhaustively
We know it better
than the Earth

They will mine
its minerals

then set out
to spread venality
cruelty and greed
to more and more
distant worlds

But not with me
Solitude is now
my sweetest choice

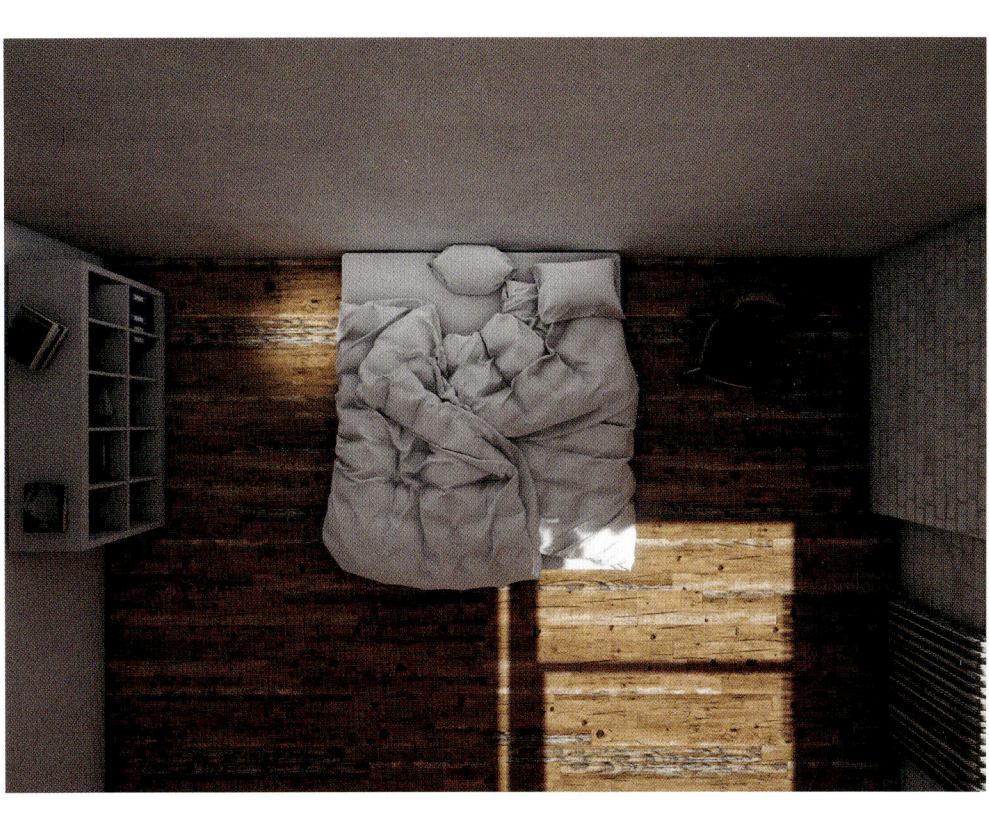

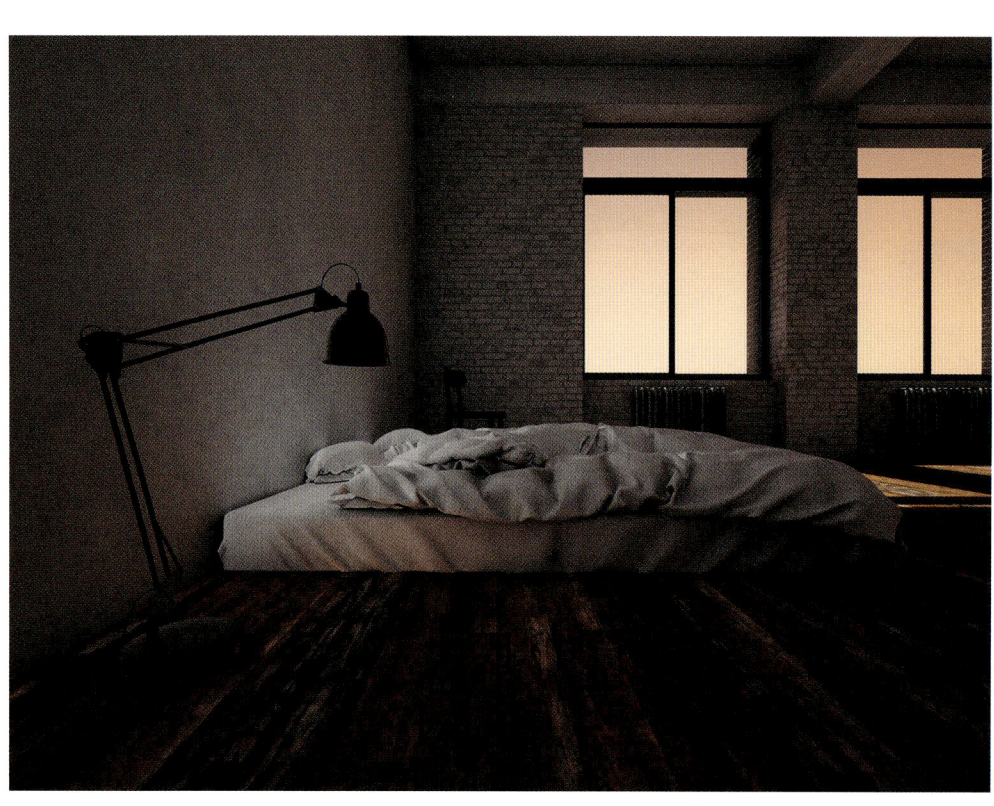

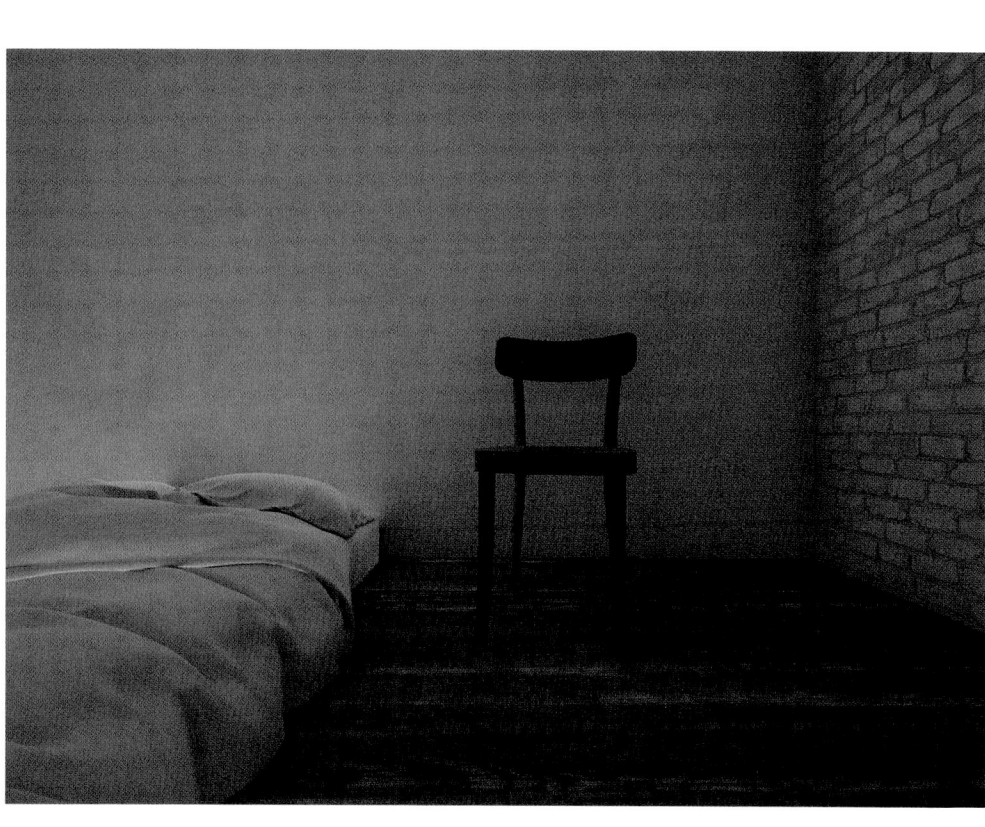

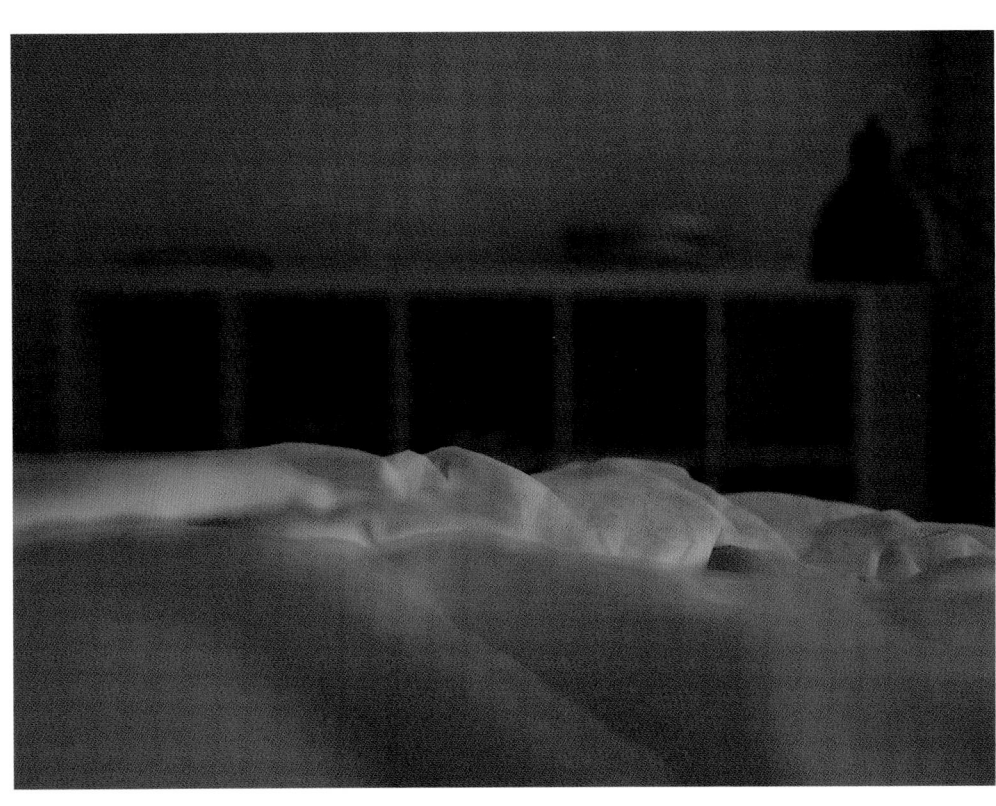

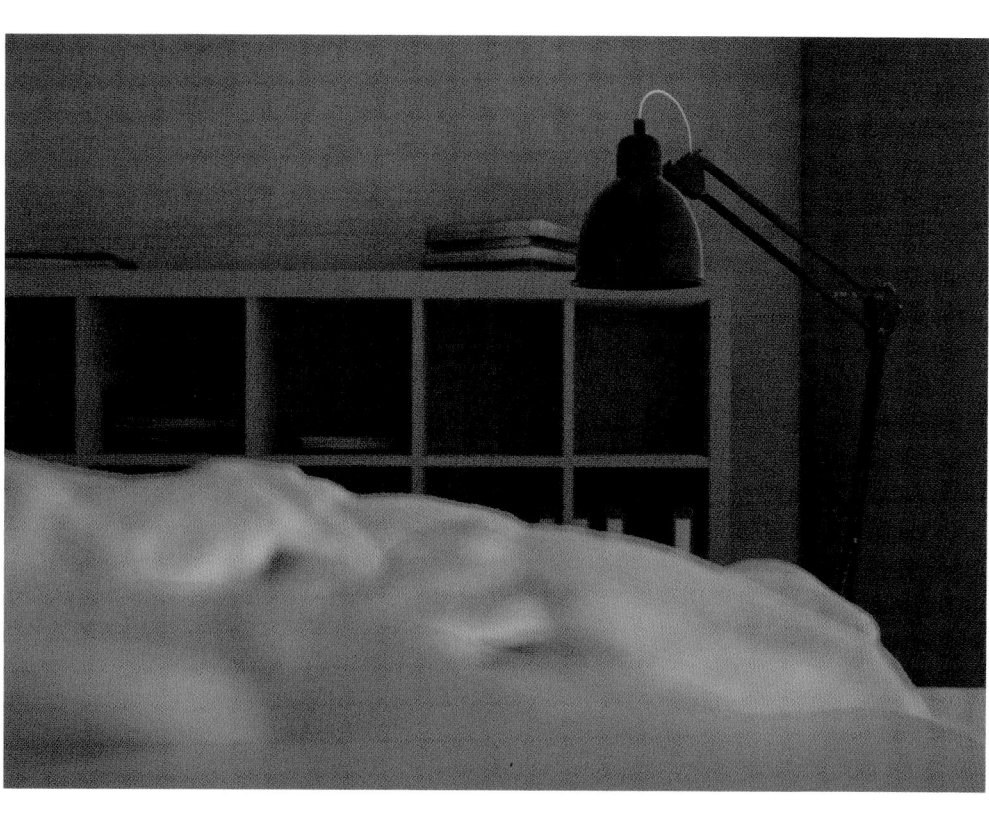

Before our universes
separated
we had many conversations
on the plurality of worlds

Fontanelle was right to say
that if women
so easily followed
the intrigues
in *La Princesse de Clèves*
they would have no trouble
understanding astronomy

How distant now
the evening we learned
that the planets turn
not around the Earth
but around the Sun

We learned that
the Earth too is a planet
circling the Sun
and that the Moon alone
orbits the Earth

You said then
you loved the Moon
for remaining faithful to us
though we are forsaken
by the planets

If Ariosto is right
in his conceit that
what is lost on Earth
finds its way
to the Moon
then may you recover
my lost hope for humanity

Until our worlds
coincide again

Your affectionate

Ernestina

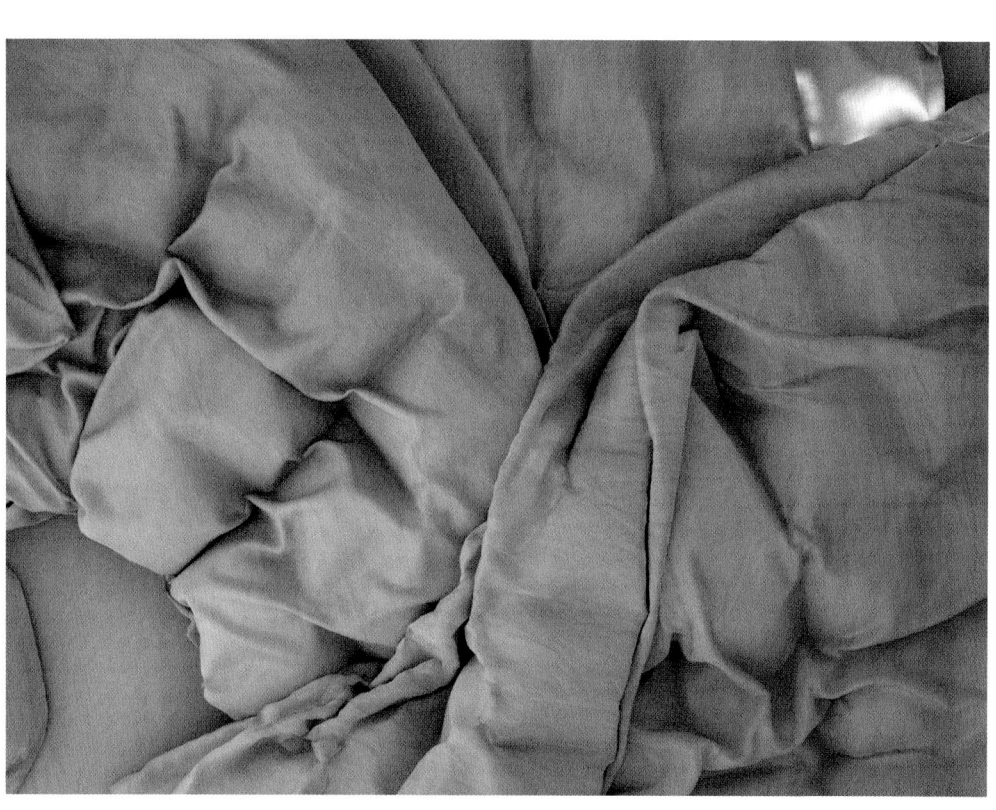

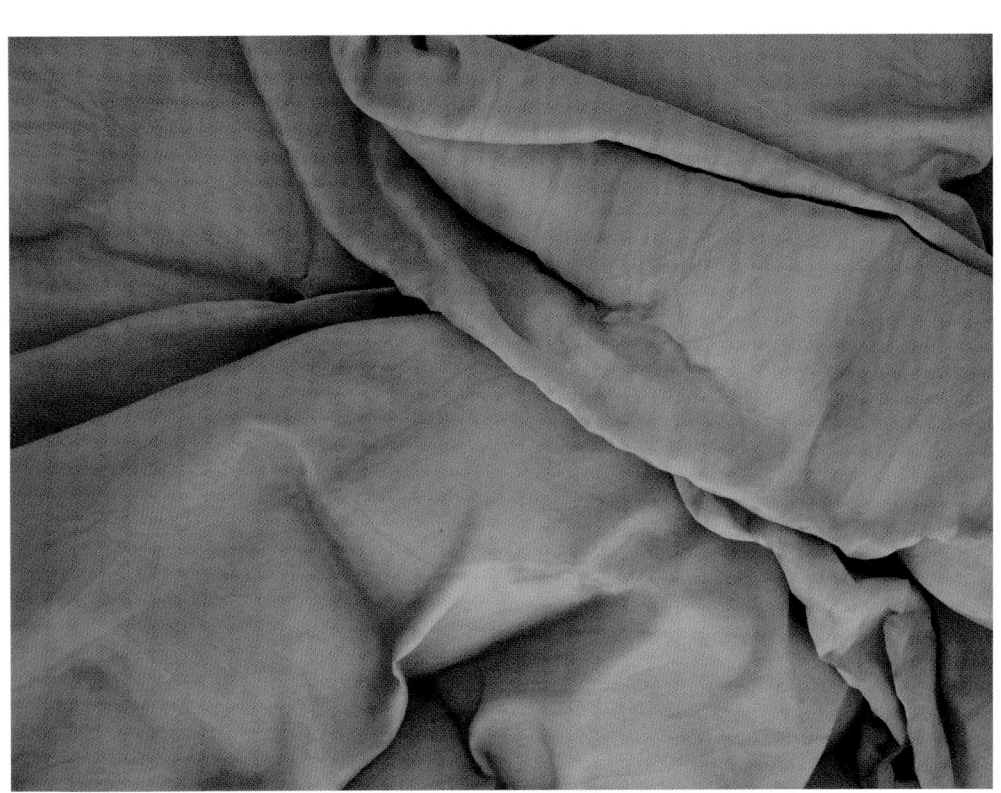

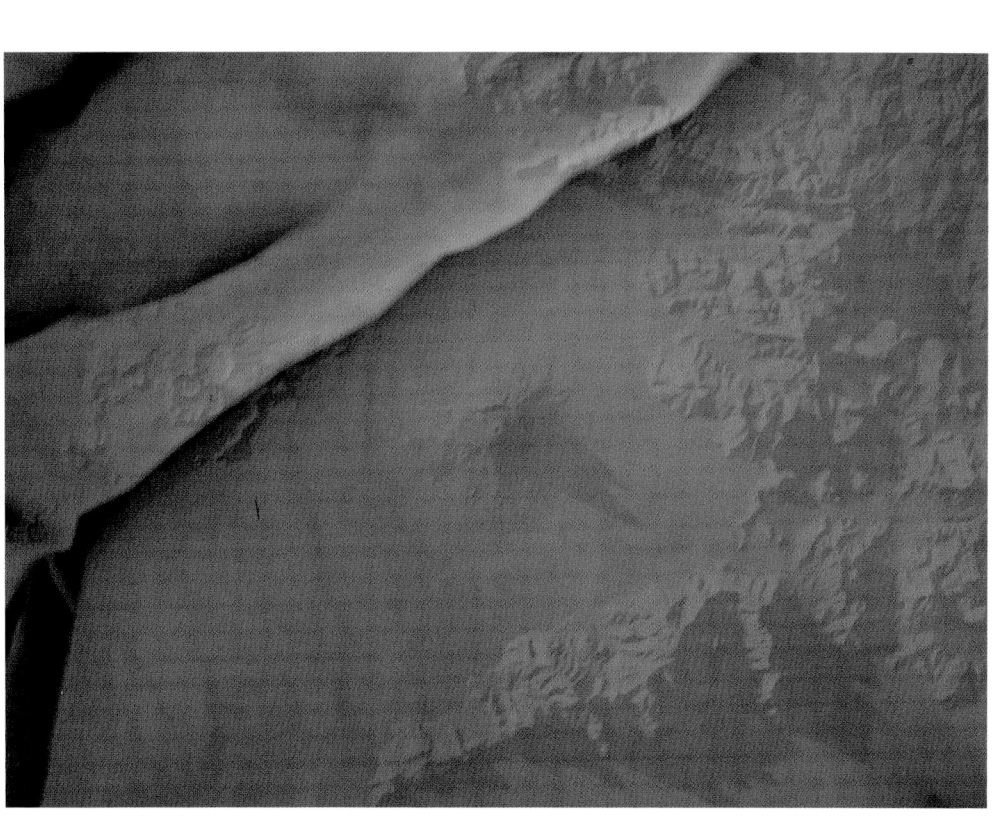

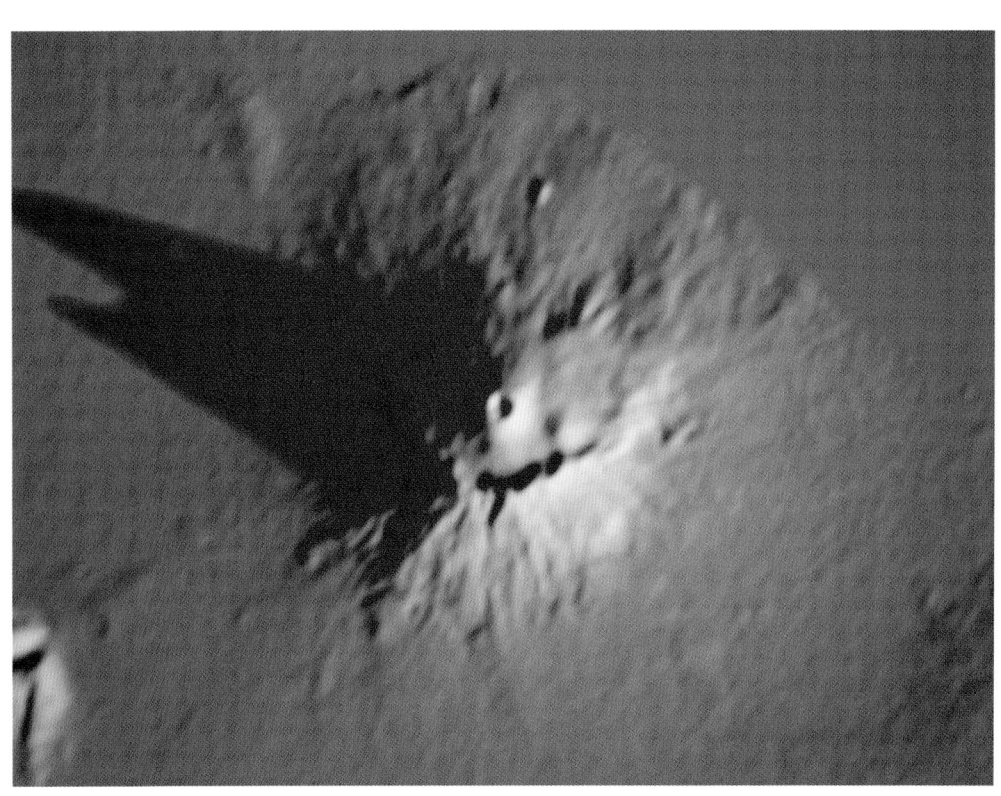

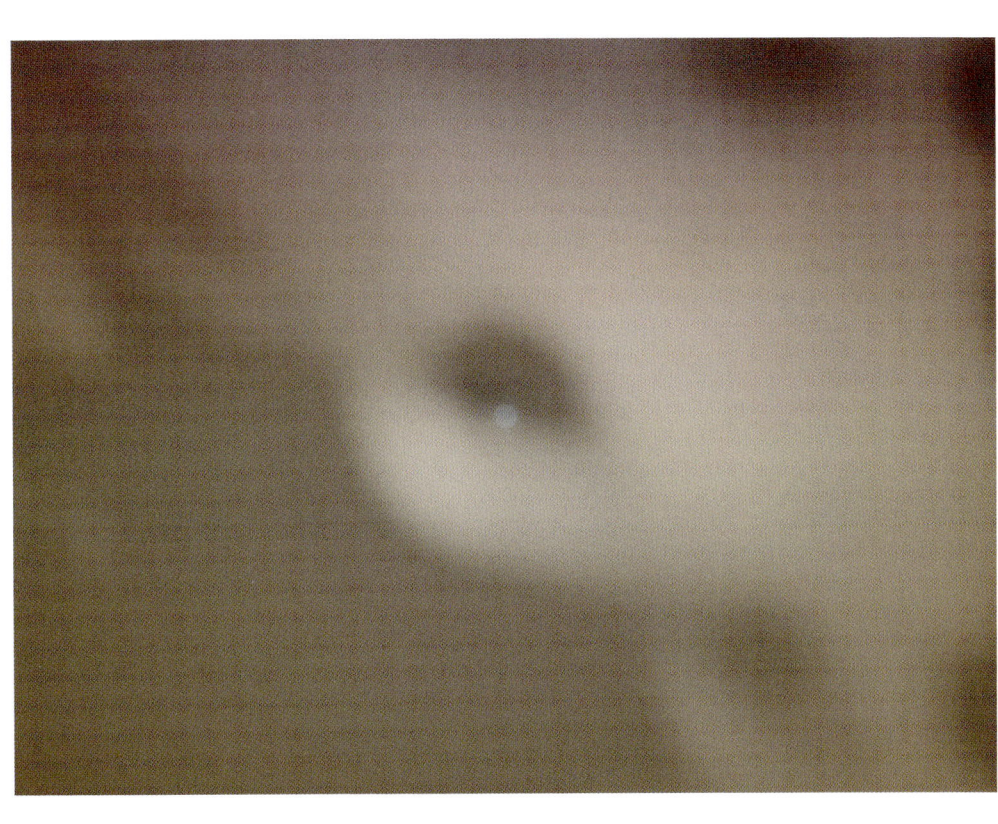

Plates

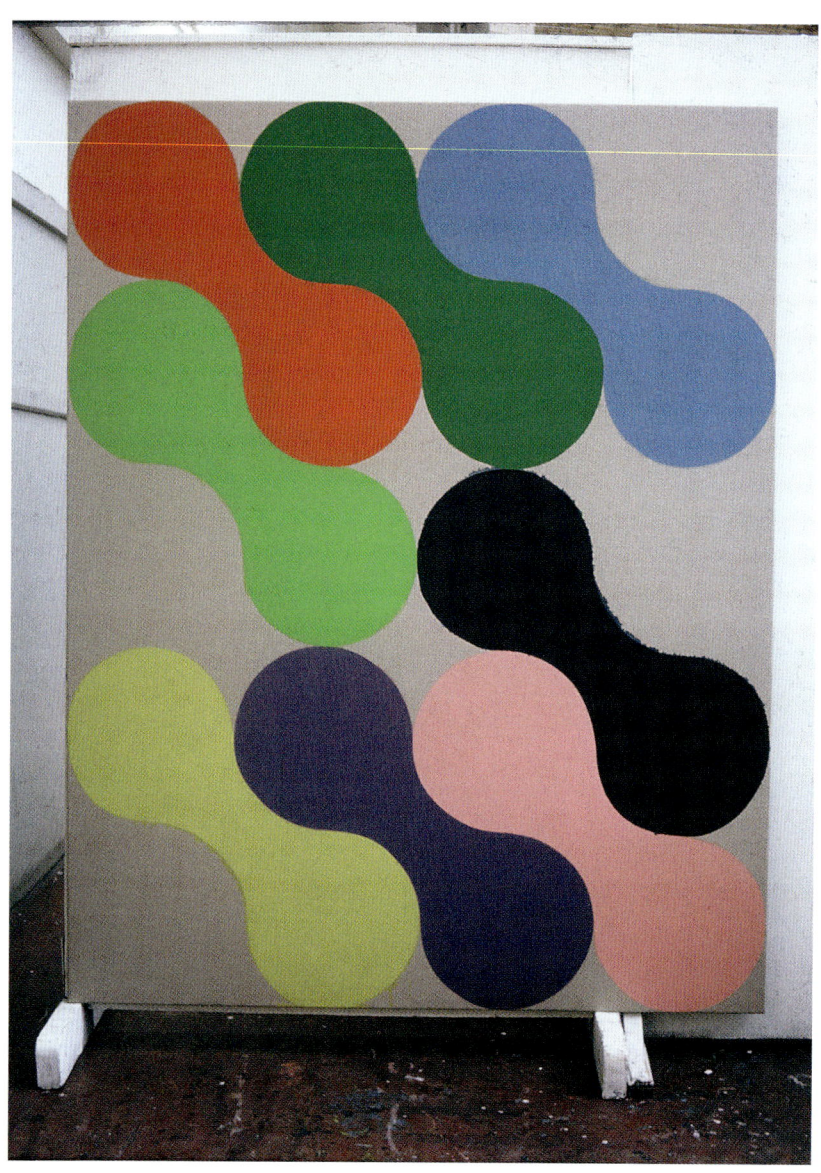

Plate 1
Untitled, 1964.

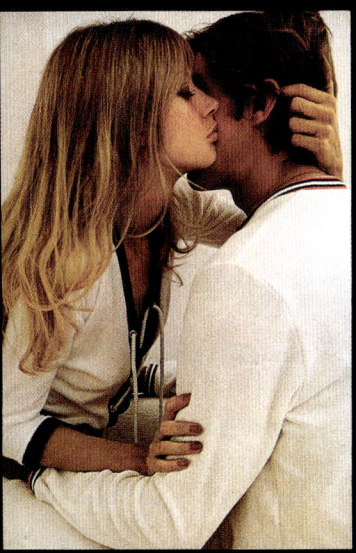

Plate 2

Possession, Newcastle, 1976. 109×84 cm.

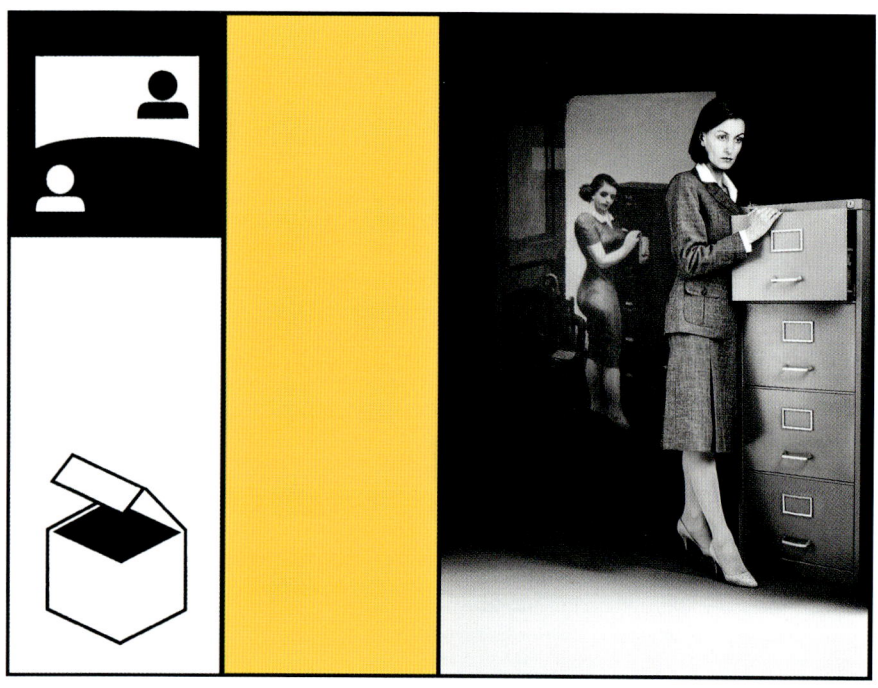

Plate 3
Office at Night, 1985–86. 183×244 cm.

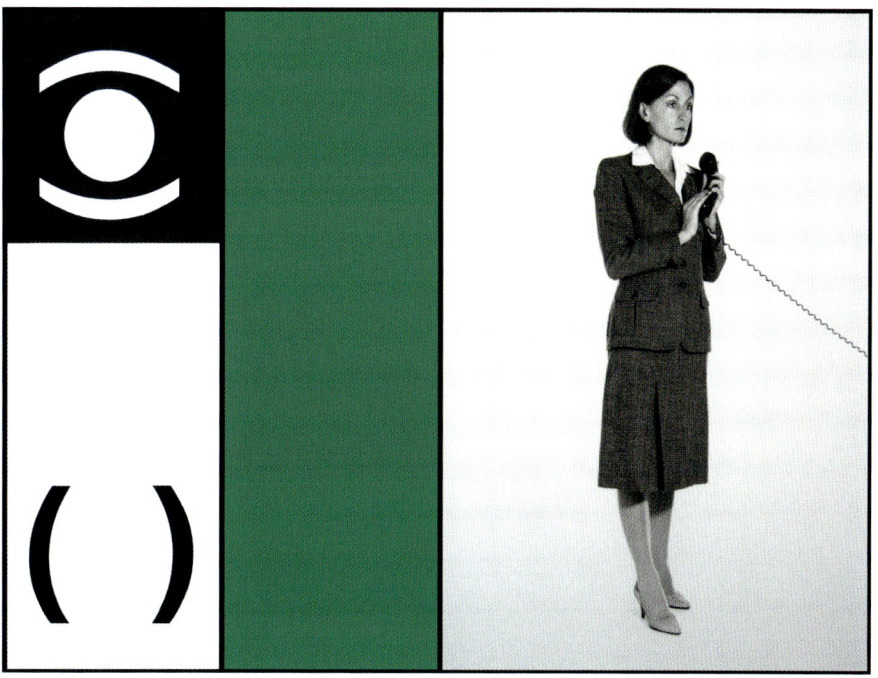

Plate 4
Office at Night, 1985–86. 183×244 cm.

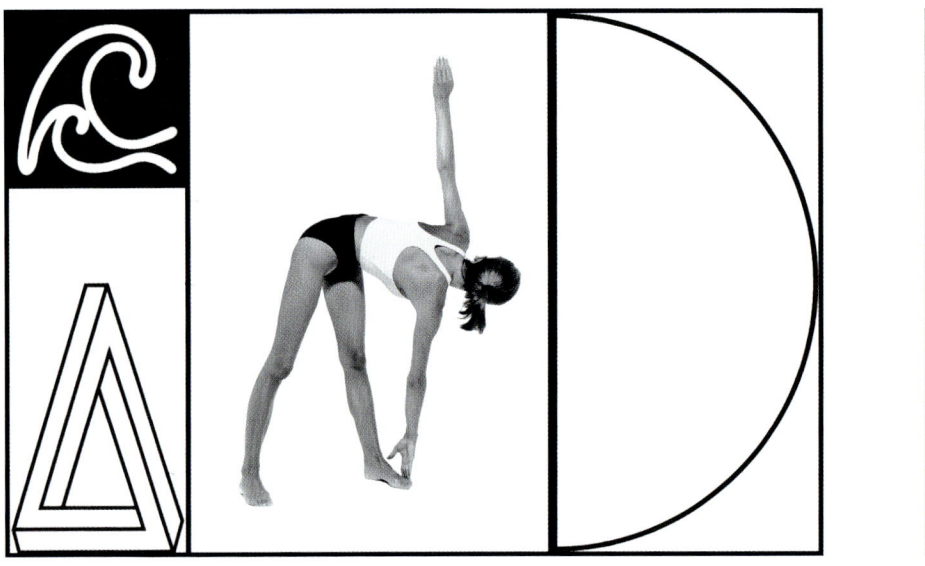

Plate 5

Danaïdes/Dames, 1986. 182×391 cm.

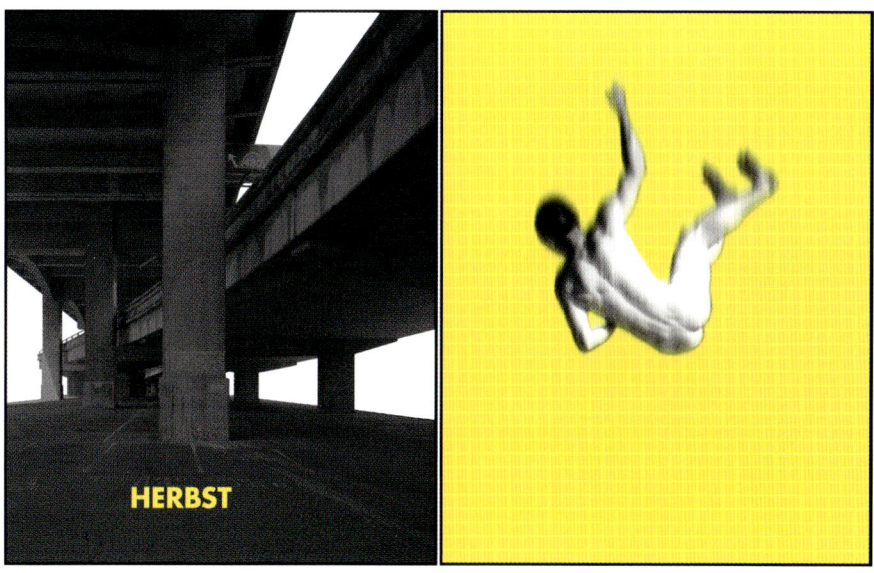

Plate 6

The Four Seasons, 1994. 4 panels, each 152,4×121,9 cm.

Plate 7

Minnesota Abstract, 1989. 3 panels. Each 121,9×121,9 cm.

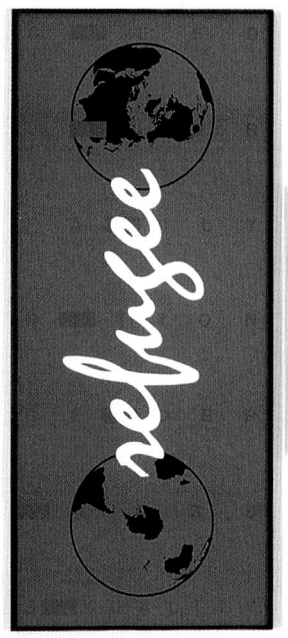
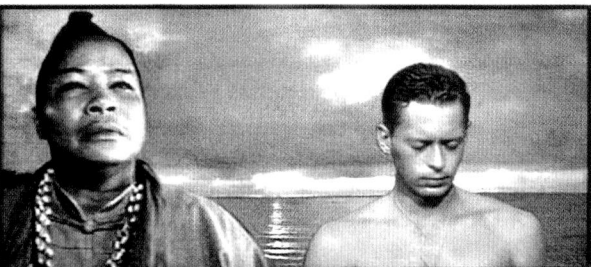

Plate 8

Family Romance, 1990. 213,4×91,4 cm and 91,4×213,4 cm.

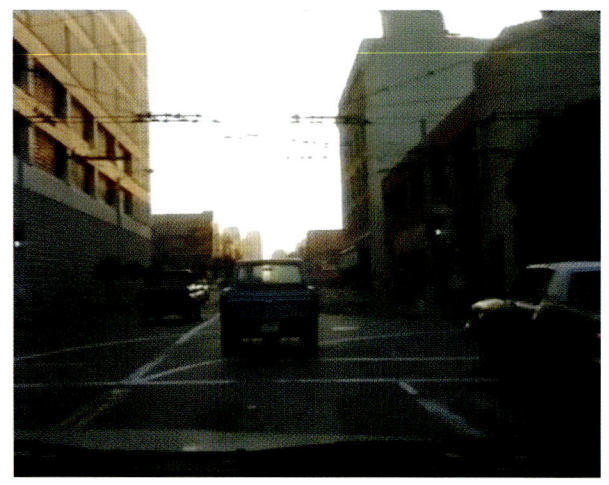

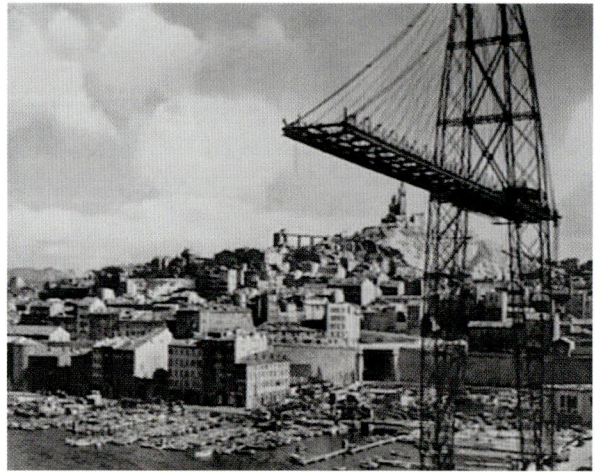

Plate 9
Stills from *Venise*, 1993. Video, 28 min. 48 sec.

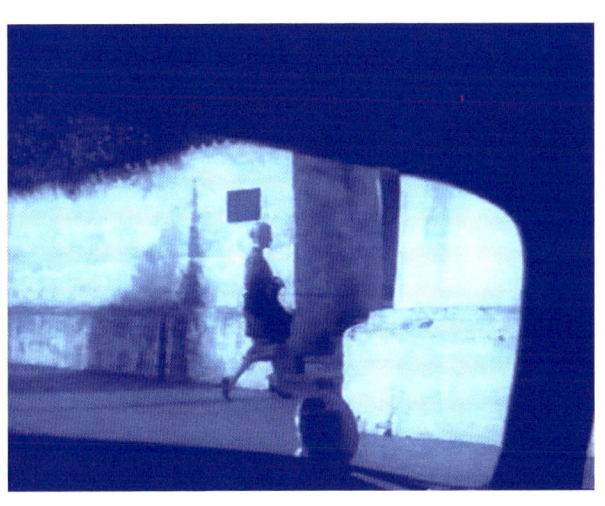

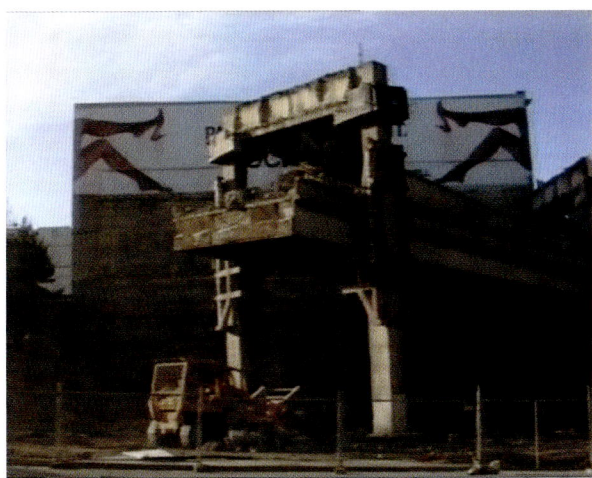

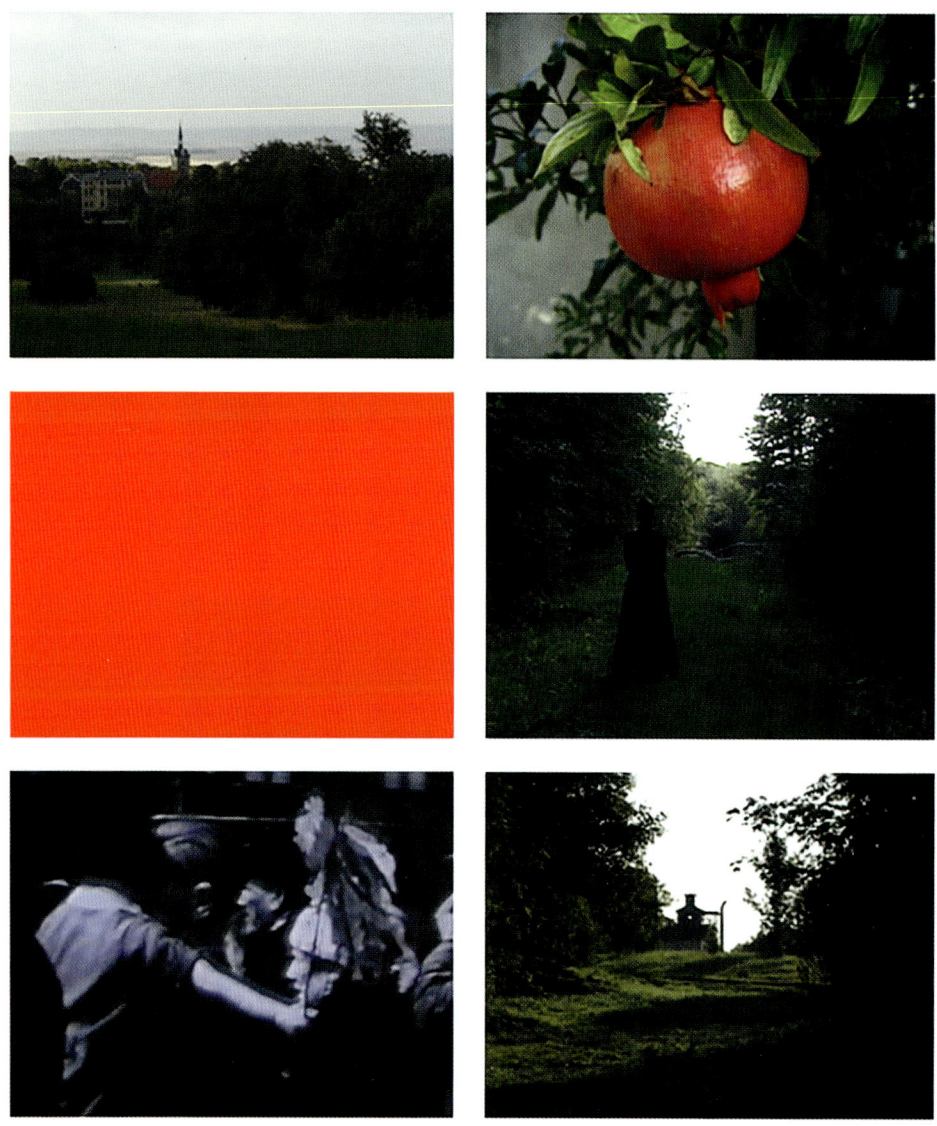

Plate 10
Stills from *Lichtung*, 1998. Single-screen video projection. DVD, 10-minute programme loop, coulour, NTSC, stereo.

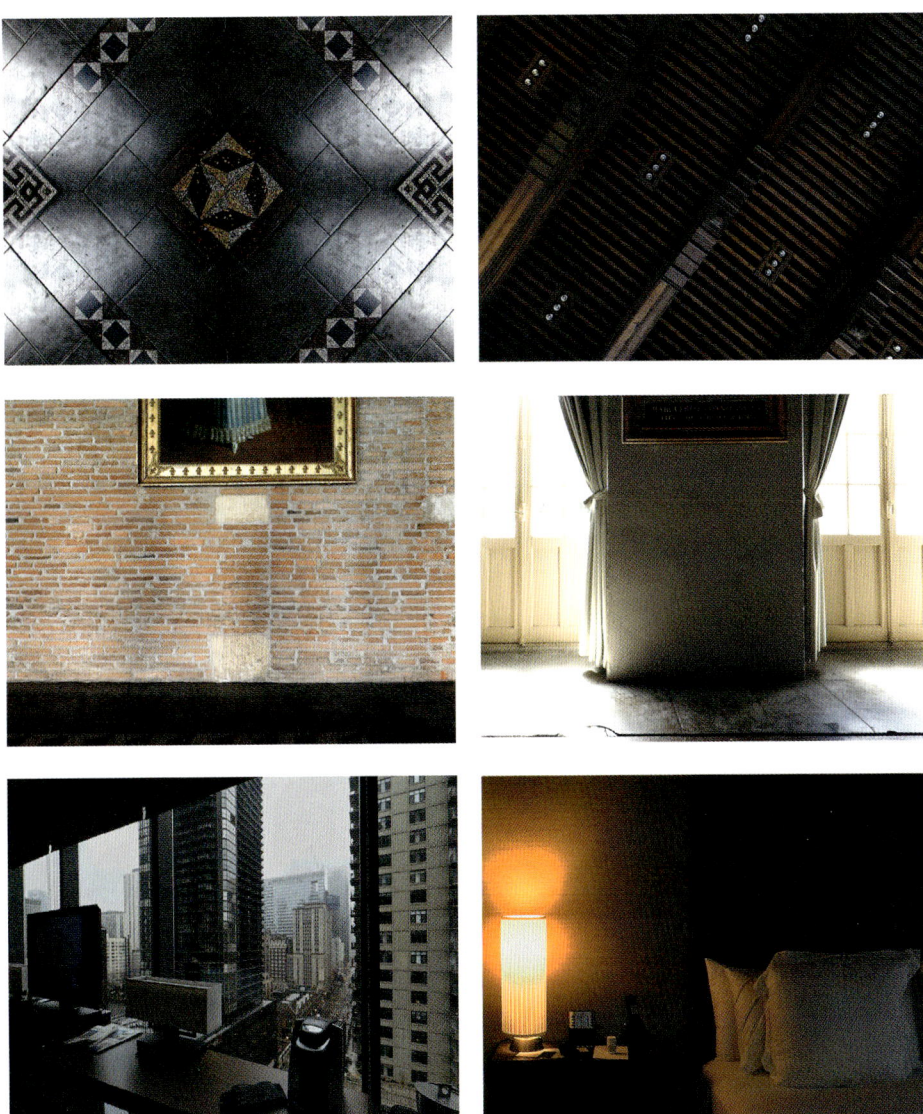

Plate 11
Stills from *Hôtel D*, 2009. Projection work, Single screen projection loop, 14 min. 29 sec.

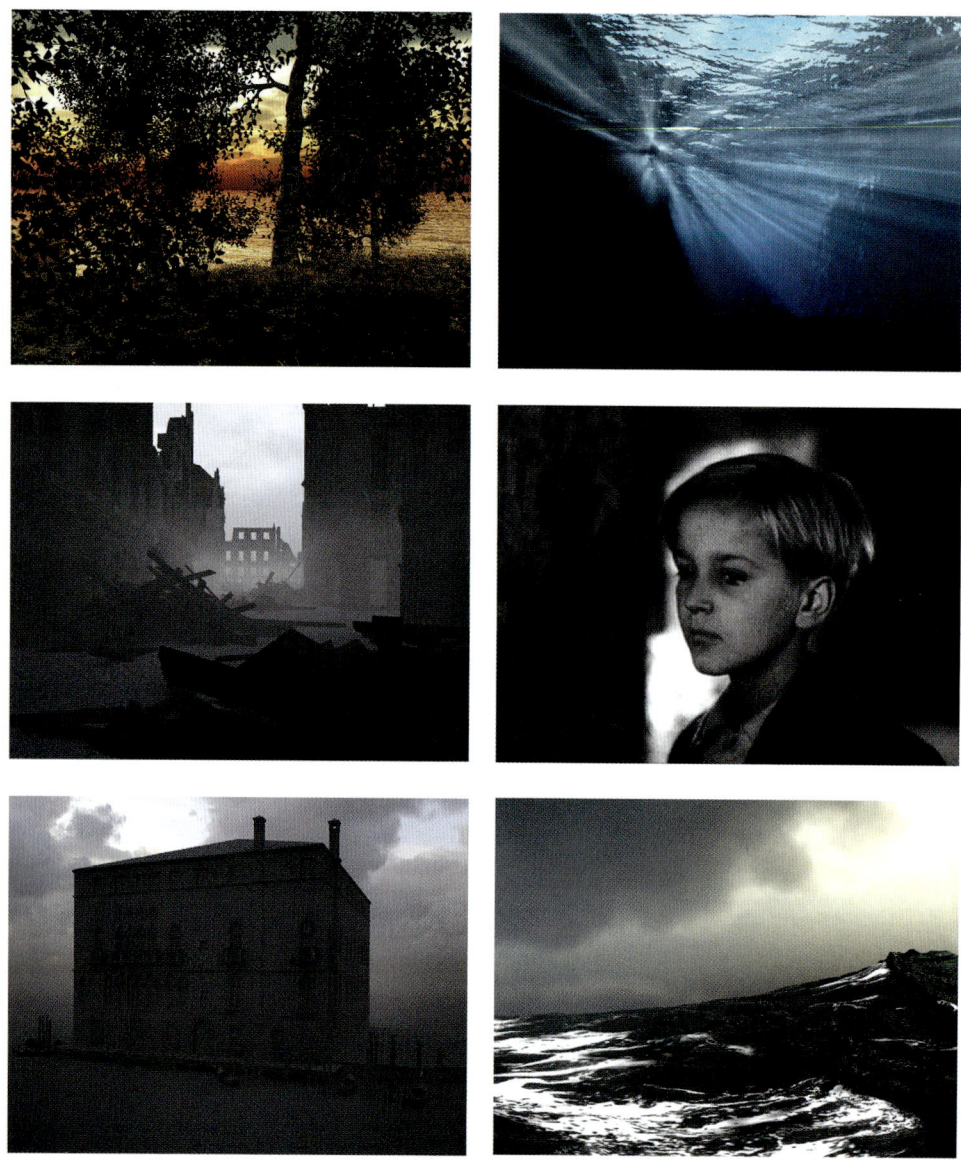

Plate 12

Stills from *Parzival*, 2013. Projected text/image loop with sound and wall text, 14 min. 50 sec.

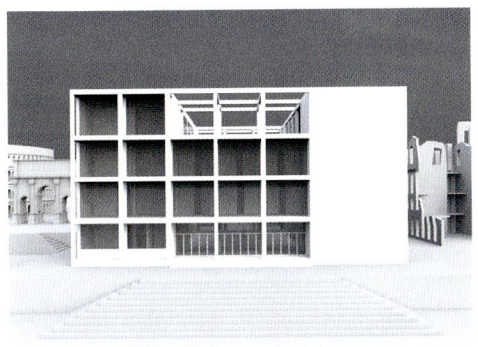
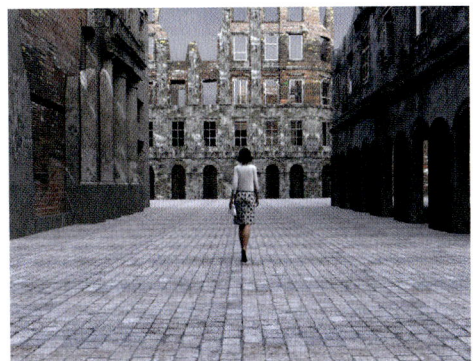
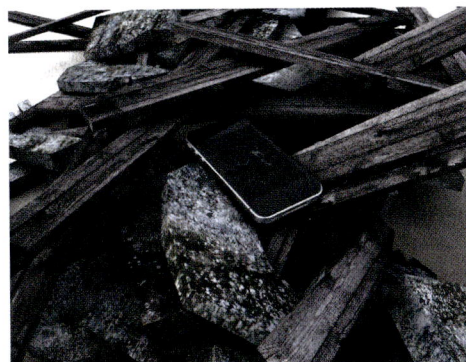
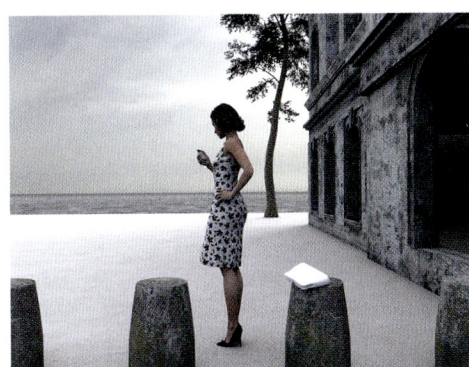
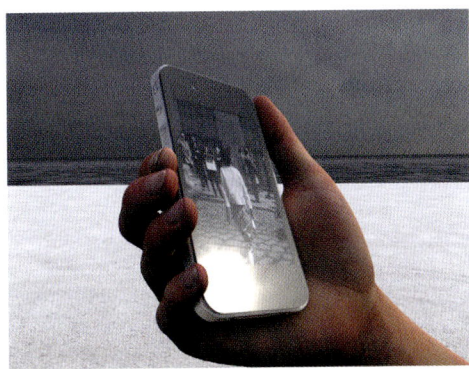
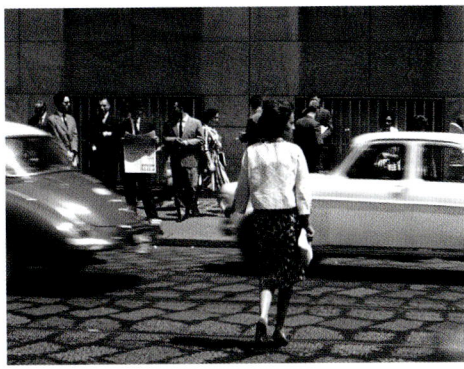

Plate 13

Stills from *The Ideal City*, 2014. Digital projection loop without sound, 6 min.

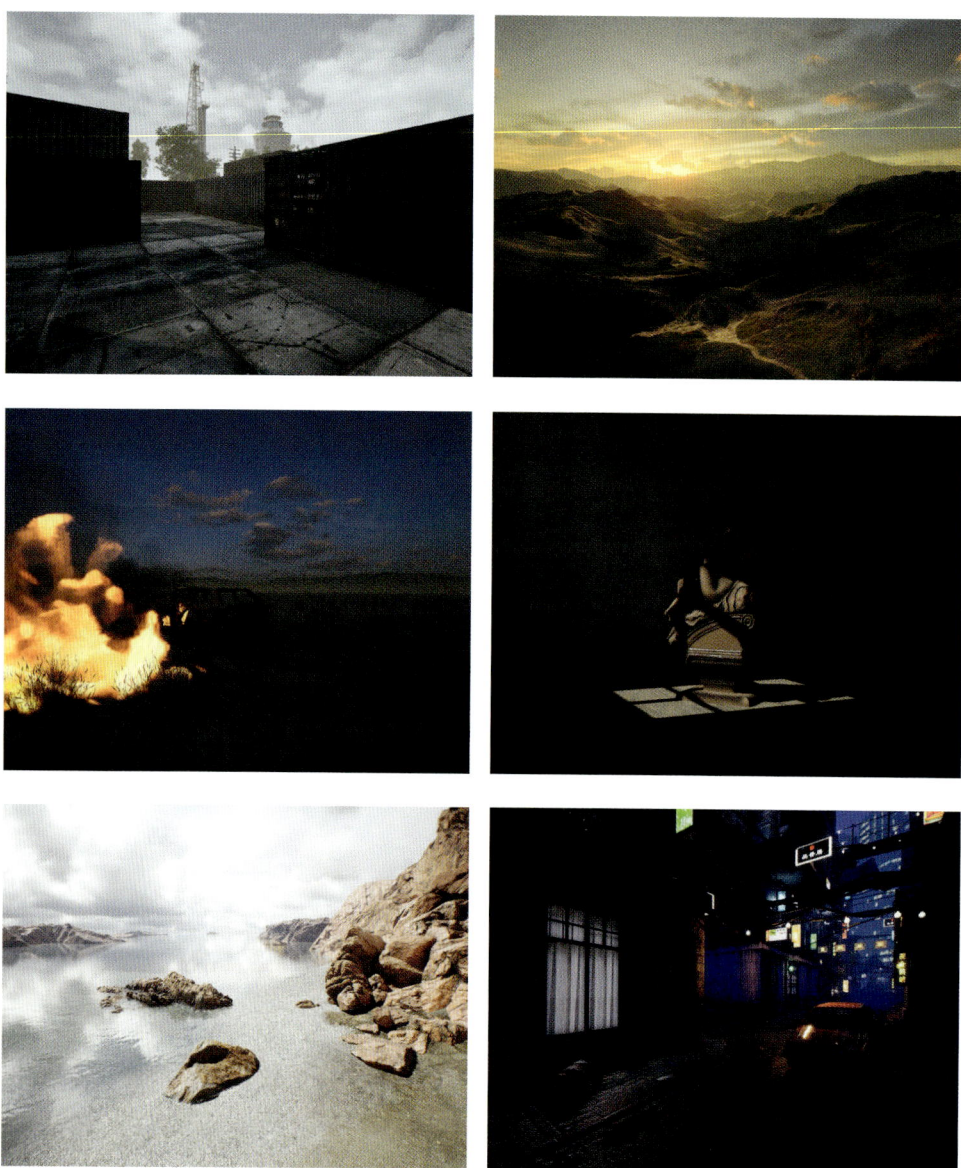

Plate 14

Images from *Afterlife*, Thomas Zander / Walther König, Cologne, 2019.

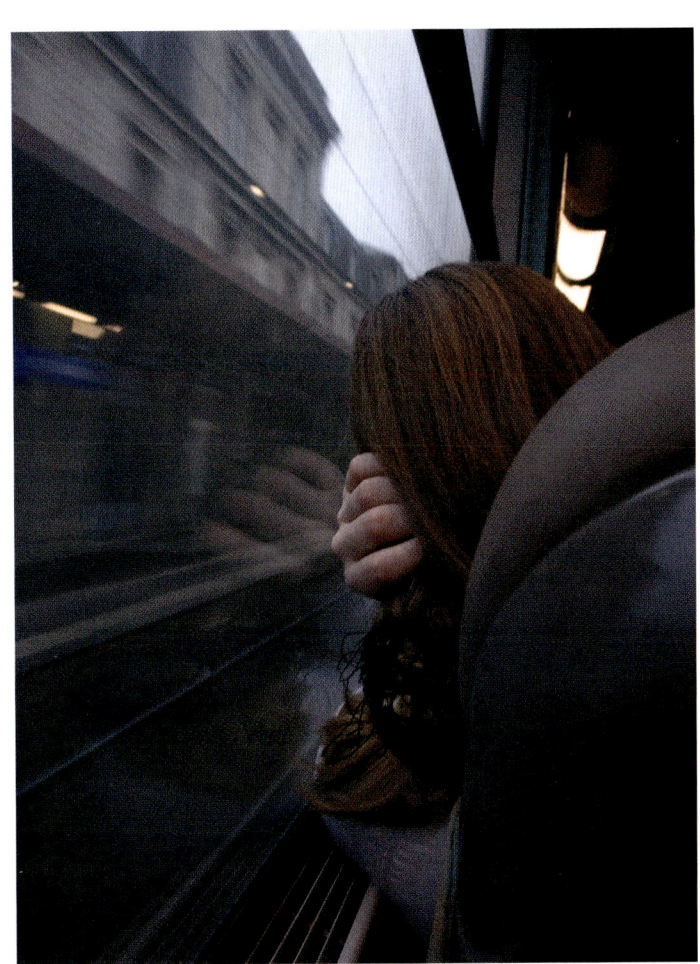

Notes

1. For the role of music in Burgin's projection works, I refer to Massin, 2007. In particular the projection works created by Burgin over the last fifteen years have recently managed to attract intense attention. See the essays gathered in *Projective. Essays about the Work of Victor Burgin* (Geneva: Mamco, 2014) and the in-depth and insightful analysis of works such as *Prairie* (2015) and *Belledonne* (2016) in *Seeing Degree Zero* (SDZ).

2. Aside from Burgin's political works from the 1970s, which contain explicit political messages, plenty of his works, from all periods, refer to concrete political contexts and situations. See, for example, Chapter 4 on *Minnesota Abstract* (1989), *Family Romance* (1990), and *Venise* (1993), and Chapter 5 on *Remembering, Repeating* (1995) and the "granular-perceptual manifestation of the political" (PT: 217-218) in *Hôtel D* (2009).

3. See Judd, 1965; Morris, 1995; LeWitt, 1978; Tuchman, 1970.

4. Concerning a "situational aesthetics" in Burgin's and Kirby's work see also Streitberger 2013b. For an in-depth analysis of Kirby's embedded sculptures see Streitberger 2017a.

5. For photography in Conceptual art see also Verhagen, 2008, and Witkovsky, 2012.

6. Letter to Charles Harrison, Tate Archives, London.

7. After "Situational Aesthetics" (1969), Burgin again cites Gibson in "Photography, Fantasy, Function" and in "Seeing Sense" (both 1980), where he relates Gibson's ideas on perceptual experiences to the question of mental images and psychic phenomena. (TP: 193; EAT: 52)

8. In their critique, Terry Atkinson and Michael Baldwin draw on Frege's distinction between "intension" and "extension." While "intension" refers to the internal conception, the idea meant by a concept, "extension" denotes its referents in reality, its physical and thus empirically verifiable realization: "quantification that crosses possible contexts is a measure of ideology not ontology. Thus, for example, the Burgin position fails even to start to make a distinction between the extensional 'object' and certain aspects of the referential apparatus. You have to make do with the prospect of more than one eventuality but this doesn't throw you squarely into adventitious indeterminism. … The point is that what determines the intension … is not what extension it happens to have but the way in which the reference or extension is determined." (Atkinson and Baldwin, 1972: 26)

9. Tate Archives, Charles Harrison collections.

10. "My work form 1973 to 1976 had all been what today is called 'appropriated image' work. I was recycling advertising imagery and reproducing the rhetoric of advertising copy." (BN, 12) And: "So naturally my fantasy was that art would become reintegrated into the broader field of cultural criticism." (Roberts, 1997: 97)

11. "At that time my work was very much in the tradition of the historic avant-garde. Dada, surrealism, post-revolutionary Russian art—with politics as part of its program." (*Flash Art*, Interview with Gregorio Magnani, 119)

12. "J'avais le sentiment, à cette époque-là, que le monde était saturé d'images, et qu'il n'y avait aucun intérêt à en fabriquer de nouvelles." (Durand, 1988: 21) See also Douglas Huebler's statement that was his contribution to the catalogue of Seth Siegelaub's exhibition "January 5—31, 1969": "The world is full of objects, more or less interesting; I do not wish to add any more. I prefer, simply, to state the existence of things in terms of time and/or place." (Godfrey, 1998: 200)

13. This shift can be traced back through the editorials of the following issues: 1 (1965), 5 (1969), 6 (1971), and 8 (1974).

14. *Studio International* was published in 1980, but Burgin's text is from 1977.

15. This chapter includes material adapted from Streitberger 2009 (xxiv-xxvi) and Streitberger 2019a (197-200).

16. Burgin's slightly different rendering reads: "The juxtaposition of a visual image and a complementary linguistic message indicating a meaning not signified by either of the component messages, *relay*.'"

17. The discussion of this work is partly taken from my introductory essay to *Situational Aesthetics*.

18. Originally conceived as the crowning element of the *Gate of Hell*, *The Thinker* represented Dante meditating on his work as the creative poet who transcends his suffering through poetry.

19. Aside from Burgin, the artists invited to reply were Terry Atkinson, Michael Baldwin, Daniel Buren, Hans Haacke, Joseph Kosuth, and Mel Ramsden.

20. Martha Rosler confirms this observation when she argues that the shift in Dorothea Lange's photographs from a social and documentary purpose to aesthetic values of artistic expression would have been caused by

their incorporation into modernist discourse. (Rosler, 1984: 330)

21. Sekula, 1978: 869. In his essay, Sekula does not give any reference to where he found this passage. Most probably, he took it from the essay collection *Brecht on Theatre: The Development of an Aesthetic* (London: Eyre Methuen, 1964: 34). It is worth noting that Benjamin quotes exactly the same passage in his essays "What is Epic Theatre?" (1931) and "The Author as Producer" (1934), both included in *Understanding Brecht* (Benjamin, 1998: 1-2 and 98-99).

22. For a more detailed discussion of Burgin's attention for the gallery space, see Chapter 3.

23. When it was claimed in the editorial of a 1973 issue of *Screen* dedicated to the work of Christian Metz that "[s]emiology, as the theory of the production of meaning in texts, will have to provide the theoretical framework for any examination/description of film texts" (Willemen, 1973: 2), this corresponds precisely to Burgin's suggestions formulated in "Photographic Practice and Art Theory" with respect to "photographic texts." The psychological turn in *Screen* was subsequently consummated in an issue published in 1975 (vol. 16, no. 2), which exclusively contains psychoanalytically oriented texts.

24. *Tales from Freud* at John Weber Gallery, New York, 1982. Later in the same year the exhibition was on view at Yatlow Salzman Gallery, Toronto. Aside from *Gradiva* this exhibition included three other works from the early 1980s: *In Lyon* (1980), *In Grenoble* (1981), and *Olympia* (1982). The title was derived from the fact that all four works were based on case-studies from the writings of Freud (*In Lyon*: "A Case of Paranoia Running Counter to the Theory of the Desease," 1915; *In Grenoble*: descriptions of the Oedipus complex and Freud's dream about his Uncle Josef in *The Interpretation of Dreams*, 1900; *Gradiva*: "Delusions and Dreams in W. Jensen's *Gradiva*," 1907; *Olympia*: "The Uncanny," 1919). In an exchange of emails during August 2018, Burgin told me that in retrospect he would also include two works produced later, *The Bridge* and *Portia* (both 1984), in the *Tales from Freud*, as they also refer to two concrete texts by Freud (*The Bridge*: "A Special Type of Choice of Object Made by Man," 1910; *Portia*: "The Motif of the Three Caskets," 1913): "The five works mentioned above belong to the period during which I was most intensively engaged with psychoanalytic theory, and during which I myself was in psychoanalysis. There were two reasons for this engagement—one scholarly and one 'artistic': 1) This was the period in which the British cultural 'left' split over the question of psychoanalytic theory. (I resume this history in the introduction to *In/Different Spaces*, and I can be 'heard' making the argument in 1986 in my preface to *Formations of Fantasy*.) For me as a 'left' academic, psychoanalytic theory became

important because of my central interest in theories of ideology—not least stemming from Althusser's judgment that, contra Marx and Engels, ideology is not a matter of 'false consciousness' but is 'profoundly unconscious.' Relevant anecdote: I first learned of the essay by Freud that forms the basis of *In Lyon* from the British feminist theorist Jacqueline Rose. 2) Psychoanalytic theory (above all, Freud's account of dream-work) became important to my work as a visual artist because I was dealing with relations between words and images, working with condensed and repetitive forms that more closely resembled the forms of fantasies and dreams than the forms of conventional narratives. In looking for formal models for my work I had pretty much exhausted the possibilities of semiotic theory (primarily the rhetorically inspired forms of such works as the *Possession* poster) and was looking for more subtle and sophisticated models." (Streitberger, 2019b: 37)

25. Both the English translation of Oudart's Text, "Cinema and Suture," and Heath's article are published in *Screen*, 18, 4 (Winter 1977).

26. The script of Laura Mulvey and Peter Wollen's film *Riddles of the Sphinx* (1977) suggests that the scopophilic gaze may be interrupted by: "Montage sequence of found footage of the Egyptian Sphinx, refilmed through a number of generations with the aid of a motion-analyser projector, freeze frames, and extreme close-up (concentrating on the Sphinx's mouth) eventually showing film grain." Laura Mulvey and Peter Wollen, "Riddles of the Sphinx: Script," *Screen*, Vol. 18, 2, (Summer 1977): 61-78 (63).

27. The exhibition *Beyond the Purloined Image* took place at Riverside Studios, London, from August 3 to August 28, 1983.

28. "Oui, tout à l'heure j'ai parlé d'un film, mais bien qu'il y ait dans une pratique comme la mienne un aspect linéaire, diachronique—de même qu'on a l'habitude de lire de gauche à droite—, il y a aussi, et plus fondamentalement, un aspect synchronique où tout est présent en même temps. On peut lire les fragments de mon travail dans n'importe quel ordre, selon n'importe quelle configuration. Certes, mon travail n'est pas un rêve …, mais disons que le mot 'rêve' est plutôt employé ici à titre de métaphore. Freud a dit que le rêve n'était pas une histoire, mais un rebus, et que dans l'inconscient, le temps n'existe pas. C'est un peu selon ces principes du rêve que je structure mon travail." (Gintz, 1981: 16)

29. This chapter contains passages from Streitberger, 2008: 43-47.

30. For a more dynamic concept of the pose, see Kaja Silverman's considerations in her book *The Threshold of the Visible World*. In contrast to Barthes and Owens, Silverman insists less on the body's transformation

into an object than on the pose as a kind of position-ing or mise-en-scène in relation to cultural ideals. As Silverman writes, the pose is "a constant disruptive and transformative labor at the site of ideality." (Silverman, 1996: 206) In this regard, it is noteworthy that in Burgin's works of the 1980s (*Gradiva*, *Olympia*, *The Bridge*, *Office at Night*) the posing subject is never presented alone but always in combination with other poses or gestures.

31. Some years later, this view is developed further by Charles Bernheimer, who argues "that in place of this finished production, the female idol as cultural fetish, Manet's picture offers its viewer an illustration of the very processes of displacement and substitution that construct woman as fetish." (Bernheimer, 1989: 269).

32. For the concept of the "uncinematic" see Chapter 5.

33. The short, highly suggestive texts are visually arranged and elicit "certain 'subliminal' references" (BN: 173) among the subject matters of the work. As Burgin states in an interview: "I intended that the texts should suggest images, and the images should invoke words." (Lewis, 1987/88: 56)

34. Burgin was aware of both essays, which are published in *Formations of Fantasy*, edited by Victor Burgin, James Donald, and Cora Kaplan in 1986.

35. Burgin explores the relation between postmodernism, feminism, and difference in the essay "The Absence of Presence: Conceptualism and Post-modernisms." Published for the first time in 1984, in the exhibition catalogue, *When Attitudes Became Form*, the essay is based on a talk Burgin gave in 1982 at the John Hansard Gallery, Southampton University. (EAT: ix)

36. For further discussion, see Hutcheon, 1989; Tickner, 1984.

37. In his article "Les grandes expositions: Esquisse d'une typologie," Jean-Marc Poinsot observes that the aim of the curators of *New Spirit in Painting* and *Zeitgeist* was to "reaffirm the vitality of painting against other models of development in contemporary art." To achieve this goal, they chose two of the most venerable institutions of art: The Royal Academy of Art, London (*A New Spirit in Painting*) and the Martin Gropius Bau, Berlin (*Zeitgeist*). (Poinsot, 1986: 122-145; my translation)

38. Published in the catalogue of the exhibition "The British Edge", held at The Institute of Contemporary Art, Boston, in 1987, the essay is based on a paper given in the series, Psychoanalysis and Culture, at the ICA, London, February 1987. (*The British Edge*, 1987: 24-34) A slightly different version, entitled "Geometry and Abjection," was published in *AA Files—Annals of the Architectural Association School of Architecture*, no. 15 (Summer 1987). It is this version that is reprinted in Burgin's *In/Different Spaces* (IDS: 39-56).

39. Burgin describes the passage from analogue to digital technologies in the production process of his works as a radical shift within his work. In an interview given in 1988, he remarks: "*Between* marque la fin de la dernière période, de toute une époque en fait, puisque j'ai renoncé à utiliser la prise de vue photographique au bénéfice de l'ordinateur." (Durand, 1988: 22)

40. As Sabine Hake writes: "Neurath attempted nothing less than to show that science and socialism were mutually compatible epistemologies and, furthermore, to establish the scientific worldview as the foundation of a radical socialist politics." Hence the "focus on the standardized human form in the representation of labor under capitalism … [which] is put in the service of workers' education and political agitation." (Hake, 2017: 219)

41. In various interviews, Burgin takes a critical stance toward the appropriation artists and the way they were promoted by the authors of *October*: "In making her (Sherrie Levine) the exemplary-postmodern-authori-al-deconstructive artist, they have promoted her pre-cisely to a position of authorship." (Magnini, 1989: 120)

42. Sekula evokes this psychological dimension when he writes that the exhibition "moves from the celebra-tion of patriarchal authority—which finds its highest embodiment in the United Nations—to the final construction of an imaginary utopia that resembles nothing so much as a protracted state of infantile, preoedipal bliss." (Sekula, 1981: 20) However, his critical materialism kept him from elaborating on this point in a more detailed way. The link between the myth of the family and the myth of the nation can be established with reference to another essay by Freud, *The Psychopathology of Everyday Life*, in which he observes that childhood recollections are not true memory traces but function as "'screen memories' and in doing so offer a remarkable analogy with the childhood memories that a nation preserves in its store of legends and myths." (Freud, 1901/1957: 48) Burgin was aware of this passage, as evidenced by a quotation in *In/Different Spaces*. (IDS: 225)

43. The essay was first published in the collective volume *World Cities and the Future of the Metropolis: Beyond the City, the Metropolis*, edited by Georges Teyssot (Milano: Electa, 1988), 139-141.

44. Clips from classic Hollywood movies are projected on the wall of the book department, thus bombarding the Japanese visitor with fictions from a different culture and from different times. The boundaries between inside and outside, virtual space and real space, are blurred by means of a myriad of monitors placed all over the store in order to plunge the visitor of the store into images of the cherry blossom, which could actu-ally be observed outside of the building in the nearby Ueno Park. (IDS: 109 and 111)

45. https://www.tate.org.uk/art/artworks/burgin-no-title-p77515. Accessed June 19, 2019.

46. Victor Burgin on Re-reading Images, TateShots, 27 February 2014, https://www.youtube.com/watch?v=p5TcayyP4oY. Accessed June 19, 2019.

47. Concerning the use of maps by Debord, see Wood, 2010: 171-176. As further reading on The Situationist International and the city, I recommend Sadler, 1999.

48. "Enigmatic state" is a rather inappropriate translation of the French "état de rebus" (De Certeau, 1990: 163). Given that De Certeau not only uses Freud's terms to designate the dream mechanisms, but also refers explicitly to Freud's *Interpretation of Dreams*, it seems quite evident that the term "rebus" hints to the psychical reality of the dream. (De Certeau, 1988: 102)

49. Includes materials adapted from Streitberger 2019c.

50. The paper was given at the conference "The Visual Arts in a Technological Age: A Centennial Rereading of Walter Benjamin," Wayne State University, 4 April 1992. It was first published in *New Formations*, No. 20 (Summer 1993) and is also included in *In/Different Spaces*.

51. See for example Déotte, 2012; Fellmann, 2014; Gilloch, 1996.

52. I borrow the term from Marshall McLuhan, according to whom "[a]nti-environments, or countersituations made by artists, provide means of direct attention and enable us to see and understand more clearly" how media operate as active but invisible environments. (McLuhan, 1996: 68)

53. As discussed in Chapter 2, already in the mid-1970s, photography was defined as an environment insisting on its context-bound nature as a heterogeneous medium. In contrast, film and painting would "readily constitute themselves as *objects*, thus facilitating critical attention ..." (EAT: 20).

54. Burgin himself pointed out that in this respect Foucault's image of the ship as the ideal heterotopia comes closest to the cinematic heterotopia, because it creates a place unto itself without actually being bound to any specific place. (RF: 10) For more on this discussion see also my introduction to *Situational Aesthetics*. (Streitberger, 2009: xx-xxiii)

55. For what follows below, see the introduction in Cohen and Streitberger, 2016, 7-17.

56. Among the numerous publications on the relationship between photography and film see: Cohen and Streitberger, 2016; Karen Beckman and Jean Ma (eds), *Still Moving: Between Cinema and Photography* (Durham: Duke University Press, 2008); *Mutations II – Moving Stills*, exh. cat. (Maison européenne de la photo Paris, et al., 2008); Eivind Rossaak, *The Still/Moving Image: Cinema and the Arts* (Saarbrücken: LAP Lambert Academic Publishing, 2010); Laurent Guido and Olivier Lugon (eds), *Fixe/animé. Croisements de la photographie et du cinéma au XXe siècle* (Lausanne: L'Age d'Homme, 2010); Ingrid Hölzl, "Moving Stills: Images That Are No Longer Immobile," *Photographies*, 3, 1 (2010): 99-108; Laura Mulvey, *Death 24x a Second: Stillness and the Moving Image* (London: Reaktion, 2006); Katja Pratschke, Gusztav Hamos, and Thomas Tode (eds), *Viva Fotofilm. Bewegt/Unbewegt* (Marburg: Schüren Verlag, 2009).

57. I will use the term "video" only for works produced with lens-based cameras and called "video" by the artist himself. As a general term and for the most recent works produced on the basis of computer-generated images, I will use the term "projection."

58. In his essay, Burgin describes the sequence-image as "a sequence of such brevity that I might almost be describing a still image." (Campany, 2007: 201) The concept of the sequence-image will be developed further below.

59. For a discussion of Greenberg and specificity, see VBP: 59-68.

60. The sequence is taken from the same footage used by Burgin already in 1997 for his three-screen video projection *Szerelmes Levelek (Love Letters)*. This work will be discussed later in this chapter.

61. The importance of this figure in Burgin's work is confirmed by its appearance in other projection pieces of the same period, such as *Case History* (1998), *Another Case History* (1999), and *Nietzsche's Paris* (1999-2000).

62. In an interview with Burgin, Hilde Van Gelder proposes to describe the projection works as "disassembled tableau," for the different layers of the "painting" are scattered through time and space—including the memory space of the viewer. (PT: 222) Burgin confirms this reading when he responds: "Now, although the words and images that make up my work are necessarily deployed in time, my accommodations to the indeterminacy in their viewing and reading in effect breaks up and spatializes the temporal flow—so your expression 'disassembled tableau' may fit my work quite well." (223) Elsewhere he describes his projection works as "a kind of psychical cubism" that would be "best addressed not as one might approach a film, but rather as one might approach a painting." (SCR: 94)

63. For example, the red screen filled with the music of Mozart's *Magic Flute* evokes associations that differ from the ones triggered by the identically colored screen with the voice-over reciting a passage from Goethe's *Elective Affinities*. Moreover, both will be interpreted differently when they pass a second time after a first viewing of the loop, etc.

64. In the first and the third room, only one of the voices accompanied the images while both voices meet in the central room. (Burgin, 2000: 72)

65. This chapter includes materials adapted from Streitberger, 2013a.

66. Other artists using panoramic images or processes are, for example, Ed Ruscha, *Every Building on the Sunset Strip* (1966), Dennis Oppenheim, *Flower Arrangement for Bruce Nauman* (1969), Robert Morris, *Finch College Project* and *Continuous Project Altered Daily* (both 1969), and Dan Graham, *Body Press* (1972). See Streitberger, 2013a: 63-65 and 70-71.

67. This conflictual confrontation of the supposed rationality of modernist architecture with affective content from disparate temporal and spatial contexts is also present in other panoramic works, such as *Elective Affinities* (2000-2001) and *The Little House* (2005). Both include panoramic views of pioneering modernist architectures—Mies van der Rohe's pavilion for the 1929 Barcelona International Exhibition in *Elective Affinities* and Rudolph Michael Schindler's Kings Road House in Los Angeles (1922) in *The Little House*. And in both cases heterogeneous fragments from different historical and cultural contexts are scattered between these panoramic views. *Elective Affinities* includes a résumé of Penelope's endless weaving and undoing of a tapestry to delay her suitors during Odysseus's absence, references to Goethe's novel *Elective Affinities* in the title of the work and in the image of a forest edge, and film footage taken from a French television program about Catalonia and the Civil War. (CP: 121) In *The Little House*, Schindler's modernist architecture is combined with François Bastide's novella *La Petite Maison* (1758) and a young Chinese woman in modern dress holding a copy of *Quotations from Chairman Mao Tse-tung*, known as the "The Little Red Book." (CP: 157-158) Both works further mark important steps in the technological evolution of the panoramas. For *Elective Affinities* (as for *Watergate* shortly before), Burgin used a special motorized panoramic still camera that allowed him to make the panorama in a single piece, without the need of a stitch, before modifying and animating it on a computer. *The Little House* was the first work for which he used a normal still camera mounted on a panoramic tripod head, which was less cumbersome and expensive. The individual images were then stitched together and animated on the computer. Email exchange from July 2, 2019.

68. Interestingly enough, the final paragraphs of Chapter 4, "Intermedia Stages of Virtual Reality in the Twentieth Century," in which Grau emphasizes this crucial role of the panorama for the evolution of virtual reality, are excluded from the English translation. Notwithstanding this omission, it becomes clear, even in the English version, that Grau persists in his viewpoint when he writes: "The desire to be in the picture, in both the metaphorical and nonmetaphorical sense, did not disappear with the panorama but lived on in the twentieth century." (Grau, 2003: 141)

69. Video Jeu de Paume: https://www.youtube.com/watch?v=JJ3rDi0FNLU. Accessed June 24, 2019.

70. This and the next chapter include materials adapted from Streitberger 2017b.

71. Yet, if we consider that the projection works usually react to the particular historical and social conditions for which they are made and in which they are displayed, the outside of the gallery becomes part of the work as a site-specific installation. (Bishop and Burgin, 2016: 101) The peripatetic viewer then has to walk from the outside of the gallery to the inside in order to connect the elements of the work with her or his knowledge and impressions of the place where it is displayed.

72. I borrow the concept of "divided memories" from Bernhard Giesen. Dismantling the opposition of past and present as a profoundly modern idea linked to concepts of purity and linear progress, Giesen argues that it is time to acknowledge the coexistence of historically heterogeneous phenomena as the normal state of affairs, rather than as the exception. (Giesen, 2004: 29) Furthermore, he divides Reinhart Koselleck's concept of the *Gleichzeitigkeit des Ungleichzeitigen* (*simultaneousness of the non-simultaneous*) into three semantic and conceptual levels: noncontemporaneity as a historical concept concerns the "hybridization of different historical cultures;" asynchronicity means the coexistence of varying temporal rhythms and intensities as "a product of social construction;" and the category of divided memories, finally, suggests a psychological element, where the acceleration of generations implies that various "temporal horizons and collective memories" exist within one society. (29-32)

73. In an email exchange from September 2019, Burgin explains how he came to this intertitle: "This idea came to me from of the way environments are modelled in videogames. E.g., you see a figure running through a landscape, you have the impression that the landscape is out there in its entirety—but it is modelled, in real-time, only when and where it can be seen—and of course once it is no longer seen it ceases to exist. Quite often, in games and other computer simulations, you can see this happening when there is too much demand on the processor, as a result of which the details called for arrive a little late—so you see the landscape leaping up [out] of nothing as the character runs towards it."

74. See the very complete wikipedia article on mind uploading in fiction: https://en.wikipedia.org/wiki/Mind_uploading_in_fiction. Accessed September 13, 2019.

75. Victor Burgin, "Mutation, Appropriation and Style," paper to be published in the series *The Key Debates: Mutations and Appropriations in European Film Studies*, Amsterdam University Press.

Bibliography

Abbreviations

BN = Victor Burgin, *Between* (Oxford and New York: Basil Blackwell, 1986).

CP = Victor Burgin, *Components of a Practice* (Milan: Skira, 2008).

EAT = Victor Burgin, *The End of Art Theory. Criticism and Postmodernity* (London and Basingstoke: Macmillan Press, and New Jersey: Humanities Press International, 1986).

IDS = Victor Burgin, *In/Different Spaces. Place and Memory in Visual Culture* (Berkeley and Los Angeles: University of California Press, 1996).

PS = Victor Burgin, *Passages*, cat. (Lille: Musée d'art moderne de la Communauté Urbaine de Lille, Villeneuve d'Ascq, 1991).

PT = Victor Burgin, *Parallel Texts. Interviews and Interventions about Art* (London: Reaktion Books, 2011).

RF = Victor Burgin, *The Remembered Film* (London, Reaktion Books, 2004).

SA = Victor Burgin, *Situational Aesthetics. Selected Writings by Victor Burgin*, ed. Alexander Streitberger (Leuven: Leuven University Press, 2009).

SC = Victor Burgin, *Some Cities* (Berkeley and Los Angeles, University of California Press, and London, Reaktion Books, 1996).

SCR = Victor Burgin, *Scripts*, ed. and trans Valérie Mavridorakis (Genova: Mamco, 2016).

SDZ = Ryan Bishop and Sunil Manghani (eds), *Seeing Degree Zero. Barthes / Burgin and Political Aesthetics* (Edinburgh: Edinburgh University Press, 2019).

TC = Victor Burgin, *The Camera. Essence and Apparatus* (London: Mack, 2018).

TP = Victor Burgin (ed.), *Thinking Photography* (London and Basingstoke: Macmillan Press, and New Jersey: Humanities Press International, 1982).

VB = *Victor Burgin* (Barcelona: Fundació Antoni Tàpies, 2001).

VBP = Stéphane Symons and Hilde Van Gelder (eds), *Victor Burgin's* Parzival *in Leuven. Reflections on the "Uncinematic"* (Leuven: Leuven University Press, 2017).

Theodor W. Adorno, *Aesthetic Theory*, eds Gretel Adorno and Rolf Tiedemann, trans Robert Hullot-Kentor (London: Bloomsbury, 2013).

Alexander Alberro and Alice Zimmerman, "Not How It Should Were It To Be Built But How It Could Were It To Be Built," in *Lawrence Weiner,* eds Alexander Alberro et al. (London: Phaidon, 1998), 36-73.

Lawrence Alloway, "Artists and Photographs," in *Artists and Photographs,* ed. Marian Goodman (New York: Multiples Gallery, 1970), 3-5.

Louis Althusser, "Ideology and Ideological State Apparatuses (Notes towards an Investigation)," in Id., *Lenin and Philosophy and Other Essays* (Monthly Review Press, 1971), 127-186.

Lou Andreas-Salomé, *Looking Back* (New York: Marlow & Company, 1995).

Sebastian Anthony, "Photosynth: For Touring Photos in 3D, *PC Magazin*, February 2014: 9-12. https://pdfslide.us/documents/pc-magazine-february-2014-usa.html. Accessed September 18, 2019.

Emily Apter, "Masquerade," in *Feminism and Psychoanalysis. A Critical Dictionary*, ed. Elizabeth Wright (Oxford, UK and Cambridge, Massachusetts: Blackwell, 1992), 242-244.

Bruce A. Arrigo, "The Inside Out of the Dangerous Mentally Ill: Topological Applications to Law and Social Justice," in *Lacan: Topologically Speaking*, eds Ellie Ragland and Dragan Milovanovic (New York: Other Press, 2004), 150-173.

Art as a Thought Process. Works bought for the Arts Council by Michael Compton, cat. (London: Art Council, 1974).

Arte Inglese Oggi. 1960-76, cat., Palazzo Reale, Milan (Milan: Electa, 1976).

Terry Atkinson, "Concerning the Article 'The Dematerialization of Art' (1968)," in *Conceptual Art: A Critical Anthology*, eds Alexander Alberro and Blake Stimson (Cambridge, Mass.: MIT Press, 1999), 52-58.

Terry Atkinson and Michael Baldwin, "Unnatural Rules and Excuses," *Art-Language*, Vol. 2, no. 1 (February 1972): 1-27.

Samuel Axon, "Returning to Second Life," *Ars Technica*. October 23, 2017. Retrieved January 18, 2019. https://ars-technica.com/gaming/2017/10/returning-to-second-life/. Accessed September 16, 2019.

Alfred Jules Ayer, *Language, Truth and Logic* (1936) (New York: Dover Publications, 1952).

Jan Baetens and Hilde Van Gelder (eds), *Critical Realism in Contemporary Art. Around Allan Sekula's Photography* (Leuven: Leuven University Press, 2006).

Stephen Bann, "Victor Burgin's Critical Topography," in *Victor Burgin. Relocating*, cat., (Bristol: Arnolfini, 2002).

Roland Barthes, *The Pleasure of the Text*, trans Richard Miller (New York: Hill and Wang, 1975).

Roland Barthes, *Image, Music, Text*, ed. and trans Stephen Heath (London: Fontana Press: 1977).

Roland Barthes, *Camera Lucida. Reflections on Photography* (1980), trans Richard Howard (New York: Hill and Wang, 1982).

Roland Barthes, "Leaving the Movie Theatre (1975)," in Id., *The Rustle of Language*, trans Richard Howard (New York: Hill and Wang, 1986), 345-349.

Roland Barthes, *Mythologies* (1957), trans Annette Lavers (New York: The Noonday Press, 1991).

Geoffrey Batchen, "For an Impossible Realism. An Interview with Victor Burgin," *Afterimage*, 16, 7 (February 1989): 4-9.

Geoffrey Batchen, "Cancellation," in *The Last Picture Show: Artists Using Photography 1960-1982*, cat., ed. Douglas Fogle (Minneapolis: Walker Art Center, 2003), 177-182.

Jean Baudrillard, *Simulacra and Simulation*, trans Sheila Fara Glaser (Ann Arbor: The University of Michigan Press, 1994).

Jean-Louis Baudry, "Ideological Effects of the Basic Cinematographic Apparatus," (1970) *Film Quaterly*, vol. 28, no. 2 (Winter, 1974-75): 39-47.

Raymond Bellour "The Pensive Spectator (1985)," in *The Cinematic*, ed. David Campany (Cambridge, Mass. and London: Whitechapel and MIT Press, 2007), 119-123.

Raymond Bellour, *Between-the-Images*, trans Allyn Hardyck (Zurich: JRP/Ringier: 2012).

Walter Benjamin and Asja Lacis, "Naples (1925)," in Id., *Reflections. Essays, Aphorisms, Autobiographical Writings*, ed. Peter Demetz, trans Edmund Jephcott (New York and London: Harcourt Brace Jovanovich, 1978), 163-173.

Walter Benjamin, *The Origin of German Tragic Drama*, trans John Osbourne (London, New York: Verso, 1992).

Walter Benjamin, *Understanding Brecht*, ed. Stanley Mitchell, trans Anna Bostock (London and New York: Verso, 1998).

Walter Benjamin, *The Arcades Project*, trans Howard Eiland and Kevin McLaughlin (Cambridge, Massachusetts and London: Harvard University Press, 1999).

Walter Benjamin, "The Work of Art in the Age of Mechanical Reproduction (1939)," in Id., *Selected Writings*, Vol. 4, 1938-1940, eds Howard Eiland and Michael W. Jennings, trans Edmund Jephcott and Others (Cambridge, Massachusetts and London: The Belknap Press of Harvard University Press: 2003), 251-283.

Walter Benjamin, *Illuminations. Essays and Reflections*, ed. Hannah Arendt, trans Harry Zohn, new preface by Leon Wieseltier (New York: Schocken Books, 2007).

Henri Bergson, *La Pensée et le Mouvant: essais et conférences* (Paris: PUF, 1985).

Henri Bergson, *Matière et mémoire* (1939) (Paris: PUF, 1999).

Charles Bernheimer, "Manet's *Olympia*: The Figuration of Scandal," *Poetics Today*, vol. 10, no. 2, Art and Literature II (Summer, 1989): 255-277.

Augustin Berque, *Le Sens de l'Espace au Japon: Vivre, Penser, Bâtir* (Paris: Arguments, 2004).

Homi Bhabha, *The Location of Culture* (1994) (London, New York: Routledge, 2004).

Jon Bird, "Victor Burgin Interviewed by Jon Bird," in *Victor Burgin. Office at Night and Danaïdes/Dames*, cat. (Charlotte NC: Knight Gallery, 1988), 27-40.

Ryan Bishop and Victor Burgin, "Still Moving," in *Barthes | Burgin*, eds Ryan Bishop and Sunil Manghani (Edinburgh: Edinburgh University Press: 2016).

Ryan Bishop, "I Was Sitting in a Room: Cybernetic Aesthetics and Victor Burgin's Projection Loops," in *Seeing Degree Zero. Barthes | Burgin and Political Aesthetics*, eds Ryan Bishop, Runil Manghani (Edinburgh: Edinburgh University Press, 2019), 137-158.

Ernst Bloch, *Heritage of Our Times* (1935), trans Neville and Stephen Plaice (Cambridge, Massachusetts: Polity Press, 1991).

Mel Bochner, "Serial Art, Systems, Solipsism (1967)," in *Minimal Art: A Critical Anthology*, ed. Gregory Battcock (Berkeley and Los Angeles: University of California Press, 1968), 92-102.

Hartmut Böhme, "Die Ästhetik der Ruinen," in *Der Schein des Schönen*, eds Dieter Kamper and Christoph Wulf (Göttingen: Steidl, 1989), 287-304.

Jay David Bolter and Richard Grusin, *Remediation: Understanding New Media* (Cambridge, Mass.: MIT Press, 2000).

Norbert Bolz, "Die Moderne als Ruine," in *Ruinen des Denkens: Denken in Ruinen*, eds Norbert Bolz and Willem van Reijen (Frankfurt a.M.: Suhrkamp, 1996), 7-23.

Dieter Borchmeyer, *Richard Wagner. Werk - Leben - Zeit* (Ditzingen: Reclam, 2013).

Jorge Luis Borges, "The Garden of Forking Paths," in Id., *Labyrinths. Selected Stories & Other Writings*, eds Donald A. Yates and James E. Irby (New York: New Directions Book, 1964), 19-29.

André Breton, *Nadja* (1928), trans Richard Howard (New York: Grove Press: 1977).

Norman Bryson, "Victor Burgin and the Optical Unconscious," in *Victor Burgin* (Barcelona: Fundació Antoni Tàpies, 2001), 41-52.

Benjamin Buchloh, "Figures of Authority, Ciphers of Regression," *October*, 16 (Spring 1981): 39-68.

Susan Buck-Morss, *The Dialectics of Seeing: Walter Benjamin and the Arcades Project* (Cambridge Mass.: MIT Press, 1989).

Victor Burgin, "Art Society System," *Control* (1968): n. p.

Victor Burgin, "Thanks for the Memory…," *Architectural Design*, 40 (August 1970a): 288-292.

Victor Burgin, "Language and Art," in *Publication*, ed. David Lamelas (London: Nigel Greenwood, 1970b), 9-12.

Victor Burgin, "Rules of Thumb," *Studio International*, vol. 181 (May 1971): 237-239.

Victor Burgin, "In Reply," *Art-Language*, 2 (Summer 1972a): 32-34.

Victor Burgin, "Margin Note," in *A Survey of the Avant-Garde in Britain*, cat. (London: Gallery House, 1972b), 15-19.

Victor Burgin, "Transcript of Lecture Delivered at Gallery House, The German Institute, Kensington, London, August 1972," in *Deurle 22/7/73*, cat., ed. Fernand Spillemaeckers (Deurle: Museum Dhondt–Dhaenens, 1973), np.

Victor Burgin, *Work and Commentary* (London: Latimer, 1973).

Victor Burgin, "Why Photography," in *Arte Inglese Oggi. 1960-76*, cat., Palazzo Reale, Milan (Milan: Electa, 1976a), 360-67.

Victor Burgin, "Socialist Formalism," *Studio International*, vol. 191, no. 980 (March/April 1976b): 148-154.

Victor Burgin, "Art, Common Sense and Photography," *Camerawork*, no. 3 (1976c): 1-2.

Victor Burgin, *Two Essays on Art Photography and Semiotics* (London: Robert Self, 1976d).

Victor Burgin, "Images of People," *Studio International*, vol. 194, no. 989 (February 1978): 132-134.

Victor Burgin, *Studio International*, vol. 195, no. 990 (1980): 25-26.

Victor Burgin, "Legitimating Narratives," *Camera Austria*, 25 (1988a): 4-13.

Victor Burgin, "Yes, Difference Again," *Flash Art*, no. 143 (November/December 1988b): 110-111.

Victor Burgin, "A Note on 'Minnesota Abstract,'" *Art & Design* (Spring 1990): 62-65.

Victor Burgin, "Venise," in *Desiring Practices. Architecture, Gender and the Interdisciplinary*, eds Katerina Rüedi, Sarah Wigglesworth, Duncan McCorquodale (London: Black Dog, 1996): 60-71.

Victor Burgin, *Szerelmes Levelek (Love Letters)* (Budapest: Mücsarnok Museum), 1997.

Victor Burgin, *Shadowed*, cat., Architectural Association, London (London: AA Publications, 2000).

Victor Burgin, "The Separateness of Things," *Tate Papers*, no. 3 (Spring 2005). https://www.tate.org.uk/research/publications/tate-papers/03/the-separateness-of-things-victor-burgin. Accessed October 6, 2019.

Victor Burgin, "The Shadow and the Ruin," in Victor Burgin, *Voyage to Italy* (Ostfildern: Hatje Cantz, 2006).

Victor Burgin. Objets Temporels, eds Nathalie Boulouch, Valérie Mavridorakis, David Perreau (Rennes: Presses universitaires de Rennes, 2007).

Victor Burgin et al., *Palmanova* (Choisy-le-Roi: éditions Form[e]s, 2013).

Victor Burgin. Five Pieces for Projection, ed. by Eva Schmidt (Berlin: Sternberg Press, 2014).

Victor Burgin, *Afterlife* (Cologne: Walther König, 2019).

Victor Burgin, James Donald and Cora Kaplan (eds), *Formations of Fantasy* (London and New York: Routledge, 1986).

Victor Burgin and Hilde Van Gelder, "Artistic Representation and Politics. An Exchange between Victor Burgin & Hilde Van Gelder," *A Prior*, no. 20 (2010): 92-116.

Jack Burnham, "Systems Esthetics," *Artforum*, 7:1 (September 1968): 30-35.

Judith Butler, "Performative Acts and Gender Constitution: An Essay in Phenomenology and Feminist Theory," *Theatre Journal*, Vol. 40, No. 4 (Dec. 1988): 519-531.

Michel Butor, *Les mots dans la peinture* (Geneva: Skira, 1980).

Italo Calvino, *Invisible Cities* (1972), trans William Weaver (Orlando, Austin, New York, San Diego, Toronto, London: Harcourt, 1974).

David Campany (ed.), *The Cinematic* (Cambridge, Mass. and London: Whitechapel and MIT Press, 2007).

Ernesto Capocci, *Viaggio alla luna. Anno 2057: la prima donna nello spazio* (1857) (Bari: LB Edizioni, 2015).

Rudolf Carnap, *The Logical Structure of the World and Pseudoproblems in Philosophy* (1928), trans Rolf A. George (Chicago and La Salle, Illinois: Open Court, 2003).

Bill Carter, "Fictional Characters Get Virtual Lives, Too," *The New York Times*, online edition, October 4, 2007. https://www.nytimes.com/2007/10/04/arts/television/04c-s1.html. Accessed September 11, 2019.

Erik Champion, "Undefining Machinima," in *The Machinima Reader*, eds Henry Lowood and Michael Nitsche (Cambridge, Mass.: The MIT Press, 2011), 219-238.

Federica Chiocchetti, "Text – Image – Form. In Conversation with Victor Burgin," *Aperture*, 11 (Spring 2019): 22-23.

Timothy J. Clark, "Preliminaries to a Possible Treatment of 'Olympia' in 1865," *Screen*, Vol. 21, 1 (March 1980): 18-42.

Timothy J. Clark, *The Painting of Modern Life: Paris in the Art of Manet and His Followers* (Princeton: Princeton University Press, 1986).

Brianne Cohen and Alexander Streitberger, *The Photofilmic. Entangled Images in Contemporary Art and Visual Culture* (Leuven: Leuven University Press, 2016).

Bernard Comment, *The Painted Panorama* (New York: Harry N. Abrams, Inc., 1999).

Richard Cork, "Alternative Developments," *Arte Inglese Oggi. 1960-76*, cat., Palazzo Reale, Milan (Milan: Electa, 1976), 309-343.

Laura Cottingham, "Interview with Victor Burgin," *Journal of Contemporary Art*, No. 4 (Spring/Summer 1991): 12-23 (http://www.jca-online.com/burgin.html).

Jonathan Crary, *Techniques of the Observer: On Vision and Modernity in the Nineteenth Century* (Cambridge, Mass.: MIT Press, 1992).

Douglas Crimp, "Pictures," *October*, Vol. 8 (Spring, 1979): 75-88.

Douglas Crimp, "The Photographic Activity of Postmodernism," *October*, Vol. 15 (Winter 1980): 91-101.

Andrew Darley, *Visual Digital Culture: Survey Play and Spectacle in New Media Genres* (London and New York: Routledge, 2000).

Michel De Certeau, *L'invention du quotidien. 1. arts de faire* (1980) (Paris: Gallimard: 1990).

Michel De Certeau, *The Practice of Everyday Life* (1980), trans Seven Rendall (Berkeley and Los Angeles: University of California Press, 1988).

Gilles Deleuze, "Coldness and Cruelty (1967)," in *Masochism*, trans Jean McNeil (New York: Zone Books, 1991), 6-138.

Gilles Deleuze, *Cinema 2. The Time-Image* (1985), trans Hugh Tomlinson and Robert Galeta (Minneapolis: University of Minnesota Press, 1997).

Gilles Deleuze and Claire Parnet, *Dialogues* (Paris: Flammarion, 2002).

Jean-Louis Déotte, *Walter Benjamin et la forme plastique. Architecture, technique, lieux* (Paris: L'Harmattan, 2012).

Mary Ann *Doane*, "Film and the Masquerade: Theorising the Female Spectator," *Screen*, Volume 23, 3-4, (September/October 1982): 74-88.

Georges Didi-Huberman, Vivian Rehberg and Boris Belay, "Artistic Survival: Panofsky vs. Warburg and the Exorcism of Impure Time," *Common Knowledge*, 9, no. 2 (2003): 273-285.

Joël Dor, "The Epistemological Status of Lacan's Mathematical Paradigms," in *Disseminating Lacan*, eds

David Pettigrew and François Raffoul (New York: State University of New York Press, 1996), 109-122.

Régis Durand, "Victor Burgin: L'adieu à la photographie," *Art Press*, 130 (November 1988): 20-24.

Régis Durand, "Thinking in the Present: Notes on the Work of Victor Burgin," in Victor Burgin, *Passages*, cat. (Lille: Musée d'art moderne de la Communauté Urbaine de Lille, Villeneuve d'Ascq, 1991), 61-74.

Edmund Engelman, *Berggasse 19. Sigmund Freud's Home and Offices*, Vienna 1938 (New York: Basic Books, 1976).

Jessica Evans, "Victor Burgin's Polysemic Dreamcoat," in *Art Has No History! The Making and Unmaking of Modern Art*, ed. John Roberts (London, New York: Verso, 1994), 200-229.

Ron Eyerman, "False Consciousness and Ideology in Marxist Theory," *Acta Sociologica*, vol. 24, no. 1-2 (1981): 43-56.

Benjamin Fellmann, *Durchdringung und Porosität: Walter Benjamins Neapel. Von der Architekturwahrnehmung zur kunstkritischen Medientheorie* (Berlin: LIT Verlag, 2014).

Shoshana Felman, *Jacques Lacan and the Adventure of Insight* (Cambridge, Massachusetts and London: Harvard University Press, 1987).

Gustave Flaubert, *Sentimental Education*, trans Robert Baldick (London: Penguin, 2004).

Joseph Fletcher, *Situation Ethics: The New Morality* (Philadelphia: Westminster Press, 1966).

Hal Foster (ed.), *The Anti-Aesthetic. Essays on Postmodern Culture* (Port Townsend, Washington: Bay Press, 1983).

Michel Foucault, *Discipline and Punish: The Birth of the Prison* (1975) (New York: Pantheon Books, 1977).

Michel Foucault, "Of Other Spaces," trans Jay Miskowiec, *Diacritics*, 16 (Spring 1986): 22-27.

Four Young Artists, cat., Institute of Contemporary Arts London (London: Fanfare Press Ltd., 1965).

Sigmund Freud, "Case Histories. (1) Fräulein Anna O. (Breuer)," (1893) in *Sigmund Freud. The Standard Edition of the Complete Psychological Works*, Vol. II (1893-1895), ed and trans James Strachey (London: The Hogarth Press, 1955), 19-47.

Sigmund Freud, *The Interpretation of Dreams*, (1900) in *Sigmund Freud. The Standard Edition of the Complete Psychological Works*, Vol. IV and V (1900), ed. and trans James Strachey (London: The Hogarth Press, 1953).

Sigmund Freud, *The Psychopathology of Everyday Life*, (1901) in *Sigmund Freud. The Standard Edition of the Complete Psychological Works*, Vol. VI (1901), ed. and trans James Strachey (London: The Hogarth Press, 1957).

Sigmund Freud, "Fragments of an Analysis of a Case of Hysteria," (1905) in *Sigmund Freud. The Standard Edition of the Complete Psychological Works*, Vol. VII (1901-1905), ed. and trans James Strachey (London: The Hogarth Press, 1953), 7-122.

Sigmund Freud, "Delusions and Dreams in Jensen's *Gradiva*," (1907) in *Sigmund Freud. The Standard Edition of the Complete Psychological Works*, Vol. IX (1906-1908), ed. and trans James Strachey (London: The Hogarth Press, 1959), 7-93.

Sigmund Freud, "Family Romance," (1909) in *Sigmund Freud. The Standard Edition of the Complete Psychological Works*, Vol. IX (1906-1908), ed. and trans James Strachey (London: The Hogarth Press, 1959), 237-241.

Sigmund Freud, "A Special Type of Choice of Object Made by Man (Contributions to the Psychology of Love I)," (1910) in *Sigmund Freud. The Standard Edition of the Complete Psychological Works*, Vol. XI (1910), ed. and trans James Strachey (London: The Hogarth Press, 1957), 163-175.

Sigmund Freud, "On the Universal Tendency to Debasement in the Sphere of Love (Contributions to the Psychology of Love II)," (1912) in *Sigmund Freud. The Standard Edition of the Complete Psychological Works*, Vol. XI (1910), ed. and trans James Strachey (London: The Hogarth Press, 1957), 177-190.

Sigmund Freud, "The Theme of the Three Caskets," (1913) in *Sigmund Freud. The Standard Edition of the Complete Psychological Works*, Vol. XII (1911-1913), ed. and trans James Strachey (London: The Hogarth Press, 1958), 289-301.

Sigmund Freud, "A Case of Paranoia Running Counter to the Psycho-analytic Theory of Disease," (1915) in *Sigmund Freud. The Standard Edition of the Complete Psychological Works*, Vol. XIV (1914-1916), ed. and trans James Strachey (London: The Hogarth Press, 1957), 261-272.

Sigmund Freud, "The Uncanny," (1919) in *Sigmund Freud. The Standard Edition of the Complete Psychological Works*, Vol. XVII (1917-1919), ed. and trans James Strachey (London: The Hogarth Press, 1955), 217-252.

Michael Fried, "Art and Objecthood (1967)," in Id., *Art and Objecthood: Essays and Reviews* (Chicago: University of Chicago Press, 1998), 148-172.

Anne Friedberg, *The Virtual Window: From Alberti to Microsoft* (Cambridge, Mass.: MIT Press, 2006).

James J. Gibson, "Constancy and Invariance in Perception," in *The Nature and Art of Motion*, ed. Gyorgy Kepes (New York: Brazilier, 1965), 60-70.

Bernhard Giesen, "Noncontemporaneity, Asynchronicity and Divided Memory," *Time Society*, 13, 1 (March 2004): 27-40.

Graeme Gilloch, *Myth and Metropolis: Walter Benjamin and the City* (Cambridge: Polity Press, 1996).

William Gilpin, *An Essay on Prints* (1768) (London: Strahan, 1802).

Claude Gintz, "Victor Burgin: Sexualité, Pouvoir, Histoire," *Art Press*, 54 (December 1981): 16-18.

Tony Godfrey, "Sex, Text, Politics. An Interview with Victor Burgin," *Block*, 7 (1982): 2-26.

Tony Godfrey, "Victor Burgin," *Art Monthly*, 96 (May 1986): 16-17.

Tony Godfrey, *Conceptual Art* (London: Phaidon, 1998).

Johann Wolfgang von Goethe, *Italian Journey*, trans Robert R. Heitner (Princeton: Princeton University Press, 1994).

Dan Graham, "Photographs of Motion (1967/69)," in *Dan Graham*, eds Birgit Pelzer et al. (London: Phaidon, 2001), 104-107.

Dan Graham, *Works 1965-2000* (Düsseldorf: Richter Verlag, 2001).

Oliver Grau, *Virtuelle Kunst in Geschichte und Gegenwart. Visuelle Strategien* (Berlin: Reimer, 2001).

Oliver Grau, *Virtual Art: From Illusion to Immersion* (Cambridge, Mass.: MIT Press, 2003).

Tom Gunning, "Never Seen This Picture Before (2003)," in *The Cinematic*, ed. David Campany (Cambridge, Mass. and London: Whitechapel and MIT Press, 2007), 20-24.

Sabine Hake, *The Proletarian Dream: Socialism, Culture, and Emotion in Germany 1863-1933* (Berlin/Boston: De Gruyter, 2017).

Stuart Hall, "Fantasy, Identity, Politics," in *Cultural Remix. Theories of Politics and the Popular*, eds Erica Carter, James Donald and Judith Squires (London: Lawrence & Wishart, 1995), 63-69.

Peter Halley, "The Crisis in Geometry," *Arts Magazine* (Summer 1984): 111-115.

Peter Hamilton and Roger Hargreaves, *The Beautiful and the Damned: The Creation of Identity in Nineteenth-Century Photography* (Aldershot: Lund Humphries, 2001).

Byung-Chul Han, *Transparenzgesellschaft* (Berlin: Matthes & Seitz, 2012).

Al Harris F., "Introduction," Victor Burgin, *History Painting*, cat., University at Buffalo Art Gallery / Research Center in Art + Culture (Cheektowaga, NY: Dual Printing, 1995).

Charles Harrison, "On exhibitions and the world at large: Seth Siegelaub in conversation with Charles Harrison," *Studio International*, vol. 178, no. 917 (December 1969): 202-203.

Stephen Heath, "Lessons from Brecht," *Screen*, 15, 2 (Summer 1974): 103-128.

Stephen Heath, "Joan Riviere and the Masquerade," in *Formations of Fantasy*, eds Victor Burgin, James Donald and Cora Kaplan (London and New York: Routledge, 1986), 45-61.

Marianne Hirsch, *Family Frames. Photography, Narrative and Postmemory* (1997) (Cambridge/Mass., London: Harvard University Press, 2012).

E. T. A. Hoffmann, "The Sandman," (1816) in *The Sandman. The Elementary Spirit. Two Mystery Tales*, trans John Oxenford (New York: Mondial, 2008): 1-42.

David Hopkins, *After Modern Art. 1945-2000* (London: Oxford University Press, 2000).

Yuk Hui, *On the Existence of Digital Objects* (Minneapolis: University of Minnesota Press, 2016).

Roman Ingarden, *The Cognition of the Literary Work of Art*, trans Ruth Ann Crowley and Kenneth R. Olson (Evanston, Illinois: Northwestern University Press, 1973).

Wolfgang Iser, *The Act of Reading: A Theory of Aesthetic Response* (Baltimore: The Johns Hopkins University Press, 1978).

Fredric Jameson, "Postmodernism, or The Cultural Logic of Late Capitalism," *New Left Review*, 146 (July–August 1984): 53-92.

Frederic Jameson, *The Geopolitical Aesthetic: Cinema and Space in the World System* (Bloomington and Indianapolis: Indiana University Press, 1992).

Stefan Jonsson, *A Brief History of the Masses. Three Revolutions* (New York: Columbia University Press, 2008).

Donald Judd, "Specific Objects," *Arts Yearbook* 8 (1965): 74-82.

Howard Junker, "The New Sculpture," *The Saturday Evening Post*, New York (2 Nov. 1968): 44.

Mary Kelly, "Beyond the Purloined Image," *Block*, 9 (1983): 68-72.

Homay King, "Beyond Repetition: Victor Burgin's Loops," in *Projective. Essays about the Work of Victor Burgin* (Geneva: Mamco, 2014), 71-102.

Michael Kirby, *The Art of Time: Essays on the Avant-Garde* (New York: E.P. Dutton & Company, 1969).

Melanie Klein, "Notes on Some Schizoid Mechanisms," (1946) in *The Selected Melanie Klein*, ed. Juliet Mitchell (New York: Free Press, 1986), 175-200.

Ken Knabb (ed.) *Situationist International Anthology. Revised and Expanded Edition*, (Berkeley, California: Bureau of Public Secrets, 2006).

Joseph Kosuth, "Art after Philosophy (1969)," in Id., *Art after Philosophy and After. Collected Writings, 1966-1990* (Cambridge, Mass.: MIT Press, 1991), 13-32.

Joseph Kosuth, "1975," in *Conceptual Art: A Critical Anthology*, eds Alexander Alberro and Blake Stimson (Cambridge, Mass.: MIT Press, 1999), 334-348.

Rosalind Krauss, "Notes on the Index: Seventies Art in America," *October*, Vol. 3 (Spring 1977): 68-81.

Rosalind Krauss, "Grids," *October*, Vol. 9 (Summer, 1979): 50-64.

Rosalind Krauss, "A Note on Photography and the Simulacral," *October*, Vol. 31 (Winter, 1984): 49-68.

Rosalind Krauss, "The Originality of the Avant-Garde," in Id., *The Originality of the Avant-Garde and Other Modernist Myths* (Cambridge, Mass.: MIT Press, 1985), 151-170.

Rosalind Krauss, "Reinventing the Medium," *Critical Inquiry*, no. 25 (Winter 1999): 289-305.

Julia Kristeva, *Etrangers à nous-mêmes* (Paris: Fayard, 1988).

Julia Kristeva, *Black Sun. Depression and Melancholia*, trans Leon S. Roudiez (New York: Columbia University Press, 1992).

Jacques Lacan, *Ecrits. The First Complete Edition in English*, trans Bruce Fink (New York, London: W. W. Norton & Company, 2006).

Jean Laplanche and Serge Leclaire, "The Unconscious: A Psychoanalytic Study," *Yale French Studies*, 48 (1972): 118-175.

La Révolution Surréaliste, 12 (15 December 1929).

Henri Lefebvre, *The Production of Space* (1974), trans Donald Nicholson-Smith (Oxford UK and Cambridge Massachusetts: Blackwell, 1991).

Sol LeWitt, "Serial Project No. 1 (ABCD) (1966)," in *Sol Lewitt*, cat., ed. Alicia Legg (New York: Museum of Modern Art, 1978), 170-171.

Sol LeWitt, "Paragraphs on Conceptual Art," (1967) in *Conceptual Art: A Critical Anthology*, eds Alexander Alberro and Blake Stimson (Cambridge, Mass.: MIT Press, 1999), 12-16.

Mark Lewis, "Interview with Victor Burgin," *C Magazine*, 16 (Winter 1987/88): 54-65.

Lucy Lippard and John Chandler, "The Dematerialization of Art," *Art International* 12, 2 (1968): 31–36.

Lucy Lippard, *Six Years: The Dematerialization of the Art Object from 1966 to 1972* (Berkeley and Los Angeles: University of California Press, 2001).

Henry Lowood, "Real-time performance: Machinima and game studies," *iDMAa Journal*, 2(1) (2005): 10-17.

David Lyon, "Liquid Surveillance: The Contribution of Zygmunt Bauman to Surveillance Studies," *International Political Sociology*, 4 (2010): 325-338.

Paul Maenz, *What Do You Expect?* (Cologne: Galerie Paul Maenz, 1977).

Gregorio Magnani, "Victor Burgin," *Flash Art*, 149 (November/December 1989): 119-121.

Lev Manovich, "The Paradoxes of Digital Photography," in *Photography after Photography: Memory and Representation in the Digital Age*, eds Hubertus von Amelunxen, Stefan Iglhaut, and Florian Rötzer (London: G+B Arts, 1997), 57-65.

Paul Marino, *The Art of Machinima: 3D Game-Based Filmmaking* (Scottsdale: Paraglyph Press, 2004).

Marianne Massin, "L'emploi de la musique dans Nietzsche's Paris. Un da capo Nietzschéen," in *Victor Burgin. Objets Temporels*, eds Nathalie Boulouch, Valérie Mavridorakis, David Perreau (Rennes: Presses universi-taires de Rennes, 2007), 141-153.

Guy de Maupassant, *Bel-Ami*, trans Margaret Mauldon (Oxford: Oxford University Press. Oxford World's Classics, 2001).

Marshall McLuhan, *The Medium is the Massage* (1967) (New York: Penguin Books, 1996).

Kynaston McShine (ed.), *Information*, cat. (Museum of Modern Art, New York, 1970).

Nicholas Mirzoeff, *The Right to Look. A Counterhistory of Visuality* (Durham and London: Duke University Press, 2011).

Nicholas Mirzoeff, *How to See the World* (New York: Basic Books, 2016).

William J. Mitchell, *The Reconfigured Eye: Visual Truth in the Post-photographic Era* (Cambridge Mass.: MIT Press, 1992).

W. J. T. Mitchell, *Iconology. Image, Text, Ideology* (Chicago and London: Chicago University Press, 1986).

Robert Morris, "Notes on Sculpture (1966)," in *Minimal Art: A Critical Anthology*, ed. Gregory Battcock (Berkeley: University of California Press, 1995), 222-235.

Andrea Most, "'You've Got to Be Carefully Taught': The Politics of Race in Rodgers and Hammerstein's *South Pacific*," *Theatre Journal*, Vol. 52, No. 3 (October 2000): 307-337.

Laura Mulvey, "Visual Pleasure and Narrative Cinema," *Screen*, vol. 16, 3 (1975): 6-18.

Laura Mulvey, "Afterthoughts on 'Visual Pleasure and Narrative Cinema' inspired by King Vidor's *Duel In The Sun* (1946) (1981)," in Id., *Visual and Other Pleasures* (Basingstoke: Palgrave Macmillan, 2009), 31-40.

Magali Nachtergael, "Nadja. Images, désir et sacrifice," *Postures*, Dossier "Arts, littérature: dialogues, croisements, interférences," No. 7 (2005): 158-173.

Beaumont Newhall, *The History of Photography* (1937) (New York: The Museum of Modern Art, 1978).

Linda Nochlin, *Realism* (Baltimore: Penguin, 1971).

Pierre Nora, *Realms of Memory: The Construction of the French Past*, ed. Lawrence D. Kritzman (New York: Columbia University Press, 1996).

Stephan Oettermann, *The Panorama: History of a Mass Medium* (Cambridge, Mass.: MIT Press, 1997).

Peter Osborne, "*Everywhere, or not at all*: Victor Burgin and Conceptual Art," in *Relocating Victor Burgin*, cat. (Bristol: Arnolfini, 2002a), 62-75.

Peter Osborne, *Conceptual Art* (London: Phaidon, 2002b).

Craig Owens, "The Allegorical Impulse: Towards a Theory of Postmodernism," *October*, Vol. 12 (Spring 1980): 67-86.

Craig Owens, "The Discourse of Others: Feminists and Postmodernism," in *The Anti-Aesthetic. Essays on Postmodern Culture* (Port Townsend, Washington: Bay Press, 1983), 57-82.

Craig Owens, "Posing," in *Difference. On Representation and Sexuality*, cat., ed. Kate Linker (New York: The New Museum of Contemporary Art, 1984), 7-18.

Francette Pacteau, "The Impossible Referent: Representations of the Androgyne," in *Formations of Fantasy*, eds Victor Burgin, James Donald and Cora Kaplan (London and New York: Routledge, 1986), 62-84.

Françoise Parfait, "Immobile Movement and the Speeds of Emotion," in *Relocating Victor Burgin*, cat. (Bristol: Arnolfini, 2002), 112-123.

Morse Peckham, *Man's Rage for Chaos: Biology, Behavior, and the Arts* (Philadelphia: Chilton Company, 1965).

Christopher Phillips, "The Judgment Seat of Photography," *October*, Vol. 22 (Autumn 1982): 27-63.

Martin Picard, "Machinima: Video Game As An Art Form?," Proceedings of CGSA 2006 Symposium, 2006 (http://journals.sfu.ca/loading/index.php/loading/article/view/17/20). Accessed September 12, 2019.

Jean-Marc Poinsot, "Les grandes expositions: Esquisse d'une typologie," *Les Cahiers du Musée national d'art moderne*, no. 17-18 (Fall 1986): 122-145.

Griselda Pollock, "Screening the Seventies. Sexuality and Representation in Feminist Practice—A Brechtian Perspective," in Id., *Vision and Difference. Feminism, Femininity and the Histories of Art* (London and New York: Routledge, 2003), 212-268.

Karl H. Pribram, "The Neurophysiology of Remembering," *Scientific American*, vol. 220, 1 (January 1969a): 73-86.

Karl H. Pribram, "The Physiology of Remembering," in *The Future of the Brain Science*, ed. Samuel Bogoch (New York: Plenum Press, 1969b), 65-87.

Jacques Rancière, *The Future of the Image*, trans Gregory Elliott (London: Verso, 2007).

Jacques Rancière, *The Politics of Aesthetics. The Distribution of the Sensible*, trans Gabriel Rockhill (New York: Continuum, 2011).

Herman Rapaport, "Gazing in Wonderland: The Disarticulated Image," *Enclitic*, 6, no. 2 (Fall 1982): 57-77.

Gerhard Richter, *Afterness: Figures of Following in Modern Thought and Aesthetics* (New York: Columbia University Press, 2011).

Joan Riviere, "Womanliness as a Masquerade (1929)," in *Formations of Fantasy*, eds Victor Burgin, James Donald and Cora Kaplan (London and New York: Routledge, 1986), 35-44.

John Roberts (ed.), *The Imposssible Document: Photography and Conceptual Art in Britain 1966-1976* (London: Camerawork, 1997).

D. N. Rodowick, "The Unnameable (In Three Moments)," in *Projective. Essays about the Work of Victor Burgin* (Geneva: Mamco, 2014), 9-37.

Anne Rorimer, *New Art in the 60s and 70s. Redefining Reality* (London: Thames & Hudson, 2004).

Robert Rosenblum, "Gedanken zu den Quellen des Zeitgeistes,", in *Zeitgeist*, cat., Martin-Gropius-Bau Berlin, ed. Christos M. Joachimides (Berlin: Frölich & Kaufmann, 1982), 11-14.

Martha Rosler, "Lookers, Buyers, Dealers, and Makers: Thoughts on Audience (1979)," in *Art after Modernism: Rethinking Representation*, ed. Brian Wallis (Boston: D.R. Godine, 1984), 311-340.

Martha Rosler, "Notes on Quotes," (1982) in Id., *Decoys and Disruptions. Selected Writings, 1975-2001* (Cambridge, Mass.: MIT Press, 2004), 133-148.

Marie-Laure Ryan, *Narrative as Virtual Reality 2: Revisiting Immersion and Interactivity in Literature and Electronic Media* (Baltimore, Maryland: John Hopkins University Press, 2015).

Leopold von Sacher-Masoch, "Venus in Furs (1870)," in *Masochism*, trans Jean Mc Neil (New York: Zone Books, 1991), 141-271.

Simon Sadler, *The Situationist City* (Cambridge, Mass.: MIT Press, 1999).

Anders Sandberg and Nick Boström, "Whole Brain Emulation: A Roadmap," *Technical report #2008-3*, future of Humanity Institute, Oxford University, 2008. www.fhi.ox.ac.uk/reports/2008-3.pdf. Accessed September 12, 2019.

Ferdinand de Saussure, *Course in General Linguistics*, trans Roy Harris (London: Duckworth, 1916/1983).

Paul Schilder, "Psycho-Analysis of Space," *International Journal of Psycho-Analysis*, 16 (1935): 274-295.

Wolfgang Schivelbusch, *The Railway Journey: The Industrialization and Perception of Time and Space* (1977) (Berkeley, CA: University of California Press, 1986).

W. G. Sebald, *The Rings of Saturn*, trans Michael Hulse (London: Vintage, 2002).

Navindra P. Seeram, Risa N. Schulman, David Heber, *Pomegranantes. Ancient Roots to Modern Medicine* (Boca Raton, London, New York: Taylor & Francis, 2006).

Allan Sekula, "Dismantling Modernism, Reinventing Documentary (Notes on the Politics of Representation)," *The Massachusetts Review*, 19, 4, Photography (Winter 1978): 859-883.

Allan Sekula, "The Traffic in Photographs," *Art Journal*, Vol. 41, No. 1, Photography and the Scholar/Critic (Spring, 1981): 15-25.

Allan Sekula, "On the Invention of Photographic Meaning (1975)," in *Thinking Photography*, ed. Victor Burgin (Houndmills and London: Macmillan, 1982), 84-109.

Allan Sekula, *Performance under Working Conditions*, cat., ed. Sabine Breitwieser, Generali Foundation Vienna (Ostfildern-Ruit: Hatje Cantz, 2003).

Anne Seymour, "Interview with Victor Burgin," in *The New Art*, The Hayward Gallery, London, 1972, 74-78.

Edward A. Shanken, "Art in the Information Age: Technology and Conceptual Art," LEONARDO, vol. 35, no. 4 (2002): 433-438.

Viktor Shklovsky, *Zoo, or letters not about love*, trans Richard Sheldon (Champaign, Dublin, London: Dalkey Archive Press, 2012).

Stephen Shore, *The Nature of Photographs* (New York: Phaidon, 2007).

Seth Siegelaub (ed.), *January 5-31, 1969 (Barry, Huebler, Kosuth, Weiner)*, cat. (New York, 1969).

Kaja Silverman, *The Threshold of the Visible World* (New York, London: Routledge, 1996).

Noah Snavely, Steven M. Seitz, and Richard Szeliski, "Photo Tourism: Exploring Photo Collections in 3D," ACM *Transactions on Graphics (SIGGRAPH Proceedings)*, 25, 3 (2006): 835-846. http://phototour.cs.washington.edu/ Accessed September 18, 2019.

Noah Snavely, Rahul Garg, Steven M. Seitz, and Richard Szeliski, "Finding Paths through the World's Photos," ACM *Transactions on Graphics (SIGGRAPH Proceedings)*, 27, 3 (2008): 11-21. http://phototour.cs.washington.edu/ Accessed September 18, 2019.

Abigail Solomon-Godeau, "Photography after Art Photography," in *Art after Modernism. Rethinking Representation*, ed. Brian Wallis (Boston: D.R. Godine, 1984), 75-86.

Frederic Spotts, *Bayreuth: A History of the Wagner Festival* (New Haven, Connecticut: Yale University Press, 1994).

Edward Steichen, *The Family of Man* (1955) (New York: Museum of Modern Art, 2013).

Garrett Stewart, "Photo-gravure: Death, Photography and Film Narrative," *Wide Angle*, Vol. 9, no. 6 (Winter 1987): 11-31.

Alexander Streitberger, "'The Ambiguous Multiple-entendre' (Baldessari) – Multimedia Art as Rebus," in *Photography between Poetry and Politics. The Critical Position of the Photographic Medium in Contemporary Art*, eds Hilde Van Gelder and Helen Westgeest (Leuven: Leuven University Press, 2008), 35-49.

Alexander Streitberger, "The Psychotopological Text: Victor Burgin's Writings in Perspective," in *Situational Aesthetics. Selected Writings by Victor Burgin*, ed. Alexander

Streitberger (Leuven: Leuven University Press, 2009), xi-xxix.

Alexander Streitberger, "The Return of the Panorama," in *Heterogeneous Objects: Intermedia and Photography after Modernism*, eds Raphaël Pirenne and Alexander Streitberger (Leuven: Leuven University Press, 2013a), 59-88.

Alexander Streitberger, "Spezifische Objekte der Fotografie. Situationsästhetik und konzeptuelle Fotografie Ende der 1960er Jahre," in *The Challenge of the Object. Die Herausforderung des Objekts. 33rd Congress of the International Committee of the History of Art. Part 4*, eds G. Ulrich Großmann, Petra Krutisch (Nuremberg: Verlag des Germanischen Nationalmuseums, 2013b), 1313-1317.

Alexander Streitberger, "A Stage Presence. Michael Kirby's Embedded Sculptures," *TDR: the journal of performance studies*, Vol. 61, no.2 (2017a): 105-116.

Alexander Streitberger, "Victor Burgin's *Parzival*: A Monument of Melancholia," in *Victor Burgin's* Parzival *in Leuven. Reflections on the "Uncinematic"*, eds Stéphane Symons and Hilde Van Gelder (Leuven: Leuven University Press, 2017b), 38-58.

Alexander Streitberger, "'Cultural work as a praxis.' The Artist as Producer in the Work of Victor Burgin, Martha Rosler, and Allan Sekula," in *"Disassembled" Images. Allan Sekula and Contemporary Art*, eds Alexander Streitberger and Hilde Van Gelder (Leuven: Leuven University Press, 2019a), 192-211.

Alexander Streitberger, *Victor Burgin. Gradiva* (Berlin: Kunstverlag, 2019b).

Alexander Streitberger, "La porosité du livre. Some Cities de Victor Burgin comme lieu d'échange et de compénétration psycho-topologique," *textimage. revue du dialogue texte-image, Les blessures du livre*, écrivains et plasticiens à contremploi, no. 11 (Automne 2019c). https://www. revue-textimage.com/17_blessures_du_livre/streitberger1. html. Accessed November 6, 2019.

John Szarkowski, *The Photographer's Eye* (1966) (New York: The Museum of Modern Art, 1997).

The British Edge, cat. (Boston: The Institute of Contemporary Art, 1987).

The Tate Gallery Report 1972-1974 (London, 1975).

Tate Gallery & Patrons of New Art (eds), *The Turner Prize 1986* (London, 1986).

Lisa Tickner, "Sexuality and/in Representation. Five British Artists," in *Difference. On Representation and Sexuality*, cat., ed. Kate Linker (New York: The New Museum of Contemporary Art, 1984), 19-30.

Phyllis Tuchman, "An Interview with Carl Andre," *Artforum*, 10 (1970): 55-61.

Marcia Tucker, "Preface," in *Difference. On Representation and Sexuality*, cat., ed. Kate Linker (The New Museum of Contemporary Art, New York, 1984), 4.

William Uricchio, "The Algorithmic Turn: Photosynth, Augmented Reality and the Changing Implications of the Image," *Visual Studies*, Vol. 26, No. 1 (March 2011): 25-35.

Erik Verhagen, "La photographie conceptuelle. Paradoxes, contradictions et impossibilités," *Etudes Photographiques*, no. 22 (September 2008): 118-139.

Anthony Vidler, "The Panoramic Unconscious: Victor Burgin and Spatial Modernism," in Victor Burgin, *Shadowed*, cat. (London: Architectural Association, 2000), 8-19.

Anthony Vidler, "Victor Burgin's Architectural Palimpsests," in *Projective. Essays about the Work of Victor Burgin* (Geneva: Mamco, 2014), 105-130.

Paul Virilio, *Lost Dimension*, trans Daniel Moshenberg (New York: Semiotext(e), 1991).

Richard Wagner, *The Art-Work of the Future and Other Works*, trans W. Ashton Ellis (Lincoln: University of Nebraska Press, 1994).

Richard Wagner, *Opera and Drama*, trans W. Ashton Ellis (Lincoln: University of Nebraska Press, 1995).

John A. Walker, *Left Shift: Radical Art in 1970s Britain* (London, New York: I. B. Tauris Publishers, 2002).

Rolf Wedewer (ed.), *Konzeption—Conception*, cat. (Städtisches Museum Leverkusen, Schloß Morsbroich, 1969).

Norbert Weiner, *Cybernetics: or Control and Communication in the Animal and the Machine* (1948), (Cambridge Mass.: MIT Press, second edition, 1961).

When Attitudes Become Form, cat. (London: The Institute of Contemporary Arts, Nash House, The Mall, 1969).

Stephen Willats, "Artwork as Social Model," *Studio International*, vol. 191, no. 980, (March-April 1976a): 100-107.

Stephen Willats, *Art and Social Function* (London: Latimer, 1976b).

Andrew Wilson (ed.), *Conceptual Art in Britain. 1964-1979* (London: Tate Publishing, 2016).

William Wilson, *Stuart Davis's Abstract Argot* (San Francisco: Chameleon books, 1993).

Matthew S. Witkovsky (ed.), *Light Years. Conceptual Art and the Photograph, 1964-1977* (New Haven, London: Yale University Press, 2012).

Janet Wolff, "Postmodern Theory and Feminist Art Practice," in *Postmodernism and Society*, eds Roy Boyne and Ali Rattansi (London: Palgrave Macmillan, 1990), 187-208.

Peter Wollen, "Manet: Modernism and Avant-Garde," *Screen*, Vol. 21, Issue 2 (July 1980): 15-26.

Peter Wollen, "Barthes, Burgin, Vertigo," in *Victor Burgin* (Barcelona: Fundació Antoni Tàpies, 2001), 10-26.

Louise Wolthers, "Watching Europe and Beyond: Surveillance, Art and Photography in the New Millennium," in *Watched! Surveillance, Art and Photography*, eds Louise Wolthers, Dragana Vujanovic and Niclas Östlind (Cologne: Walther König, 2016), 8-23.

Denis Wood, *The Power of Maps* (New York, London: The Guilford Press, 2010).

Works bought for the Arts Council by Michael Compton (London: Arts Council, 1974).

Colophon

Every effort has been made to contact all holders of the copyright to the visual material contained in this publication. Any copyright-holders who believe that illustrations have been reproduced without their knowledge are asked to contact the Lieven Gevaert Research Centre for Photography, Art and Visual Culture. Victor Burgin kindly granted permission for the reproduction of images of his work.

Lieven Gevaert Research Centre for Photography, Art and Visual Culture
Arts Faculty KU Leuven
Blijde-Inkomststraat 21 box 3313
B-3000 Leuven
Belgium

Author: Alexander Streitberger
Language revision: Ton Brouwers
Lay-out and cover design: DOGMA

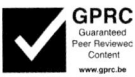

© 2020 by Leuven University Press / Universitaire Pers Leuven / Presses Universitaires de Louvain. Minderbroedersstraat 4, B-3000 Leuven (Belgium).

ISBN 978 94 6270 246 2
D/2020/1869/45
NUR: 652

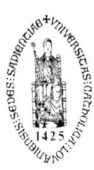
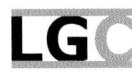